CAR AND DRIVER

Y E A R B O O K 1993

LOTUS ESPRIT BY DICK KELLEY

CAR AND DRIVER

YEARBOOK 1993

 GROLIER ENTERPRISES, INC.
Danbury, Connecticut

Published by Grolier Enterprises, Inc.

The publisher wishes to thank *CAR AND DRIVER* Editor William Jeanes and his staff for the creation of the articles upon which this yearbook is based, as well as for creation of new texts and photos. Special thanks go to *CAR AND DRIVER*'s Phil Berg, the project editor, and Julianne Purther, photo assistant.

Book design: Nancy Norton, Norton & Company Design
Composition: Dix Type Inc.
Cover Photo: Don Johnston

Grolier Enterprises staff:

President: Dante Cirilli
Vice President & Publisher: Rosanna Hansen
Editorial Director: Neil Soderstrom
Assistant Editor: Cindy Stierle
Vice President Annual/Yearbook Division:
John Weggeman
Senior Product Manager: Sara Stringfellow
Vice President Manufacturing: Joseph J. Corlett
Senior Production Manager: Susan Gallucci
Production Manager: Diane Hassan

Grolier Enterprises, Inc., offers a varied selection of both adult and children's book racks. For details on ordering, please write:

Premium Department
Grolier Enterprises, Inc.
Sherman Turnpike
Danbury, CT 06816

ISSN: 1050-9682
ISBN: 0-7172-8305-4

Manufactured in the United States of America

10 9 8 7 6 5 4 3 2 1

CONTENTS

(Continued)

PREVIEWS

ENVIRONMENTAL ISSUES

PEOPLE AND PAST

RACING

DRIVING

PREFACE

By William Jeanes

PHOTO BY JEFFREY G. RUSSELL

Welcome to our third annual yearbook. In the past year the auto industry has seen bad times, and not-so-bad times. Competition remains keen, so keen that giant GM re-assigned its captains and took drastic cost-cutting measures. In the closing of some GM factories, we saw a groundswell of anti-Japanese sentiment. We see things differently here, that it is not the motive of any country that we need to concern ourselves with but the rules our government sets for the auto industry.

A report crossed my desk recently, ominously titled "The Case for Saving the Big Three." The study, commissioned by the University of Michigan, was undertaken by the Economic Strategy Institute, a Washington think tank that, in its words, is "dedicated to achieving American leadership in technology and industry."

The study plainly holds that saving the U.S. auto industry is necessary, noting that though it doesn't theoretically matter who owns the works, the achievement of industrial and technological leadership would be difficult without a healthy auto industry operating in the United States.

The ESI study cites our country's loss of leadership—and market share—in consumer electronics, machine tools, ceramics, and other industries. Consumer electronics alone makes the point: from a position of dominance in 1970, when the U.S. industry claimed nearly 70 percent of the worldwide market share, American-made consumer electronics now accounts for perhaps 5 percent. American jobs disappeared with the market share. So look at your television sets before you take to the streets with your "Buy American" banner.

Though the millions of Big Three stockholders would disagree, it theoretically does *not* matter who owns the car companies. We have all heard it said that only

so many assembly-line jobs are required to build enough cars to serve the U.S. market. Does it matter, therefore, whose badge is on those cars?

We would do well to remember that, although the assembly-line jobs might remain constant—even though they might be geographically relocated—there are a great many other jobs to consider.

Assembly jobs are but a part of the total job population required to build a car. For example, engineering, research, and development functions must be performed before a car reaches the assembly stage. Financing must be secured. Tools and equipment must be purchased. Raw materials must be mined and processed. Factories—and workers—somewhere must fabricate electrical components, weave upholstery fabrics, make glass, build rack-and-pinion steering mechanisms, and do the thousands of things necessary to see that a car reaches a customer.

The ESI study tells us that sixteen design and R&D facilities have been established in the U.S. by overseas automakers. These sixteen facilities have, in total, fewer than 2000 employees. By contrast, Chrysler's new engineering and technical center employs 7000.

It's clear, then, that even though a company from beyond the seas builds cars in a factory that it built in this country, and that employs American workers, it nonetheless leaves a substantial number of jobs at home. It's equally clear that such a company has sound, non-sinister business reasons for doing this.

Even supposing that this job deficit can somehow be absorbed in a country as large and diverse as ours, it takes no great leap of reason to see that the same situation ought not be allowed where the materials used in making those cars are concerned. If all the raw materials are mined and processed elsewhere, and if all the thousands of components are built in or purchased from other countries, there can be no argument that U.S. jobs will begin to disappear—as indeed they have.

Oversimplifying, consider what might happen if a new restaurant opened in the heart of a U.S. farming area. It would provide jobs for cooks, waiters, hosts, and janitorial personnel...but if the restaurant is successful, established restaurants might lose business and therefore jobs. Yet, the argument can be made —and soundly—that no loss of jobs has occurred.

Suppose then that our new restaurant does not buy its food or its beverages locally. In this situation, farms and other restaurant suppliers would lose business, with a corresponding loss of jobs in those areas—areas unseen by those who dine at the new eatery.

Returning to the auto industry, we can say that it is important—and critically so —to this nation's underlying economy that a large percentage of all the materials used in an automobile built in the U.S. be made and purchased in the U.S. That way, jobs will be preserved all across the broad manufacturing spectrum that works together to build cars.

To be considered an American car, an automobile must contain 75 percent "local content." Which I would take to mean U.S. content. Under the current rules, many cars meet this standard.

There is room, however, to question that. The Environmental Protection Agency has somehow wound up in charge of this. Its rules count only the cost of materials directly imported by transplants as "foreign content." Such things as salaries of home-country (non-U.S.) executives, interest paid to foreign banks, depreciation on machinery and equipment purchased elsewhere, distributor profit margins, and even exchange-rate losses are counted as U.S. content.

It is only fair to point out that any transplant manufacturer that takes advantage of these oddly written regulations is only doing what businesses traditionally do: attempting to make the largest profit possible. Such a manufacturer has violated no laws. Its morals cannot be called into question.

What can be called into question is our own government's approach to the issue of local content. Keeping in mind that the Big Three by no means use 100 percent American-made components, we must realize that there is no simple answer to the problem. Lord knows, nothing is simple when the government gets involved.

It does not seem unreasonable, however, to suggest that when the Washington grandstanders are making out the next schedule of vote-getting Congressional hearings that they put the issue of U.S. content—and U.S. jobs—at the top of their agenda.

Though we spend time hoping for a more enlightened government, we spend far more time driving. During the past year, we savored some terrific cars, and we delighted in learning more about some of the people who make the world of cars what it is. Enjoy this compendium of our favorite stories of the year.

Facing page: Pillars of Car and Driver, *past and present, Csaba Csere, Tony Assenza, William Jeanes, Rich Ceppos, Brock Yates, Larry Griffin, Nicholas Bissoon-Dath (partially hidden), Patrick Bedard, Arthur St. Antione.*

COLUMNS

EAT YOUR SPINACH

By Patrick Bedard

California's imperial bureaucracy—seeking to desmog its air and simultaneously kink the flow of petrodollars to the Arabs—has decreed that electric cars *will* be sold in that state beginning in 1998. Is this a good idea?

I've been calling around, trying to find exact emissions and energy-efficiency data for electrics. Larry O'Connell at the Electric Power Research Institute couldn't answer my questions. Instead, he said something *really* interesting.

"The real reason we need electric cars is not for emissions or efficiency. We need them because petroleum is too precious to burn."

For sure, oil is wonderful stuff. You can make fuel from every ounce. Or lubricating oil. Or pop-back-to-original-shape bumpers. Or keep-coffee-hot-forever cups. Or packing peanuts that will cushion the Post Office's speediest handling. Oil is twentieth-century man's most versatile building block, and I can't imagine life without the plastic chair I'm sitting in and the plastic keyboard I'm working at. And the plastic phone over which Mr. O'Connell reminded me of the value of oil.

At the same time, I can buy all the oil I want on the world market for twenty bucks a barrel. That's exactly how valuable it is.

Exactly! say the Larry O'Connells of this world. Oil is too cheap! High-school dropouts can afford to burn it by the tankfuls in their strutting Trans Ams. Spendthrift man is piddling away this fabulous petroleum legacy. If we don't end up back in the cave, cold and naked, then our children will. Because it's just a matter of time until the petroleum runs out.

Historians will recall the same lamentations 200 years ago about the running out of whale oil. But I don't notice that our lives are made bleak by its chronic absence down at Wal-Mart.

Will our children, and their children, have lives less good than ours? Give that idea the history test. Would you go back and trade lives with your father when he was your age? Or your grandfather? How about with the pioneers trekking westward? Or the boat people on the *Mayflower?*

Not at gunpoint, I'll bet. We have it better. And when I look back over history, I see the remarkable story of man: always adapting, always inventing, always making things better. He started his betterment program long before he discovered oil, and he'll keep it long after the last drop is gone.

The Larry O'Connells of this world are saying, "Yeah, but this time is different."

No, it's never different. And don't tell me that man has been perfecting the computer so we can ease our transition back to the cave.

It must be said, too, that man's entire

advancement from shank's mare transit to supersonic jets happened without "public policy." This is the term Big Brother uses now that "central planning" has been discredited. CAFE is public policy. The national maximum speed limit is public policy. Electric cars are public policy. Methanol programs and car-pool lanes and the shunned mass-transit systems are public policy. Notice that all of these programs exist, wholly or in part, to preserve oil.

Public policy has to be the fastest growing industry in the country. I recently picked up the Fuels Report from the California Energy Commission. This was done by the Fuels Planning Committee, the people deciding which fuels Californians will use in the future rather than just pulling up to pumps down at the Circle K. This 39-pager has 33 names on the masthead, about the same as this magazine if you leave out the art department.

Of course it takes a lot of people if you're trying to alter the direction of mankind's advancement. That's what public policy is about—making people do what they never would on their own, making them eat their spinach, so to speak.

Traffic congestion is one of the items on every public-policy maker's to-do list. The Fuels Report says, "In 1990 more than 197,000 hours per day were lost due to traffic congestion. These time delays cost Californians $5 million per day." Another public-policy report, from the California Air Resources Board, says, "A car that takes 30 minutes to drive 10 miles will produce two and one-half times more pollution than a car making the same trip in only 11 minutes. In other words, 19 minutes of delay will increase hydrocarbon emissions 250 percent!"

You're thinking that those statistics cry out for more roads, right? Uh-uh. Eat your spinach. "Using a wide array of strategies," including toll roads and higher prices at rush hour, the public-policy peo-ple will take care of the problem without pouring another yard of concrete.

CAFE is classic public policy. It's the conceit of these people that they can "save" oil. They can't. They *can* make us eat our spinach by driving little cars at the national speed limit. But they can't save oil. Because, in the real world, any cutback in our domestic oil consumption merely lowers world demand a little, which lowers price a little, which makes oil a little better deal, which means every other consuming nation uses a little more of it. Oil *must* sell. Look at how many countries rely on selling oil to keep their economies afloat.

Sure, petroleum is a finite resource and the last well someday will suck air, but public policy won't change the time it happens by one sweep of your second hand. The last barrel will be pumped exactly when somebody—perhaps from Texas but just as likely from Tokyo or Timbuktu—is willing to pay the world price for it. Slurp, end of oil. And if that somebody wants to use the last barrel to propel an old Buick down the road, he'll damn well do it, although the price by that time pretty much assures a more admirable use.

The point is, nothing we Americans do will influence the end of oil because, never mind how important we Americans think we are, our public policy stops at the border.

Still, the public-policy committees grow fat on ever-increasing government budgets. Remember how it was said that the military had enough weapons to kill every Ruskie ten times yet it still wanted more, just to keep itself going? What would you say about public policy that has already mandated cars 99.3 percent clean on hydrocarbons and 95 percent clean on NOx yet goes on to require electric cars at fantastic cost?

I would say the military never got its Star Wars, but the public-policy people are getting theirs.

CAFE, THE SUCKER TAX

By Csaba Csere

Get your lynch ropes ready. I've got a bright idea—it's really a tax, but it's a cheaper, better replacement for a hidden tax we're already paying. The tax we've been paying for almost twenty years is called CAFE (Corporate Average Fuel Economy), and recent rumblings from Washington suggest that the politicians are itching to jack up this tax.

Consider this: only 35 percent of the oil we consume is burned by cars and light trucks. And yet the government's righteous plan for conservation is pinned squarely on us 35-percenters. Heavy trucks, boats, mobile homes, jet aircraft, industry, home owners, and just about everyone else gets off virtually scot-free.

The idea behind CAFE is simplicity itself. The feds require an average-fuel-economy number for every carmaker that sells in America, currently 28.5 mpg. If the average fuel economy of the entire fleet of cars that a company sells in a given year doesn't meet the standard, the hapless firm gets hit with a penalty, currently $100 for every mile per gallon on every car sold.

You can see why the politicians went for the idea. It seems free of cost, at least superficially, which is the way people in Washington think. It's up to the auto industry to figure out how to build these econoboxes and get us to buy them.

So far this system hasn't hurt too much because the 28.5-mpg standard has resulted in cars that are acceptable to most of us. But if the folks in Washington jump the standard to 40 mpg, we're all going to take it on the chin.

The reason is that CAFE picks your pocket in more ways than a Calcutta street urchin. CAFE results in higher car prices because manufacturers have to pay for the expensive technology that is needed to improve fuel economy. The price of this technology is one of the reasons that car stickers have been rising substantially faster than has the rate of inflation for the past decade or so.

And it would get a lot worse with a 40-mpg standard because all of the easy fuel-economy tricks—four-speed automatic transmissions, lockup torque converters, fuel injection, low-rolling-resistance tires, and superficial weight loss—have already been put into play.

Consider this: Joe Average in the seventies drove 12,000 miles a year in a 15-mpg car. The 800 gallons of fuel he burned every year cost maybe $800. Offered a car that got 5 more miles to the gallon, he took it, and his fuel use dropped to 600 gallons, saving him about $200 a year. Car companies could make that improvement fairly easily, so they only added about $250 to the sticker price.

Joe could see that his $250 investment would pay off in little more than a year. He and a lot of other buyers went for it. In fact, until about 1985, fuel economy went up faster than CAFE required because it made economic sense to buy fuel economy.

It's a different deal today. Now Joe's driving a 25-mpg car that burns 480 gallons of fuel annually—costing him about $576. But now, when Joe is offered a car with another 5-mpg boost, he hesitates. Sure, his fuel bill would drop to 400 gallons ($480), but now the sticker price is up at least $500 because each added mpg is much tougher to deliver when you're starting at 25 mpg. Forking over $500 up front to save $96 a year, Joe wouldn't break even until the sixth year, and by then he's traded the car.

So, Joe passes up that offer, and so do most customers. Rest assured that if CAFE ever demands 40 mpg, only traveling salesmen with long careers will ever make money on their fuel-economy specials.

Unfortunately, it may not be so simple to pass up that offer. That's because CAFE will be picking your other pocket. Because no matter what car you want, the manufacturers must achieve the mandated fleet average. So if it doesn't make sense to buy the little fuel miser, they'll make it make sense by jacking up the price of the larger, less fuel-efficient model you had your heart set on. That's right. *CAFE will force the car company to discourage you from buying the car you want.* The law gets you coming and going.

What makes this especially ludicrous is that after CAFE gets done hosing us, it doesn't even save that much fuel. For one thing, those who end up buying the little misers will likely drive more than they ever did because these superfuelers will be cheaper to run than the cars they replaced. Other customers will rebel and shift out of cars into pickups and SUVs, and we know how economical they are.

Finally, CAFE takes forever to take effect because only about ten percent of America's 150 million cars are replaced every year. And that rate might well slow down once people figure out that the only way to beat CAFE is to hold on to their old cars.

A recent study by Charles River Associates, a Boston-based economics think tank, examines the costs and benefits of CAFE. Although this study was sponsored by the Motor Vehicle Manufacturers Association, the authors ran their economic model using three different scenarios, ranging from the assumptions of the CAFE advocates in the Department of Energy to more sanguine industry projections. CAFE turned out to be a bad deal no matter what the assumptions.

The cost of raising the standard to 40 mpg by 2000, even by the most CAFE-favorable estimate, would be about $7 for each barrel of oil we wouldn't use. A more realistic estimate puts the cost at more like $45 per barrel saved. On the other hand, the estimates for saving the same amount of fuel through a gasoline tax range from $4 to $10 per barrel.

The economic arguments for a gas tax are simple: a gas tax encourages buyers to drive more efficient vehicles; it discourages driving, unlike CAFE, because it makes trips more expensive no matter what you're driving; and finally, it affects consumption on all vehicles right now.

Going one step further, why shouldn't the tax be on each barrel of crude oil itself? Why shouldn't the users who account for the other 65 percent of America's oil appetite be forced to diet as well? As one might expect, by spreading the pain, an oil tax is even more cost effective, with the estimates ranging from 75 cents to $2 per barrel saved.

CAFE is a sucker tax on driving and a dumb way to save oil. If we want to conserve, we should end this farce and replace CAFE with an oil tax. We'll save both our money and our freedom to buy the cars we want.

DREAMERS FINISH FIRST

By Brock Yates

I owe Soichiro Honda a posthumous apology.

In the final line of my biography of Enzo Ferrari (an excerpt from which begins on page 146), I described the great Italian as "the last automotive titan." That, clearly, was a statement of absurd hyperbole, because at the time of Ferrari's death in 1988, Soichiro Honda was still operating in the role of "supreme adviser" to the incredible automobile and motorcycle empire he created from the rubble of World War II.

With all due respect to Ferrari's role as an entrepreneur of the car business, his stature as a "titan" must be chopped at the knees when compared with that of the tough little ex-racer from Hamamatsu. While Ferrari's accomplishments as the maker of high-performance sports and racing machines are the stuff of legend, Honda not only achieved notable success with similar automobiles but also revolutionized small cars and motorcycles with his exquisitely conceived machines.

There is only one legitimate counterpart to Honda in the modern era. That is Ferdinand Porsche. A vast spectrum of intense interest and enthusiasm was what set both men apart from their rivals. Certainly others equaled them as managers or engineers or financiers or salesmen, but as multitalented creators of great machines they were nonpareil.

Consider that both Porsche and Honda not only developed super racing cars (Auto Unions and McLaren Hondas), but created milestone economy cars as well. The Volkswagen was perhaps Porsche's crowning achievement, while many might agree that Honda's 1973 Civic was an equally significant effort. Admittedly, the Civic was a refinement of Englishman Alec Issigonis's brilliant 1960 Austin Seven/Morris Mini-Minor, which the somnambulant British automobile industry had permitted to stagnate, but Honda's faster, better-built version electrified the world and served as the triggering mechanism for this fledgling company (which had been in the car business only eleven years!).

Porsche and Honda alone among automakers achieved success in a variety of vehicular disciplines (racing cars, sports cars, motorcycles, economy cars, and even tanks). Their portfolios are jammed with wildly daring designs and innovations. Not all were successful. Some of Porsche's military creations were abject failures. Honda's first foray into Formula 1 racing in 1966–67 ended in shame. But until their final days, both men were prepared to operate at the edge of their imaginations and their financial resources. They were daring, audacious, endlessly curious engineers and entrepreneurs.

Ironically, both came from modest backgrounds: Porsche's father was an Austrian tinsmith, Honda's a blacksmith. Both were fascinated by raw speed and high performance. Both were tough, totally committed men with iron wills. Both were crushed by World War II but rose from its smoking ruins to build automotive empires.

The first car to bear Porsche's name was the first-generation Type 356, introduced in 1950. Honda, already an international power in motorcycles, came to market twelve years later with a tiny two-seat sports car powered by a miniature DOHC four-cylinder engine. He was hardly welcomed into the business. Never a member of one of Japan's elite and immensely powerful *keiretsu* business and financial cartels, like rivals Datsun and Toyota, Soichiro Honda was openly discouraged from poking into the tightly controlled automotive realm. Always the maverick, he defied the powerful establishment and within 25 years ascended to the very pinnacle of the business: World Championships in cars and motorcycles and world-class products ranging from the still-superb Civic to the magnificent NSX supercar. At the time of his recent death at the age of 84, Soichiro Honda, by dint of his own brilliance and pugnacity, dominated a business that he was not supposed to enter and that current wisdom says digests newcomers like a pack of killer whales dining on hors d'oeuvres of smelt.

All of which begs the question: If Soichiro Honda made it big, why not someone else? Where is it mandated that the club is closed to new members, that the entry fee is beyond the reach of anyone, no matter how rich, and that the qualifications are too exclusive for any mortal to meet?

It has long been business dogma that no organization, much less an individual, possesses the muscle to enter the automobile business. The recent failures of John Z. De Lorean and Malcolm Bricklin are inevitably dredged up as prima facie evidence that such an enterprise is akin to creating cold fusion, perpetual motion, and an efficient postal system. It simply cannot be done and that is that, say the business gurus.

But do not forget that the same thing was being claimed in the early 1960s when Soichiro Honda poked his foot in the door. At that time, America's Big Three were all-powerful. General Motors alone controlled nearly half the world market and faced the constant threat of breakup under the Sherman Antitrust Act. The Japanese car industry was a joke. The Germans, with the exception of Volkswagen, were still rebuilding both product and reputation from the war. The British were descending into an abyss where they remain to this day, and the French and Italians had already set a pattern of jingoism that was to curse them as exporting nations.

Today, the patterns appear as rigid and unyielding as they did to Honda in the early 1960s. There would seem to be no room at the bottom, much less the top. Yet I am sure the same logic prevailed when Steven Jobs and Steve Wozniak launched Apple Computers from a garage in 1977. No doubt they were informed that IBM was unassailable in the field and advised not to quit their day jobs. Surely the same was true for Fred Smith, the man who started Federal Express—a delivery concept considered implausible by the experts at UPS.

So too for the car business. For the dreamers and the crazies and the visionaries, there is always room to compete. In more cases than not, revolutionary developments in a given industry have come from outsiders, not from the haughty and often isolated establishment. If only we could ask Mr. Honda, the last titan (until the next one comes along).

TOM DREW

TECHNOLOGY

TEN BEST CARS OF 1992

By William Jeanes

This is the tenth year we've winnowed the season's new cars down to Ten Best. We regard it as a heavy responsibility, and yet—and yet—for a troop of car guys, what could be lighter work?

Each autumn, we round up the cars that we think have a chance of earning a spot on Ten Best. This *thinking* is based on what we learn driving every new car as soon as it becomes available. Each staffer then drives the entire field of nominees and files his rating sheet. Combining the ratings produces the Ten Best.

Only a few restrictions apply. There has always been a price limit—$30,000 at first, raised to $35,000 in 1988, and raised again this year, to $40,000. Sure, cars priced higher are great, but greatness for less is Best. We used to reserve five spots each for domestic and imported cars, until foreign labels built in U.S. plants blurred the distinction. Now, instead, we limit to two cars per brand on the final Ten Best list, our version of the Olympics limit of three athletes per nation.

Ten Best Cars is unique in that it's untethered by rules of strict categories. It doesn't care what's the best sports car or the best family hauler. It seeks overall bests, homing in on a model year's best achievements like a heat-seeking Stinger sniffing out an Iraqi helicopter. If the world's automakers were to unleash ten breakthrough four-doors in a given season, it's entirely possible that those ten sedans would bump everything else off the winning list.

A best-seeker is every consumer's dream, wouldn't you agree? But after ten years of Ten Best Cars, we see something more. We see a record—a database of automotive achievement—from which trends emerge, trends that forecast the future of the automobile in America. When viewed as a leading indicator, Ten Best Cars has been predicting the following:

The rise of Japan as a source of Best Cars. On the first Ten Best list in 1983, Japanese brands tied the Europeans at three cars each. Last year, the Japanese earned eight spots, nine if you credit Mazda engineering for the Mercury Tracer LTS's success. Clearly the Japanese have taken the lead in providing nimble, efficient cars with nifty mechanisms that reward the driver. If our enthusiast's bias for fun-to-drive cars is showing here, it knows no national boundaries—it works for BMW and the Taurus SHO, too. More to the point, American buyers are responding to these same pleasures as they choose more and more Japanese cars.

Ten Best trends suggest that the appeal of Japanese cars will keep on rising.

The weakening of Europe as a market force. Historically, Europe was the leading source of imported cars. The high point came in 1986, with four Europeans on the list. It's been fast fade since: no Europeans made it in 1990 and 1991.

Think back to the mid-eighties. The Volkswagen Rabbit GTI was the fun car of choice then. Where is the popularly priced European fun car now? In the sports-car business, Porsche was a real contender over a wide price range: the 944 made the first four Ten Bests. Now there isn't a single Porsche priced under $40,000. What European maker can you turn to for an affordable sports car?

Ten Best trends point to Europe's fading competitiveness in the U.S. market. The fact that a lone European, the BMW 325i, did make the list this year doesn't change the trend.

The emergence of the minivan as the new family car. It's a measure of the minivan's rightness that it has managed to break through our fun-to-drive bias in 1985 (Chrysler), 1990 (Mazda MPV), and in a big way last year (Mazda MPV and Toyota Previa). Minivans aren't fun, but their efficiency and usefulness is so compelling that they often push aside some perfectly wonderful cars in our ratings.

Ten Best trends predict a bright future for this only-a-decade-old type of automobile, which already sells almost a million units a year.

The resurgence of Nissan as a carmaker of note. Nissan this year took a hit from the two-winner limit: the Maxima SE was dropped. Nissan (then Datsun) was strong in the seventies; then it lost the scent. But the company has placed two cars among the Ten Best for four consecutive years now, which predicts a strong future.

How reliable is this indicator? After a similar showing by Ford in the four years beginning in 1986 (accompanied by phenomenal success in the market), the company dropped back to one winner in 1990. Very quickly, Ford's sales softened.

Honda (before the two-winner limit) had three cars on the list in 1985 and 1988. Over the Ten Best history Honda has averaged 1.9 cars per year on the list, a record unmatched by any other maker. Honda's growth in sales over the period is also unmatched.

The magic of Ten Best is the way it crosses body-style distinctions and national borders in a straight-ahead quest for goodness. The insight it gives into cars and car markets is simply unmatched. Other car magazines apparently agree, or they wouldn't be jumping in with imitations of their own.

BMW 325i

Vehicle type: front-engine, rear-wheel-drive, 5-passenger, 4-door sedan
Base price: $28,365
Engine: DOHC 24-valve 2.5-liter 6-in-line
Power (SAE net) ....189 bhp @ 5900 rpm
Transmission 5-speed
Wheelbase ....106.3 in
Length...174.5 in
Curb weight ....3000 lb
EPA fuel economy, city driving...............................18 mpg

Vehicle type: front-engine, front-wheel-drive, 5-passenger, 4-door sedan
Base price: $39,433
Engine: 4.9-liter V-8
Power (SAE net) ....200 bhp @ 4100 rpm
Transmission ....4-speed auto
Wheelbase ....111.0 in
Length...203.9 in
Curb weight ....3700 lb
EPA fuel economy, city driving...............................16 mpg

Vehicle type: front-engine, 4-wheel-drive, 2+2-passenger, 3-door coupe
Base price: $17,221–19,217
Engine: turbocharged and intercooled DOHC 16-valve 2.0-liter 4-in-line
Power (SAE net) ....195 bhp
Transmission 5-speed
Wheelbase ....97.2 in
Length...172.4–174.8 in
Curb weight ....3100 lb
EPA fuel economy, city driving..........................18–20 mpg

BMW 325i

Few occurrences are as heart-warming to car enthusiasts as the appearance of a new BMW. Three cheers, then, for the 325i, a new BMW that we identified as "a BMW you can actually afford."

This car is the lineal and spiritual descendant of the BMW 2002, the little giant-killer that became a cult car in 1968. The 2002's achievement of cult status was aided by your pals at *Car and Driver,* who couldn't find enough good things to say about it.

We found more than enough good things to say about the new 325i: more exciting, more practical, the performance of a wing-footed god, an engine that can sing Mozart, and German good looks.

We also believe that the 325i is the most handsome 3-series car ever—both without and within. And that its 24-valve 2.5-liter in-line six—the same engine found in the larger 525i sedan—and the Getrag five-speed gearbox make a perfect setup for those of us who demand the satisfaction of perfect driving.

CADILLAC SEVILLE TOURING SEDAN

In the event that Detroit is listening, let us note that, as good as the Cadillac STS is, it's not perfect. But it's the brightest ray of sunshine that we've seen from the Motor City in years, and we're pleased that it earned a spot on our Ten Best list.

Distinguished by its restraint, the STS proves that Detroit can build a tasteful American car that doesn't depend on BMW for its styling cues. At $39,433, the car is within our parameters but too close for comfort to the import luxury cars. Still, the STS should gain market share for Cadillac among the younger buyers it must attract to succeed in the long term.

What's not perfect? Two things—one small, one larger, both important. In the $40,000 luxury class, the paint quality and the interior fit and finish must be above reproach, and a world-class engine belongs under the hood. Our test car was an early-production model, so we assume the first criticism is fixed by now. The engine, in the form of the 32-valve Northstar, arrives for 1993.

CADILLAC SEVILLE TOURING SEDAN

DIAMOND-STAR AWD TURBOS

The Diamond-Star Turbos remain dear to our hearts despite 1992 being the swoopy coupes' third year in the U.S. marketplace. It's hardly surprising, then, that 1992 marks the third year that Diamond-Star Turbos have appeared on our Ten Best Cars list, an honor earned by giving the enthusiast as fine a combination of value, good looks, and tummy-tightening performance as could be found anywhere at any price.

This year, however, we've added a qualification to the Diamond-Star Turbos win: the award goes only to those models with all-wheel drive. That means the Eagle Talon TSi AWD, the Plymouth Laser RS Turbo AWD, and the Mitsubishi Eclipse GSX take home the crystal trophy.

For a more than reasonable price, beginning at $17,221 for the Plymouth Laser RS Turbo AWD, you get a car that can be enjoyed in everyday driving, looks good on social occasions, and provides a generous 195 horsepower to enjoy during those special times on the road.

PLYMOUTH LASER RS TURBO AWD

FORD TAURUS SHO

FORD TAURUS SHO

Victimized largely by advancing competition, the Taurus line, which had made our Ten Best Cars list for each of the past six years, has been replaced for 1992 by Ford Division's premium standard-bearer, the Ford Taurus SHO.

Constant readers will recall that this version of the Taurus—which, like the entire line, got a sheetmetal redo for 1992 —is Ford's Q-ship, a quietly styled sedan with the heart of a lion beating beneath its skin. The feline power and smoothness of the Yamaha 24-valve 3.0-liter V-6 makes the SHO a true high-performance sports sedan that can take on anything in its price range and emerge from the contest with its head high and its 220-hp heart unbroken.

The SHO has suffered in the marketplace because it has, until this fall, lacked an automatic-transmission option. The new four-speed automatic transmission and larger engine will surely broaden the appeal of the SHO. We're happy for Ford but readily admit that we liked having the SHO as our secret.

Vehicle type: front-engine, front-wheel-drive, 5-passenger, 4-door sedan
Base price: $24,262
Engine: DOHC 24-valve 3.0-liter V-6
Power (SAE net) ....220 bhp @ 6200 rpm
Transmission 5-speed
Wheelbase .... 106.0 in
Length .... 188.4 in
Curb weight ....3450 lb
EPA fuel economy, city driving.............................. 18 mpg

HONDA PRELUDE Si

HONDA PRELUDE Si

We don't know this to be fact, but it may be impossible to do a Ten Best list without a Honda on it (one has appeared on all ten of our Ten Best Cars lists). This year's Honda representative is the spanking-new Prelude Si—the two-wheel-steer version only. This fine distinction is made because we did not feel that the added four-wheel-steer capability justified the added cost for this option. Trust us, you won't miss it.

Nor will you miss one of the best driving experiences available. The Prelude Si sports coupe is completely redone for 1992. Taking several years of criticism into account, Honda changed the Pre-

LEXUS SC400

lude's personality from plain vanilla to cayenne pepper, a change that went down well with the *Car and Driver* troops.

The Prelude Si for 1992 has a softer yet more massive presence and is powered by a 160-hp 2.3-liter version of the Accord engine. The balance and execution of this car made it the surprise vote-getter among a powerful Honda contingent that included both the Civic and the Accord.

Lexus SC400

Our technical director, the redoubtable Mr. Csere, summed the new Lexus SC400 up by calling it frustrating. Why? Because he couldn't think of one single thing to do to the new Lexus coupe that would make it better.

Powered by the 250-hp Lexus V-8, the SC400 exhibits a personality that's a welcome counterpoint to the seamless LS400 sedan that preceded it to the U.S. Though the coupe shares what one of us called "the crypt-like silence, silky smooth engine, and supple, well-controlled suspension behavior" found in the sedan, the coupe is a car built for drivers. You get not only luxury but also a 6.7-second 0-to-60-mph time. And our testers reached 145 mph on the test track. Serious motoring? You bet.

And it's good-looking in the bargain (which, relatively speaking, the SC400 represents, even at nearly $40,000 as tested). The styling, by designers at Toyota's Calty Design in California, exhibits enough beauty of line to supply most of the world's auto industry. The SC400's as handsome as they come.

Vehicle type: front-engine, front-wheel-drive, 2+2-passenger, 2-door coupe
Base price: $19,540
Engine: DOHC 16-valve 2.3-liter 4-in-line
Power (SAE net) ....160 bhp @ 5800 rpm
Transmission 5-speed
Wheelbase ....100.4 in
Length ....174.8 in
Curb weight ....2900 lb
EPA fuel economy, city driving...................22 mpg

Vehicle type: front-engine, rear-wheel-drive, 2+2-passenger, 2-door coupe
Base price: $38,690
Engine: DOHC 32-valve 4.0-liter V-8
Power (SAE net) ....250 bhp @ 5600 rpm
Transmission ....4-speed auto
Wheelbase ....105.9 in
Length ....191.1 in
Curb weight ....3700 lb
EPA fuel economy, city driving...............18 mpg

MAZDA MX-5 MIATA

Mazda MX-5 Miata

If ever a car earned the title "America's Sweetheart," or the perhaps more correct "America's Significant Other," it's the Mazda Miata—everyone's secret automotive heartthrob.

There are better cars than the Miata. Some of them are made by Mazda. But the Miata makes our list for the simple reason that it's a one-of-a-kind execution of those automotive values that got so many of us interested in cars to begin with.

It sounds good. It shifts and turns with an élan not found in most small cars. If driven properly, which is to say vigorously, its performance is stout enough to reward the driver with smiles. Its top may be removed, revealing a whole new world of motoring pleasure.

It is interesting to note that, though aimed squarely at the fortysomething or fiftysomething crowd—drivers who experienced similar cars in all their oil-leaking and temperamental glory—the Mazda Miata has found fans in every age group and at every income level, which is what happens when you get it right.

Vehicle type: front-engine, rear-wheel-drive, 2-passenger, 2-door convertible
Base price: $14,650
Engine: DOHC 16-valve 1.6-liter 4-in-line
Power (SAE net)..105–116 bhp
Transmissions ....5-speed, 4-speed auto
Wheelbase ....89.2 in
Length...155.4 in
Curb weight...2200–2250 lb
EPA fuel economy, city driving.........................23–24 mpg

Nissan Sentra SE-R

Is it homely? Or at best a bit on the retro side? Yes. Is it wonderful? Also yes. And not the least of its attractions is a price tag that won't stun you.

The SE-R has been called the BMW 2002 of the 1990s, and we won't quarrel with that. What's more, this being the 1990s, you get a car that doesn't require the kind of skilled and often expensive attention once demanded by a small BMW. Gain without the pain, as it were.

At the heart of our attraction to the SE-R is its engine, a DOHC, sixteen-valve, all-aluminum 2.0-liter four that graces its taskmaster with 140 horsepower in highly usable form.

NISSAN 300ZX TURBO

NISSAN 300ZX TURBO

As our group of Ten Best voters drove the 300ZX Turbo and compared this two-seat beauty with its competition, the adjective "civilized" once more came into wide use. As well it should, for this car—at what could be defended as a modest $37,000—brings a new feel to touring in the grand manner. It is particularly rewarding to the enthusiast to see how far Nissan has taken the idea of the sports car. The 300ZX is a distant mechanical relative of the 240Z that appeared twenty years ago, but it remains close in spirit to that groundbreaker.

Nissan's 300ZX line offers you two engines, normally aspirated or turbocharged and intercooled, but unless you're averse to owning the best thing of its kind, at a nominal price penalty, we say get the turbocharged version ... which is again the one that gets our Ten Best nod.

For the purest kind of driving satisfaction on that perfect road on that perfect day, the Nissan 300ZX Turbo gets our vote as the perfect car.

Vehicle type: front-engine, rear-wheel-drive, 2-passenger, 3-door coupe
Base price: $36,809–$37,845
Engine: twin-turbocharged and intercooled DOHC 24-valve 3.0-liter V-6
Power (SAE net)..280–300 bhp
Transmissions ....5-speed, 4-speed auto
Wheelbase ....96.5 in
Length...169.5 in
Curb weight ....3550–3600 lb
EPA fuel economy, city driving...............................18 mpg

NISSAN SENTRA SE-R

The SE-R made our list last year because we felt that it delivered about as much fun for as little money as you could reasonably expect a car to do. This conviction continues, though it's softened somewhat by the base price having risen from less than $11,000 to just over $12,000. But the good news is that you can have an SE-R with air, a stereo, and ABS for just over $14,000. Good news indeed.

Vehicle type: front-engine, front-wheel-drive, 5-passenger, 2-door sedan
Base price: $12,150
Engine: DOHC 16-valve 2.0-liter 4-in-line
Power (SAE net) ....140 bhp @ 6400 rpm
Transmission 5-speed
Wheelbase ....95.7 in
Length...170.3 in
Curb weight ....2600 lb
EPA fuel economy, city driving................................24 mpg

TOYOTA CAMRY XLE

Toyota Camry V-6

Remember when Nissan and Toyota made four-door sedans that, despite being as dependable as the sun and as trouble-free as an anvil, were sort of dumb-looking? It's time to file those memories away with your eight-track tapes and your Bob Dylan records. The times have indeed changed, and there's no more stunning example than the new Toyota Camry.

The Nissan Maxima was the first car from Japan that we felt gave normal humans the choice of modern, sporty four-door transport with all the convenience of a family sedan. The Camry has expanded on this theme and in its new intermediate-size configuration figures to give such mainstay cars as the Taurus and the Lumina a run for the customer's money.

The Ten Best award goes to the V-6–powered versions of the Camry. With its *au courant* looks, superb interior appointments, plus excellent power and handling for a family sedan, the Kentucky-built Toyota Camry V-6 stands as a benchmark in the building of a mainstream sedan. We predict big sales for this new Toyota.

Vehicle type: front-engine, front-wheel-drive, 5-passenger, 4-door sedan
Base price: $17,103–20,803
Engine: DOHC 24-valve 3.0-liter V-6
Power (SAE net) .... 185 bhp @ 5200 rpm
Transmission .... 4-speed auto
Wheelbase .... 103.1 in
Length .... 187.8 in
Curb weight .... 3300 lb
EPA fuel economy, city driving .... 18 mpg

TEN BEST PERFORMERS, 1991*

Acceleration, 0–60 mph .... Ferrari F40, 4.2 sec
Quarter-mile .... Ferrari F40, 12.1 sec @ 122 mph
Top-gear acceleration** .... GMC Syclone, 7.6 sec
Top speed .... Ferrari F40, 197 mph
Braking, 70–0 mph .... Chevrolet Corvette ZR-1, 155 feet
Roadholding .... Ferrari F40, 1.01g
Interior sound level @ 70 mph . Mercedes-Benz 400SE, 66 dBA
Road horsepower @ 50 mph .... Ford Escort LX, 10 hp
Geo Metro LSi Convertible, 10 hp
EPA city fuel economy ..... Geo Metro LSi Convertible, 41 mpg
C/D observed fuel economy Geo Metro LSi Convertible, 34 mpg

*Includes only U.S.-specification production cars tested by *C/D* in 1991
**Sum of 30-to-50-mph and 50-to-70-mph acceleration times

TEN WORST PERFORMERS, 1991*

Acceleration, 0–60 mph ...... Ford F350 XLT Lariat, 17.3 sec
Quarter-mile ...... Ford F350 XLT Lariat, 20.5 sec @ 65 mph
Top-gear acceleration** .... Ford Ranger Sport, 49.6 sec
Top speed .... Isuzu Rodeo LS, 89 mph
Braking, 70–0 mph ... Chev. Suburb. 1500 4x4 Silverado, 264 ft
Roadholding .... Toyota 4Runner 4WD SR5 V6, 0.62 g
Interior sound level @ 70 mph .... Ferrari F40, 89 dBA
Road horsepower @ 50 mph .... Isuzu Rodeo LS, 26 hp
EPA city fuel economy .... Aston Martin Virage, 11 mpg
C/D observed fuel economy ..... Ford F350 XLT Lariat, 8 mpg

*Includes only U.S.-specification production cars tested by *C/D* in 1991
**Sum of 30-to-50-mph and 50-to-70-mph acceleration times

FULL SLATE OF TEN BEST NOMINEES

Our Ten Best Cars nominating process was designed to err on the side of including too many cars rather than too few. Any new car that we haven't driven much gets included, just in case. The previous year's Ten Best are automatic nominees, as are winners of comparison tests. Any other car can be nominated by a majority vote of the staff.

The result is a long list of possibles. Then the driving begins.

We cannot overstate the knowledge to be gained from driving more than three dozen good cars back-to-back in a compressed time frame (six to seven days in this instance). Cars we thought were wonderful turn out to be less so when driven in the same afternoon against their competition. It's fun, but more important it's a learning experience—one that we wish each one of you could share with us.

Acura Legend
Acura Legend Coupe
Audi 100CS
BMW 325i
Buick Park Avenue Ultra
Cadillac Seville Touring Sedan
Chevrolet Corvette
Chevrolet Lumina Euro 3.4
Diamond-Star AWD Turbos
Dodge Caravan
Eagle Summit Wagon
Ford Escort LX-E
Ford Mustang LX 5.0
Ford Taurus
Ford Taurus SHO
Honda Accord
Honda Civic
Honda Prelude Si
Lexus ES300

Lexus SC400
Mazda 929
Mazda MX-5 Miata
Mazda MPV V-6
Mazda MX-3 GS
Mazda Protegé LX
Mercury Sable
Mercury Tracer LTS
Nissan Maxima SE HO
Nissan NX2000
Nissan Sentra SE-R
Nissan 300ZX Turbo
Pontiac Bonneville
Pontiac Grand Am
Saturn Coupe
Subaru SVX
Toyota Camry V-6
Toyota Previa
Volvo 960

OTHER NOMINEES

GARY RICHARDSON ILLUSTRATION

By Phil Berg

Every year we at *Car and Driver* test the newest and most promising cars of that year to determine our Ten Best. We nominated 38 cars for the 1992 model year, then gathered all the nominees and drove them at our test site. The jury was out for about a week as merits and shortcomings were compared. Then the verdict was read. The Ten Best appear on the preceding pages. The remaining 28 cars, some of which just missed the Top Ten, are shown here alphabetically.

ACURA LEGEND
Mechanical excellence, superb quality of fit and finish, and thoughtful details are sometimes not enough for us. We seek a Legend that inspires us to drive.

ACURA LEGEND COUPE
Two inches shorter than the Legend sedan, the two-door coupe feels slightly more compact. But perhaps it's not as sporty as we'd like a two-door to be.

AUDI 100CS
It looks terrific inside and out, and is powered by a smooth, new V-6 engine. But its $34,000 price belies the fact that it's slower than half-a-dozen of its competitors.

BUICK PARK AVENUE ULTRA
A smooth, quiet, and likable big luxury car, the supercharged Buick doesn't feel as composed at high speeds as it does cruising on slower streets.

CHEVROLET CORVETTE
A power boost to 300 hp for 1992 makes the Corvette great fun to drive, but every now and then a stray rattle or clunk gets in the way of our enjoyment.

CHEVROLET LUMINA EURO 3.4
Featuring the largest twin-cam V-6 engine you can buy, the sportiest of Chevy's mid-size sedans promises drivers more fun than it delivers.

DODGE CARAVAN
The new Chrysler minivan is as good as they get. Trouble is, there are so many great cars on our list, the best of minivans got squeezed out.

EAGLE SUMMIT WAGON
A fun and incredibly useful little van, this tall wagon/mini-minivan offers convenience for those with adventurous lifestyles. It's thrifty, too, but it's slow.

FORD ESCORT LX-E
Consider this small sedan an Escort GT with two extra doors. We love its 1.8-liter four-cylinder engine, and rank this compact sedan just below the refined Sentra SE-R in the fun-to-drive category.

FORD MUSTANG LX 5.0
A favorite, affordable performance car, the aging V-8 Mustang keeps up with much newer machinery in speed and handling. Rough roads tend to upset the Mustang's ride.

FORD TAURUS
Newly refined for 1992, the Taurus is three inches longer than before and has a smoother, quieter ride. The refinements are evolutionary rather than revolutionary.

HONDA ACCORD
America's most popular car lacks the power of Toyota's new V-6 Camry, though the Honda features top-line fit and finish and a thoughtfully designed interior.

HONDA CIVIC
Of the four models of new Civics we drove, we thought the best-outfitted versions were too expensive. However, the superb refinement on these cars usually has no price limit.

LEXUS ES300
Most of the goodness of this sedan can be found in the similar V-6 Toyota Camry; think of the Lexus as a highly styled variation with more flair and a quicker steering ratio.

MAZDA 929
Every one of us thinks this is a gorgeous car both outside and inside. But we feel a few details, such as interior space and at-the-limit handling, could be improved.

MAZDA MPV V-6
This minivan has been one of our Ten Best before, but newer cars, and Chrysler's newly refined minivan, have proved to be stiff enough competition to keep it off this year's list.

MAZDA MX-3 GS
It's cute, and the little Mazda's 1.8-liter V-6 engine runs smoothly and sounds like a Maserati. But this specialized MX-3 isn't as quick as the Diamond-Star coupes, nor is it quicker than the less-expensive Sentra SE-R.

MAZDA PROTEGÉ LX
We like the interior and styling of the Escort LX-E better than the Mazda, though mostly for subjective reasons. It remains a small sedan we could drive anywhere.

MERCURY SABLE
This sedan received all of the same refinements as the new Taurus, which earned it high marks. It's competent but not outstanding.

MERCURY TRACER LTS
Sharing the same driveline as the Escort LX-E and the Protegé LX, the top-line Tracer sedan is a capable, fun car. All it needs is a little more refinement.

NISSAN MAXIMA SE HO
A 30-hp boost to 190 hp makes the sportiest Maxima great fun to drive. It's slightly noisier than the Camry, and its major controls are just a touch heavy.

NISSAN NX2000
Based on the same drivetrain as the Sentra SE-R, the 2.0-liter NX coupe is heavier and substantially more expensive. A few of us aren't sold on the front-end styling.

PONTIAC BONNEVILLE
Better looking, we feel, than its faster SSEi sibling, we think Pontiac's largest car could be a world-class sedan with a bit more refinement.

PONTIAC GRAND AM
The 180-hp GT model is plenty fast and capable, but it loses its composure on rough roads, and its steering and shifting could feel better.

SATURN COUPE
The two-door Saturn is a great value, but its driving fun is not exceptional. It's quite buzzy when you rev its twin-cam 1.9-liter four-cylinder engine, too.

SUBARU SVX
This expensive coupe rewards its driver in 98 percent of all driving conditions. But at its near-$30,000 price, you should be able to expect 100 percent.

TOYOTA PREVIA
The Toyota is another minivan that's made our list in the past. Like the Chrysler and Mazda minivans, better cars leave less room for this slick van.

VOLVO 960
The big Volvo's 201-hp six-cylinder engine is smooth and powerful, but it's trapped in an aging body that feels tuned for slower driving than its competitors.

PHOTOGRAPHY BY AARON KILEY

FORD TAURUS LX

By Frank Markus

In 1985, Ford completed a $3 billion investment in the most radically aerodynamic American sedan since the Chrysler Airflow. As if to evince its bullish aspirations for the car, Ford called it the Taurus. In spite of some recalls and minor quality problems, the bold style and European ride and handling have won the car a place in some two million garages and on every *C/D* Ten Best list since 1986.

Now Ford is releasing an updated Taurus. The Dearborn company has spent $650 million on the 1992 Taurus (and, of course, its sister car, the Mercury Sable) to refine its appearance, improve assembly quality, and hone its driving characteristics. These revisions are expected to sustain the model until it is replaced by an all-new car in 1995.

The styling revisions are as evolutionary as those we've come to expect from

Volvo, although all exterior body panels except the doors are new this year. Rear overhang is extended 2.5 inches, which increases trunk volume slightly. The familiar face now sports wider, lower headlights and is even more rounded than before, protruding an inch further into the wind. These changes, plus new wheels and body cladding, combine for subtle improvements in both appearance and aerodynamics. The drag coefficient is down from 0.33 to 0.32. The Taurus SHO version gets its own distinctive front fascia and side cladding, as well as a hood, fenders, headlights, and marker lights borrowed from the new Sable.

Inside, the 1992 car has new seat fabrics and door trim panels, a swoopy new dash, an optional passenger-side air bag (available mid-year), and some pleasant ergonomic refinements. The power window and door-lock switches are horizontally arrayed on the armrest and backlit for night visibility. The radio buttons are larger and are augmented by redundant volume, seek, and memory seek buttons located high on the instrument panel, next to the steering wheel. They're too far away for hands-on-the-wheel operation though, unless you can reach a three-octave piano chord. The overall shape and design of the interior pleases the editorial eye, but the plastic and vinyl grained to match the leather seats in our luxo version just weren't convincing. A contrasting accent color or some different materials might help.

If what's been described so far doesn't seem like 650 million clams' worth, we agree. But much of the money was spent where it doesn't show, on a number of small but intelligent high-tech refinements to the vehicle structure and suspension to improve noise level, vibration, harshness, drivability, and (hopefully) customer satisfaction.

New upper strut mounts reduce rear-suspension noise. A retuned tire and wheel package avoids exciting the body's natural vibration frequency. Increased torsional rigidity of the unibody allowed a reduction in the rear anti-roll-bar stiffness to improve ride without compromising handling. A recalibrated version of the speed-sensitive power steering borrowed from the Continental provides higher effort at low speed and less variation in effort throughout all speed ranges. The list of technical revisions goes on and on—and pays off.

Our first impression upon driving the new Taurus is that the cabin is quiet enough for golf broadcasters and librarians to carry on a conversation. Our measurements back up this perception, with levels down 7 dBA at idle and 2 to 3 dBA under acceleration, cruise, and coast, compared with the last Taurus LX we tested. And it's quieter than the Acura Legend and the Cadillac Sedan de Ville. At 9.2 seconds from 0 to 60 mph, it's also the quickest automatic Taurus we've measured, including the police version. Ride and handling remain classic Taurus, taut but very supple with excellent control and no surprises. One serious drivetrain problem with the Taurus is that during braking the electronic overdrive automatic transmission seems somehow to go into neutral, then grab and make the car lurch forward when the accelerator is reapplied.

That flaw notwithstanding, the new Taurus remains a good value among family sedans. Although our fully loaded LX cost over $20,000, one can obtain nicely outfitted examples for much less. As a high-value, multifariously capable family sedan, the Taurus remains hard to beat.

Highs: *Hushed cockpit, supple ride.*

Lows: *Indecisive automatic transmission, overly synthetic interior trim.*

The verdict: *No longer the standout it once was, but updates keep it among the class leaders.*

COUNTERPOINT

Ford executives like to claim that Japanese car manufacturers carry over a lot of old parts when they redesign their products every four years. They understand such thinking in Dearborn and happily adopted it when they face-lifted the Taurus after six years of production. However, even if many redesigned Japanese models do take full advantage of existing parts, they also incorporate significant mechanical or styling changes. Although a fine car, the new Taurus offers neither. As a result, it's no longer the phenomenon it was six years ago. —*Csaba Csere*

Mom and Pop need a new car. They're asking my advice. The problem is we don't see eye to eye when it comes to wheels. Mom checks the speedometer. I check the tachometer. Dad likes engines with "pep." I prefer ones that melt pavement. And so on. It's not that Mom and Dad are fuddy-duddies. They're mainstream new-car buyers looking for the most rational car in this hotly contested sedan market. This new Taurus LX, with all its improvements, will do just fine for the 'rents. And that still leaves the SHO for less rational types, like me.
—*Don Schroeder*

Six years for one model is the automotive equivalent of middle age. But the Taurus hasn't had its midlife crisis yet. It's aged well, with no glaring wrinkles or gray hairs, and the new face-lift keeps it as fresh as it was in 1986. The smoother nose and tail, the new instrument panel, and the revised automatic transmission are attractive and welcome changes. The superb JBL sound system and classy leather interior in our test car rival those available in the Continental. All told, the new Taurus maintains its substantial and mature feel—it's as if somebody discovered Grecian Formula.
—*Martin Padgett Jr.*

Ford Taurus LX

Vehicle type: front-engine, front-wheel-drive, 6-passenger, 4-door sedan

Estimated price as tested: $22,000

Major standard accessories: power steering, windows, seats, and locks, A/C, tilt steering

Sound system: Ford JBL AM/FM-stereo radio/cassette/compact-disc player, 4 speakers

ENGINE
Type ....V-6, iron block and aluminum heads
Bore x stroke...........................3.81 x 3.39 in, 96.8 x 86.0mm
Displacement..............................232 cu in, 3797cc
Compression ratio 9.0:1
Engine-control system...............Ford with port fuel injection
Emissions controls........................3-way catalytic converter, feedback fuel-air-ratio control, EGR
Valve gear ....pushrods, hydraulic lifters
Power (SAE net) ....140 bhp @ 3800 rpm
Torque (SAE net) ....215 lb-ft @ 2200 rpm
Redline ....5300 rpm

DRIVETRAIN
Transmission.......................................4-speed automatic with lockup torque converter
Final-drive ratio...3.19:1

Gear	Ratio	Mph/100 rpm	Max. test speed
I	2.77	8.3	44 mph (5300 rpm)
II	1.54	15.0	79 mph (5300 rpm)
III	1.00	23.1	116 mph (5000 rpm)
IV	0.69	33.5	115 mph (3450 rpm)

DIMENSIONS AND CAPACITIES
Wheelbase...106.0 in
Track, F/R...61.6/60.5 in
Length..192.0 in
Width...71.2 in
Height ....54.1 in
Frontal Area...22.9 sq ft
Ground clearance..5.5 in
Curb weight ....3383 lb
Weight distribution, F/R 64.1/35.9%
Fuel capacity ....16.0 gal

Oil capacity...4.5 qt
Water capacity ....11.6 qt

CHASSIS/BODY
Type ....unit construction with a rubber-isolated powertrain cradle
Body material ....welded steel stampings

INTERIOR
SAE volume, front seat...53 cu ft
                      rear seat..47 cu ft
                      luggage space ....18 cu ft
Front seat...bench
Seat adjustments ....fore and aft, seatback angle, front height, rear height, lumbar support
Restraint systems, front ....manual 3-point belts, center lap belt, driver air bag
                      rear ....manual 3-point belts, center lap belt
General comfort ....poor fair **good** excellent
Fore-and-aft support ....poor fair **good** excellent
Lateral support................................poor **fair** good excellent

SUSPENSION
F:..............................ind, strut located by a control arm, coil springs, anti-roll bar
R:................................ind, strut located by 2 lateral links and 1 trailing link, coil springs, anti-roll bar

STEERING
Type ....rack-and-pinion, power-assisted
Turns lock-to-lock 2.8
Turning circle curb-to-curb...38.6 ft

BRAKES
F:...10.0 x 1.0-in vented disc
R:...8.9 x 1.5-in cast-iron drum
Power assist...........................vacuum with anti-lock control

WHEELS AND TIRES
Wheel size ....6.0 x 15 in
Wheel type ....cast aluminum
Tires ....Michelin XW4 205/65R-15
Test inflation pressures, F/R.....................................35/35 psi

---

CAR AND DRIVER TEST RESULTS

ACCELERATION
	Seconds
Zero to 30 mph	.2.9
40 mph	.4.6
50 mph	.6.7
60 mph	.9.2
70 mph	.12.6
80 mph	.17.0
90 mph	.22.2
100 mph	.29.6
110 mph	.45.9
Street start, 5–60 mph	.9.3
Top-gear passing time, 30–50 mph	.4.5
50–70 mph	.6.7
Standing 1/4-mile	.17.0 sec @ 80 mph
Top speed	.116 mph

BRAKING
70–0 mph @ impending lockup......................202 ft
Fade ....**none** moderate heavy

HANDLING
Roadholding, 300-ft-dia skidpad ....0.76 g
Understeer ....**minimal** moderate excessive

COAST-DOWN MEASUREMENTS
Road horsepower @ 30 mph...........................6 hp
                              50 mph.............................14 hp
                              70 mph.............................30 hp

FUEL ECONOMY
EPA city driving...18 mpg
EPA highway driving..28 mpg
C/D observed fuel economy ....20 mpg

INTERIOR SOUND LEVEL
Idle ....43 dBA
Full-throttle acceleration....................................74 dBA
70-mph cruising ....68 dBA
70-mph coasting ....68 dBA

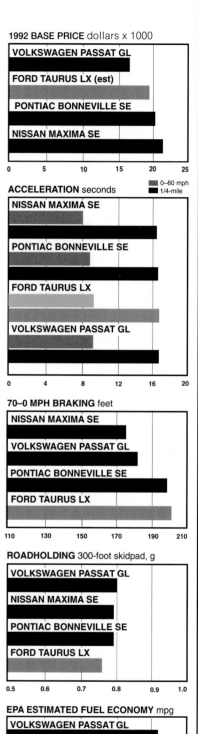

1992 BASE PRICE dollars x 1000
- VOLKSWAGEN PASSAT GL
- FORD TAURUS LX (est)
- PONTIAC BONNEVILLE SE
- NISSAN MAXIMA SE

0   5   10   15   20   25

■ 0–60 mph
■ 1/4-mile

ACCELERATION seconds
- NISSAN MAXIMA SE
- PONTIAC BONNEVILLE SE
- FORD TAURUS LX
- VOLKSWAGEN PASSAT GL

0   4   8   12   16   20

70–0 MPH BRAKING feet
- NISSAN MAXIMA SE
- VOLKSWAGEN PASSAT GL
- PONTIAC BONNEVILLE SE
- FORD TAURUS LX

110   130   150   170   190   210

ROADHOLDING 300-foot skidpad, g
- VOLKSWAGEN PASSAT GL
- NISSAN MAXIMA SE
- PONTIAC BONNEVILLE SE
- FORD TAURUS LX

0.5   0.6   0.7   0.8   0.9   1.0

EPA ESTIMATED FUEL ECONOMY mpg
- VOLKSWAGEN PASSAT GL
- NISSAN MAXIMA SE
- FORD TAURUS LX
- PONTIAC BONNEVILLE SE

0   5   10   15   20   25

Base price includes freight, applicable luxury and gas-guzzler taxes, and any performance options.

CADILLAC STS

By Csaba Csere

Since its 1976 debut, the Cadillac Seville's mission has been to win back some of the Americans who, in increasing numbers, were buying imported luxury cars. The approach was simple. Mainstream Cadillacs were big, flashy, and soft. So Cadillac made the Seville smaller, more subtle, and tauter.

The result was a successful failure. Despite its departures from the Cadillac norm, the Seville was still too glitzy and too slow to compete with the imported competition. On the other hand, it did find plenty of buyers who simply wanted a smaller, sleeker Cadillac.

The second- and third-generation Sevilles achieved no more success against the imports than the original. But the fourth-generation 1992 model, especially the Seville Touring Sedan (also known as STS) we've tested here, may finally fulfill its mission and win back some of those American luxury-car defectors.

For starters, this is the best-looking Seville ever. Chief exterior stylist Richard Ruzzin and his Cadillac team have spawned a design with long, flowing lines that combine a contemporary aerodynamic look—yielding a 0.33 drag coefficient—with a broad-shouldered crispness that's distinctly American.

From the front, the Seville presents a fresh face incorporating only a few traditional cues that reveal its Cadillac bloodline. Even the brightwork is applied with taste and discrimination. Parked next to a Mercedes 300, a BMW 735i, or a Lexus LS400, this Seville looks distinctive but very much in the proper company.

More important than the new Seville's exterior styling is the new interior-decorating philosophy that Cadillac brings to this car. For although the previous model was reasonably clean and smooth from the outside, when you opened its doors you were overcome by tiny, shiny switches scattered haphazardly about a boxy dashboard, enough fake-looking wood to stock the contact-paper aisle in the local builder's supply center, and numerous instrument displays scattered throughout the cockpit.

Highs: *Crisp styling that stands out in a crowd, ultrasmooth and responsive powertrain.*

Lows: *Back-road ride, the occasional ergonomic fumble.*

The verdict: *A Cadillac that an enthusiast can drive and enjoy.*

All of these elements have been banished from the new model. Instead, we find a smooth, flowing instrument panel, a black switch gear, and a white-on-black round tachometer and speedometer set squarely in front of the driver. The digital information center is now set to the left of the main instruments rather than being buried at the bottom of the central console. And although there's still wood trim, it now keeps the look of the real article, thanks to fewer, larger, and simpler panels and a less glossy finish. Finally, there's a general softening to all of the elements, which gives this interior the organic look that the Seville's targeted buyers seek in the luxury imports.

The new interior also offers more room now, due primarily to a three-inch wheelbase stretch that has gone mostly into additional rear-seat leg room. Shoulder and hip room are also more generous, thanks to the 1992 Cadillac Seville's 2.4-inch increase in overall width. The result is a car that now seems as roomy as its competitors.

Unfortunately, the rear seating position is a little low, basically because the Seville, overall, is on the low side, measuring 54.0 inches high. That's up a fraction from last year's car but still much lower than most foreign competitors (a Mercedes 300E is 57.1 inches high).

We have a few other nits to pick with the interior. The square panel that regulates the climate-control system is set just to the right of the main instruments, and the steering-wheel rim blocks the driver's view of it. The lumbar-support switches on the console are far away from the rest of the seat switches on the door. And some of us were not crazy about the shade of gray chosen for the interior of our test car. It does little to complement the rich warmth of the zebrano-wood trim. Give us the beige interior, please.

Finding fault with the STS powertrain is a far more difficult exercise. Cadillac's 4.9-liter V-8 collaborates beautifully with the 4T60-E four-speed automatic transmission to provide a wonderfully smooth and quiet flow of power. Upshifts are virtually imperceptible at any throttle setting, and foot-to-the-floor kickdowns are crisp and unusually shock-free. Although the button on the shifter makes a rather junky clang whenever it's depressed to shift out of park, we can't think of another car that changes gears as smoothly as the STS.

We're also happy to report that there's plenty of punch to go along with these manners. Starting from rest, the transmission makes the most of the V-8's 275 pound-feet of torque to move off smartly, reaching 30 mph in 2.5 seconds. An LS400 needs 3.0 seconds to hit the same speed, and even the powerful Infiniti Q45 takes a tenth longer than the STS. Of course, once the cars are rolling, the 200-hp STS falls behind the 250-hp Lexus and the

Details on the Seville STS speak better than any advertisement. Like the body. Cadillac could have taken the easy route, adding yet another Mercedes bar-of-soap look-alike to the luxury fold. Instead, it worked a crisply creased design that looks distinctive yet pleasing. The 4.9-liter pushrod aluminum V-8 is of humble origin, but Cadillac makes the best of it: its curved intake plenums and sparkling aluminum rocker covers beg to be shown off. And, it's athletically tuned, with a hefty low-end punch and a barking exhaust note that give the engine a lively flavor of its own. What's missing? Some of the smoothness of an Infiniti Q45 or a Lexus LS400 wouldn't hurt. The upcoming Northstar V-8 wouldn't hurt, either. This Seville needs few apologies, though. It just goes about its driving fun a little differently. Trend-setting car buyers like this kind of stuff. Could Cadillac become a hip marque of the nineties?

—*Don Schroeder*

What's gone is perhaps more significant than what's new in this car. Gone: the "boingy" ride found in American yachts (you encounter a protuberance in a highway at 65 and the suspension goes *boing, boing, boing,* up and down, long after the bump has been negotiated). Gone: spongy, sinker seats. These seats feel like the Amish made them, and that's good. Gone: the lunging, howling passing gear that scares all the womenfolk. Gone: the corporate chrome fetish (a single thin, shiny line runs through the waist of the body). Gone: the old leisure-suit look of

the interior. Cadillac at last has produced the feel and look of a Euro cockpit; the center console is very Germanic, sensible and clean. If there's a mistake in this country-club cruiser, it can be found glued to the side window—the sticker price. Cadillac's engineers have hit the target, but the bean counters need to lower their sights.

—*Steve Spence*

A confession: I'm the guy who, in 1985, told you that the Merkur XR4Ti was so good and cheap that Lincoln-Mercury would have to convert domed stadiums into showrooms and BMW would be wrecked. See, car guys can wax encyclopedic about hardware, but they don't know sweetpeas about marketing.

Okay? Fine. So here I go again. The STS has been sabotaged by marketing: it costs too much. Cadillac knows that to survive the nineties it must attract younger buyers. The Allanté was an ambitious try: right car, wrong price.

So why are we looking at an instant replay here? At $39,000, the STS nuzzles up against the intoxicating power hitters from Infiniti and Lexus, where it competes in neither refinement nor quality control. I say Cadillac must sell this desirable sedan—even if it's at a loss—for $30,000 or so. At $30K, the STS dazzles as it battles the likes of the Acura Legend, the Audi 100CS, the Mazda 929, and the Saab 9000. At $30K, the STS would become, as Carroll Shelby is fond of saying, stronger than chicken manure.

—*John Phillips III*

278-hp Infiniti. Still, the STS hits 60 mph in 8.1 seconds and covers the quarter-mile in 16.4 seconds—reasonable performance for a big car. Its 121-mph top speed is about 30 mph shy of its high-powered rivals, though.

What all this means is that the STS can easily hold its own against its rivals in the cut and thrust of urban traffic, but it seems a bit weaker during two-lane-road passing, and it's at a serious disadvantage in an autobahn shoot-out. If that shortcoming in top end bothers you, wait for the new 290-hp Northstar engine coming in 1993 models.

The distinctive Cadillac STS is a choice you won't have any problem defending at the country club.

Underneath the new STS skin lies a reworked version of the previous Seville's chassis. The structure benefits from a host of design changes and additional braces that improve stiffness; redesigned bushings and recalibrated shocks, springs, and anti-roll bars upgrade the suspension.

The results work as well on smooth California freeways as on broken-up Midwestern equivalents. The suspension pro-vides tight control of body motions over bumps, yet it allows the wheels enough motion to round off the sharp edges on potholes and expansion joints.

When the road gets twisty, the STS gives an equally good account of itself. It bends into corners precisely and surely with very little sense that you're in a front-drive car. There's 0.80 g of grip to play with, and the mild understeer at the limit encourages an enthusiastic driver to use every bit of it.

Much of the credit for this performance belongs to the STS's computer-controlled shock absorbers, which increase their damping in three stages with speed. This adaptive system allows relatively soft springs without giving up much control.

The soft springs do, however, require stiff anti-roll bars to minimize body roll. Although there's nothing wrong with this approach on most surfaces, on lumpy back roads with large one-wheel bumps, the anti-roll bars produce some side-to-side head-tossing motions that are decidedly not luxurious.

Otherwise, the STS performs the duties of a luxury sedan in exemplary fashion. It simply provides more comfort, more convenience, and more performance than most lesser cars. And it should, with an as-tested price of more than $41,000.

That puts it within about $3000 of a comparably equipped Lexus LS400—everybody's favorite luxury-sedan value. The Lexus has the edge in high-speed performance, build quality, and ergonomics, but the STS looks distinctive and has quicker reflexes in city traffic. We would still probably give our editorial nod to the Lexus, but if the STS strikes your fancy, you won't have any problem defending your choice at the country club.

Cadillac STS

Vehicle type: front-engine, front-wheel-drive, 5-passenger, 4-door sedan

Price as tested: $41,359

Price and option breakdown: base Cadillac STS (includes $600 freight and $858 luxury tax), $39,433; premium sound system, $972; heated windshield, $309; pearlescent paint, $240; heated front seats, $120; auto-dimming rear-view mirror, $110; luxury tax on options, $175

Major standard accessories: power steering, windows, seats, and locks, A/C, cruise control, tilt steering, rear defroster

Sound system: Delco-Bose Gold series AM/FM-stereo radio/cassette/compact disc player, 4 speakers

ENGINE
Type ....V-8, aluminum block and iron heads
Bore x stroke.........................3.62 x 3.62 in, 92.0 x 92.0mm
Displacement ....299 cu in, 4893cc
Compression ratio...9.5:1
Engine-control system................GM with port fuel injection
Emissions controls............3-way catalytic converter, feedback fuel-air-ratio control, EGR
Valve gear ....pushrods, roller hydraulic lifters
Power (SAE net) ....200 bhp @ 4100 rpm
Torque (SAE net) ....275 lb-ft @ 3000 rpm
Redline...4800 rpm

DRIVETRAIN
Transmission ....4-speed automatic with lockup torque converter
Final-drive ratio 3.33:1

Gear	Ratio	Mph/1000 rpm	Max. test speed
I	2.92	7.9	38 mph (4800 rpm)
II	1.57	14.6	70 mph (4800 rpm)
III	1.00	23.0	110 mph (4800 rpm)
IV	0.70	32.8	121 mph (3650 rpm)

DIMENSIONS AND CAPACITIES
Wheelbase ....111.0 in
Track, F/R..60.9/60.9 in
Length ....203.9 in
Width ....74.4 in
Height ....54.0 in
Frontal area...23.3 sq ft

Ground clearance ....6.0 in
Curb weight ....3689 lb
Weight distribution, F/R 63.2/36.8%
Fuel capacity ....18.8 gal
Oil capacity...5.0 qt

CHASSIS/BODY
Type.....unit construction with 2 rubber-isolated subframes
Body material.................................welded steel stampings

INTERIOR
SAE volume, front seat..55 cu ft
rear seat ....50 cu ft
luggage space ....14 cu ft
Front seats ....bucket
Seat adjustments ....fore and aft, seatback angle, front height, rear height, lumbar support
Restraint systems, front......................manual 3-point belts, driver air bag
rear......................manual 3-point belts, center lap belt
General comfort.............................poor fair **good** excellent
Fore-and-aft support ....poor fair **good** excellent
Lateral support ....poor fair **good** excellent

SUSPENSION
F: ....ind, strut located by a control arm, coil springs, electronically controlled shock absorbers, anti-roll bar
R:.................................ind, strut located by a control arm, transverse leaf spring, electronically controlled shock absorbers, anti-roll bar

STEERING
Type ....rack-and-pinion, power-assisted
Turns lock-to-lock 2.7
Turning circle curb-to-curb.......................................40.0 ft

BRAKES
F:..10.9 x 1.3-in vented disc
R:..11.0 x 0.4-in disc
Power assist ....vacuum with anti-lock control

WHEELS AND TIRES
Wheel size ....7.0 x 16 in
Wheel type...cast aluminum
Tires ....Goodyear Eagle GA, P225/60HR-16
Test inflation pressures, F/R.............................28/26 psi

CAR AND DRIVER TEST RESULTS

ACCELERATION
	Seconds
Zero to 30 mph..	2.5
40 mph..	4.0
50 mph..	5.8
60 mph..	8.1
70 mph..	11.1
80 mph..	15.3
90 mph..	21.0
100 mph..	28.7
110 mph..	51.3

Street start, 5–60 mph..8.2
Top-gear passing time, 30–50 mph 3.9
50–70 mph.......................5.8
Standing 1/4-mile..........................16.4 sec @ 82 mph
Top speed...121 mph

BRAKING
70–0 mph @ impending lockup ....196 ft
Fade..none **moderate** heavy

HANDLING
Roadholding, 295-ft-dia skidpad.......................0.80 g
Understeer ....minimal **moderate** excessive

COAST-DOWN MEASUREMENTS
Road horsepower @ 30 mph ....7 hp
50 mph ....16 hp
70 mph ....35 hp

FUEL ECONOMY
EPA city driving...**16 mpg**
EPA highway driving ....25 mpg
C/D observed fuel economy ....**18 mpg**

INTERIOR SOUND LEVEL
Idle...46 dBA
Full-throttle acceleration ....73 dBA
70-mph cruising..69 dBA
70-mph coasting..69 dBA

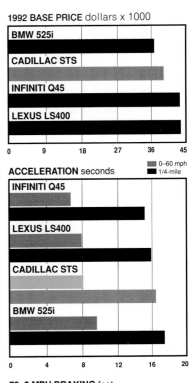

1992 BASE PRICE dollars x 1000
BMW 525i
CADILLAC STS
INFINITI Q45
LEXUS LS400
0 9 18 27 36 45

☐ 0–60 mph
■ 1/4-mile

ACCELERATION seconds
INFINITI Q45
LEXUS LS400
CADILLAC STS
BMW 525i
0 4 8 12 16 20

70–0 MPH BRAKING feet
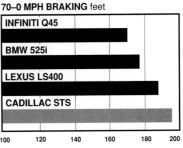
INFINITI Q45
BMW 525i
LEXUS LS400
CADILLAC STS
100 120 140 160 180 200

ROADHOLDING 300-foot skidpad, g
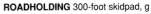
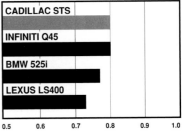
CADILLAC STS
INFINITI Q45
BMW 525i
LEXUS LS400
0.5 0.6 0.7 0.8 0.9 1.0

EPA ESTIMATED FUEL ECONOMY mpg
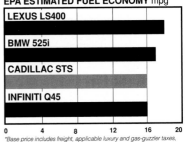
LEXUS LS400
BMW 525i
CADILLAC STS
INFINITI Q45
0 4 8 12 16 20

Base price includes freight, applicable luxury and gas-guzzler taxes, and any performance options.

PONTIAC SSEi

PHOTOGRAPHY BY LARRY GRIFFIN

By Brock Yates

Okay, Waldo, you want a Pontiac Bonneville? *Here's* a Pontiac Bonneville: 389 cubic inches, 10.0:1 compression ratio, three two-barrel Rochester "Tri-Power" carburetors, 315 horsepower at 4600 rpm, and enough torque to haul Mount Rushmore into downtown Rapid City. How about "Wide Track Cats," with road-crusher two-ton weight and twenty-foot hardtop convertible styling that comes with enough brightwork to make a Wurlitzer look like a shipping crate? Big speed, big acceleration, big body, big balls. That, Waldo me boy, *was* a Bonneville.

As luck would have it, you're about thirty years too late. Little zigzags in the car biz in the form of Naderism, oil embargoes, Washington busybodies, and urban air that looks like Mount Saint Helens with a head cold have altered things from the heady days in the late 1950s when the then-new division general manager Bunkie Knudsen and his boy racers almost overnight transformed Pontiac from a nanny's favorite to a NASCAR fire-breather. At the head of the performance renaissance rumbled the Bonneville.

This is not to suggest that the latest permutation of the Bonneville is a counterpart to Joan Claybrook's sensible shoes. Far from it. It stands as yet another example of how modern materials and the miracle of the microchip have created cars

that are vastly better—our sentiments for raw size and power notwithstanding. Today's Bonneville is lighter and smaller, yet it produces better performance. Early Tri-Power Bonnevilles strained hard to thunder through the quarter-mile in under seventeen seconds, whereas the best of the current breed, the supercharged six-cylinder SSEi, cuts the beam in 15.9 seconds (at 87 mph). So much for the legend of the muscle-car mastodons—many of which can be humbled by contemporary machinery with engines half as large.

The vaunted Bonneville nameplate has been employed since 1957. The basic SE, with its 3.8-liter V-6 and value-packed $19,000 base price, was celebrated in the October 1991 *C/D*. In his review, writer Larry Griffin plunged deep into the hyperbolic thicket on the subject of the top-of-the-line SSEi, lamenting it as a body cursed with "gonzo aerodynamic furbelows." Indeed, the SSEi begins as an essentially pleasing four-door shape that is then laden with a curvaceous deck spoiler, an arrogant air dam with aircraft-issue landing lights, and a fluted beltline that appears to have been scavenged from a Chippendale highboy. Adding to the visual zaniness are overwrought, multi-finned sixteen-inch alloy wheels that can be color-keyed to the paintwork. In the case of our refrigerator-white test car, one is stricken with the impression that it squirted out of a can of Redi-Whip. It may

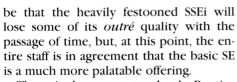

be that the heavily festooned SSEi will lose some of its *outré* quality with the passage of time, but, at this point, the entire staff is in agreement that the basic SE is a much more palatable offering.

There is, however, one hook. Pontiac only offers the 205-hp supercharged V-6 and the sixteen-inch Goodyear Z-rated rubber on its SSEi and SSE models. We wish Pontiac would offer the puffer and the stiffer underpinnings on the more restrained SE, which would then produce a properly civilized big four-door for a reasonable price.

This is not to suggest that the SSEi is not packed with value. At $28,600, the SSEi is a gilded lily of standard features. Goodies include dual air bags up front, GM's superb 4T60-E four-speed automatic (with dual shift modes), full instrumentation, traction control, and twelve-way seats (leather is an option). Some thoughtful additions include a pass-through between the trunk and the rear seats and dual drink holders in the back.

A debatable addition is the "head up" optical speedometer windshield display, which on our test car offered a reading fully three miles an hour slower than the speedo on the instrument panel (the HUD had the true speed). We would also de-

bate the efficacy of the bogus wood paneling, the cluster of nine seat-adjustment buttons that crowd the center console, and the radio controls mounted in the steering-wheel hub. They're fussy and overdone. Truth be known, a viable standard of ergonomic efficiency has been reached in recent years, first on European sedans and finally on better American and Japanese products. Stalk controls, radio buttons, gauges, the shift lever, door latches, window switches, and such are now properly located on most cars, and to fiddle with their placement is to dabble with change simply for the sake of change.

The SSEi works best on long Interstate hauls. Wide semi-bucket seats and interior room are excellent, and cabin sound levels permit normal conversation at velocities of up to 90 mph. (Top speed—with an electronic limiter in third and fourth gears—is 125 mph.) For the businessman seeking an American-made machine that gobbles up the miles with a modicum of effort, the Bonneville is a viable candidate. The V-6, with its Eaton-made supercharger (like that on the Thunderbird, but minus an intercooler), provides good acceleration (0 to 60 in 7.5 seconds), but it works best for midrange passing. The SSEi performs the 50-to-70-mph passing maneuver in a sprightly 5.6 seconds, without complaint from the balance-shafted V-6.

Despite its nose-heaviness, the front-wheel-drive SSEi corners rather neatly, although mushy understeer can be produced if an imprudent throttle application happens to wake up the supercharger. The biggish machine (110.8-inch wheelbase, 201.2 inches overall, 3667 pounds) is rigged with the same coil-sprung strut suspension at all four corners that is found on the Buick Park Avenue Ultra. An

Putting the radio controls on the steering-wheel hub is a debatable move. But there is no argument with the SSEi's spacious interior or the 205-hp supercharged V-6.

SSEi driver will never be deluded into thinking he's at the wheel of an active-suspension Infiniti Q45, but the machine is workmanlike, if uninspired, on most of the smooth road surfaces we face in the United States.

Sadly, despite all the attention to what the Pontiac guys perceive as sporting gadgetry, the company's bean counters have cursed the Bonnevilles with smallish brakes—albeit assisted with anti-lock control. Up front are 10.9-inch vented discs, which are acceptable, but in back one finds an ancient set of 8.9-inch drums dating perhaps from the first Bonnevilles of 35 years ago. We prefer high-performance sedans with rear drive and four-wheel disc brakes. Pontiac has largely masked its front-drive handling, but hard driving bares the weak brakes like an automotive harelip. Drum brakes simply cannot be concealed from the serious driver, and but a few miles of brisk motor-

ing in the SSEi produces a mushy pedal and the acrid odor of barbecued linings. Despite the legends built up around anti-lock systems, they are effective only for emergency stops (and the SSEi's 197-foot stopping distance from 70 mph is strictly average), and anti-lock control adds nothing to a car's ability to slow repeatedly during, say, a fast mountainside descent. In the case of the SSEi, as with many modern automobiles, bigger four-wheel disc brakes are the only solution.

Still, we like the new Bonnevilles. One can debate the swoopy bodywork and some of the gadgetry, but the basic package offers solid value in the American big-car idiom. Our favorite is the low-line SE, but the blown V-6 of the SSEi is a major attraction. We hope it won't be too long before the two are combined (with four-wheel discs, of course) to produce an outright All-American winner. That would make Bunkie and his boys proud indeed.

Highs: *Comfy seats and interior, loads of standard goodies, solid performance.*

Lows: *Hysterical Euro-style overkill, fussy gadgetry, flabby brakes.*

The verdict: *Solid American tourer that needs a dollop of subtlety.*

COUNTERPOINT

Pontiac calls this "excitement." What I see is a four-door with solid credentials, to which Pontiac has added more slots, vents, flares, claddings, overlays, wings, and Goldfinger badges than you'd find in a Saudi prince's entire fleet. Build a house this exciting and it would depress property values for blocks around—until the neighbors burned it down. American party animals have a right to their kind of car. But I think Pontiac got the name wrong. It should be "SEEi." The grammar is kinda bumpy, but culture was never meant to be this car's message, was it?
—*Patrick Bedard*

Rather than do the hard thing—produce a sports sedan with exceptional poise and refinement—Pontiac has done the adolescent thing and plumped up the SSEi with lots of gadgetry and flash. Along with its flamboyant "ground effects," this car has enough buttons to embarrass an IBM keyboard. My question is: Who's going to fall

for this dress-up? The customer who's just test-driven a BMW 325i? No, and that's too bad, because the basic Bonneville SE is a fine piece. With smart thinking and good hardware, the SSEi could have built nicely on the SE's foundation. Instead, it looks like the automotive equivalent of Liberace.
—*Arthur St. Antoine*

I know that some consumers measure the desirability of a product by the sheer tonnage of gadgetry it contains. But I still think cars and driving should be taken seriously, and unless a feature makes my life at the wheel more pleasant, accomplishes something I want done, and otherwise doesn't interfere with my control of a moving vehicle, I'd rather do without it. The SSEi's complex dash panel makes me feel as if I were alone in the control room of a nuclear power plant. I don't feel in imminent danger, but neither am I eager to start touching things.
—*Kevin Smith*

Pontiac SSEi

Vehicle type: front-engine, front-wheel-drive, 5-passenger, 4-door sedan

Price as tested: $29,605

Price and option breakdown: base Pontiac SSEi (includes $555 freight), $28,600; leather seats and overhead console, $779; sound-system upgrade, $226

Major standard accessories: power steering, windows, seats, and locks, A/C, cruise control, tilt steering, rear defroster

Sound system: Delco AM/FM-stereo radio/compact-disc player, 8 speakers

ENGINE
Type	supercharged V-6, iron block and heads
Bore x stroke	3.80 x 3.40 in, 96.5 x 86.4mm
Displacement	231 cu in, 3791cc
Compression ratio	8.5:1
Engine-control system	GM with port fuel injection
Emissions controls	3-way catalytic converter, feedback fuel-air-ratio control, EGR
Supercharger	Eaton model 62, Rootes type
Waste gate	integral
Maximum boost pressure	8.0 psi
Valve gear	pushrods, hydraulic lifters
Power (SAE net)	205 bhp @ 4600 rpm
Torque (SAE net)	260 lb-ft @ 2600 rpm
Redline	5600 rpm

DRIVETRAIN
Transmission ....4-speed automatic with lockup torque converter
Final-drive ratio 2.97:1

Gear	Ratio	Mph/1000 rpm	Max. test speed
I	2.92	8.8	49 mph (5600 rpm)
II	1.57	16.4	92 mph (5600 rpm)
III	1.00	25.7	125 mph (4850 rpm)
IV	0.70	36.8	125 mph (3400 rpm)

DIMENSIONS AND CAPACITIES
Wheelbase	110.8 in
Track, F/R	60.5/60.2 in
Length	201.2 in
Width	73.6 in
Height	55.5 in
Frontal area	24.3 sq ft
Ground clearance	5.6 in
Curb weight	3667 lb
Weight distribution, F/R	64.0/36.0%
Fuel capacity	18.0 gal
Oil capacity	5.0 qt
Water capacity	11.8 qt

CHASSIS/BODY
Type ....unit construction with rubber-isolated powertrain cradle
Body material.................................welded steel stampings

INTERIOR
SAE volume, front seat...57 cu ft
rear seat...............................51 cu ft
luggage space ....18 cu ft
Front seats ....bucket
Seat adjustments ....fore and aft, seatback angle, front height, rear height, lumbar support, upper side bolsters
Restraint systems, front......................manual 3-point belts, driver and passenger air bags
rear ....manual 3-point belts, center lap belt
General comfort............................poor fair **good** excellent
Fore-and-aft support ....poor fair **good** excellent
Lateral support ....poor fair **good** excellent

SUSPENSION
F: ....ind, strut located by a control arm, coil springs, anti-roll bar
R: ....ind, strut located by a control arm and a lateral link, coil springs, automatic-leveling shock absorbers, anti-roll bar

STEERING
Type ....rack-and-pinion, power-assisted
Turns lock-to-lock 3.0
Turning circle curb-to-curb ....40.3 ft

BRAKES
F: ....10.9 x 1.3-in vented disc
R: ....8.9 x 1.8-in cast-iron drum
Power assist ....vacuum with anti-lock control

WHEELS AND TIRES
Wheel size ....7.0 x 16 in
Wheel type...cast aluminum
Tires ....Goodyear Eagle GT+4, 225/60ZR-16
Test inflation pressures, F/R.................................30/30 psi

---

CAR AND DRIVER TEST RESULTS

ACCELERATION
	Seconds
Zero to 30 mph	2.5
40 mph	3.7
50 mph	5.3
60 mph	7.5
70 mph	10.1
80 mph	13.0
90 mph	17.2
100 mph	23.2
110 mph	30.6
120 mph	41.7
Street start, 5–60 mph	7.7
Top-gear passing time, 30–50 mph	3.5
50–70 mph	5.6
Standing 1/4-mile	15.9 sec @ 87 mph
Top speed	125 mph

BRAKING
70–0 mph @ impending lockup ....197 ft
Fade.....................................none **moderate** heavy

HANDLING
Roadholding, 295-ft-dia skidpad......................0.78 g
Understeer ....minimal **moderate** excessive

COAST-DOWN MEASUREMENTS
Road horsepower @ 30 mph ....7 hp
50 mph ....17 hp
70 mph ....34 hp

FUEL ECONOMY
EPA city driving..**18 mpg**
EPA highway driving ....25 mpg
C/D observed fuel economy ....**19 mpg**

INTERIOR SOUND LEVEL
Idle	43 dBA
Full-throttle acceleration	72 dBA
70-mph cruising	68 dBA
70-mph coasting	67 dBA

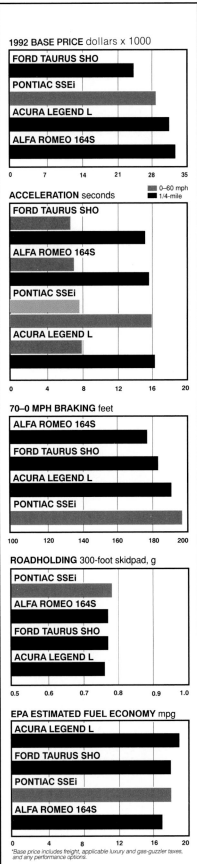

1992 BASE PRICE dollars x 1000
- FORD TAURUS SHO
- PONTIAC SSEi
- ACURA LEGEND L
- ALFA ROMEO 164S

(0, 7, 14, 21, 28, 35)

Legend: ■ 0–60 mph ■ 1/4-mile

ACCELERATION seconds
- FORD TAURUS SHO
- ALFA ROMEO 164S
- PONTIAC SSEi
- ACURA LEGEND L

(0, 4, 8, 12, 16, 20)

70–0 MPH BRAKING feet
- ALFA ROMEO 164S
- FORD TAURUS SHO
- ACURA LEGEND L
- PONTIAC SSEi

(100, 120, 140, 160, 180, 200)

ROADHOLDING 300-foot skidpad, g
- PONTIAC SSEi
- ALFA ROMEO 164S
- FORD TAURUS SHO
- ACURA LEGEND L

(0.5, 0.6, 0.7, 0.8, 0.9, 1.0)

EPA ESTIMATED FUEL ECONOMY mpg
- ACURA LEGEND L
- FORD TAURUS SHO
- PONTIAC SSEi
- ALFA ROMEO 164S

(0, 4, 8, 12, 16, 20)

Base price includes freight, applicable luxury and gas-guzzler taxes, and any performance options.

43

MITSUBISHI DIAMANTE LS

By Patrick Bedard

I f we had to sum up the Mitsubishi Diamante in one sentence, we'd say,
"Look out, Buick!"

Actually, Oldsmobile and Mercury and
Chrysler are just as threatened. For two
reasons: first, this is the sort of quiet,
comfy, gadget-rich four-door that the upscale Detroit brands have always regarded
as their exclusive franchise; second, it's a
harbinger from Japan of many more fancy
family four-doors to come.

Let's take the second reason first. This
car made its Japanese debut in May 1990,
just about the time that government decided to let its people live a little. Taxes
on large cars (exceeding 2.0 liters in engine displacement, 185 inches in length,
and 67 inches in width) were substantially reduced—not just the new-car tax
but also the ownership tax that's due
every year. Insurance rates were lowered
too. As a result, Japanese buyers rushed to
bigger cars, lifting sales of the Diamante
to more than twice the level Mitsubishi
had projected. Other makers benefited

too: Lexus LS400s and Infiniti Q45s are
now as common as fireplugs in Tokyo.

How does this threaten Buick? Easy.
The Japanese have long dominated the
small-car category because they've been
catering to home-market demand, which
gave them the economy of volume production. As the home market shifts to bigger cars, so will the Japanese advantage.
Expect plenty of Japanese action in the
above-$20,000 sedan category from now
on.

And Detroit's in for a real siege too,
judging by the Diamante. This car, in the
heavily optioned form tested here
($29,622), excels at the pleasures for
which people have traditionally bought
Buicks. What it loses in a showdown of
pure, curbside bulk—the Diamante is
about four inches shorter and two inches
narrower than a Buick Regal four-door—
it more than makes up for in gadgets you
can point at and make the neighbors say
wow. Mitsubishi proffers more acronyms
than the Houston Space Center: TCL, ECS,

ABS, EPS-II, MSS, MVIC, ECL-M. It's part of a carefully considered plan. The company knows that the country-club set doesn't genuflect—yet—to the name Mitsubishi. But people associate technology with value, so the Diamante is laden with buttons, switches, and systems that people will take for technology. It's the ultimate Sharper Image car.

If anything, the buttons distract from the classy act of a well-bred automobile. Certain aspects of the Diamante are very appealing. The test car's leather interior is a knockout, charming in a Jaguar-like fashion. The 24-valve V-6 makes a sexy growl as you toe into it, a sound that seems to be showcased in an otherwise whisper-quiet interior. And the ride is controlled yet magic-carpet silky, provided you leave the Euro-Handling package's Active-ECS switch in its default position. Diddle with the buttons, however, and you can easily screw up a good thing.

We're talking about the top-of-the-pile Diamante LS, a car of the same size and shape as the $20,000 no-suffix Diamante but so different in detail that this review can't apply to both. The LS's 202 horsepower (compared with 175 in the twelve-valve base engine), smoother-shifting computer-controlled transmission, and optional leather interior gave our test car a level of sophistication appropriate to its price. Incidentally, the wood trim is fake, but it's the best fake in the industry.

In size, the Diamante fits in the middle, between the Nissan Maxima and the Acura Legend. Back-seat room is good for adults, particularly in toe space under the front seat. Trunk room, at only 13.6 cubic feet, is stingy. Given the exterior size and interior room, the Diamante LS, at 3668 pounds, is decidedly overweight.

Yet performance is quite spritely, particularly at those times when you let the engine rev. The 0-to-100-mph time of only 24 seconds is impressive. In most contests, though, an Acura Legend would be the quicker machine.

Although Mitsubishi has invested heavily in the Sharper Image approach to motoring, we are generally not very enthusiastic about electronic adjustments—why not just make the car work right instead of making it adjustable?—and we find nothing of great value in the Mitsubishi way. In fact, the LS's speed-dependent, electronically controlled steering effort (not driver adjustable) gives some phony feedback under certain circumstances that's plain annoying.

Automatic transmissions such as Mitsubishi's, with driver-operated switches for overdrive on-off and for power-or-economy shift schedules, are probably harmless enough. The big electronic item on the test car was the Euro-Handling package ($1670 extra), which includes electronically controlled suspension and traction control.

This suspension allows you to select Sport, which makes the ride hard. Leave it alone and the computer stiffens the dampers at higher speeds and when you turn or brake beyond nominal g-levels. All you feel is a car that seems well behaved. (Isn't that the point?)

This suspension, when left alone, also adjusts car height: 1.2 inches higher for low speeds on very rough roads, normal for routine driving, 0.4 inch lower on smooth roads above 56 mph. A switch allows you to override this schedule too, although the computer disregards your

Highs: *Seductive leather, growling V-6, wowee features.*

Lows: *Phony steering effort, compact trunk, wowee features.*

The verdict: *A four-door for the Sharper Image crowd.*

orders if it thinks you're trying something foolish—over 43 mph in the high position, for example.

The traction control has an additional function called Trace Control. The basic traction-control feature performs as you'd expect, reducing power in the event of wheelspin by first retarding the spark, then moderating the throttle. Trace Control, which the driver can switch off, is Mitsubishi's way of using the traction control's power-controlling functions to limit cornering capability to a level at which it thinks the driver will be comfortable. Funny, we always thought that's what the right pedal was for. Anyway, Trace Control, at moderate highway speeds, gives you only enough power in corners to maintain 0.7 g. As speed increases, power in turns is gradually pared back, finally allowing you only 0.3 g. Our skidpad-testing speed is typically about 40 mph. We tried it with Trace Control, recording 0.72 g. Without it, the figure was 0.75 g. The numbers don't appear much different, but the cut in power is unmistakable.

What's the point? Well, Mitsubishi just wants to help . . . and help and help. This is one of those cars that locks its doors automatically as soon as it's up to jogging speed. At first thought, that's kind of neat. But they don't unlock when you slow or stop. Well, of course not. How could a machine possibly know when it's safe to unlock the doors? But that means it's just trading one set of problems for another. Now *you* have to do the unlocking, either individually or by pressing the master "Unlock" button. And you're going to forget. You stop, get out to load a package, and all the doors are locked but the one you exited. If this car really wanted to help, it would find a way, when you're standing there with two arms full, to unlock the door that *it* had the bright idea to lock in the first place.

Our test car, with all its options, is a lot like one of those fancy restaurants where the waiters never stop hovering, fussing with your glassware. Some people think that's fine service. And they will never stop saying wowee about this car.

People who dress better than I do say this car looks like a BMW. At first I didn't agree, but I'm beginning to come around. Maybe the styling of the Diamante will be its real appeal. Never mind the slick four-wheel-steering system, the fine response of the revvy V-6, or any of the electro-contraptions that control ride, handling, and shifting. None of these features is new. Forget the opulent upholstery, too. But the styling, in a Japanese luxury car, is new. It's grown-up, hip, and doesn't look like Japanese styling. If it sells well, I'll change my wardrobe.   —*Phil Berg*

I wish Mitsubishi would sometimes give its technology a rest. The Diamante doesn't need variable damping and ride-height suspension, computer-controlled power steering, or "trace" control. None

of these features complements the character of this competent and comfortable, if somewhat bland, sedan. In fact, this technology doesn't even work particularly well. A Diamante without these features is not only better, it's a better buy.
    —*Csaba Csere*

The new Mitsubishi Diamante, much like the new Acura Vigor, strikes me as belonging to the gray porridge area of the automobile world—good as it is. It is a car difficult to find fault with—but just as difficult to fall in love with (unlike, say, the Nissan Maxima SE). The Diamante stops, goes, turns, and looks just fine. The dashboard seems a bit gimmicky, as does the exterior, but the driving position is excellent. If this car lacks anything, it's excitement.   —*William Jeanes*

Mitsubishi Diamante LS

Vehicle type: front-engine, front-wheel-drive, 5-passenger, 4-door sedan

Price as tested: $29,622

Price and option breakdown: base Mitsubishi Diamante LS (includes $368 freight), $25,503; luxury package (includes leather trim, power passenger seat), $2100; Euro-Handling package, $1670; sound system, $259; floor mats, $90

Major standard accessories: power steering, windows, driver's seat, and locks, A/C, cruise control, tilt steering, rear defroster

Sound system: Panasonic AM/FM-stereo radio/cassette with Mitsubishi U006 compact-disc player, 6 speakers

ENGINE
Type.............................V-6, iron block and aluminum heads
Bore x stroke.........................3.58 x 2.99 in, 91.0 x 76.0mm
Displacement..181 cu in, 2966cc
Compression ratio 10.0:1
Engine-control system......Mitsubishi with port fuel injection
Emissions controls ......3-way catalytic converter, feedback
     fuel-air-ratio control, EGR, auxiliary air pump
Valve gear ....belt-driven double overhead cams, 4
     valves per cylinder, hydraulic lifters
Power (SAE net) ....202 bhp @ 6000 rpm
Torque (SAE net) ....199 lb-ft @ 3000 rpm

DRIVETRAIN
Transmission............4-speed automatic with lockup torque
     converter
Final-drive ratio..3.96:1

Gear	Ratio	Mph/1000 rpm	Max. test speed
I	2.55	7.3	51 mph (7000 rpm)
II	1.49	12.5	87 mph (7000 rpm)
III	1.00	18.5	128 mph (6900 rpm)
IV	0.69	27.1	130 mph (4800 rpm)

DIMENSIONS AND CAPACITIES
Wheelbase...107.1 in
Track, F/R ....60.4/60.2 in
Length..190.2 in
Width ....69.9 in
Height ....55.5 in
Frontal area ....23.0 sq ft
Ground clearance ....6.5 in

Curb weight...3668 lb
Weight distribution, F/R 63.4/36.6%
Fuel capacity...19.0 gal
Oil capacity ....4.5 qt
Water capacity ....9.5 qt

CHASSIS/BODY
Type.....unit construction with 2 rubber-isolated subframes
Body material ....welded steel stampings

INTERIOR
SAE volume, front seat ....54 cu ft
     rear seat ....41 cu ft
     luggage space ....14 cu ft
Front seats ....bucket
Seat adjustments....................fore and aft, seatback angle,
     front height, rear height, lumbar support
Restraint systems, front ....manual 3-point belts,
     driver air bag
     rear..........manual 3-point belts, center
     lap belt
General comfort ....poor fair **good** excellent
Fore-and-aft support ....poor fair **good** excellent
Lateral support ....poor fair **good** excellent

SUSPENSION
F:...........................ind, strut located by a control arm, coil
     and air springs, electronically controlled
     shock absorbers, anti-roll bar
R:................... ind, 1 trailing arm and 3 lateral links per side,
     coil and air springs, electronically controlled shock
     absorbers, anti-roll bar

STEERING
Type ....rack-and-pinion, power-assisted
Turns lock-to-lock..3.2
Turning circle curb-to-curb ....36.7 ft

BRAKES
F:.......................................10.9 x 0.9-in vented disc
R:.......................................10.5 x 0.7-in vented disc
Power assist ....vacuum with anti-lock control

WHEELS AND TIRES
Wheel size...6.0 x 15 in
Wheel type ....cast aluminum
Tires ....Yokohama Radial 376, 205/65VR-15 M+S
Test inflation pressures, F/R ....30/26 psi

CAR AND DRIVER TEST RESULTS

ACCELERATION
	Seconds
Zero to 30 mph...3.3
40 mph 4.7
50 mph 6.6
60 mph 8.8
70 mph 11.2
80 mph 14.3
90 mph 18.6
100 mph 24.0
110 mph 31.0
120 mph 44.3
Street start, 5–60 mph.....................................9.3
Top-gear passing time, 30–50 mph 5.2
50–70 mph........................6.1
Standing ¼-mile ....16.8 sec @ 86 mph
Top speed.......................................130 mph

BRAKING
70-0 mph @ impending lockup ....194 ft
Fade ....**none** moderate heavy

HANDLING
Roadholding, 300-ft-dia skidpad ....0.75 g
Understeer.....................minimal **moderate** excessive

COAST-DOWN MEASUREMENTS
Road horsepower @ 30 mph...............................7 hp
     50 mph...........................16 hp
     70 mph...........................33 hp

FUEL ECONOMY
EPA city driving...18 mpg
EPA highway driving......................................24 mpg
C/D observed fuel economy ....19 mpg

INTERIOR SOUND LEVEL
Idle...43 dBA
Full-throttle acceleration.................................76 dBA
70-mph cruising..67 dBA
70-mph coasting...67 dBA

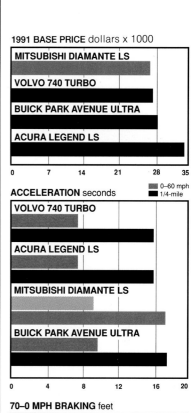

1991 BASE PRICE dollars x 1000

MITSUBISHI DIAMANTE LS
VOLVO 740 TURBO
BUICK PARK AVENUE ULTRA
ACURA LEGEND LS

0   7   14   21   28   35

0–60 mph
1/4-mile

ACCELERATION seconds

VOLVO 740 TURBO
ACURA LEGEND LS
MITSUBISHI DIAMANTE LS
BUICK PARK AVENUE ULTRA

0   4   8   12   16   20

70–0 MPH BRAKING feet

VOLVO 740 TURBO
ACURA LEGEND LS
MITSUBISHI DIAMANTE LS
BUICK PARK AVENUE ULTRA

160   170   180   190   200   210

ROADHOLDING 300-foot skidpad, g

VOLVO 740 TURBO
ACURA LEGEND LS
BUICK PARK AVENUE ULTRA
MITSUBISHI DIAMANTE LS

0.5   0.6   0.7   0.8   0.9   1.0

EPA ESTIMATED FUEL ECONOMY mpg

ACURA LEGEND LS
BUICK PARK AVENUE ULTRA
MITSUBISHI DIAMANTE LS
VOLVO 740 TURBO

0   4   8   12   16   20

Base price includes freight, applicable luxury and gas-guzzler taxes, and any performance options.

SPEEDING BEAUTIES

By Patrick Bedard

We know what the term "sports car" meant in the sixties—wire wheels and tweedy caps and elbows-out dashes down those twisting country roads.

We know what the term meant in the seventies and eighties, too—mostly Madison Avenue hype applied to any sedan with separate seats and a shifter between them.

But this is the nineties, a period when carmakers overrev their engineering departments trying to outdo each other in to-the-death global competition. What's the state of the sports car today?

Give Mazda credit for raising this question. It heralds its new RX-7 as the "return of the pure sports car." It says of this third-generation two-seater: "... at a time when other manufacturers are introducing sports cars that are larger, heavier, and more complex, Mazda has made the new-generation RX-7 smaller and lighter, yet more powerful than its predecessor—as well as simpler, with no gimmicks to de-

viate from the original intent of building a pure sports car."

The first half of that statement should make every auto builder in the world—and maybe every car enthusiast—a little uncomfortable. Cars *are* getting heavier and more complex. Too heavy? Too complex? Today's family haulers have comfort and economy and reliability and environmental friendliness to the degree that they stand as engineering wonders. But sports cars are different. They exist for the fun of driving. Are they getting too heavy and too complex for their own good? Are we losing sight of what made them fun back in the glory days of MGs, Triumphs, Healeys, Alfas, and Jaguars? Remember, back in 1960, very few sports cars had side windows. They were open two-seaters with removable side curtains. In the three decades since, we've passed

right through the crank-up-window era and into the "full power" condition once reserved for the fat-cat Buicks and Cadillacs—power windows, power brakes, power steering, power seats, power mirrors, and air conditioning. Heavy, complicated stuff is standard equipment in sports cars now.

Are we having more fun?

It's time somebody did a reality check on sports cars. Mazda, with the RX-7, promises a return to the original concept, speed unburdened by unnecessary weight. How does Mazda's answer compare with the state of the art, A.D. 1992? Sounds like this is a job for a comparison test, doesn't it?

The price of the new RX-7 is around $35,000. What other sports cars can you buy without winning the lottery—say, around $40,000?

Clockwise, left to right: The Nissan 300ZX Turbo; Chevrolet Corvette; Lotus Elan; and Mazda RX-7.

The Nissan 300ZX Turbo, since its introduction in 1990, is a two-time winner of our comparison tests. At this price, the sports-car art knows no finer state.

America's Only Sports Car has undergone another renewal: now 300 horsepower is standard equipment under the Corvette's hood, and more refinement is apparent everywhere else.

We are intrigued, too, with the Lotus Elan—in part because it's British, and the British arguably invented the sports car. And in part because it still carries forward the recipe that made sports cars famous: it's a four-cylinder, open-air two-seater.

Porsche, by virtue of its accomplishments in the sports-car field, deserves a place in this comparison too. Alas, our deadlines came a month before the new 968's arrival in this country.

So the Nissan, the Chevy, and the Lotus met the new Mazda RX-7 in the Carolina hill country for three days of track testing, twisty-road driving, and soul-searching on the topic of What Makes Driving Fun?

The answers are in. As usual, we're saving the best for last.

4TH PLACE
LOTUS ELAN

LOTUS ELAN

Highs: *Turbo-doorstop styling, easy-down top, slick shifter.*
Lows: *Frenetic four-cylinder tempo, lo-cal power, hi-cal price.*
The verdict: *The Richard Simmons of the speedsters.*

The Elan scores highest on one of the most sought-after sports-car qualities— rarity. Only 300 have been sold in the U.S. as this is being written, which means the Elan is now—and probably always will be —a jaunty little roadster that most people have never seen. Bystanders are drawn to this car. The Elan single-handedly emptied an Asheville carwash of its patrons, none of whom were particularly fascinated by the RX-7's equally new shape.

This is a tiny car, a bit narrower than the RX-7 (the next-smallest of the group) and 16.3 inches shorter in length. The cockpit is plenty wide, but tall drivers would like another notch or two of rearward seat travel. Don't expect to stow your briefcase behind the seats. No room. There is a trunk, however, and it easily accepts enough soft luggage for two people going across country, all without encroaching on space for the top when it's down.

Driving the Elan awakens old sports-car memories. The body is a bit shaky, as small open cars always have been. You hear air rushing over the top if it's up, or over your ears if it's down. The shifter is wonderfully light and slick. The little engine gets buzzy at high revs, reminding you that it's a four.

Still, sporting driving does not seem to have been the designers' highest priority. The seats have prominent lumbar support but not much side support, which means you brace against the door panel for cornering—and the door panel is a long distance away. There's no dead pedal for your left foot, although the footwells are remarkably spacious—ten inches of open floor space lie to the left of the clutch pedal. The high-style treatment of the dash sometimes gets in the way of function. Sunlight from certain directions makes the instrument lenses go opaque, and the red dial markings (instead of white) on black background have too little contrast to be read easily.

Yet this car has promise. Mazda cites light weight as the sports car's basic requirement. At 2452 pounds, this Lotus weighs a full 350 pounds less than the RX-7, a nifty accomplishment considering that Lotus didn't start with a pure sports car in mind. The turbocharged 1588cc four and its front-drive unit are taken from the Isuzu Impulse coupe. From that engine size, you can see that Lotus is continuing its traditional lightweight, small-bore approach to speed. The turbo lags, although you could say it adds a dose of excitement when the boost comes on.

On the road, the Elan is a nimble handler with little indication that the front wheels are driving. It's surprisingly well balanced on the track, too. Adding power widens the arc through turns but never makes the front tires go numb, as happens in many front-drive sedans. Still, at the limit, this car skims over the pavement with little of the feedback so prized in sports cars.

Moreover, front drive really does require a special technique for high-performance work, as one of our drivers was rudely reminded at the track. He was flat out in a 100-mph right-hander when he concluded that his exit path would be about six inches wider than the pavement. His rear-drive response was to ease the power back enough to slip off the road at zero acceleration and zero engine braking. Wrong! The understeering front wheels at full power were angled smartly into the turn. Reducing power left them more traction for turning, and it transferred load to the front as well, pressing those tires more firmly against the pavement. The Elan promptly hooked to the right, just as it was dropping off the edge, and commenced a lurid slide that lasted for about a day and a half.

It's not the car's fault that the chauffeur forgot which wheels were driving. But this story should be a vivid reminder that the front-drive Elan is fully as idiosyncratic as it looks. And, it must be added, more interested in being idiosyncratic than in going fast.

3RD PLACE
CHEVROLET CORVETTE

The Corvette represents a peculiarly American approach to the sports car, the Big Iron approach: big engine (300 horsepower, 5733cc V-8), big transmission (six speeds), big tires (Goodyear Eagle GS-C 275/40ZR-17s on 9.5-inch-wide wheels), and big visual statement (it's nine inches longer than the Nissan, the next-longest of the group). This is Dirty Harry blowing a big hole in the wind.

There's nothing easy about the Corvette. You have to be a contortionist to maneuver over the frame that blocks too much of the door opening, to duck under the low edge of the roof, and to get past the high sides of the deep-bucket seats. You have to get used to the starship instrument panel with its pumpkin-colored markings. The steering, shifter, and clutch require manly forces, too. But then again, you'd hardly complain about the effort to pull back the hammer on a .44 Magnum.

This is big iron, and it makes a big bang.

CHEVROLET CORVETTE

Highs: Hormone-injected V-8, painless ride (optional), chiseled good looks.

Lows: Junky-sounding drivetrain, contortionist entry and exit, bulky exterior.

The verdict: The hairy-chestedest of the speedsters.

The new-for-'92 LT1 engine pulls strongly all the way to its 5500-rpm redline now, making this the quickest car in the group —13.6 seconds at 104 mph in the quarter-mile. The V-8 broadcasts a wonderful noise, too.

The big tires provide tremendous grip, enough to stop from 70 mph in 166 feet, enough to circle the skidpad at 0.92 g (the pad used for this test produced slightly higher-g results than our usual pad).

Grip, though, is not the same as handling. Corvette handling gets mixed reviews among staffers. Those who have raced Corvettes in Showroom Stock have nothing but high praise for it. Others say the brakes have too little pedal feel on light applications and the too-quick steering doesn't allow smooth turns into corners. Lift-throttle transients tend to be squirmy, too, although dialing the optional Ride Control to the performance setting helps.

Having said all that, we must also say that the Corvette (with one of the staff Corvette enthusiasts at the wheel) did produce the fastest lap around the road course by the slenderest of margins— one-tenth of a second quicker than the RX-7. Given the few laps that were run, this result probably wouldn't withstand statistical analysis. Still, the Big Iron Corvette was fastest.

We are used to Corvettes being fastest. But this 1992 version had qualities we're not so used to. With the adjustable shocks in the softest position, the ride was darned near plush. The car had relatively few squeaks and rattles, too, although the drivetrain still makes junky noises. And it achieved 17 mpg during our road-driving segment, 1 mpg better than the Nissan 300ZX and 2 mpg better than the Mazda RX-7, thanks mostly to the long sixth gear on the highway.

Because there's general agreement that sports cars are supposed to be nimble and light, the Big Iron approach is controversial. When it came time for overall evaluations, the voters scattered their ratings wider on the Corvette than on any other car. Significantly, though, no one ranked it higher than third—or lower.

2ND PLACE
MAZDA RX-7

RX-7s have always been interesting, and they've always been fun, but what's this? A second-place ranking against arguably the best front-engine sports cars in the world? Moreover, it missed winning top honors by just two points. Did somebody tilt the board, or what?

Actually, Mazda did the tilting when it decided to go for a "pure sports car." Weight is the enemy of performance. It's a burden on driving pleasure, too. So

weight was ruthlessly pared (the dipstick handle, for example, has been reduced in size to a thin wire). This new car weighs only 2800 pounds, more than 600 pounds less than the Corvette, more than 700 less than the Nissan.

This is a lean automobile, with its skin pulled tight as a bubble pack around two passengers and a beer-keg-size rotary engine. The RX-7 is ten inches shorter in length than the Corvette.

Yet it has more head room and leg room inside, plenty of elbow room, good briefcase space behind the seats, and reasonable cargo room under the hatch (unless you opt for the Touring package, which comes with a Bose sound system that sounds terrific but sprawls around the load floor).

To the lightweight formula, Mazda added more power—the rotary has two turbos acting sequentially, like the primary and secondary barrels of a carbure-

Left: The new-for-'92 LT1 engine made the Corvette the quickest car in the group—13.6 seconds to 104 mph in the quarter-mile.

tor. There is an intercooler. Because the primary turbo gets to work early, turbo lag is minimal and the torque curve is generous for a rotary. Flow of power is a bit jerky when the throttle is first opened or closed, though.

Nowhere did Mazda skimp on the performance details. The limited slip is a Torsen. Anti-lock control is standard. All four brakes are vented. Dual-cone synchros are used on first, second, and third gears. In the cockpit, the largest dial on the panel is the tachometer, centered and looking right at you. The dials are all round and clearly marked, and the small controls are especially easy to reach. The seat backrests give tremendous lateral support. A big, spacious dead pedal is right where you want it. The clutch and brake pedals are bare aluminum for maximum feel and minimum weight.

The RX-7 has plenty of heavy stuff—power steering, brakes, and windows, plus air conditioning—but it manages to pack all that equipment without being fat. We tested the bespoiled R1 version, which has more drag than the standard car but less lift (the R1's coefficient of drag is 0.32, vs. 0.29 for the base car). The R1 also includes Z-rated tires.

The details of the RX-7 are all aligned in the direction of usable performance. And the car delivers—13.7 seconds at 101 mph in the quarter, the highest top speed of the group at 159 mph, and the best cornering grip at 0.97 g on the high-traction skidpad we used for all cars in this test. The RX-7 definitely *feels* like a sports car, too. The controls are light and extremely direct.

At times, however, the car feels nervous. The low-profile tires make the steering darty on some roads, much like the Corvette used to be, though not as bad. And when we pushed it hard on high-speed turns, the tail began twitching in a threatening way. Every editor who drove the car mentioned the intimidating oversteer. Mostly, though, there was only admiration for a clean and lean little machine that knows exactly why it exists —for the fun of driving.

Serious disagreement arose over only one issue—the molded–Jell-O shape of the body. One staffer thought it the best-looking car in the bunch; another thought it the worst. But no one was ambivalent. In fact, the RX-7 threatens to knock that word right out of your vocabulary.

1st Place
Nissan 300ZX Turbo

There was no ambivalence—and no controversy—over this car. And virtually no scatter in the Overall Rating. We all loved it.

Not because of specifications. It's too heavy at 3533 pounds. You might be surprised to learn that the 300ZX is 109 pounds heavier than the Big Iron Corvette. But like an Olympic athlete, this Nissan carries its weight *so* well. From the driver's seat, it does not seem heavy. Only perfect.

But pure sports cars were never perfect. Their lightness (and the rustic state of the engineering art in the old days) made them noisy and fidgety as well as quick. Did we love the whole package? Or were we hooked on the speed and merely tolerant of the rest?

We think the latter. Nissan engineers have found a way to eliminate the bothers, albeit at the cost of pounds. The resulting 300ZX Turbo may be impure as sports cars go, but the perfection of it completely wins us over. Speed *with* refinement is surely the greater joy.

The test results show that this is not the speediest of the speedsters. The Corvette edges it in the quarter-mile, both the Corvette and the RX-7 eke out more top end (although the 300ZX's speed is limited by

Mazda RX–7

Highs: *Feels lean, mean, and born to boogie—and it is.*

Lows: *Darty steering, lurchy throttle response.*

The verdict: *The raciest of the speedsters.*

a governor, not drag), and they both produce more cornering grip than the Z. But when you drive these cars each in turn, those test-track accomplishments are less apparent than this Nissan's refinement.

Refinement? Does that word suggest amenities sought by bald guys too old to stand on the gas? Then consider another word that applies just as well—correctness. This car seems so correct: in design,

in detail, in response. The instruments are *so* well grouped and *so* legible. The twin-turbo V-6 is *so* powerful yet unobtrusive. The shifter is *so* light and precise. The brakes respond *so* predictably.

Yes, the cockpit is terrifically comfortable, too. The leather seat offers support without being obnoxious about it. And the ersatz-suede–covered padding down where your knees bang into the walls dur-

		acceleration, sec											
		0–30 mph	0–60 mph	0–100 mph	0–120 mph	1/4-mile	street start, 5–60 mph	top gear, 30–50 mph	top gear, 50–70 mph	top speed, mph	braking, 70–0 mph, ft	roadholding, 196-ft skidpad, g
C/D Test Results	**CHEVROLET CORVETTE**	1.9	5.0	12.6	19.0	13.6 @ 104 mph	5.4	10.1	10.1	157	166	0.92
	LOTUS ELAN	2.3	6.6	19.7	—	15.1 @ 91 mph	7.7	11.2	9.6	131	190	0.87
	MAZDA RX-7	1.9	5.0	13.4	19.4	13.7 @ 101 mph	6.0	10.7	7.5	159	157	0.97
	NISSAN 300ZX TURBO	2.0	5.0	13.1	19.5	13.7 @ 102 mph	6.1	10.3	8.3	153	168	0.88

		'92 price, base/ as tested	engine	SAE net power/torque	transmission/gear ratios:1/ maximum test speed, mph/ axle ratio:1	curb weight, lb	weight distribution, % F/R
Vital Statistics	**CHEVROLET CORVETTE**	$34,604/ $40,273	V-8, 350 cu in (5733cc), iron block and aluminum heads, GM engine-control system with port fuel injection	300 bhp @ 5000 rpm/ 330 lb-ft @ 4000 rpm	6-speed/ 2.68, 1.80, 1.29, 1.00, 0.75, 0.50/ 44, 65, 90, 118, 157, 151/ 3.45	3424	51.5/48.5
	LOTUS ELAN	$40,989/ $40,989	turbocharged and intercooled DOHC 16-valve 4-in-line, 97 cu in (1588cc), iron block and aluminum head, Lotus/GM-Delco engine-control system with port fuel injection	162 bhp @ 6600 rpm/ 148 lb-ft @ 4200 rpm	5-speed/ 3.33, 1.92, 1.33, 1.03, 0.83/ 37, 64, 92, 119, 131/ 3.83	2452	66.7/33.3
	MAZDA RX-7	$34,000/ $34,000 (estimated)	twin-turbocharged and intercooled 2-rotor Wankel, 80 cu in (1308cc), aluminum rotor housings, iron end plates, Mazda engine-control system with port fuel injection	255 bhp @ 6500 rpm/ 217 lb-ft @ 5000 rpm	5-speed/ 3.48, 2.02, 1.39, 1.00, 0.72/ 40, 69, 100, 139, 159/ 4.10	2800 (mfr.)	50/50 (mfr.)
	NISSAN 300ZX TURBO	$36,809/ $38,212	twin-turbocharged and intercooled DOHC 24-valve V-6, 181 cu in (2960cc), iron block and aluminum heads, Nissan engine-control system with port fuel injection	300 bhp @ 6400 rpm/ 283 lb-ft @ 3600 rpm	5-speed/ 3.21, 1.93, 1.30, 1.00, 0.75/ 38, 63, 94, 122, 153/ 4.08	3533	54.3/45.7

ing hard driving is a thoughtful gesture.

Correctness like this suggests that the engineering task was easy. It wasn't. This car may be heavy, but the equipment is packed into a remarkably dense envelope only one inch longer than the pared-down RX-7. Big power—300 horsepower, same rating as the Corvette—comes from a small engine room. And we found no distress from the heat of those two turbos in such tight confinement.

In back, the Super-HICAS (rear steer) suspension is compactly packaged. You

don't see it and you don't notice it when driving. The driver notices only that this car has well-behaved transient handling. And that's the point, isn't it?

We were less impressed with the two-position adjustable shocks—the Sport setting made the ride hard with no apparent benefit in handling. In Tour, ride was not quite as plush as that of the Corvette in its soft setting, but it wasn't as floaty either.

Are you ready for the clincher? All of the Nissan's refinement and correctness is

maneuverability, 1000-ft slalom, mph	interior sound level, dBA				fuel economy, mpg			racecourse, min:sec
	idle	full throttle	70-mph cruising	70-mph coasting	EPA city	EPA highway	*C/D* 600-mile trip	
64.3	53	88	77	75	17	25	17	1:31.5
65.7	51	86	78	78	24	31	24	1:37.2
67.6	50	84	75	74	17	25	15	1:31.6
66.5	47	80	74	73	18	24	16	1:33.2

dimensions, in				fuel tank, gal	suspension		brakes, F/R	tires
wheelbase	length	width	height		front	rear		
96.2	178.5	70.7	46.3	20.0	ind, unequal-length control arms, transverse plastic leaf spring, 3-position cockpit-adjustable electronically controlled shock absorbers, anti-roll bar	ind; fixed-length half-shaft, 2 lateral links and 2 trailing links per side; transverse plastic leaf spring; 3-position cockpit-adjustable electronically controlled shock absorbers; anti-roll bar	vented disc/ vented disc; anti-lock control	Goodyear Eagle GS-C, P275/40ZR-17
88.6	152.2	68.2	49.2	10.2	ind, unequal-length control arms, coil springs, anti-roll bar	ind, unequal-length control arms, coil springs, anti-roll bar	vented disc/ disc	Goodyear Eagle GS-D, 205/45ZR-16
95.5	168.5	68.9	48.4	20.0	ind, unequal-length control arms, coil springs, anti-roll bar	ind, unequal-length control arms with a toe-control link, coil springs, anti-roll bar	vented disc/ vented disc; anti-lock control	Bridgestone Expedia S-07, 225/50ZR-16
96.5	169.5	70.5	49.2	18.7	ind, unequal-length control arms with a two-piece hub, coil springs, 2-position cockpit-adjustable shock absorbers, anti-roll bar	ind; 1 diagonal link, 2 lateral links, and 1 control arm per side; coil springs; 2-position cockpit-adjustable shock absorbers; anti-roll bar	vented disc/ vented disc; anti-lock control	Goodyear Eagle ZR, F: 225/50ZR-16; R: 245/45ZR-16

priced under the Lotus and Corvette.

Regarding the opening question—What is the state of the sports car today?—we have an optimistic answer if not a clear one. The Overall Rating shows an extravagantly impure sports car winning out over one aggressively pure and doing so by a mere two points. Which suggests that neither purity nor impurity is the key ingredient of a sports car.

It's execution that counts. And as you will surely conclude from the way these cars perform, execution in the nineties is simply breathtaking.

Editors' Ratings		engine	trans-mission	brakes	handling	ride	ergo-nomics	comfort	room	styling	value	fun to drive	OVERALL RATING*
	CHEVROLET CORVETTE	9	7	8	8	8	8	7	8	8	8	9	82
	LOTUS ELAN	6	9	7	7	8	8	8	7	8	5	7	68
	MAZDA RX-7	8	8	9	9	6	9	8	7	8	9	10	90
	NISSAN 300ZX TURBO	9	9	8	8	9	9	9	8	9	9	9	92

HOW IT WORKS: Editors rate vehicles from 1 to 10 (10 being best) in each category. Then scores are collected and averaged, resulting in the numbers shown above.

*The Overall Rating is not the total of those numbers. Rather, it is an independent judgment (on a 1-to-100 scale) that includes other factors—even personal preferences—not easily categorized.

FERRARI 512TR

By William Jeanes

The latest Testarossa is by no means all-new, but Ferrari has improved it in so many ways that it might as well be. In the process, the maestros of Maranello have also made the car more beautiful than its predecessor and have given it a new alphanumeric designator: the 512TR.

Each year, about 4000 exotic cars emerge from the Ferrari works. The factory is a marvel of microcosmic industrial excellence, from its own foundry—where street and racing engines are built—to its state-of-the-art paint system and finally to its spotless assembly lines.

"We buy only the best," Ferrari's manufacturing chief Walter Vignale told us, pointing out the vast concrete pads where three huge Japanese boring machines would soon rest. Vignale, a nephew of the famed Parisian coachbuilder, makes a strong case for Ferrari quality. "We not only replace our machinery when it's worn out," he says, "we replace it if we find something better." Tweed-coated and mustached, the trim Vignale looks more like a retired Guards officer than the man dedicated to, in his words, "producing cars that perform *and* are reliable."

Consider the 512TR. More development time—and expense—has gone into the updating of this car, which was first introduced at the Paris auto show in 1984, than most small manufacturers have invested in their entire organization. And the result is a car costing about $200,000 that almost seems worth it . . . if you believe the oft-rendered pronouncement: "With a Ferrari, you are not just buying a car, you are buying art." Only 1300 of these artworks were built in 1992, with 300 allotted to North America.

Ferrari had ambitious goals for the Testarossa update: it wanted to improve engine performance while reducing NOx levels, to incorporate an engine-management and self-diagnostic system that would enable the car to meet Swiss and California emissions regulations, and to improve aerodynamics, handling, safety, braking, and ergonomics—especially regarding the shifter. How did Ferrari score? Quite high except for the shifter: *Ferraristi* will tell you this device makes the car a Ferrari, and ordinary persons will say it makes your arm tired.

From the moment you slide into the hard leather seat—which is adjustable to fit persons of reasonable height if not breadth—you must resist the onset of giddiness that comes with Ferrari operation, a condition brought on by inhaling Connolly-leather fumes and knowing that hordes of otherwise rational people would feel more honored to be in your place than to be lunching at Harry's Bar with the Holy Father.

Turn the key and the engine snaps to life with a surprise: it sounds more like a Ferrari ought to than did the previous model. "The sound is different and is something you will like," Ferrari of North America boss Giuseppe Greco had confided to us on the road to Maranello. He was right. The effort put into the aural rewards of the exhaust note means that persons of all stations will be enriched by the mere passing of a 512TR.

The source of the sound is the "boxer" flat twelve with the red-painted valve covers (hence the name *"testa rossa,"* which

Seated in this Ferrari, the driver must resist a feeling of giddiness. But with Connolly-leather fumes and an engine that sounds like a Ferrari ought to, some lightheadedness is pardonable.

in Italian means "red head"). The engine's 4943cc displacement is unchanged, but it now delivers a maximum of 421 horsepower at 6750 rpm (up from 380 hp at 5750 rpm). This has been accomplished by more than two dozen engine modifications, led by a redesigned air-intake system and a new Bosch Motronic engine-management system. The compression ratio has been raised to 10:1, there are new pistons, new Nikasil cylinder liners, larger-diameter intake valves, and a redesigned exhaust system.

There's more in the way of technical minutiae, but most important to drivers is the new engine's flatter torque curve in its peak operating territory. Maximum torque of 360 pound-feet is reached at 5500 rpm, and the power levels off between 6250 and 7250 rpm (near 420 hp). Ferrari claims that's good for a 0-to-62-mph time of 4.8 seconds and a top speed of 192 mph. Given room, the 512TR will run all day at 7250, which is 50 rpm below its redline.

The gearbox retains the slotted gates and stiffness we expect from Ferrari but shifts a bit easier thanks to sliding ball bearings and a new angle to the shifter itself. A new single-plate clutch with reduced inertial force makes the other part of shifting gears easier as well.

The four-wheel ventilated disc brakes now benefit from cross-drilling all around, larger front rotors, new ducting, and a new proportioning valve. The new brakes provide stunning stopping power with excellent pedal feel.

Handling, already in the superb range, benefits from a shorter steering ratio (3.3 turns lock-to-lock, from 3.4), new eighteen-inch wheels, and even lower-profile tires (which, with the removal of the black paint on the rocker panel, have the visual effect of lowering the car enormously), new shock absorbers, and a number of material changes aimed at reducing unsprung weight.

The cabin has been simplified in upholstery design and in instrumentation location. The center console is gone. Not only have the air-conditioning controls been improved, but the system itself has been given a larger capacity.

Outside, every single thing that the Pininfarina stylists did was worth doing. The front air dam is better integrated, as is the one-piece rear bumper, which now encloses the exhaust pipes in a sculpted opening that harmonizes with the rest of the exterior. The new five-spoke wheels

are see-through numbers that some will like (we did), and some won't. Everyone should like the new engine-cover treatment and the removal of the black vent strips from the buttresses that flow rearward from the roof. The styling touches effect a major improvement on a look that had nothing to apologize for to begin with.

We drove the 512TR at the Ferrari test track in Maranello, at the Mugello track near Florence, and on public roads between the two venues. On road or track, the car rewards the driver generously. After we put the 512TR through a full road test, we'll provide an in-depth evaluation. But we can sum up our preliminary assessment in three letters: wow!

FERRARI 512TR

Vehicle type: mid-engine, rear-wheel-drive, 2-passenger, 2-door coupe

1992 base price: $212,160

Price and option breakdown: base Ferrari 512TR (includes $16,560 luxury tax, $4500 gas-guzzler tax, and $1600 freight), $212,160

Major standard accessories: power windows and locks, A/C, tilt steering, rear defroster

Sound system: none

ENGINE
Type . . . . flat 12, aluminum block and heads
Bore x stroke . . . . 3.23 x 3.07 in., 82.0 x 78.0mm
Displacement . . . . 302 cu. in., 4943cc
Compression ratio 10.0:1
Engine-control system . . . . . . Bosch Motronic M 2.7 engine-control system with port fuel injection
Emissions controls . . . . . 3-way catalytic converter, feedback fuel-air-ratio control, auxiliary air pump
Valve gear . . . . belt-driven double overhead cams, 4 valves per cylinder
Power (SAE net) . . . . 421 bhp @ 6750 rpm
Torque (SAE net) . . . . 360 lb-ft @ 5500 rpm
Redline . . . . 7300 rpm

DRIVETRAIN
Transmission 5-speed
Final-drive ratio . . . . 3.21:1, limited slip
Transfer-gear ratio 1.11:1

Gear	Ratio	Mph/1000 rpm	Speed in gears
I	2.92	7.2	53 mph (7300 rpm)
II	1.88	11.2	81 mph (7300 rpm)
III	1.42	14.8	108 mph (7300 rpm)
IV	1.09	19,3	141 mph (7300 rpm)
V	0.82	25.8	192 mph (7450 rpm)

DIMENSIONS AND CAPACITIES
Wheelbase . . . . 100.4 in.
Track, F/R . . . . 60.3/64.7 in.
Length . . . . 176.4 in.
Width . . . . 77.8 in.
Height . . . . 44.7 in.
Curb weight . . . . 3650 lb
Weight distribution, F/R 42/58%

Fuel capacity . . . . 28.5 gal.
Oil capacity . . . . 12.2 qt.
Water capacity . . . . 21.1 qt.

CHASSIS/BODY
Type . . . . full-length frame bolted to body
Body material . . . . welded steel and aluminum stampings, fiberglass-reinforced plastic

INTERIOR
SAE volume, front seat . . . . 47 cu. ft.
luggage space . . . . 5 cu. ft.
Front seats . . . . bucket
Seat adjustments . . . . fore and aft, seatback angle
Restraint systems, front . . . . motorized shoulder belts, manual lap belts

SUSPENSION
F: . . . . ind, unequal-length control arms, coil springs, anti-roll bar
R: . . . . ind, unequal-length control arms, coil springs, anti-roll bar

STEERING
Type . . . . rack-and-pinion
Turns lock-to-lock 3.3
Turning circle curb-to-curb . . . . 39.4 ft.

BRAKES
F: . . . . 12.4 x 1.3-in vented disc
R: . . . . 12.2 x 1.1-in. vented disc
Power assist . . . . vacuum

WHEELS AND TIRES
Wheel size . . . . F: 8.0 x 18 in., R: 10.5 x 18 in.
Wheel type . . . . cast aluminum
Tires . . . . Pirelli P Zero, F: 235/40ZR-18
R: 295/35ZR-18

MANUFACTURER'S PERFORMANCE RATINGS
Zero to 62 mph . . . . 4.8 sec
Standing ¼-mile . . . . 12.8 sec.
Top speed . . . . 192 mph

FUEL ECONOMY
EPA city driving . . . . 11 mpg
EPA highway driving . . . . 16 mpg

VECTOR W8 TWINTURBO

By Csaba Csere

9:00 a.m., a spring Monday in 1991, Wilmington, California—We arrive at Vector headquarters, nestled in an industrial ghetto between the Los Angeles and Long Beach harbors. Jerry Wiegert has lured us with the promise of an exclusive first crack at testing his audacious supercar, which has been the subject of great intrigue and speculation since we covered his first running prototype in December 1980.

The decade since then has been long and hard for Wiegert, who, like Ferruccio Lamborghini in the early sixties, decided to take on the established supercar order. Unlike Lamborghini, however, who was a

wealthy industrialist, Wiegert was a young industrial designer without a personal fortune. Although Wiegert often boasts of the Vector's ten years of development, he spent much of the eighties scratching for cash. That he survived is a testament to his dedication to his brainchild and his gift for self-promotion.

He scored a financial victory in November 1988, when a public stock offering in the newly reconstituted Vector Aeromotive Corporation raised $6 million. Wiegert's company got $4.9 million and the remainder went to his underwriter, Blinder, Robinson & Company, which has since filed for bankruptcy.

That cash infusion and a later one inflated what had been Wiegert's shoestring operation into a 40,000-square-foot plant employing 82 workers—the plant we have just entered. Palletized engines, bins of suspension parts, stacks of complex castings, half a dozen cars under construction, and a score of busy employees fill the final assembly area. The Vector operation is real indeed.

David Kostka, Vector's vice president for engineering, shows us the gray and red engineering prototypes that we are to test as we wait for the truck he has ordered to haul the cars up to our designated testing sites.

11:30 a.m., Angeles Crest Highway— We unload the Vectors in the San Gabriel Mountains. Although the W8's styling is about fifteen years old, the car is still an ocular magnet. Its snout is higher and longer than the current fashion and the body creases are too sharp, but like the late Lamborghini Countach, the Vector has a timeless visual appeal.

Inside, the Vector has the blocky, hand-tailored, somewhat homemade look indigenous to most limited-production cars, but the fashion theme is jet-fighter cockpit. There's a computerized instrument display on which the driver can choose one of four information displays. And the black-anodized aluminum eyeball air vents, the Allen-head cap screws, the push-to-reset circuit breakers, and the illuminated square switches not only look like aircraft parts, they *are* aircraft parts—

Although the Vector W8's styling is about fifteen years old, it has a timeless visual appeal. Its snout is higher than current fashion, and its creases may be too sharp. Yet the smooth bodywork, gleaming finish, and admirably even gaps convey quality in keeping with the $400,000+ price.

very expensive ones at that.

Not surprisingly, the seating position is very low, but visibility forward is excellent, gradually deteriorating as one's view traverses toward the rear. The Recaro C seats are superbly comfortable, the driving position is good, and there's ample leg and headroom in the wide cockpit.

The tilting, air bag-equipped steering wheel is a pleasant surprise, but the shifter is a disappointment. Buried in a well to the *left* of the driver's seat, a short lever topped by a crossbar controls the Vector's three-speed automatic transmission—a much modified version of the GM unit developed for the original Olds Toronado more than 25 years ago.

The handle moves through the usual park-reverse-neutral-drive sequence to allow fully automatic operation. When you lift the handle, it becomes a ratchet shifter, shifting up or down a gear with each fore or aft movement.

Upon firing up the Vector, we find that the shifter, buried in its tight little well, does not fall readily to hand. When you do grab it, screws protrude from its underside and there's a heavy, sticky action. With the gearbox in drive, the transmission upshifts at very low rpm and refuses to kickdown when you floor the accelerator at anything above city speed.

Under way though, the red prototype feels tight and solid, although the engine is loud. During our cornering passes for the photographer, the suspension seems supple and well controlled. The power steering is too light, however, and it doesn't provide as much self-centering action as we like in 200-mph cars.

Our photography completed, we head toward our desert test sight. The 3680-pound Vector is quick, with the twin-turbocharged 6.0-liter V-8 building boost and thrust quickly. Above 4000 rpm, the push is strong enough to make Vector's claim of 625 hp believable.

Soon, however, we find ourselves coasting. The engine is still running, but the transmission has ceased communication with the rear wheels. We glide to a halt on the shoulder of Angeles Forest Highway. After a few minutes of fiddling, Kostka suggests we press on with the gray car, while his mechanic coasts down the mountain with the red car toward a nearby restaurant to summon the truck.

3:00 p.m., C/D desert test site near Edwards AFB—Instruments in place, we start our testing. Although Vector literature calls the W8 the fastest production car in the world, Kostka asks us to refrain from top-speed testing because of insufficient high-speed development. Since we're not paid enough to be 200-mph guinea pigs, we agree, but wonder privately about the overseas owners of the cars already delivered.

Top-gear acceleration is strong, but the transmission is slipping out of third gear. The brakes are powerful; only premature rear lockup extends the stopping distance from 70 mph to 191 feet.

We're ready to do the acceleration runs, but the coolant-temperature gauge has surged to 250 degrees, and wisps of steam are wafting through the louvered engine cover. Kostka suspects an air bubble in the cooling system and suggests waiting a bit before adding water.

After two hours of waiting and dribbling water into the Vector's expansion tank (to avoid cracking the hot head or block with a sudden deluge of cold water), darkness is approaching, and we decide to go to the nearby skidpad. Although the surface is wet, the Vector circulates at an admirable 0.91 g, with a touch of tail-happiness at the limit. We suspect it would probably pull in the area of 0.95 g on dry pavement.

The skidpad testing overheats the engine again, so we spend another hour cooling the cooling system. Kostka finally suggests we try an acceleration run. Not only does the temperature skyrocket as soon as we leg it, but the engine detonates fiercely and the transmission resolutely resists shifting into third gear. We decide to pack it in while the Vector can still limp home under its own power.

*9:00 a.m. Tuesday, Wilmington—*While the mechanics are puzzling over the gray Vector's cooling system, Mark Bailey, vice president for production, gives us a tour of the premises.

Bailey learned his trade fabricating aerospace components at Northrop, and he is simultaneously enthusiastic about the Vector and frank about the problems gearing up the assembly line. "We're just now finishing the engineering drawings and fixtures for the parts. Many of the first sheetmetal pieces had to be traced from prototype components."

Despite these handicaps, chassis number 14 is in progress at the frame shop, one of the dozen or so cars somewhere in the production process at any one time.

The Vector's core is formed by a welded chrome-molybdenum steel-tubing roll cage reinforced by riveted aluminum panels and an aluminum honeycomb floorpan. Riveted and bonded aluminum monocoque structures extend from this central core to mount the suspension and driveline components, as well as to pro-

The wide cockpit
provides ample leg and
head room, and the twin-
turbocharged 6.0-liter
V-8 provides more than
ample 625 hp.

vide crush zones and bumper supports. Bailey bemoans the cost of pumping the 6000 or so rivets that go into each Vector, but the superbly crafted chassis easily passed the Department of Transportation's crash tests.

The body is made of fiberglass, carbon fiber, and Kevlar composite panels. Each set of panels is individually fitted to a matched chassis, then finished with catalyzed paint. The result is smooth bodywork, a gleaming finish, and admirably even gaps—quality in keeping with the Vector's $400,000-plus price.

The running gear is equally top-drawer. The front hubs and uprights are Grand National stock-car pieces. The brakes are huge Alcon rotors and aluminum calipers all around. The engine is a race-prepped small-block Chevy, assembled by a subcontractor using top-grade aftermarket components such as a Rodeck aluminum block, Air Flow Research aluminum heads, TRW pistons, and Carrillo rods.

The powertrain tucks into the engine compartment bolted to a pair of intricate blue-anodized aluminum plates the size of doormats, which attach from the rear bulkhead. The glittering array of polished aluminum, braided stainless-steel plumbing, and heavy-duty heat exchangers is an impressive sight.

As we photograph the engine, Kostka promises to have the gray car's overheating problem solved by evening.

7:00 p.m. same night, Wilmington— We leave for another crack at testing, this time at a most unofficial track. Kostka and I make for the nearby Terminal Island Freeway, which should be deserted at this hour. In the five-minute drive to the free-

way, the engine overheats again. We return to the factory with the Vector bleeding steam from its haunches.

Wiegert is tense and unhappy. "The car is sound, you can see that. It has been tested and punished to the max." He attributes the breakdowns to obsolete parts in the development cars we've been driving, explaining: "You put the best stuff in the cars you have to ship."

Wiegert seems desperate for us to complete a successful test and presses us to stay until the cars can be fixed. Unfortunately, we're scheduled to leave for Michigan the next morning. But we offer him another shot if one of the cars is repaired before flight time.

2:30 a.m. Wednesday, Los Angeles— The phone jars me awake in my hotel room near Los Angeles International. Kostka says he has the red car running again. We agree to meet in the lobby at 3:00 a.m.

Even in the dark of early morning, the arrival of the Vector perks up the hotel's skeleton staff. Kostka and I hop in, followed by one of his mechanics in a Suburban. This time we head toward Pershing Avenue—a limited-access divided four-lane road just west of the airport that should be barren at this hour.

The red car is running strong. Its temperature stays in the low 200s and there is no sign of detonation. After four runs, our best 0-to-60 time is 3.8 seconds, and we measure a standing quarter-mile in twelve seconds flat at 118 mph. Those times are good enough to edge out a Ferrari F40. There was room to go faster, but the car refused to upshift into third gear and the engine was hitting its rev limiter well short of its 7000-rpm redline.

I drive over to the waiting Kostka so that he can check it out. He confirms the problems, and we find that reverse is also gone. We call it a night, and I am back in my room at 4:00 a.m.

"It costs us substantially more to build this car than it costs Ferrari to build an F40," says Jerry Wiegert. Judging by the premium components, fine craftsmanship, and excellent finish of the cars he is shipping, that may well be true. But in development and engineering, we suspect Ferrari has outspent Vector.

Will the Vector satisfy the demanding supercar buyer? Perhaps. But this question doesn't frighten Jerry Wiegert. "My customers are big guys, they've got attorneys, they know what to do if they're not satisfied."

Is Wiegert himself satisfied? No perfectionist ever is. "I will improve this car through my team and efforts."

We wish him success.

VECTOR W8 TWINTURBO

Vehicle type: mid-engine, rear-wheel-drive, 2-passenger, 2-door coupe

Base price: $421,270 (includes $35,570 luxury tax and $7700 gas-guzzler tax)

Major standard accessories: power steering and windows, A/C, cruise control, tilt steering

Sound system: Sony RM-X2001 AM/FM-stereo radio with Sony CDX-A2002 10-disc CD changer and Sony XE-8 equalizer, 8 ADS speakers

ENGINE
Type . . . . twin-turbocharged and intercooled V-8, aluminum block and heads
Bore x stroke . . . . 4.00 x 3.63 in, 101.6 x 92.1mm
Displacement . . . . 364 cu in, 5972cc
Compression ratio 8.0:1
Engine-control system . . . . Vector/Electromotive with port fuel injection
Emissions controls . . . . 3-way catalytic converter, feedback fuel-air-ratio control, auxiliary air pump
Turbochargers . . . . 2 Garrett H32
Waste gates . . . . 2 proprietary
Maximum boost pressure . . . . .10.0 psi
Valve gear . . . . pushrods, hydraulic lifters
Power (SAE net) . . . . .625 bhp @ 5700 rpm
Torque (SAE net) . . . . 630 lb-ft @ 4900 rpm

DRIVETRAIN
Transmission . . . . 3-speed automatic
Final-drive ratio . . . . 2.43:1, Torsen limited slip

Gear	Ratio	Mph/1000 rpm	Max. test speed
I	3.00	10.1	75 mph (6200 rpm)
II	1.57	19.1	122 mph (6400 rpm)
III	1.00	30.2	136 mph (4500 rpm)

DIMENSIONS AND CAPACITIES
Wheelbase . . . . 103.0 in
Track, F/R . . . . 63.0/65.0 in
Length . . . . 172.0 in
Width . . . . 76.0 in
Height . . . . 42.5 in
Ground clearance . . . . 5.5 in
Curb weight . . . . 3680 lb

Weight distribution, F/R 42.9/57.1
Fuel capacity 28.0
Oil capacity 14.0
Water capacity 24.0

CHASSIS/BODY
Type . . . . . . steel-tube central cage reinforced with sh[...] aluminum, aluminum monocoque front a[...] rear extensio[...]
Body material . . . . . carbon fiber-, Kevlar-, and fibergla[...] reinforced plas[...]

INTERIOR
SAE volume, front seat . . . . 50 cu[...] luggage space . . . . 5 cu[...]
Front seats . . . . buc[...]
Seat adjustments . . . . fore and aft, seatback ang[...] lumbar support, upper side bolste[...] thigh supp[...]
Restraint systems, front . . . . manual 3-point bel[...] driver air b[...]
General comfort . . . . poor fair good **excelle**[...]
Fore-and-aft support . . . . poor fair good **excelle**[...]
Lateral support . . . . poor fair good **excelle**[...]

SUSPENSION
F: . . . . ind, unequal-length control arms, coil sprin[...] anti-roll b[...]
R: . . . . de Dion rigid axle located by 4 trailing lir[...] and a Panhard rod, coil springs, anti-roll b[...]

STEERING
Type . . . . rack-and-pinion, power-assist[...]
Turns lock-to-lock . . . . 2[...]
Turning circle curb-to-curb . . . . 46.2[...]

BRAKES
F: . . . . 13.0 x 1.1-in vented d[...]
R: . . . . 13.0 x 1.1-in vented d[...]
Power assist . . . . nc[...]

WHEELS AND TIRES
Wheel size . . . . .F: 9.5 x 16 in, R: 12.0 x 16[...]
Wheel type . . . . 3-piece modular alumin[...]
Tires . . . . Michelin Sport XGT Plus; F: 255/45ZR-1[...] R: 315/40ZR-[...]

CAR AND DRIVER TEST RESULTS

ACCELERATION
	Seconds
Zero to 30 mph	1.6
40 mph	2.2
50 mph	2.9
60 mph	3.8
70 mph	4.8
80 mph	5.8
90 mph	7.0
100 mph	8.3
110 mph	10.2
120 mph	12.4

Top-gear passing time, 30–50 mph 5.0
50–70 mph 5.5
Standing ¼-mile . . . . 12.0 sec @ 118 mph
Top speed (mfr claim) . . . . 218 mph

BRAKING
70–0 mph @ impending lockup . . . . 191 ft

Modulation . . . . poor fair good **excellent**
Fade . . . . **none** moderate heavy
Front-rear balance . . . . poor **fair** good

HANDLING
Roadholding, 300-ft-dia skidpad . . . . 0.91 g
Understeer . . . . **minimal** moderate excessive

PROJECTED FUEL ECONOMY
EPA city driving . . . . .7 mpg
EPA highway driving . . . . 15 mpg

INTERIOR SOUND LEVEL
Idle . . . . 75 dBA
Full-throttle acceleration . . . . 95 dBA
70-mph cruising . . . . 90 dBA
70-mph coasting . . . . 90 dBA

PHOTOGRAPHY BY JEFFREY G. RUSSELL

FUTURE SHOCKS

By Csaba Csere

After examining the workings of active suspensions in recent years, we predicted that it would be at least five years before the radically new technology saw production. As it turned out, Nissan and Toyota rushed the first production versions to the gadget-hungry Japanese market barely two years after that story. The Toyota Active-Sports Celica has since fallen by the wayside. The Infiniti Q45 with the "Full-Active" option, however, not only remains in production but arrived in America as an option on the 1991 Q45. Is it true, as Infiniti claims, that the active suspension creates "a luxury sedan with a smooth, comfortable ride and the ability to outpower and outhandle many sports cars"? We spent three months with an active-suspension Q45 to find the answer to that question.

First, how the system works. Conventional suspensions are called passive because the springs, shock absorbers, and anti-roll bars can only *react* to the wheel and body motions created by road and driving conditions. When a bump pushes a car's wheel up, the springs and shocks resist the movement and also transfer an upward motion to the car's body; when the road flattens again, the wheel drops down and so does the body, usually compressing the suspension excessively and bouncing around a bit before settling back to its original position.

Passive suspensions cannot differentiate between ride motions caused by bumps and those caused by cornering and braking forces, even though ride motions usually occur much faster than handling motions. An ideal suspension would allow very easy wheel motions over bumps but would tighten up during handling maneuvers. And it would be smart enough to detect a bump in the middle of a corner and release the suspension just enough to deal with it.

Rent-a-Data-Maker: the $107,000
Datron EEP-2 with speed and ride
height sensors.

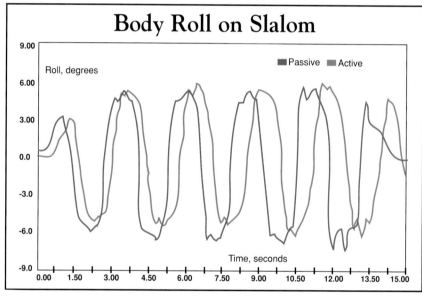

Body Roll on Slalom

Roll, degrees

■ Passive ■ Active

Time, seconds

Single-Bump Performance

Wheel Travel, inches

■ Passive ■ Active

Time, seconds

That's what an active suspension does. In the Q45's "Full-Active" system, two sixteen-bit microcomputers listen to ten sensors that constantly monitor the forces acting on the car's wheels and body. The computers determine whether the forces acting on the car originate from ride or handling activities. And the sophisticated program pinpoints the ideal position of each of the car's four wheels at every instant in time.

To implement this information, an active suspension replaces the passive-suspension components with positively controlled hydraulic actuators at each wheel. The system's computers then signal the hydraulic actuators to move each wheel in the optimal fashion. An ideal system can even lift a wheel to exactly match the contour of the bump it is rolling over. A good analogy is a downhill skier who by scanning and feeling the snowy surface moves his legs to anticipate bumps and moguls before they throw him.

As you might expect, the machinery needed to control and move four heavy wheel/tire/suspension combinations virtually instantaneously in response to ever-changing ride and handling dynamics is extremely complex and expensive. And the hydraulic pump that energizes the hydraulic cylinders consumes some of the engine's horsepower.

To deal with these problems, Nissan engineers took a few technical shortcuts when they designed the Q45 active suspension. They added coil springs to each wheel to help support the weight of the car. This reduces the exertions of the hydraulic cylinders, which need only flex their muscles when something is actually happening to the suspension.

Another shortcut is the use of one-way rather than two-way hydraulic cylinders. The simpler design cannot lift a wheel off the ground to follow the rising curve of a bump; it can only provide additional pressure downward on the wheel. This further reduces complexity and power consumption.

Finally, the Infiniti system is designed to operate relatively slowly. Blow-off valves in the hydraulic cylinders' main control valves open and allow the system to operate passively when the system encounters suspension motions faster than one cycle per second. This further reduces complexity and power requirements. The drawback is that the system cannot react actively to short, sharp bumps.

These compromises depart so much from the active-suspension ideal that we would describe this system as semiactive rather than "Full-Active." Still, the active setup performs very differently than the standard Q45 suspension. To examine these differences, we put two Q45s—one with each suspension—through a battery of handling and ride evaluations.

To accurately measure what the suspensions were doing, we rented a Datron EEP-2 computer equipped with an optical speed sensor and four optical ride-height sensors. This $107,000 instrumentation package let us monitor ride height at all four corners of the car. As long as the

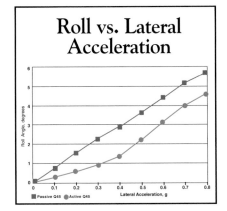

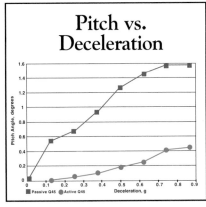

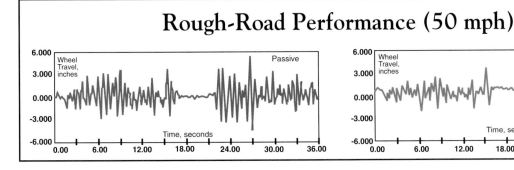

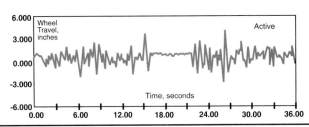

		acceleration, sec				braking, 70–0 mph, ft	roadholding, 300-ft skidpad, g	maneuverability, 1000-ft slalom, mph	fuel economy, mpg		racecourse, min:sec
	curb weight, lb	0–60 mph	1/4-mile	top gear, 30–50 mph	top gear, 50–70 mph				EPA city	EPA hwy	
INFINITI Q45 (passive)	3992	6.7	15.2 @ 93 mph	4.2	4.5	182	0.78	60.0	16	22	1:24.2
INFINITI Q45 (active)	4194	7.1	15.5 @ 93 mph	4.4	4.6	184	0.77	57.9	14	19	1:24.1

wheels are in contact with the ground, ride height is proportional to suspension travel; therefore, this system let us keep tabs on what the wheels were doing. Using this data, the system could also calculate roll and pitch angles.

We went first to the skidpad to measure the two cars' maximum grip and their body roll. The cars were equipped with identical Michelin Sport XGT V 215/65VR-15 tires, so any differences would be attributable solely to the suspensions.

Surprisingly, the passive Q45 outgripped the active car by a hair—0.78 to 0.77 g. We suspect the difference was due to the passive car's lighter weight and more balanced handling. The active car tended to scrub its front tires much harder, whereas the passive car could gently hang its tail out at the limit.

The passive car did roll more (see graph of roll versus lateral acceleration on previous page). The passive car rolls twice as much as the active car up to 0.4 g, although beyond that level roll increases at about the same rate. In the easy cornering of everyday driving, we found this difference very apparent.

Even more apparent is the active car's reduced pitch. As the graph shows, the active car's nose dips only about one third as much as the passive car's during braking. We didn't measure pitch under acceleration, but we would expect similar results.

The active car's reduced pitch and roll didn't yield many dividends on our standard 1000-foot slalom course. The passive car outperformed it by a pretty large margin—threading its way through the cones at 60.0 mph rather easily. It tended to hang its tail out when pressed to the limit, but the transition to oversteer was smooth and progressive.

In contrast, the active car was a handful even at its lower, 57.9-mph speed. The lunging switchbacks of the slalom course came too quickly for the active suspension to react. A comparison of the body roll of the two cars through the slalom bears out our impression, because the active car rolls just about as much as the passive one.

The active suspension seemed to react to each turn just as we were reversing our direction to get around the next cone. This reaction had the unfortunate effect of transforming the car's initial understeer to oversteer, which upset the car at the worst possible time.

The active car's shortcomings through the slalom were disappointing, but redemption came during our rough-road testing. We used the ride-evaluation roads at Chrysler proving grounds, concentrating on two sections that duplicate some of Ann Arbor's choppiest streets. We also tested the cars on a single smooth six-inch-high bump.

We drove each car over the rough-road sections and the calibrated bump at 35, 50, and 60 mph. At all of these speeds, the active suspension easily came out on top. As the graphs of ride height and pitch demonstrate, the active car remained on an even keel, while the passive car bounced and darted around.

The source of this stability is revealed in a comparison of the two cars' performance in the single-bump test. Not only does the active suspension use less wheel motion during the compression and extension part of the bump, but it also damps out the aftershocks almost instantaneously. In contrast, the standard suspension goes through at least two more cycles of oscillation. These benefits also translate into less pitch over the bump. And although we had no way of measuring the shocks transmitted to the passengers, the active car didn't feel harsher than the passive one.

The ability of the active car to quickly return to an even keel after a bump helps in dealing with successive bumps because full suspension travel is available more quickly. The passive car, because it takes longer to regain its equilibrium, gets caught out more easily by successive bumps and simply gets further and further out of shape.

Such composure is always welcome in a suspension, and it paid off on Chrysler's 1.7-mile handling course. Despite the active car's poorer skidpad, slalom, and acceleration capabilities, it lapped at the same speed as the passive car and was easier to drive in the process.

Both cars were nicely balanced on the track, but the active car was more poised. It transitioned to oversteer more smoothly and controllably, which was particularly beneficial in the tight esses. And the generally reduced body motion enhanced the suspension's ability to cope with the cornering demands and also increased driver confidence.

On the open road, these benefits are magnified. With the more stable platform, it is easier to make the mid-course corrections needed to counter the surprises and ambushes that an unknown road can spring on an aggressive driver.

Even in less aggressive driving, the active suspension is more comfortable and permits higher speeds over virtually all manner of rough roads. The humpbacked pavement found where a crowned side road joins a crowned main road no longer produces instant bottoming and flying. The gutters that run across intersections in southern California can also be taken with greater margins.

We think these benefits are definitely worthwhile. Unlike many of the four-wheel-steering systems on the market, whose advantages are highly dubious, Infiniti's exotic suspension pays off with a more controlled ride over rough roads and greater composure in most kinds of hard driving.

The system costs $5500 and leads to other costs (see below), but about eleven percent of 1991 Q45 buyers made the investment. What's more, if even a simplified active suspension like this can produce such clear advantages over a very good riding and handling passive setup that already rides and handles well, then this technology will likely become the dominant high-end suspension as it matures in the next decade.

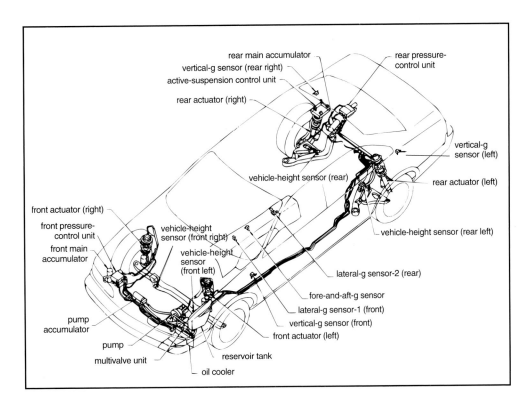

The Price of Active Suspension

The active suspension option on the Q45 costs $5500, including luxury tax. As hefty as that sum is, you won't stop paying for the system once you've written the check in the showroom.

You also pay for the active suspension's elaborate components with 202 additional pounds. That additional weight is a constant sap on performance, as the comparison chart shows. The differences aren't huge, but they're in the wrong direction for an enthusiast.

Another penalty is the power required by the system's high-pressure hydraulic pump. Circulating up to sixteen quarts of hydraulic fluid per minute at 1500 psi, the six-plunger pump draws three to five horsepower. That won't slow down the Q45's 278-hp V-8 very much. But at normal speeds, when the engine is only delivering 20 or 30 hp, it becomes a significant power drain, which shows up very clearly on the EPA driving cycles. The standard Q45's 16/22 mpg city/highway figures drop to 14/19.

These hidden costs don't necessarily make the active suspension a bad deal, but they confirm that even the most modern technology usually involves some compromises. They also suggest areas for improvement before active systems become commonplace. —CC

PHOTOGRAPHY BY DAVID DEWHURST

HONDA BEAT

By Kevin Smith

For the first time since the premiere of "Night Court," the American legal system has given us something truly worthwhile: the new term "hedonic loss." It has popped up in our highly litigious times in personal-injury and wrongful-death lawsuits, and it means *missed good times.* We're going to borrow that term, because "hedonic loss" aptly describes how American car enthusiasts are denied driving pleasure, aesthetic delight, and unbridled fun on account of boring old crashworthiness regulations.

In short, the U.S. government won't allow the sale of the Honda Beat in this country because not enough of the car remains standing after it meets a concrete wall.

Maybe we should sue.

Okay, in a serious scrap with a Peterbilt, the improbably tiny Beat would lose. But so would anything else you could stand to drive. And look: this thing has an air bag, door beams, and high-center brake light (because Japanese consumers wanted them), so don't be too hasty to judge its safety.

Meanwhile, the astonishingly compact, puny-engined Beat addresses other great issues of this decade—congestion, air pollution, oil consumption, collagen-plumped lips—better than a lot of proposed future cars. If there's an electric car on the drawing boards as stylish as the Beat, we ain't seen it; if one of those *voltswagens* is anywhere near this fun to drive, we'll eat our electric bill. Barbara Hershey's, too. (She'd get such an elevated sense of I'm-okay-ness from just being near this car, see, that she wouldn't need to inflate her already quite-inviting lips.)

In truth, the 10.8-foot-long, 0.66-liter Beat only seems quirky because of how *our* driving environment evolved. We're a vast country, and we've developed a taste for crossing our vast distances in vast automobiles. Our whole motive landscape, from lane widths to the lines at the Department of Motor Vehicles, is drawn in units of several yards—its *dot pitch,* if you will, is quite coarse.

Honda's Beat exists on a different scale, a finer scale. A Japanese scale. It may appear to be out of register here, but it's really just slipping into the vacuous spaces around our dots. (That's the way it felt in San Diego Freeway traffic, certainly. Its high-decibel yellow paint was our only hope against disappearing in the shadows of the enormous Geo Metros and CRXs that loomed menacingly all around.)

On its Oriental home turf, the Beat speaks to two everyday realities: first, the unaffordability of energy and space, and second, the unwaveringly wacky tastes of its public. The 660cc minicar category represents completely legitimate transportation over there, and there's a thriving market for it. Since Honda introduced this first mid-engine sports roadster to the class last spring, folks have been lining up like Muscovites to pay $10,800 for the little zipper.

We can see the Beat's appeal. But performance, in the objective sense, is not part of its act. The three-cylinder engine's 657cc displacement is smaller than that of just one Corvette cylinder. And at 1675 pounds, the Beat is light but hardly feathery. So while the stubby car does nip through holes in traffic that aren't there

for other vehicles, power is not your partner. Even the issue of which wheels are driven (the rears, for the record) is academic; nothing you can do with the throttle has more than an incidental effect on the car's balance or behavior.

Which is not to say the Beat is a dull drive. When you're concentrating on conserving speed, planning ahead, and savagely whipping a little motor that you outweigh, who has time for dull? To extract its full 63 horsepower (which you must), you spin the tiny twelve-valve triple right to the 8500-rpm redline. Six grand (about 70 mph in fifth) is the useful bottom of the power band. You are into top gear before the end of a freeway on-ramp. Full steam is 80-something mph.

Reflex-quick steering magnifies the impression of maneuverability, the Beat's predominant handling trait. Though its wheelbase is not exactly elfin—at 89.8 inches, it's half an inch *longer* than a

For such a small car, the cockpit is surprisingly roomy—it's big enough for six-foot-plus Westerners. Alas, it is not big enough to have the crunch zones necessary to make government-pleasing numbers in the barrier test.

Miata's—the car attacks direction changes so voraciously that at freeway speeds it's all atwitter, juking and darting anxiously. Yet the Beat feels firmly planted on the road, thanks to tires that are pretty meaty for the car's mass and power.

As entertaining as the Beat is to drive, however, its most endearing qualities are its design and packaging. It is so *tiny* (a foot and a half shorter and almost a foot narrower than a CRX), but it doesn't really look undersized unless something provides a scale of reference—like another car, a person, a nickel. Designers will tell you it's easier to make a vice-president look brilliant than to make a short car look handsome, so hurray for Honda's stylists.

Even the Beat's cockpit is shockingly roomy. It easily accepts six-foot-plus Westerners. But the car ends some 30 inches ahead of your feet and about 50 inches behind your back pockets.

In a nutshell, there is the problem: an automobile cannot be scaled like this (rather like a nutshell, come to think of it) and still have the crush zones necessary to make government-pleasing numbers in the barrier test. All humankind would benefit from the compact size and modest appetite of cars like the Beat, now that the automobile must soften its environmental impact. But "impact" is the dirty word where shoe-sized cars are concerned. The feds shake their heads and deny us such ingenious cars because The Gang That Can't Drive Straight might stumble into one and go fulfill a statistical destiny.

Our hedonic loss is downright criminal. There ought to be a law. And a zillion bucks compensation for every one of us who has been officially denied—on pain of death and tax audit—the right to run life's little risks in the zany contraption of our choice.

HONDA BEAT

Vehicle type: mid-engine, rear-wheel-drive, 2-passenger, 2-door convertible

Price (Japan): $10,800

Engine type: SOHC 12-valve 3-in-line, aluminum block and head, Honda PGM-FI engine-control system with port fuel injection

Displacement	40 cu in, 657cc
Power (SAE net)	63 bhp @ 8100 rpm
Transmission	5-speed
Wheelbase	89.8 in
Length	129.7 in
Width	54.9 in
Height	46.3 in
Curb weight	1675 lb

Manufacturer's performance ratings:

Zero to 50 mph	8.1 sec
Top speed	84 mph
Fuel economy, Japanese city cycle	41 mpg
steady 37 mph	64 mpg

TRUCKS AND VANS

LOVE YOUR MOTHER

STOP ARMS RACE
SAVE HUMAN RACE

DEAD FEAT
JUNE 23 & 24, 1990 · EUGENE, OR

VOLKSWAGEN
WHO ARE THE GRATEFUL DEAD
AND WHY DO THEY KEEP FOLLOWING ME

RESCUE THE RAINFORESTS

FOOD NOT BOMBS

The VW bus, built between 1949 and '79, is a "negative status symbol," and has long been the vehicle of choice for followers of the Grateful Dead (top). Cheap to buy, cheap to run, cheap to fix. Just toss in a mattress, hot plate, and portable fridge for a cosmic journey. One of the faithful, Angie Padgett (above, right), shows off the tie-die work of boyfriend Steve Yatson.

THE VAN Of AQUARIUS

By Steve Spence

A palpable buzz of electricity was in the air of the pretty, clapboard towns surrounding Richfield Coliseum south of Cleveland, even though the excitement— a three-night stand by the cosmic old fogeys, the Grateful Dead—was still two days away.

The buzz began with the first wave of wiggy old Volkswagen buses that began appearing on the suburban landscape. Soon the local folks could be seen leaning forward over the steering wheels of their cars, squinting out at all the strange messages decorating the buses. Look at that bumper sticker, Glenda!

"WE ALL LIVE DOWNSTREAM."

"I NEED A MIRACLE."

"MEAT STINKS."

The "Deadheads" had arrived, the camp followers of the middle-aged rock group who will travel any distance to attend these mini-Woodstock gatherings of their musical tribe. They pulled their buses and vans off roads near busy intersections and set up shop, hanging up tie-dyes—sheets, shirts, hippie-style dresses, T-shirts, Grateful Dead posters and paraphernalia, rastafarian hair-wraps—on clotheslines. Overnight, the landscape was transformed. It was as if a traveling sixties roadshow of gypsy hippies had come to town.

One supposes the locals appreciated the atmosphere of festival. There was a lot of grinning and shaking of their heads in local coffeeshops, but it was all good-natured. (In the sixties, there would have been a local brick-throwing contingent, for those gypsies brought with them strange ideas and mind-expanding chemicals.)

The night before the Cleveland concert, some Deadheads, suited up in their tie-dyed finery and sporting serious big hair and T-shirts with messages like "Eat, Drink and See Jerry," appeared to drink beer and eat among the locals at the nearby Winking Lizard Tavern, one of those places that employ clean-cut college kids who have the exuberant look of having experienced farm work. You could feel the excitement, you could even smell the perfume of patchouli in the barroom.

The bartender, a strapping college-age youth, was asked if he was going to the concert. He grinned widely. "I was thinking of going," he said, "but I'm kind of afraid it'd change my life." A waitress his age heard that, and laughed somewhat uneasily. She understood what he meant; strange ideas still have their allure, and there was always the possibility of moral defection, the temptation to dump tired old values. Who among these nineties kids had not heard stories of the wicked sixties, the sexual revolution, the Age of Aquarius?

So while the bartender laughed it off, maybe he considered the vague possibility of being overcome by a strange desire to drop out, to buy a beat-up VW bus for $500, to toss in a mattress, a hot plate, and a portable fridge, and to head off after the Grateful Dead. What a trip! Thousands of Deadheads do just that, and they manage to make a living in the process.

VW buses and other provocative forms of weird transport were everywhere: lined up behind filling stations, parked in vacant lots and behind motels, and, most of all, jammed into a nearby state-park campground. Down in that park, the Age of Aquarius had returned.

The VW bus has gone by many names—Microbus, Panel Van, Kombi, Crew Cab, Camper, Station Wagon, Vanagon—but it is the simplest van, the bus, built between 1949 and '79, that has been the vehicle of choice for those who have turned their backs on convention, or those who have wished to make personal statements about their values via their mode of transport.

The VW bus, like the Beetle, has been "a negative status symbol" for most of its 43 years—plain as a brick, simple as a lawnmower, slow as glue, cheap to buy, cheap to run, and cheap to fix, it has

A gathering of "Deadheads" (below left) transforms the landscape. Conrad Neil of Manitoba (below right) sells posters out of his 1978 VW.

Deadheads like to twist popular icons, like the VW logo, which becomes "Darkstarvergnugen."

hauled a lot of people (and surfboards) around in a style that *disdains* style. If you're a Deadhead, it's not just a vehicle —it's home.

Something on the order of 6.7 million VW buses have been built since 1949. Oddly enough, the idea for this simple "hauler" was not hatched in VW's Wolfsburg plant in Germany, but in the head of an ambitious Dutchman named Ben Pon, who saw the potential of VW after the war and was to become an early exporter of its products (he personally brought the first Beetle to America).

Pon thought VW needed to offer more than just the Beetle, and with a simple sketch in a spiral notebook that is now a museum artifact at Wolfsburg, he drew a rendering of what he had in mind.

Pon's idea so captivated Heinz Nordhoff, the late head man at VW, that to launch the bus in 1950 he had to cut back on production of the Beetle at a time when Volkswagen could not keep up with orders for its inexpensive car. It was called the "Type 2" (Type 1 being the Beetle). Nordhoff and Pon had guessed correctly—by the mid-fifties, VW had to build a plant in Hanover just to build the Type 2s. Eventually the homely hauler would be sold in 140 countries.

Imagine a 2300-pound van that promised to carry as many as nine people but was propelled—hardly the right word— by a 25-horsepower engine! By 1962, when the one-millionth "Bully" (named for its bulldog, workhorse stance) came off the line, its output had been increased to 34 hp and it finally got a synchronized transmission.

VW offered its bus in countless configurations, with varying interior heights and bed plans and door arrangements. American buyers, who had to get up to speed on freeways, soon got a model with a 1.5-liter, 42-horsepower engine. (Still, it was an adventure to be hit by a gust of wind in a VW bus while crossing the Golden Gate Bridge.) The first major facelift came in 1967; the two-piece windshield was replaced by a single pane, its nose was flattened, and the doors, which had opened like those on a barn, were now sliding. The VW bus craze in this country reached its peak in 1969, with a record 65,069 sold that year. More minor facelifts continued, and in 1972, a bus arrived with a Porsche 914 engine. The following year, an automatic transmission was offered. In 1974, the Hanover plant was able to build an astounding 1200 buses in a single day, and sales went over the four-million mark.

The modern-day bus, the Vanagon, appeared in 1979. It now had an all-wheel-drive model and a squared-off, all-business front. It was the best bus ever made, but it had lost its goofy charm. Sales, which had begun to slide in the seventies, slipped even further in the eighties (5147 in 1989). The heyday of the VW bus was over.

John Hollander, who goes by the name Emmett and is just 23, had parked his '77 VW bus behind a truck stop among a crazy quilt of Deadhead vehicles, including a couple of converted yellow school buses reminiscent of Ken Kesey's Merry Pranksters' bus of sixties psychedelic fame ("Positive Vibrations," it announced). Kids roamed through the area, girls in muslin tie-dyes, and Jerry Garcia's voice boomed forth from the open doors of cars. Hollander had driven all the way from Seattle, and he was digging around inside looking for something; the inside of his bus looked like a twister had visited it recently. His hair was wild in rastafarian fashion, and he was slight of build, looking as if he hadn't spent much time eating.

The bus was painted a flat white, as if he'd done it with a paintbrush. The entire bus was covered with hand prints in various bright colors.

Emmett is a budding entrepreneur learning the tie-dye ropes. It has not been all gravy. At a Denver concert of the Dead, "the cops busted me for vending without a license. They took twenty shirts off me. I went home with $4." It's not easy being

a Deadhead, although Emmett did not want to be described as one.

"What's the deal with the hand prints?" he was asked.

"Well, I had a stencil of a hand, so . . ." He thought for a moment. What was his purpose? ". . . so, I figured I'd put a black hand on one side, and, well, it just went from there."

Like a lot of the independent-thinking Deadheads, he gave me an answer that had the ring of Zen when I asked what it was he liked about his bus, which has a rebuilt engine and cost him $2000.

"Uh, I kind of liked the idea of an air-cooled engine, you know?"

We wished him luck, and headed off for

Anthony Vanderford (top, center) uses his VW bus to set up shop. In the trees. He sells his wares to other Deadheads who are in the same business. There's a whole iconography of the Dead and the VW bus (far left). Concessionaire in cowboy hat (near left) sells healthful "stir-fry," not hot dogs.

With a sink, stove, refrigerator, and bed, the VW bus is a home away from home.

the park campground. A long gravel road led finally to a gated checkpoint, where we paid a $10 fee to get in. "Are there any Deadheads down there?" we asked a young woman wearing a khaki uniform and a Smokey the Bear hat. She rolled her eyes around in her head, like it was a question not worth answering.

Coming down the hill's incline to a meadow where the tribe of Deadheads suddenly came into view, where Grateful Dead music filled the air, I was somehow reminded of Custer, and how he must have felt so momentarily strange coming upon the sight of an entire nation of Sioux camped at the Little Big Horn. It is reflexive upon seeing a sight like this to utter Christ's first name, though not in vain. "Jesus."

The first VW bus that caught my eye belonged to Anthony Vanderford of Casper, Wyoming. Vanderford, who was 20, had been following the Dead since high-school graduation. He had set up a table with all sorts of things for sale, and tie-dyed sheets were pinned to trees forming a canopy above his bus.

The cheerful Vanderford invited me to look inside the bus. Poking out from under a pile of bedding and clothing was a sleeping woman's head. There was a sink and a stove and a refrigerator and running water, and a series of bunk beds.

"It's a little home. It's got everything you need," he said proudly. Meanwhile, some potential customers poked over his goods. But these were Deadhead camp followers like himself, and I wondered out loud if it was possible to sell stuff to other Deadheads, who were in the same business as he was.

He gave me a cosmic grin, like the whole thing was a mystery to him, too. "I know what you're saying, but I've only been here a couple of hours and I've already made two hundred dollars!"

I came upon Conrad and Dan Neil, brothers from Manitoba, Canada. Conrad was selling exotic posters for $10 each. This was Dan's third concert, but his brother has traveled to 30 of them.

Asked what it was about the Dead's music that he found so alluring, Conrad had to think a moment. Finally he said, "The feel, man. It talks to you. It's a natural high, and everybody's calm. I like the calmness of it."

An upholsterer by trade, Conrad had a fine '78 bus loaded with amenities. He summed up his affection for it: "It can sleep six and it's great on gas. What else

can I say? The guy I bought it from wanted $5000, but I got it for $3600. You can't beat that."

But in fact Jeff Johns of Pottstown, Pennsylvania, who was parked fifty feet away, beat that. His '73 bus cost him $475 just five months earlier. Okay, it wasn't as nice as Conrad's. Johns, 20, a cycle mechanic "on and off," said he bought the bus from a Czech who "buys them, fixes them up and sells them." The Czech, it turned out, wasn't setting any entrepreneurial records. "He bought this van for $400, and he was asking $550 for it. We told him our situation, which basically was we don't have any money. So he sold it to us for $475."

Intrigued by an old '72 bus with a humorous protective vinyl bra strapped over its nose, I came around the back and ran into Angie Padgett, who would be, hands down, *The Prettiest Freckled Girl in the World* were there such a contest. She was posing for a picture when her boyfriend, Steve Yatson, showed up. They are both in their early twenties, and he'd given up the yuppie lifestyle to follow the Dead for awhile, learning tie-dying.

"I went from a Porsche 944 to this," he said laughing, amused by his own change of lifestyle. "I paid $400 for this bus, but I did tons of work on it."

Angie said, "At some places, if you've got problems with your bus, there are mechanics around who will work for beer."

Yatson said, "I used to sell construction materials, and did very well. But you can make money here, too." Pointing to a tie-dyed sheet he'd made that was draped over his van, he said, "That sheet cost about $2 to make, and we sell it for $35." It was clear that for Angie and Steve, this was a temporary lark. "I'm going to have to do the real-life thing again pretty soon." Sometime soon he will be headed for college in San Jose, California.

We wandered around, and I was reminded of a conversation I'd had with Blair Jackson, a Dead historian from Berkeley, California, who puts out a periodical of Grateful Dead lore called *The Golden Road.* "The Volkswagen bus is the cheap warhorse vehicle of the seventies.

"There's a whole iconography of the Dead and the VW." I had to look that up. It means the images and pictures that become the symbols that describe a culture.

"The Dead has a tradition of taking traditional items from the culture and then twisting them—in a friendly way. Like [a depiction of] Calvin and Hobbes, only they're smoking a bong or doing nitrous oxide." Just then I saw a Charlie Brown T-shirt, with Charlie's head ballooned to watermelon size, making him "Cosmic Charlie." Another shirt declared, "Bo Knows Jerry." A Disney-like theme park reads, "Deadheadland."

No one, including the Grateful Dead, now in their 26th year, can quite explain their popularity. Says leader Jerry Garcia: "Here we are, we're getting into our fifties, and where are these people who keep coming to our shows coming from? What do they find fascinating about these middle-aged bastards playing basically the same thing we've always played? I mean, what do 17-year-olds find fascinating

A deadheader campaigns for his favorite plant (far left). John Steinbach, Deadhead fashion king (center). Emmett ("I'm not a Deadhead") Hollander is a budding entrepreneur learning the tie-dye ropes.

adventure" to it. "It's rock 'n' roll with a bit of country-western. And blues. Actually, it's like a jazz band—they never play the same set twice. They have such a large body of music—probably 110 to 120 songs at any given time. They played six shows in the Bay Area, and during all that, they repeated just one song—'Promised Land.' "

Whatever the case, in the first half of 1991, Dead concerts grossed $20 million. Their average take per show, according to Pollstar, a firm that reports on the music industry, was more than $1.1 million, or nearly twice that of that summer's second biggest touring act, Guns n' Roses. The Dead played nine nights in New York's Madison Square Garden, three in Cleveland, and six at Boston Garden—and all of them were sold-out performances.

about this? . . . So what is it about the 1990s in America? There must be a dearth of fun out there in America. Or adventure. Maybe that's it: maybe we're just one of the last adventures in America. I don't know."

Blair Jackson says there's a "sense of

"We didn't invent the Grateful Dead," says Garcia. "The crowd invented the Grateful Dead. We were just in line to see what was going to happen."

Like the popularity of the VW bus, it defies explanation.

Wendy Terhune (above) has her priorities straight. Will Deadheads make the EuroVan (right) the choice of radicals in the future?

Volkswagen EuroVan GL

Many among us were raised to be Democrats in families that were propelled by Generation One and Generation Two VW Microbuses. They were homely, slow, rare, and cheap.

Now there's a new VW minivan, Generation Four, called the EuroVan. It's homely, slow, and rare. Cheap, it's not. The five models introduced in 1992 range from about $17,000 to $24,000. That sug-

gests the van will instead appeal to today's upscale Eurofans rather than radical families. We're not sold: Despite its name, the EuroVan (called the Caravelle in Europe) hasn't got the chic presence of other stylish European products, namely Audi cars, Braun coffee makers, or Krups food processors.

The EuroVan is ten inches taller than a Chrysler mini. You climb high into the driver's seat or the front passenger's optional swivel seat. Front-seat occupants sit tall and can see over the tops of other minivans. The rear floor, however, is relatively low, and entering through the sliding side door is easy.

The EuroVan is larger inside than other minivans. Camper models, the fifteen-inch-longer wheelbase RV (Recreational Vehicle), and the CV (Camping Vehicle) are available with beds, one a double in a pop-up roof. Passenger vans come in three models: the low-line CL, the GL, and the MV (Multiuse Van), differentiated by amenities and seat placement. The RV seats two in back, the CV seats four, and the other models seat five rear passengers.

The EuroVan's front wheels are powered by a transverse in-line five-cylinder engine. Older, rear-engined VW Microbuses had horizontal steering wheels, and to parallel-park you had to remember the left front wheel was under your butt. The EuroVan's front wheels are in front of the driver's feet, but its bus-style horizontal steering wheel makes it feel similar on the road to the rear-engined VWs. The EuroVan rides better than the Vanagon (Generation Three), though drivers will feel as much body roll. Wind buffeting feels substantially reduced because the new VW van is more aerodynamic. The EuroVan's vast flanks, which dwarf its fifteen-inch wheels, are large enough for the biggest flower decals. The windows, too, are large, and provide superb rear and side visibility for the driver.

Nobody ever bought a VW van to drive fast, and the EuroVan upholds this tradition. The 109-hp EuroVan jumps quickly away from a stop, but acceleration slows when you reach 20 mph. Its five-cylinder engine was developed from Audi's 2.2-liter, and it is the least powerful engine you can buy here in any van except the four-cylinder Dodge Caravan or Plymouth Voyager. The new VW powerplant doesn't have the throaty growl of the Audi engine; it sounds more like a small truck engine, the kind you're likely to hear in downtown Frankfurt or Munich. Acceleration to 60 mph takes 15.8 seconds, just one second faster than the latest "waterboxer" Vanagon, but five seconds slower than a 3.3-liter Dodge Caravan. Top speed is 95 mph—a Vanagon will reach only 83 mph.

The standard electronically controlled four-speed automatic (also used in the Passat) shifts like a rental truck and is not as refined as the transmissions in other U.S.-sold minivans.

The EuroVan was developed in the mid-eighties to compete with Europe's Ford Transit, currently the best-selling minivan over there. The bulk of sales (over 60 percent) are to plumbers and carpenters and the like. The U.S. models have more soundproofing but still are slightly noisier than other minis for sale here. VW expects Americans will buy about 20,000 per year—one for every 20 Chrysler minivans sold.

In the age of the Chrysler minivan, a VW van designed for European plumbers can't compete as transportation for the average American family. Maybe it can for the *radical* American family, and thereby uphold a good tradition. Peace, baby.

—*Phil Berg*

Volkswagen Eurovan GL

Vehicle type: front-engine, front-wheel-drive, 7-passenger, 4-door van

Estimated base price: $19,000

Engine type: SOHC 5-in-line, iron block and aluminum head, Bosch Motronic engine-control system with port fuel injection

Displacement	150 cu in, 2459cc
Power (SAE net)	109 bhp @ 4500 rpm
Transmission	4-speed automatic with lockup torque converter
Wheelbase	115.0 in
Length	187.4 in
Curb weight	3950 lb
Zero to 60 mph	15.8 sec
Street start, 5 to 60 mph	16.4 sec
Standing 1/4-mile	20.2 sec @ 67 mph
Top speed	95 mph
Braking, 70–0 mph	218 ft
Roadholding, 100-ft-dia skidpad	0.55 g
Road horsepower @ 50 mph	18 hp
EPA fuel economy, city driving	17 mpg
C/D observed fuel economy	15 mpg

EUROVAN PHOTOS BY DICK KELLEY

POLAR MOMENTS

By John Phillips III

An Alaskan's advice on driving the Dalton Highway in November: "Take spare windshields and tires. Take money. Take colorful clothes you can spread on the tundra to signal aircraft. Take Alaska Airlines south to Maui."

This came, of course, *after* William Jeanes and Csaba Csere had warmly embraced the notion of driving the entire population of four-wheel-drive minivans as far north as possible on planet Earth.

William or Csaba came up with this idea *before* they knew anything about avalanches in the Brooks Range, grizzly-bear warnings, minus-40-degree temperatures, and four hours of daily sunlight. Before they heard that the 28-foot-wide Dalton

Highway is entirely gravel, its 500-mile length punctuated by exactly two settlements that, on any given day, might or might not have fuel or electric lights or vegetarian lasagna. Before either knew we had to get permission from the state even to *use* the Highway—which is there to service the 800-mile-long trans-Alaska oil pipeline and not motoring journalists, one of whom is carrying his sleeping bag in a brown-paper sack that says, "Let's Go Krogering."

But by the time they'd learned enough to want to reconsider, it was too late. By then, five minivans, a GMC Yukon tow vehicle, and eleven people were already loitering in Fairbanks. (The Chevy Astro

arrived via Federal Express. Really.) By then, *C/D* staffers were already grinding through stacks of reindeer sausage at the Westmark Fairbanks hotel, this despite warnings from our guides—John and Suzy Fouse—who had both arrived wearing tent-sized parkas and six inches of layered clothing that made them look like miniature submarines.

Alaskan veterans both, the Fouses had helped assemble the outpost whence the pipeline's oil emanates, which was also our destination: the otherworldly Prudhoe Bay, half on land and half atop the Arctic Ocean, a place that might have been a setting for *Mad Max IV* or *Return of the Alien* except that, as a backdrop for sci-fi movies, it is not sufficiently believable.

"It's warm here now," explains John Fouse as he gestures at Fairbanks's minus-15-degree weather. "But where we're going, it may get cold. And we only have an 18,000-pound winch on the Yukon."

Our heaviest minivan—the Astro—

weighs 4449 pounds. So why a problem?

"Because you have the weight of the van added to the weight of what it's stuck in," he replies. "Which could be a chunk of the Brooks Range slightly larger than Alabama."

We set out anyway. Fouse ominously announces on the CB radio, "Gather up the wagons." (The Donner Party tried to cross the Sierra Nevada—a Wally Cox of mountain ranges compared with what we are facing—in wagons roughly the size of our own but without cruise control. A subject for Geraldo: People who have eaten people.)

A mere 30 miles north of Fairbanks, all traces of festering civilization conclude, even the neon Coors signs. One by one, the radio stations go dead. And there is a twenty-foot homemade white cross by the roadside, in memory of one Chuckie Kelly, who evidently erred here from the path of righteousness and the northbound lane. We are now officially On Our Own. Walk 50 feet off the Highway and you may

Dear Diary:

1. Guide Fouse delivers opinion of Fairbanks: "You see a guy barf on the sidewalk in September and it's still there in March." Nonetheless recommends nearby saloon: Skinny Dick's Halfway Inn.

2. Aerostar center-punches two ptarmigans in flight; air fills with white feathers, like a Beautyrest explosion. Jensen explains, "I'm sorry, but it was as if Mother Nature just shouted, 'Pull.'"

3. Technical director Csere, standing before urinal, is photographed by local child who has recently acquired Kodak flash attachment. Same child later observed climbing into glass display case.

4. CB-radio conversation:
Trucker: "You guys testing them little things?"
Us: "Yessir, ten-four."
Trucker: "Who won?"
Us: "We'll let you read about it in the March issue of *Car and Driver*."
Trucker: "Hey, great. I watch that every week on PBS."

5. Disaster Creek. Permit-holders' checkpoint. Permit checkers not on duty today, last week, next month. Also, there aren't any.

6. Associate editor Berg, overcome by vastness of landscape: "You could come up here with Las Vegas hookers and just do weird things right out in the open." We encourage associate editor to get more air.

7. Associate editor yet again, questioned about excess speed in pitch darkness on ice-covered road subject to avalanches and grizzly-bear conventions, replies, "It is amazing what you can learn by watching ESPN."

8. Dalton Highway rips MPV's rear tire into angel-hair pasta. Chance to light flare, which ignites inside Mazda, showering colorful sparks on steering wheel. Excellent effect inside—beacon could draw passing aircraft—but of minimal effect atop vast North Slope, which is size of California and occupied this night only by car journalists with Fudgsicle intelligence.

9. GMC Yukon's tail-gate latch, chilled to minus 38 then slammed, breaks into shrapnel.

10. At minus 70, oil workers stop working because, Fouse recalls, "things start breaking." Things? "Oh, you know, stuff like shock absorbers and steering racks." Group falls silent; all minivans slow markedly.

11. Executive editor falls into Arctic Ocean.　　　　—JP

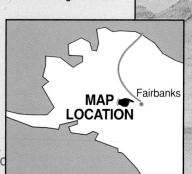

MAP LOCATION　　Fairbanks

well be standing in a spot just as it was 50 or 500 or 5000 years ago.

The Dalton Highway is narrow, and much of its loose granite surface—which is as sharp as Wilkinson sword blades and will soon chew up tires on both the Aerostar and the MPV—is mixed with coarse granular snow so dry and crunchy that it is like driving on dirt.

The road is named after James W. Dalton, a durable guy who was much in demand as an Arctic-construction expert after he directed the assembly of the DEW line for our Department of Defense. Construction of the highway—known originally simply as the Haul Road—began in 1974. The road crosses one-third of Alaska and spans the state's highest mountain pass. Dalton did not leave the project

Trans-Alaska pipeline daily carries 1.5 million barrels rather than the 3.0 million it is capable of carrying, this despite C/D's earnest annual expenditure of $40,000 on test-car fuel. Aluminum radiators dissipate heat that would otherwise thaw permafrost. Nearby sign warns: "If you see liquid escaping under severe pressure . . . vacate area."

Left to right: Toyota Previa, Mazda MPV, Ford Aerostar, Dodge Caravan, Chevrolet Astro.

in the hands of government. The proof: the highway was completed in 154 days.

On this road—which has no stop signs, traffic lights, or no-passing zones for some 500 miles—there is room enough only for an eighteen-wheeler in the oncoming lane and a large accident in yours. Which we almost have as we meet our first southbound tanker, whose driver has evidently watched way too much pro bowling or is paralyzed at the sight of six civilian vehicles. He throws his rig into a 50-mph 18-wheel drift on an intercept guaranteed to demolish every minivan in our convoy. Then he gets off the brakes. Miraculously, the rig straightens and hurtles past in a hail of blue-white snow and granite shrapnel. Two of the minivans' windshields are now cracked. All but the

Previa's will be starred, scored, or spider-webbed by day's end. (Our motto: "It's only funny until someone loses an eye.") The Dalton Highway's rules of etiquette are different from ours. They do not apply on holidays, evenings, weekdays, and mornings. Also, there aren't any.

Guide Fouse, who evidently failed to see this feat of Third World driving, gets on the CB and repeats rules he mentioned at this morning's sausage fest:

1. Drink lots of water, because the humidity is only five percent and will fall as we get farther north.

2. Don't touch a door handle with your bare hands or a bumper with your tongue.

3. Assume the road beyond a hill or around a corner is entirely clogged with Peterbilt.

CHEVROLET ASTRO

The Chevrolet Astro, which first appeared in 1985, constituted the General Motors reply to the enormously successful Chrysler minivans. Yet, if one looked closely at the Astro, one saw that it offered an entirely different atmosphere than the Chrysler people-haulers. The Astro was more industrial, more trucklike.

This trucklike personality did not happen by accident. Whereas the Chrysler minivans were built to find a place in the family garage, the Astro was aimed at a dual target: the family garage *and* the workplace. GM frankly expected that its Astro would send more copies to the working world than to the softer demands of the suburbs. The Astro retains this duality of personality, not always to its advantage when compared with minivans that make commercial use a secondary goal, if it's a goal at all.

At an as-tested price of $21,656, the Astro was our lowest-priced entry, though the range was intentionally narrow (the Caravan, at $22,104, was the most expensive). The Astro was the heaviest, by well over 200 pounds, but it was by far the most powerful. Its 4.3-liter V-6 pumped out 200 horsepower and 260 pound-feet of torque.

The Astro's commercial heritage is reflected in its dimensions: it was the tallest and widest of our vehicles, but missed by only one inch being the shortest. The rear-door design, side-by-side doors with small square windows in them, also say "truck."

Chevrolet Astro

Put frankly, the Astro just didn't do very well on our test. Despite a power advantage, it wasn't the quickest, and despite a cargo volume that led the pack (152 cubic feet), the Astro would not hold the ubiquitous four-by-eight-foot sheet of plywood, and it had the least capacity for hauling lengths of pipe.

Tools were required to remove unwanted seats. What did work well was the Astro's all-wheel anti-lock braking system.

The Astro's poor finish was no doubt colored by an engine malfunction that still had us puzzled at deadline time. In Prudhoe Bay, we spotted oil drips, and then saw what appeared to be oil and water pumping out of the dipstick: normally a sure sign of failed head gaskets or loss of the separation between the oil and water systems. Stormin' Norman's Garage in Deadhorse allowed otherwise. "A seal," quoth Norman. Indeed, with extra oil aboard, we nursed the Astro back to Fairbanks, using only one quart of Mobil 1 in the process.

But there was more. This is not a new criticism, but this driver-side footwell is a feature that simply should never have been allowed to reach the consumer. In order to operate a modern vehicle, one should not find it necessary to hike one's left foot up on the wheel-well impingement in order to have room for the other foot on the floor. Size eleven, if you're curious.

Even assuming its engine malfunction to be unusual, our Astro just seemed out of phase with the rest.

—William Jeanes

This time, nobody laughs.

Nor do they laugh at the next roadside signs, which bear a message we don't often see back home: SPEED LIMIT 50, NEXT 416 MILES.

At mile 56 we cross the Yukon River, its surface an overlapping jigsaw puzzle of ice floes the size of the USS *Vincennes* and the same color. This is the fifth-longest river in North America and the point at which most summer tourists turn tail and make tracks back to Skinny Dick's Halfway Inn. The Yukon here is as wide as the Mississippi. It is spanned by a wooden-decked bridge 2290 feet long. To celebrate this crossing, Chris Jensen (a reporter for the *Cleveland Plain Dealer* and the only non-*C/D*er who inexplicably failed to say "no" when invited) inserts his Rinkbinders cassette so that we can sing the chorus to "The Yukon—She's Callin' Me Back." It is also Jensen who explains the lack of humidity to the liberal-arts majors: "See, any water in the air tends to get hard and fall on the ground. Gravity: it's a law we can live with."

We dismount here to swap minivans. Nobody knows the temperature, but it nonetheless establishes conclusively that all those people who have told you, "Once it gets below minus 15, it never really feels any colder," have never stood next to the Yukon River at sunset (3 p.m.) on November 20. The cold here is not just an annoyance, not merely a part of winter's quirky charm. It is a vital, physical force, a sucker punch in the solar plexus the moment you open a door.

In the time it takes to walk 50 yards from the Previa to a roadside plaque, the

Toyota Previa All-Trac

4TH PLACE
TOYOTA PREVIA ALL-TRAC

As we prepared for our Alaskan onslaught, we questioned the inclusion of the Previa. Here was the lone four-wheel-drive minivan sold in the U.S. that offered no power choice other than its 2.4-liter in-line four-cylinder. Would it, we worried, stand up against minivans with V-6 power? In the end, we reasoned that it would be unfair not to include the Previa, for it was, after all, an all-wheel-drive minivan, and besides we were interested to see how its mid-mounted engine affected performance on snowy and icy roads. Would its favorable weight distribution overcome a horsepower deficit in hard winter use?

We should first define this horsepower deficit. The other competitors had engines with horsepower ratings ranging from 200 (the Astro) to 150 (the Caravan), with the other two providing 155 hp each. Thus, the Previa fell far below the Astro, but gave away no more than 17 hp to the other three. Is this a lot of horsepower when it's godzilla below zero and icy? You bet. But, as it turned out, the Previa was able to overcome the difference.

To arrive at a competitive price, $22,013 as tested, our Previa lacked a few creature features. It was the only vehicle fitted with roll-up windows, for example. Even in its stripped form, however, the Previa soon gained a following among the *C/D* explorer scouts.

The reasons for its popularity were subtle, yet pronounced. We've written before about the excellent design of the Previa's interior. This atmosphere, plus the excellent ergonomics within the cabin, plus seats that cradle you in an orthopaedically responsible embrace, made the car just plain pleasant to occupy.

On the speed front, the Previa was the slowest of the quintet, but this consideration loses some steam when the roads are in a condition that lessens your desire to floorboard the throttle.

In normal use, if one can apply that term to Alaska driving, the Previa just did not seem underpowered enough to matter. At cruising speeds it was quiet, and on the utility front, it can carry an astonishing amount of luggage with its seats remaining in place. Removing its center seat requires tools, however.

The Toyota All-Trac system worked just fine on our 1100-mile excursion, though there's no provision for locking the center differential.

The operation of the Previa, aside from the lower horsepower, was superb. The ride was matched only by the Caravan's for smoothness and comfort, and the four-wheel disc brakes (unique among our group) were unexcelled for performance.

As a measure of how well overall the Previa did, consult the Editors' Ratings. You will note that the Previa scored the highest of any minivan in styling (nine on a scale of ten), and that none of its competitors outscored it in handling, ride, ergonomics, comfort, or fun to drive.

In sum, we no longer doubt the Previa's ability to compete in this company.

—*William Jeanes*

---

cold penetrates my two pairs of gloves and one pair of mittens, then forces its way through $240 worth of Vasque boots, two pairs of cotton socks, and a mismatched set of polypropylene boot liners. By then, my fingers are drunk. Grasping a pencil to take notes is difficult. (I had long since abandoned pens, whose ink ceased to flow even inside the minivans.) I am wearing a black rubberized face mask—apparel that tech editor Don Schroeder says resembles "some sort of medical device for persons with ruptures"—and when I remove it, a dime-size chunk of my iced mustache breaks off with it.

Alaska adventurer Joe McGinniss wrote: "In this sort of cold, you do not think of normal things—upset stomach, fatigue, financial problems, whether there was life after death. You were able to think only of the cold: it monopolized every facet of your being, like first love, or the news of a death in the family."

Yet it is here, hard on the banks of the rock-solid Yukon River, that one brave soul has dropped a few Atco aluminum boxes that double as a coffeeshop. The cold has not frozen his sense of humor. A sign next to the entrance warns, "No shoes, no shirt, no service."

We do not know when or if we will eat during this trip, so associate editor Phil Berg has laden each minivan with freezer bags full of "survival gorp." This mix is created by combining pretzels, Wheat Chex, Rice Chex, Cheese Nips, peanuts, M&Ms, dried prunes, apricots, and bananas. He refuses to divulge quantities, lest the recipe be widely copied. The bananas and apricots stick together to resemble dried human ears and other body parts even more unappetizing.

SPEED LIMIT 50

NEXT 416 MILES

Wrapped in enough goose down and Thinsulate to keep 3M profitable until Easter, we cannot walk quickly and shouldn't anyway. Fall and you become a snow-dusted Galapagos tortoise on its back. Breathe too rapidly and the air has no chance to warm as it is inhaled, frosting your lungs. It is like taking God's own gulp from the top of a mug of Vernors ginger ale. Followed by a dry cough. This is not a place that man was intended to inhabit.

Nor was our first night's destination, 250 miles north of Fairbanks and 60 miles above the Arctic Circle: the village of Coldfoot. Except, calling Coldfoot a village—each of its three buildings is a variation on an Atco aluminum mobile home —is an insult to villages. But that is where we sleep. The Arctic Acres Hotel smells like a combination of Lysol, napalm, and the common involuntary gastrointestinal response to power-gulping Everclear.

Coldfoot was a gold-mining camp named in 1900, when Alaskan stampeders got as far as the Koyukuk River (which, in Eskimo, means "place where one makes love repeatedly," proving what all of us have long suspected about twenty-hour nights), then got cold feet and ran. In its heyday, which is not now, Coldfoot consisted of gambling halls (one), whorehouses (two), stores (two), and saloons (seven).

We plug each minivan into 110-volt sockets, called bull rails, and hope for the

3RD PLACE
MAZDA MPV

Travel enough and you learn to travel light. The Mazda MPV was not the lightest of our group of five four-wheel-drive minivans. At 4126 pounds it's a whole person heavier—127 pounds—than the Caravan, and 34 pounds more than the Previa. It's the most compact, however, so it forces you to pack slim.

The MPV was the shortest van in our group and had the least space for people in its second and third rows of seats. Luggage room is less than half that of the Toyota or Chevy with all the seats in place. Maximum capacity is only two-thirds that of the Toyota. So the MPV feels small and nimble, more like a car than any of the other minis except the Dodge. We like that feeling of a pint-sized van, but wish it involved less weight.

The 155-hp MPV accelerates less swiftly than the Chevy or the Ford and reaches a top speed of 105 mph, a bit shy of the less powerful Dodge. Still, the Mazda V-6 revs smoothly.

The electronically controlled four-speed automatic, which is standard, has a unique gear-holding feature, which means you can delay the transmission from upshifting by pressing a button on the shift lever. This is useful if you're descending a hill. The button will also downshift the transmission from fourth to third gear. The transmission's computer will signal for an upshift if the engine is revved above redline in any gear. It's smart and handy, but the same feats can be done manually.

The MPV can be switched easily into rear-drive mode, though its four-wheel-drive system has a center differential and can be used full-time. Mazda says you'll gain better fuel mileage and lower wear and tear on the front driveline by running in rear-drive mode in fair weather. Our MPV got 16 mpg; it remained in four-wheel-drive for almost the entire tundra trek. There is a center differential lock for improved traction on the slick paths around places like Prudhoe Bay.

We noticed the MPV was more stable while accelerating on icy corners with the center differential locked. The MPV was competent braking on icy roads, too, though we were never in a situation that called on the standard rear-only anti-lock system to work. In fact, we drove the MPV as if it had no anti-lock control and suggest you do too.

The MPV's other virtues—direct steering, linear handling, and controls that work without surprise—place it at mid-pack in the four-wheel-drive minivan class. Why? In spite of all of the MPV's accomplishments, this mini has a ride problem when compared with the Toyota and the winning Dodge. The MPV rides stiffly, and its solid rear axle can bounce the tail of the van sideways on frost heaves. The MPV is sportier than the other four vans, and its stiff suspension is best suited to curvy, dry pavement.

A lack of space and the he-man ride keep the MPV out of first place, though one other flaw may have affected our judgment: The MPV's heater only warms sufficiently when the ambient temperature rises to 0 degrees Fahrenheit and warmer. For colder climates, it's tough to dress warm enough when you're traveling this light. —*Phil Berg*

Mazda MPV

best. Our Arctic winterization program consists only of filling the crankcases with Mobil 1 and installing battery warmers. And every night, we feed each vehicle two bottles of Heet, like vitamins, to forestall condensation. It is, after all, at Coldfoot that the temperature once fell to minus 60 and stayed there for seventeen days. It is at Coldfoot that the thermometer plunged to minus 82 one January, then rose to 97 the following August: a seasonal swing of 179 degrees. Mother Nature, as played by the late Sam Kinison.

The weather accounts for a lot of unusual behavior on the part of the reclusive residents. Some of the winter's diversions: an outhouse race (the "Iditapotty"), a survival-suit race, a banana-eating contest, an ore-truck pull, an ugly animal contest, a moose-decorating fest, a greased-pole walk, and—*C/D*'s favorite by a unanimous show of still-attached limbs—a chainsaw toss.

Around midnight, as we sleep in our Arctic Acres aluminum cubbyholes ($98 per night), Coldfoot's resident cook falls in an 86-proof heap outside my door. Cackling like Joan Rivers and bellowing, "Don't tell my mother," she is then dragged feet-first to her room. Jensen counterattacks, belting out Rinkbinders' lyrics: "I take a lot of pills to stay awake/ wash them down with antifreeze/ and that's my big mistake."

The next morning, she suffers in silence in the cafe, her head facedown on a

Ford Aerostar XL Plus

2ND PLACE
FORD AEROSTAR XL PLUS

Ford's Aerostar and Chevrolet's Astro, introduced as 1986 models, were the two oldest minivans in this test. The next-oldest was Mazda's MPV, which is fully three years newer. That age might seem an insurmountable handicap, but the Aerostar is rolling proof that consistent development and improvement can keep an old van competitive.

For example, in 1990, Ford added the four-wheel-drive option that included a new 4.0-liter V-6 engine (derived from the ancient European V-6). That drivetrain (combined with an optional 3.73 axle ratio) resulted in the quickest acceleration of all the four-wheel-drive minivans—turning a quarter-mile in 17.3 seconds at 77 mph. Moreover, the big V-6 and the four-speed automatic transmission also produced silky upshifts and responsive downshifts in the mountains as well as in the flats. On the down side, the Aerostar got 15 miles to the gallon, the largest appetite of the group.

Ford's "Electronic" four-wheel-drive system worked flawlessly during the drive. The electronics engage a mechanical lockup device in the center differential when there's excessive slippage between the front and rear axles (our car also had the optional limited-slip rear axle). Though we were never aware of the system's operation, traction remained excellent at all times.

The Aerostar's braking system was less impressive. Not only did it take the longest distance to stop on dry pavement (though not by a large margin), the antilock control only acts on the rear wheels —it is still quite possible to lock up the front wheels and lose steering control on snow and ice.

Despite being a relatively low-line XL Plus model and spot-on our $22,000 as-tested target price, our Aerostar was a lavishly equipped machine. Features new for 1992 included a redesigned instrument panel, a driver's air bag, three-point belts for all outboard seating positions, and flush headlamps.

In addition, our Aerostar came with several useful options. The preferred equipment package and the power convenience group provided air conditioning, tilt steering, cruise control, tinted glass, and power windows, locks, and mirrors. The high-capacity A/C-heater option provided the coziest heat output in the group. The optional seven-passenger seating setup has a nice feature: the rear bench seats fold flat to form a bed.

The result was a machine that seemed the plushest, most luxurious vehicle in the test. It provided plenty of space for seven passengers. It offered as many power options as any other. It most easily coped with the intense cold. And it generally offered the smoothest ride and the highest performance. As a winter-ready people mover, the old Aerostar offers plenty of advantages.   —*Csaba Csere*

1st Place
Dodge Caravan SE AWD

Does this rounded box on wheels define the typical minivan to you? Yes? Perhaps it is because the Dodge Caravan and Plymouth Voyager twins are so familiar. Chrysler has built more than three million of them since 1983. In marketing-speak, one could say Chrysler hit the nail on the head. With a steam-powered pile driver.

Chrysler's make-over of this minivan in 1991 was hardly revolutionary. That means the current version remains a distant relative of the once-ubiquitous K-car, the small front-wheel-drive sedans and wagons that saved the company's financial heinie a decade ago. The K-car was a bare-bones car. It was also practical, simple, and budget-priced. And if the present-day Caravan bears any resemblance to the K-car, it's in its virtues, not its vices.

Interestingly, this passenger-car heritage was to the Caravan's advantage on the Dalton Highway. The 3.3-liter V-6, which also appears in many of Chrysler's luxury cars, was smooth and unobtrusive. The Dodge kept up with the truck-based entries (the Ford, the Chevy, and to a lesser extent, the Mazda) through the mountains without breathing hard, while tying the Toyota Previa for first place in ride quality over the Dalton's ruts, bumps, and ice. The Caravan's drivetrain generated nary a complaint, with a front torque bias that provided useful traction in snow and mild understeer. With regard to the somewhat-notorious four-speed Ultradrive transmission, either Chrysler has improved it or we were lucky: it was the smoothest-shifting automatic in the group, and it avoided all the busyness we've associated with Ultradrives past.

The inside of the Caravan was hospitable, with comfortable front seats, decent ergonomics (an exception was the distant radio placement), and pleasing switch and control feel. The heater warmed frigid subzero air with ease, although the lack of a split defroster/floor setting annoyed some editors. The boxy exterior translates to similar interior proportions; while not the roomiest in the comparison, the interior was handy and nicely finished, with removable rear seats yielding a low and flat load floor. Simple and practical.

Our Caravan was adept at the numbers game. *C/D*'s observed mileage was 17 mpg, tied for best with the four-cylinder Previa. The window sticker showed $22,104, a higher number made respectable with the standard air bag.

This was one of the more inconspicuous vans on the test, making its way along the 1100-mile test route without incident. In fact, the logbook for this car was filled not with superlatives, but mostly consistent praise. Check the Editors' Ratings chart: the Dodge did most things well without committing any unforgivable sins, which, in the less-than-favorable circumstances of Arctic Alaska, is enough to make it exceptional indeed.

The first-place honors for Chrysler's minivan shouldn't come as a surprise. After all, the company's been at it longer than anyone else.   —*Don Schroeder*

simulated-pine countertop. Breakfast is delayed. A waitress cheerily chats about the Coldfoot Classic sled-dog race and the difference between Alaskan and Siberian huskies, then concludes this brief discourse when she reports: "We had a dog once. Something ate it."

At this time of year in the Arctic, the sun rises at eleven and sets at three. And we are fast approaching November 24, the day the sun sets 27 minutes after noon and stays set for 54 days, 22 hours, and 51 minutes. We are, however, in luck. There is a full moon, which reflects off the snow and bathes the afternoon landscape in aqua-neon luminescence. Outside Coldfoot, I douse the Mazda's headlamps and drive for ten miles on moonlight alone. This makes associate editor Berg very nervous. He asks several times, "What did she *mean,* 'We had a dog once, something ate it'?"

For Arctic dilettantes like us, the weak sun induces a kind of polar jet lag, as each

How to Get There

1. Travel is restricted north of Disaster Creek. (It did not come by its name capriciously.) Get written permission from the Alaska DOT's director of maintenance and operations (907-451-2209).

The state, however, expects to open the final 200 miles to everyone, saying, "The overall theme for the Dalton Highway interpretation is the Arctic, where solar astronomy touches the Earth, affecting all aspects of life in the area." Write us if you know what this means.

2. Make reservations at Coldfoot Acres (907-678-9301) and the Prudhoe Bay Hotel (907-659-2449). Study our "husky ratings" first.

3. Don't feed the bears, wolves, foxes, Dall sheep, moose, falcons, wolverines, or inebriated short-order cooks at Coldfoot.

4. Take two spare tires, flares, a winch, drinking water, a sleeping bag in a brown-paper bag, and more clothes than are currently in all of the closets in Des Moines.

5. Take enough fuel to last 250 miles per day, plus an hour or two of idling, plus whatever you require for eye-catching rescue bonfires.

6. Take the locals' advice.

7. Take a Halcion.   —*JP*

Hotel Verdict:

C/D's "husky ratings," for Arctic hotels:

Fairbanks Westmark: Three huskies, because three of its eight pay-TV channels are triple-X-rated and breakfast includes reindeer sausage. 🐕🐕🐕

Coldfoot Arctic Acres: Two huskies, because, despite a sometimes-open bar, the hallway smells of, ah, never mind, and the hotel's dog was recently eaten by an as-yet-unidentified predator, and because Berg refers to his room as "the minimum-security wing at Betty Ford." 🐕🐕

Prudhoe Bay Hotel: One-half husky, because the billiard table has striped balls only, baths are shared, there is no bar—although there is an astounding supply of cherry Nyquil—and the management makes 100-dB public-address announcements at 7 a.m., giving the ambiance of a Cal Worthington used-car lot. 🐕   —*JP*

Above left: Executive editor breaches two or three laws by hand-feeding dried prunes to an Arctic fox that does not know enough to fear motoring journalists with Fudgsicle intelligence. Outside Prudhoe Bay Hotel, the GMC Yukon's tail-gate latch shattered into shrapnel the size of Rice Krispies.

day is foreshortened. By 4 p.m., in total darkness, we are hungry for dinner. By 6 p.m., we are thinking about bed. To while away the many dark hours, Coldfoot (known to the truckers as "Coldfood") offers its guests a paperback library with as many as 21 titles. The most popular: Tom Bodett's *The End of the Road.*

Except that it isn't the end. In fact, the next day's drive takes us another 250 miles due north, clean through the forbidding Brooks Range—the northernmost mountain range in the world. Few of its peaks have been climbed, fewer still named. Few portions are charted. Few Alaskans have ever even *seen* them. These white-and-brown granite peaks are sculpted grotesquely—saw-toothed, jagged, razor-backed. They are arrayed unnaturally, as if they had fallen from the sky. Since the last ice age, the Brooks Range has remained in a huge Amana deepfreeze, largely unaffected by the smoothing influence of erosion. This range marks the Arctic Divide: all water south flows to the Pacific Ocean, all north to the Arctic Ocean.

We approach Atigun Pass—elevation 4800 feet—and observe two warnings. The first is merely for grizzly bears, whereas the second actually gets our attention. It is a sign with the self-canceling message: AVALANCHE AREA NEXT 40 MILES; DO NOT STOP. Berg insists I slip on my red high-top sneakers and pose next to a likely looking avalanche. Then he blows the Aerostar's horn four times. This commands the attention of a Dall sheep, who eyes us with deserved suspicion. Observes photographer Dewhurst, "The sheep's horns are far more impressive than the Aerostar's."

Cresting the Brooks Range, our sturdy group again falls silent. Before us stretches the North Slope, the final 100 miles of the continent. Not a single tree or bush. Just flat, frozen tundra and permafrost that extend to the horizon, where there is no distinction between terra firma and sky. The atmosphere here is so quintessentially cold and clear that you can often see right to the Beaufort Sea, except there is no telling where seawater begins. It too is uniformly hard, flat, and white. ARCO oilmen later tell us such stupendous visibility is dangerous. People tend to say things like, "I'll just walk to that hill over there," but the hill turns out to be a pingo (a frozen lake bed that has risen as much as 300 feet above the surrounding tundra), and instead of being "just over there," it is, in fact, 34 *miles* over there.

McGinniss says the North Slope—under which languishes nobody knows how many billion dollars' worth of natural

C/D Test Results

	acceleration, sec						top speed, mph	braking, 70–0 mph, ft
	0–30 mph	0–60 mph	¼-mile	street start, 5–60 mph	top gear, 30–50 mph	top gear, 50–70 mph		
CHEVROLET ASTRO	3.2	10.3	17.9 @ 76 mph	10.4	4.9	7.7	101	204
DODGE CARAVAN SE AWD	3.9	12.3	18.5 @ 74 mph	12.2	6.8	8.7	108	201
FORD AEROSTAR XL PLUS	2.8	9.5	17.3 @ 77 mph	9.9	4.7	7.4	99	209
MAZDA MPV	3.7	11.4	18.4 @ 74 mph	11.6	5.8	8.4	105	202
TOYOTA PREVIA ALL-TRAC	4.1	12.8	19.2 @ 71 mph	13.1	5.9	9.6	101	196

Vital Statistics

	1992 price, base/as tested	layout/ 4-wheel-drive system	engine/transmission	SAE net, power/torque	exterior dimensions, in			
					wheel-base	length	width	height
CHEVROLET ASTRO	$17,790/$21,656	front-engine/ rear-biased full-time 4wd, non-locking viscous center differential	4300cc V-6, iron block and heads, port fuel injection/ 4-speed auto with lockup torque converter	200 bhp @ 4400/ 260 lb-ft @ 3600	111.0	176.8	77.5	76.2
DODGE CARAVAN SE AWD	$19,127/$22,104	front-engine/ front-biased full-time 4wd, non-locking viscous center differential	3300cc V-6, iron block and aluminum heads, port fuel injection/ 4-speed auto with lockup torque converter	150 bhp @ 4800/ 185 lb-ft @ 3600	112.2	178.1	72.0	65.9
FORD AEROSTAR XL PLUS	$18,549/$22,000	front-engine/ rear-biased full-time 4wd, automatic-locking center differential	3996cc V-6, iron block and heads, port fuel injection/ 4-speed auto with lockup torque converter	155 bhp @ 4000/ 230 lb-ft @ 2400	118.9	190.3	72.0	73.2
MAZDA MPV	$20,535/$21,780	front-engine/ rear-biased full-time 4wd, manually lockable center differential	SOHC 18-valve 2954cc V-6, iron block and aluminum heads, port fuel injection/ 4-speed auto with lockup torque converter	155 bhp @ 5000/ 169 lb-ft @ 4000	110.4	175.8	72.3	70.8
TOYOTA PREVIA ALL-TRAC	$20,313/$22,013	mid-engine/ rear-biased full-time 4wd, non-locking viscous center differential	DOHC 16-valve 2438cc 4-in-line, iron block and aluminum head, port fuel injection/ 4-speed auto with lockup torque converter	138 bhp @ 5000/ 154 lb-ft @ 4000	112.8	187.0	70.8	68.7

* Cargo utility with "seats out" is measured with all quick-release seats removed. The middle row of seats in the Previa and Astro required tools for removal and thus were left in place.

roadholding, 300-ft skidpad, g	interior sound level, dBA				fuel economy, mpg		
	idle	full throttle	70-mph cruising	70-mph coasting	EPA city	EPA highway	C/D 1100-mile trip
0.67	52	79	72	71	15	20	16
0.71	48	82	73	72	16	20	17
0.69	49	76	73	73	15	19	15
0.72	46	77	74	73	15	19	16
0.71	47	87	72	72	17	20	17

gas and crude—is "that part of North America which could make you believe that the earth was indeed flat and that, at last, you had come to its edge." It is also large. The North Slope's surface in square miles is meaninglessly immense, like the budget deficit or the Reverend Al Sharpton. We cannot grasp its enormity until a local explains, "Our school district is approximately the size of California." And there are far fewer students here than caribou, two of which loiter astern the Previa and stare glassy-eyed at it, as if reflecting upon its ovoid styling. The pipeline here is kinked by a "sag bend"—a short buried section that acts as a caribou crosswalk, although the caribou have not yet read the memo on this and cross wherever they please, using the steel supports to scratch their backs.

We continue north to Prudhoe Bay and Deadhorse, which are, like Paul Reubens and Pee-wee Herman, inexplicably the same thing. Still, it offers fuel. What remains in the tanks of the Caravan and the MPV would not fill a urologist's Dixie cup. An Arctic fox emerges from the shadows. Perhaps to observe these fellow polar travelers who mysteriously pound their mittens on their thighs. He watches our refueling. Every inch of his fragile two-foot-long body is covered in willowy, snow-white fur that is so supple it blows every which way in the wind, like hair. I approach on my stomach—yet another

weight distribution % F/R	fuel tank, gal	passenger-area volume, cu ft F/M/R	cargo volume, cu ft, seats in/out*	what fits in back			suspension		brakes, F/R	tires
				# long-neck cases: seats in/out*	length of pipe, in	sheet of plywood, in (l x w)	front	rear		
57.3/42.7	27.0	60/50/55	23/152	6/52	116.2	51.5 x 50.3	ind, unequal-length control arms, torsion bars, anti-roll bar	rigid axle, fiberglass-reinforced leaf springs	vented disc/drum; anti-lock control	Uniroyal Tiger Paw XTM M+S, P215/75R-15
58.5/41.5	18.0	49/52/43	13/115	5/56	127.3	80.8 x 48.0	ind, strut, coil springs, anti-roll bar	rigid axle, leaf springs	vented disc/drum; anti-lock control	Goodyear Invicta GA M+S, P205/70R-15
55.1/44.9	21.0	57/50/47	13/136	5/43	124.0	86.0 x 48.5	ind, unequal-length control arms, coil springs, anti-roll bar	rigid axle, coil springs	vented disc/drum; rear anti-lock control	Michelin XA4 M+S, P215/70R-14
56.1/43.9	19.8	54/43/38	9/103	5/45	130.0	79.0 x 48.5	ind, strut, coil springs, anti-roll bar	rigid axle, coil springs, anti-roll bar	vented disc/drum; rear anti-lock control	Dunlop SP Sport D31J M+S, P215/65R-15
53.8/46.2	19.8	56/51/49	23/147	12/23	146.0	60.0 x 48.0	ind, strut, coil springs, anti-roll bar	rigid axle, coil springs	vented disc/disc	Toyo A05 All Season, P215/65R-15

GMC YUKON

We took a GMC Yukon far north—north of Alaska's Yukon River and 360 miles north of the Arctic Circle—as the rescue truck for our stable of 4wd minivans. The vans were riding on all-season tires, which a right-thinking Alaskan never uses in winter. Our Yukon was the exception —it had real monster-mudder tires and a winch with 125 feet of cable in case a van or two slipped off the icy Dalton Highway. New for 1992, the Yukon replaced the big Jimmy sport-utility wagon. The body is based on the 1988 GMC and Chevy pickups, and it's three inches longer than the previous Jimmy. Chevy's Blazer is identical to the Yukon.

The Yukon does two things exceptionally well: it carries a big bunch of stuff, and it looks good. Its styling is unobtrusive: it wouldn't be out of place parked in the lot at Skinny Dick's Halfway Inn between Fairbanks and Nenana. Nor would it be turned away from valet parking at Le Dome on Sunset Boulevard.

But one thing it doesn't do particularly well is travel fast over slick roads. This is a truck, remember, with a wagon body on it. It steers like a truck. We detected about an inch of play and a numb on-center feel in the steering of our test Yukon.

Its ride is also trucklike, and hitting a bump with the right-front wheel sends a big slow-motion jiggle through the frame all the way to the left rear.

Our Yukon was powered by the standard 210-hp, 5.7-liter V-8, bolted to a four-speed automatic transmission (a five-speed manual is available). All Yukons come with part-time four-wheel drive that you can engage "on-the-fly." We left it engaged the entire trip.

Even Chevy's not-much-lighter, V-6-powered Astro can match the Yukon's 10.4 seconds to 60 mph. Adding to the impression of sloth is a stiff throttle pedal, apparently engineered for a driver wearing something as heavy as a trucker's Tony Lamas. We also needed heavy feet to engage the standard ABS when our Yukon was in 4wd, and sometimes we could lock a front wheel.

Still, there's more to the Yukon than good looks. The interior is roomy—the front seats are more spacious than those of any of the minivans on our trip. The driving position places the steering wheel far enough back that six-foot-plus drivers don't need the arms of NBA forwards to reach it. It's a tough climb over the folding front seatbacks and into the rear three-person bench, but once you're in the seat, space is generous. With the seats in place, the cargo capacity is larger than in any of our five minivans. With the rear seat folded, it has twice the cargo volume of the MPV.

We never had to pull a van out of a frozen ditch, and we looked good not doing it. And we're doubtless among the small number of people who will ever drive the Yukon over the river that bears the same name. *—Phil Berg*

The Dalton Highway is dangerous. Chuckie Kelly erred here from the path of righteousness and the northbound lane.

Vehicle type:	front-engine, rear/4-wheel-drive, 5-passenger, 3-door wagon
Price as tested:	$26,335 (base price: $20,113)
Engine type:	V-8, iron block and heads, GM engine-control system with 1x2-bbl throttle-body fuel injection
Displacement	350 cu in, 5733cc
Power (SAE net)	210 bhp @ 4000 rpm
Transmission	4-speed automatic with lockup torque converter
Wheelbase	111.5 in
Length	188.0 in
Curb weight	5048 lb
Zero to 60 mph	10.4 sec
Zero to 100 mph	50.5 sec
Street start, 5 to 60 mph	10.4 sec
Standing 1/4-mile	17.8 sec @ 75 mph
Top speed	105 mph
Braking, 70–0 mph	208 ft
Roadholding, 300-ft-dia skidpad	0.74 g
Road horsepower @ 50 mph	24 hp
EPA fuel economy, city driving	13 mpg
C/D observed fuel economy	12 mpg

new tourist floor show calculated to amuse the wildlife—offering dried human ears from Berg's gorp. The fox rejects these, as did we, as did Berg, in favor of Planters' peanuts and prunes—the latter not an indigenous foodstuff, but a sub-

stance that can be relied upon to make *Alopex lagopus* unpopular in his den. Fouse calmly points out that our group now includes a triple felon. Feeding the wildlife here is a breach of state, park, and Bureau of Land Management laws, and the

Phillips (top) ridicules miniature crevasse atop Artic Ocean, then moments later falls through ice, experiencing the heartbreak of frozen pants. Four-story drilling rig (right) is powered by locomotive engines. For three nights in a row, we sleep in structures whose walls are festooned with vehicular running lights (bottom).

leftover Rice Chex scattered on the tundra may constitute felony littering.

The frost-encrusted settlements of Prudhoe Bay and Deadhorse are a tightly packed hodgepodge of spectral shapes and surreal shadows poking out of unremitting gloom. Cranes, derricks, lengths of pipe, abandoned Chevy Suburbans whose cabs are filled with snow, and yet more Atco trailers stacked in rows like freight trains. One of them is the Prudhoe Bay Hotel—where we spend yet another night in accommodations whose walls are festooned with vehicular running lights.

Nothing here is familiar. No stoplights. No street signs. Few signs of any sort, even on the grocery store, one of whose shipments accidentally wound up scattered along the Dalton Highway. A tow truck could not reach the scene at a speed that exceeded the bears', whose variety here is sobering: black, brown, Kodiak brown, polar, grizzly. When the tow-truck driver arrived, he took one look, said "Grizzly groceries," and left.

Prudhoe's population varies between 3500 and 8500, depending on America's thirst for crude and the number of persons killing one another in the Middle East. On the two days we visit, however, the number of sentient beings actually conducting business appears to be, perhaps, twenty.

The next morn, we decide that beating a Deadhorse is worth a try. Fouse somehow endears himself to ARCO, whose chief of public affairs (of which there are understandably few in Deadhorse) has invited us to tour the Kuparuk oil field. We did not think it possible, but the ARCO site is 40 miles *north* of Prudhoe. The company at least possesses one traffic sign. It says, CAUTION: CARIBOU HAVE THE RIGHT OF WAY.

ARCO's oil wells are scattered right to the horizon in a 180-degree arc. They are housed in aluminum one-car garages. Like the pipeline, they are so unobtrusive in this vast lunar landscape that, were they painted white, nobody would be able to locate them, which is why they aren't. Perhaps 100 yards from ARCO's main employee residence—an orange high-school-size aluminum pod on stilts whose architecture may have been the handiwork of Dennis Hopper—are nine caribou dozing in the snow.

Nowhere in this alien expanse, as far as we can determine, has a drop of petroleum been unloosed. No grease. No oil. Not a smudge. Which is ironic, because it is at this moment that the Astro inexpli-

cably vomits an impressive quantity of Mobil 1 out its dipstick tube onto the final few miles of the oilfield service road. Fouse dubs the Chevy the "Astro Valdez." Assistant art director Tom Cosgrove says, "We had an Astro once; something ate it."

We reach our goal, Olik Tok Point, at noon. There is a desalinization plant here, where ARCO collects seawater that will be pumped underground to pressurize the oil. This is as far north as you can drive a vehicle without pontoons or tank treads. Mile zero. There is no manmade structure that now stands between us and the North Pole, and the wind knows it. (On February 25, 1991, the breeze here reached an invigorating 109 mph.) If we drove twenty yards farther we'd be atop the Arctic Ocean. Although except for 45 days each summer, the ocean here looks exactly like the road on which we're standing, which looks exactly like the previous 100 miles of tundra. Frost from the Previa's windows peels off in six-inch onion-ring shavings. The temperature

ARCO desalinization plant. The end of the road. Mile zero. Twenty yards from here, we confidently step off the edge of the continent.

here is 40 below. "That doesn't sound too bad if you say it fast," says Fouse.

We suit up for the obligatory photo and walk the few steps to the ice—which Fouse confidently asserts is "five or six feet thick this time of year." Then we *step off the edge of the continent.*

So.

After I fell through the ice up to my knees—catching any further descent into the Arctic Ocean by hooking both arms on the lips of a small crevasse—my blue-jeans, within twenty seconds, achieved the same consistency as ballistic Kevlar. When I fingered the cuffs, they broke off in chunks, like peanut-butter cookies.

Jeanes is on the CB: "It's getting dark again. We should turn around and repeat the whole trip backward."

Inside the warm Previa, Cosgrove watches me tear my frozen pants off, which stand upright without me in them, like hip waders. He announces to no one in particular, "We had an executive editor once. Something ate it."

Editors' Ratings

		drive-train	handling	ride	ergo-nomics	comfort	utility	room	styling	value	fun to drive	OVERALL RATING*
	CHEVROLET ASTRO	7	8	7	6	7	8	8	7	7	6	75.4
	DODGE CARAVAN SE AWD	9	9	9	8	9	9	8	8	9	8	89.0
	FORD AEROSTAR XL PLUS	8	8	8	8	8	9	9	7	8	8	84.4
	MAZDA MPV	9	9	8	9	8	8	8	8	8	8	84.2
	TOYOTA PREVIA ALL-TRAC	7	9	9	9	9	8	8	9	7	8	84.0

HOW IT WORKS: Editors rate vehicles from 1 to 10 (10 being best) in each category, then scores are collected and averaged, resulting in the numbers shown above.

*The Overall Rating is not the total of those numbers. Rather, it is an independent judgment (on a 1-to-100 scale) that includes other factors—even personal preferences—not easily categorized. (The Overall Ratings have been carried to one decimal place to break a three-way tie.)

DETROIT AUTO SHOW

By Martin Padgett Jr.

What it couldn't offer in glamour or glitz, Detroit's 1992 North American International Auto Show paid back in sheetmetal. Near-record crowds at the Motown show witnessed the debuts of more than 40 production and concept cars, spread over 600,000 square feet in maybe the world's biggest garage.

Detroit's batch of concept cars echoed the Tokyo and Frankfurt environmental theme with electric cars and two-stroke powerplants. But the lingering recession made practical ideas, not long-term prognostications, the order of the day. Some of the features on these concept cars—five-speed automatic transmissions, variable-tint glass, and traction control—are already with us.

One of the concepts pictured here, the Hyundai HCD-1, is already headed for production. If public response is a good indicator, we'll soon be seeing the rest of them in showrooms.

PONTIAC SALSA

The Salsa is Pontiac's variation on the modular theme pioneered by the Nissan Pulsar NX. It can be converted into a minitruck, a five-passenger convertible, or even a snappy hatchback. John Middlebrook, general manager of Pontiac, says the Salsa can succeed in spite of the Pulsar's failure because "we've got a good-looking car." The Salsa's unconventional body cloaks conventional mechanicals: a five-speed transmission, front-wheel drive, and a front-strut/rear-twist-axle suspension.

HYUNDAI HCD-1

"Hyundai came to this market to build fun, affordable cars," said marketing v.p. Tom Ryan. From the looks of its HCD-1 show car, we think Hyundai's serious. The upstart Koreans plan to build the HCD-1 by 1996. Hyundai designers created the anti-cab-forward retro roadster in their new design facility in Fountain Valley, California. An all-aluminum, DOHC 2.0-liter four-cylinder engine with variable valve timing will power the car. With air bags, ABS, and traction control, the HCD-1 will sell for 12,000 of today's dollars.

BUICK SCEPTRE

That distinctive Buick front end won't be going away soon, if the concept Sceptre is any indicator. "The grille," explains Buick chief Ed Mertz, "is a natural evolution of Buick's distinctive front-end appearance." Grille and all, the rear-drive Sceptre leads the way toward the styling and content of the 1994 Regal sedan. Safety is emphasized, with air bags for front and rear passengers, traction control, and integral seatbelts. If built, it would be powered by a 250-hp 3.5-liter supercharged V-6 linked to a five-speed automatic transmission.

The interior of the Hyundai HCD-1 is full of sculptured, rounded shapes and pleasing colors. Strangely, the steering wheel is ribbed, as if intended to encourage palming the hub.

LINCOLN MARQUE X

The Lincoln Marque X concept car showcases glass technology Ford has developed with its Libby-Owens-Ford subsidiary. The windshield incorporates LCD-operated visors that dim automatically. Its side mirrors do double duty: they appear as brake lights from behind and as mirrors from the cockpit. The Marque X's adjustable air dam and air suspension both lower at 45 mph.

OLDSMOBILE ANTHEM

A supercharged Quad 4, tilted 85 degrees forward, sits under the hood of the Anthem. Its aero-smart body has a drag coefficient of 0.26. Described as a test bed for the 1994 Cutlass Supreme, its new-generation ABS, traction control, and active noise cancellation are all possible for production by then.

CHRYSLER CIRRUS

Chrysler's solution to the fuel-economy quandary lies in two-stroke engine technology, according to engineering v.p. Francois Castaing. Aside from fuel-economy advantages, two-stroke engines allow more efficient packaging. The Cirrus's small engine compartment and exaggerated cab-forward stance are complemented by a turbocharged two-stroke six-cylinder engine producing 400 horsepower when operated with alcohol. It's a strong indicator, a Chrysler official said, of the 1995 JA mid-size sedans.

GM ULTRALITE

GM pegged this concept vehicle's carbon-fiber shell at just 420 pounds, which means, at $25 per pound, the shell would cost more than $13,000. The Ultralite's 1.5-liter two-stroke three-cylinder engine churns out 111 horsepower. Formidable performance specs—a 0-to-60 time of 7.8 seconds, a top speed of 135 mph, a drag coefficient of just 0.13, and 100 mpg at a steady 50 mph—don't make it any more likely for production.

CHEVROLET SIZIGI

In Chevy-speak, Sizigi means the Lumina APV. The Sizigi's fluid body panels and dash look like candidates for the next Lumina minivan. A spokesperson said Chevrolet would like to get most of the ideas displayed on the Sizigi—captain's chairs, dual sunroofs, hidden running boards —into production.

DODGE EPIC

Expect the 1995 Voyager/ Caravan replacements to look something like this EPIC (Electric Power Inter-urban Commuter). For now, the EPIC is powered by nickel-iron batteries that allow a 120-mile driving range.

FORD CONNECTA

"Consider it a family taxi," said Ford stylist Jack Telnack. The Connecta, Ford's concept of an electric minivan, is a four-plus-two passenger vehicle designed by the Ghia studios in Turin. Although there's only a single door on the driver's side, the passenger side has two doors with no central pillar. The carbon-fiber-and-Kevlar body has a glass roof with solar venting. Ford estimates the Connecta's range during the EPA's city cycle at 100 miles, with a top speed of more than 75 mph.

TOKYO MOTOR SHOW

In the market for a polished aluminum car? Check out an Audi Avus. But don't look for it at your local Audi dealer. Like all the showy stuff on the next few pages, it's a "concept" car. They call these one-of-a-kind vehicles "idea" cars or "dream" cars or "show" cars. There were all kinds of them—gull-wings and bubble tops and tiny cars with tiny two-stroke engines side by side with mammoth twelve-cylinder bombers—at the 29th Tokyo motor show.

A concept car provides an idea of what the car companies are thinking about for the future. Trying to determine which concept cars are corporate playthings (the Toyota Avalon definitely tops that list) and which have a shot at reality (both Subaru products, the jazzy family wagon and the Gucci-styled Rioma, don't seem far-fetched) is often anyone's guess.

Sometimes an aspect of a concept car later becomes a reality—if you were around in 1938, you know that GM's "Y-Job" car featured the first power windows.

These days, the Japanese automakers, who apparently have been watching a lot of American television, are out milking the environmental cow for all it's worth. (Copywriters at one automaker went over the edge and lifted a line from George Bush, describing a new car as "a gentler sedan, to people and to the Earth." Have you hugged a tree today?)

You don't see anything American here because the Big Three didn't show up with much more than a handful of '92 models and no new concept cars—not even a Corvette. In light of the current business mood between the two countries, that's no surprise.

AUDI AVUS
Audi's audacious Avus was the star of the show. Its design recalls the great pre-war Auto Union Grand Prix racers. The styling emphasizes the midship location of its 502-hp, 60-valve 6.0-liter W-12 aluminum engine. Power is distributed via a front-mounted six-speed gearbox to all four twenty-inch, high-profile tires. The gleaming exterior finish mirrors the aluminum construction of this 211-mph, 2750-pound projectile.

TOYOTA AVALON
Produce a knockout car like the Lexus coupe—as did Toyota's American design shop, Calty Design Research of Newport Beach—and the head office will write a big check for a play project. Hence the Avalon, "a socializing cruiser" for the L.A. beach set. This four-seater yupmobile's windshield folds down and a rear section comes forward, and then the cabin disappears completely, leaving a locked cocoon impervious to theft.

HONDA EP-X
Behold the 100-mpg car! Designed as the ultimate fuel squeezer, the EP-X places its two passengers in a line to minimize frontal area, with a slick shape to further reduce aerodynamic drag. All-aluminum construction holds weight to 1360 pounds, so as not to overburden the 1.0 liter VTEC-E three-cylinder engine. In an unusual move for Honda, the front-mounted engine drives the rear wheels. Although pared down, the EP-X employs front and rear air bags.

NISSAN COCOON
The Cocoon is a narrow station wagon with two bucket seats in front, two in the middle, and a two-place bench in the rear. It's designed for the family of the future, but don't expect it soon.

MITSUBISHI mS.1000
Mitsubishi's four-seat toy-like mS.1000 has just one backseat door and inward-canting passenger seats to create a lounge-like environment. The paint on the roof changes from mica red to beige when the temperature exceeds 104 degrees Fahrenheit.

MITSUBISHI mR.1000
Built as "a snuggly-crafted two-seater runabout for tomorrow," the Mitsubishi mR.1000 has a clever motorized roof panel that stows itself flat on the rear deck. The tiny car has a 997cc twenty-valve four-cylinder engine, an automatic transmission, and four-wheel steering.

SUZUKI CUE AND SPRY
Suzuki's response to heavier, overoptioned sporty cars: the Cue (top left) is a featherweight 1720-pound 4wd vehicle with a part-paneled, part-zippered fabric top that opens up to become a roll-barred convertible; the Spry (bottom left) is a mid-engined 139-inch-long two-seater weighing just 1742 pounds. It would be powered by a sixteen-valve 1.3-liter four linked to a six-speed manual transmission.

HONDA FS-X
Honda broke its tradition of eschewing concept cars at this year's Tokyo show with two futuristic models. The FS-X suggests an Acura Legend of the future. Although about the same size as the current Legend, the FS-X is jam-packed with hardware. It uses a new four-wheel-drive system that not only varies the front-rear torque split to maximize traction, but also varies the side-to-side split to improve handling stability. Power is provided by a DOHC 3.5-liter VTEC-equipped V-6. All four bucket-seated passengers are given air bags and convenient visual monitors. Despite an aluminum body, it weighs nearly 3700 pounds.

JAGUAR XJ220

Only 350 examples of the sleek, svelte, and indescribably sexy Jaguar XJ220 supercar are planned, and the price may exceed $600,000. The car uses a development of Jaguar's twin-turbocharged 3.5-liter V-6 race engine, rated at 542 hp in road tune. That is reportedly enough to push the 194-inch-long, 45-inch-high, 3032-pound XJ220 to 212 mph in testing.

ISUZU NAGISA

Here Isuzu contemplates a return to the amphibious personal-transportation niche vacant since the Amphicar's demise. Once afloat, the Nagisa's wheels retract, and skirts seal the carbon-fiber tri-hull body for reduced drag. The hull is then bilged, and the DOHC 3.2-liter V-6's hydrojet drive propels the boat to a top speed of 20 knots.

ISUZU COMO

A Geo El Camino? The Como explores the four-seat, mid-engined, V-12 pickup-car niche. Features include a tailgate that retracts into the bumper and a uselessly shallow pickup bed located above the entire drivetrain and cooling system. The engine is a detuned version of Isuzu's new Group C and F1 3.5-liter V-12. Geo marketing seems unlikely, due to inevitable cannibalization of Syclone sales.

NISSAN DUAD
With its 1.0-liter engine mounted alongside the driver, the four-wheel-drive Nissan Duad takes the mid-engine concept to new lengths. With this layout, the passenger sits sixteen inches behind the driver, but then the passenger has no windshield, either.

SUBARU RIOMA
Maybe the Rioma, a 4wd targa-type two-seater, wasn't the heartthrob of the show, but its Gucci-glitz interior caused heart flutters among the silk set. Inside, the lipstick-red color is everywhere, even on the faces of all instrumentation, complimented by delicate dial hands that look like those on expensive watches. Power comes from a flexible-fuel sixteen-valve 2.0-liter four.

SUBARU AMADEUS
With this "sports wagon," Subaru seems to be asking if families feel left out in this age of overwhelming sportiness. Probably the flashiest two-toned wagon ever, the SVX-based Amadeus has a DOHC 24-valve 3.3-liter six mated to a five-speed automatic and a 4wd system that automatically detects wheelspin at each wheel and distributes torque accordingly. But seriously impractical—if you have kids—is the white leather interior.

ENVIRONMENTAL ISSUES

COMTESSE DE PROVENCE SEDAN CHAIR

By Bruce McCall

*Technical Specifications
by Robert Whitworth*

What is it all, a K-mart plot? Spartan battery-powered economodules the size of a King Midget. One-man, 400-miles-per-gallon Japanese micro-globules without doors. Hydrogen-spiked Yugos. Solar-powered shopping carts. The world industry's current frenzy to go further on every precious drop of fossil fuel—or to come clean altogether and save Los Angeles, California, and America itself via alternative nonpolluting energy sources—

appears to derive from a definition of the average licensed circa-1999 U.S. driver as a bucks-down masochist with all the *joie de vivre* of a *Consumer Reports* toaster tester.

But what of the lucrative, significant, and expanding luxury market segment? Won't tomorrow's high roller demand something more from his personal transport than just low emissions and good citizenship? Didn't the demise of the Cadillac Cimarron teach us anything about where the fat cats draw the line in comfort and convenience and cachet?

Enter—at a brisk trot—the Comtesse. And right up front, let's set aside all quibbling about technology that predates not only Morgans of Malvern but technology itself. Technology that hasn't significantly evolved since Copernicus was in knee britches. About a model cycle of approximately three centuries seeming a tad hidebound by current standards. About a leading-edge magazine like *Car and Driver* testing something built in 1768. Because this brocade-upholstered French-built *bébé* just could be the ecological sine qua non of luxu-boite transport for the 1990s and beyond.

With but two moving parts, the Comtesse (short for Comtesse de Provence, the sister-in-law of Louis XVI for whom this prototype was constructed in Versailles) is simplicity itself. And the only known form of land transport to combine its motive, suspension, steering, and braking functions into in-line fore-and-aft detachable units, highly articulated and separate from the chassis itself. Curses as old as man's pact with the infernal combustion engine—road rumble, axle whine, drivetrain vibration—are almost eerily absent.

But that's not all. Withhold boiled cabbage, whey, and refried beans from the power source and this Comtesse generates zero emissions. Acceleration, handling, braking, even steering are all voice-activated, leaving hands and feet free. Ground clearance in the standard ride mode is four times Range Rover height—yet the ride quality of that non-steel, infinitely adjustable, speed-sensitive suspension is soft and supple. And so dainty in parking and back-and-fill maneuvers that it seems to be reading not only your mind but also your lips.

Weight isn't distributed but compacted at dead center, and 100-percent sprung. Curb weight is you and the box you're ensconced in, period. But with its abnormally high center of gravity and inherently pancake-flat torque and power curves, you'd yell yourself hoarse attempting to keep the Comtesse even with a Cadillac STS in a twenty-foot driveway drag. It's a stately carriage that feels less at home on a cinder track than tooling along amid the noonday rabble and tumbril traffic of the Arrondissement, or gently swaying its way cross-country en route to the masked ball by sundown.

The Comtesse's solo throne is gained via the twist-type clasp on its solo door—front-opening, in a flash forward to the mid-1950s Isetta bubble car. (Nothing new under the Sun King!) Accommodations of this airy monoposto interior are indeed fit for a comtesse: plump silk pillows atop a plank-type seat that can be

Given a willing brace of footmen and a following wind, the Comtesse de Provence sedan chair can attain a surprising rate of speed.

Cornering is adequate, though the passenger may experience considerable body roll.

slipped into any of several grooves for custom height adjustment; upholstery in brocaded gold-yellow silk over horsehair padding; a genuine leather floor mat; pull-up glass windows. Safety furbelows include standard hang-down braided grip straps, invaluable in off-road excursions or during evasive maneuvers with *Les Misérables* in hot pursuit.

Pickup is brisk; you are lifted up to shoulder level in a trice. Other than the slight stumble we detected in early acceleration runs—traceable to a pulled hamstring—the Comtesse pulled smoothly and willingly from a standstill straight up to its comfy cruising gait, rated by *Car and Driver*'s test equipment as faster than a mailman but slower than a cutpurse or footpad.

Navigating close urban quarters underscored the quicksilver agility of a vehicle seven feet long from pole tip to pole tip. Our standard 180-degree "hand-brake turn" maneuver smashed all *Car and Driver* records, not to mention a plate-glass bakery window. A loud and sudden reminder, to rookies unused to voice-

activated handling, that orders barked are orders instantly—blindly—executed.

Once out on the open road, the Comtesse settles into a not unpleasant rocking motion, and so do you. Even sudden directional shifts produce no more severe sway or pitch than you'd feel being borne on a sofa through the doorway of your own living room by two Bekins men. Despite the airstream-battering shape and flat windscreen, we detected no wind noise; in fact the only audible concantonation was the honking of trucks and buses and the cursing of their drivers as our Comtesse loped along on the inside lane of 20th-century highway at its 18th-century clip.

Traffic jams, gridlock, and other enforced pauses provide welcome energy-recuperation intervals for the power system. It's also an opportunity for the pilot to learn, on pain of a sore posterior and an aching pate, that this is for all its seeming brute simplicity a *precision* instrument—i.e., the precise command is never a grunted "Down!" but an almost simpering, "Down, very slowly, please?"

The Comtesse's unique diurnal system of fuel consumption reduces fill-ups to twice or at most three stops daily regardless of mileage accumulated. And compare the notoriously poky recharging pauses required for even today's most ballyhooed electrics with the time it takes to whisk in and out of the drive-thru at McDonald's.

Premium fuel has no performance-enhancing effect on the Comtesse. To the contrary: filling the power team with a three-course French dinner was followed by the most sluggish pickup and cruising speeds of our entire test. Let them eat Big Macs, to paraphrase La Comtesse de Provence's sister-in-law. Yet the turbocharger-like effect of direct caffeine injection, via optional belt-mounted twin twelve-ounce thermoses, is dramatic.

Our slalom test so quickly produced such heart-rending groans and squeals that it was abandoned. On ice, those four puny leather contact patches create an ABS effect—*A Big Slide.* Virtually all-wooden construction makes the Comtesse rust-free but hardly termite-proof, a trade-off the buyer will have to carefully weigh.

Will tomorrow's luxury traveler be pulling up to the Polo Lounge of the Beverly Hills Hotel in a grisaille-finished phone booth suspended on two pairs of poles? If the Comtesse is any indication, we'd say the answer is—who knows?

The interior of our test chair reveals considerable wear and the unexplained absence of a seat cushion.

Perhaps the most rewarding quality of the Comtesse de Provence sedan chair is its flexibility in the event of a sudden power loss.

Vehicle type: front- and rear-engine, 4-foot-drive, one-passenger, one-door sedan

Price as tested: 182,000 francs ($35,000) F.O.B. Versailles

Major options: grisaille and polychrome finish by François Boucher, cellular phone, chamber pot

Major standard accessories: tilt steering, drop-down windows, interior safety straps, leather roof

ENGINE
Type 2-servant-in-line
Displacement ....5200 cu in, 85,228cc
Engine-control system ....chattel/indenture
Emissions controls ....no-whey diet
Power (SAE net) ....380 bhp (body heft power)
Torque (SAE net) ....366 lb-ft
Redline......................................22 sps (steps per second)

DRIVETRAIN
Transmission ....2-speed manual, dual-torso, limited slip

Gear	Ratio	Mph/sps	Max. test speed
I	2.79	0.14	3.0 mph (22 sps)
II	1.00	0.39	8.5 mph (22 sps)

DIMENSIONS AND CAPACITIES
Wheel/foot-base ....54.0 in
Track, F/R.......................................30.0/28.0 in
Length (including poles) ....84.0 in
Length (without poles) ....30.0 in
Width ....25.0 in
Height...62.0 in

Ground clearance ....18.0 in
Curb weight ....48 lb
Weight distribution, F/R 50.0/50.0%
Fuel capacity ....10.0 liters V.S.O.P

CHASSIS/BODY
Type ....carriage construction with hand-forged isolated subframe
Body material ....European pine subframe, body panels, and carved trim, leather top and floor mat

INTERIOR
SAE volume, front seat............................39 cu ft
         luggage space ....2 cu ft
Front seat ....padded bench
Seat adjustments ....up and down
General comfort...........................poor fair **good** excellent
Fore-and-aft support ....poor fair **good** excellent
Lateral support ....poor **fair** good excellent
Fabric ....2-tone gold silk damask

SUSPENSION
F/R ....ind, twin-pole (lancewood), dual arm

STEERING
Type ....ball/joint-hip, leg, and foot
Turns lock-to-lock 1
Turning circle curb-to-curb ....0.0 ft

BRAKES
F: ....9C leather
R: ....13D leather
Power assist ....Cognac reservoir

BORN-AGAIN ENGINES

By Csaba Csere

The simple two-stroke engine, last seen muttering about in a '67 Saab and relegated in modern times to unpleasant drudgery duty in noisy chain saws and snarling dirt bikes, may find its way back into the engine bays of cars in the environmentally touchy nineties.

The world's automakers are hard at work solving the classic two-stroke bugaboos of lousy fuel economy and prodigious exhaust emissions. Their goal is a powerplant that's smaller, lighter, cheaper, more fuel efficient, and easier to manufacture than existing four-stroke engines. If they succeed, two-strokes could become the engine of choice for small cars. In fact, they would become overwhelmingly attractive for cars of all kinds.

The man responsible for the reemergence of the lowly two-stroke is Ralph Sarich, an Australian who has developed a new fuel-injection system that transforms two-stroke combustion and promises to solve its efficiency and pollution problems. Since his breakthrough, Ford, General Motors, Honda, and some eight other major manufacturers have purchased development licenses from him. Chrysler and many other manufacturers have observed this activity and initiated extensive two-stroke programs of their own. These expansive engineering programs could one day lead to fleets of two-stroke–powered cars on American roads.

Simple, small, light, and cheap, two-strokes have long been the bargain-basement choice of the internal-combustion engine family. They pump out lots of power for their size, but they also pump out lots of pollution, and they guzzle fuel in the process.

The biggest problem is that the thermodynamic and mechanical shortcuts taken to make the engine produce power with every crankshaft revolution also result in the intermixing of intake and exhaust gases. A sizable amount of unburned air-fuel mixture can escape through the exhaust port, boosting hydrocarbon (HC) emissions rather than power and efficiency. The intake charge that stays in the cylinder gets contaminated by plenty of

trapped exhaust gas, so a rich mixture is needed to burn properly, and that doesn't help emissions or fuel economy either. Finally, the two-stroke engine's abbreviated compression and power strokes extract less energy from the charge when it finally does burn.

The classic two-stroke does benefit from less friction than a four-stroke, thanks to its roller bearings, the absence

Chrysler's two-stroke engine departs from the Orbital design with its diesel-type fuel injection, Roots blower for scavenging, and conventional crankshaft.

OLD RELIABLE

The four-stroke engine used in modern cars runs on the Otto cycle, invented in 1876 by Nikolaus Otto, the German engine pioneer. As the name suggests, his engine employs four distinct operations spread over four full strokes of each of its pistons.

The first is the intake stroke, which begins with the intake valve open and the piston at the top of its cylinder. As the rotating crankshaft drives the piston downward, the resulting suction draws a mixture of air and fuel from the intake manifold into the cylinder.

Near the bottom of the piston's stroke, the intake valve closes and the piston is forced upward by the crankshaft. The air-fuel mixture is compressed, raising its temperature and pressure and greatly increasing the work that can be extracted from a given charge of air and fuel.

Near the top of the piston's stroke, a spark plug ignites the compressed charge of air and fuel. As the charge quickly burns, the temperature and pressure in the cylinder increase dramatically, forcing the piston down and transferring power to the crankshaft.

Just before the piston reaches the bottom of the power stroke, the exhaust

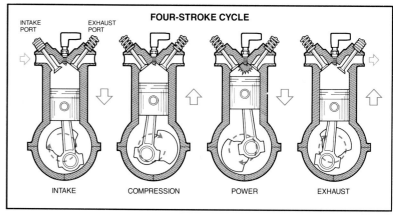

FOUR-STROKE CYCLE

INTAKE PORT — EXHAUST PORT

INTAKE — COMPRESSION — POWER — EXHAUST

ROBIN HITE

valve opens, releasing most of the burned mixture, which, even after its expansion in the power stroke, is still several times greater than atmospheric pressure. After the high pressure blows down, the low-pressure exhaust gas remaining in the cylinder is driven out when the crankshaft forces the piston up again. The exhaust valve then closes, the intake valve opens, and the entire cycle begins again.

Each phase of the cycle is performed thoroughly and completely, thanks to a dedicated stroke of the piston. But there's a price for this neatness—two revolutions of the crankshaft for each power stroke.

—*CC*

---

of all valve gear, and the lack of oil-control rings on its pistons. It also has lower pumping losses (the energy expended to pump intake and exhaust gases in and out of its cylinders). But the bottom line is that the traditional two-stroke engine is easily 30 percent thirstier and pollutes far more than typical four-strokes.

A fairly obvious solution to these problems is to run only air through the two-stroke's intake system while injecting the fuel directly into the cylinder after the exhaust port closes, much the way a diesel engine does. Unfortunately, diesel injection pumps are very expensive, high-precision devices.

That's where Sarich came in. An inveterate tinkerer, Sarich spent much of the seventies fooling around with a strange rotary powerplant that he dubbed the Orbital engine. It flopped, but during its development, Sarich and his engineers learned a few things about combustion and applied them to the two-stroke engine. They called their approach the Orbital Combustion Process, or OCP.

The key element of the OCP engine is an air-assisted direct fuel injection that's far cheaper and simpler than diesel-type systems. It consists of a small chamber directly above each cylinder that is pressurized to about 95 psi by an air pump. An electronically controlled valve—essentially a conventional fuel injector—meters fuel into this chamber. Another similar valve connects this chamber to the cylinder. When this second valve opens, the pressurized air blasts the fuel into the combustion chamber, atomizing it into extremely fine droplets. This atomization is critical because there isn't much time for the fuel to disperse and mix with the air in the cylinder before the spark plug fires. For the same reason, the spark plug and the fuel spray must be precisely positioned to ensure that there is always a combustible mixture of air and fuel near the spark during ignition. When you achieve this with a lean mixture, it's called "stratified charge combustion." Sarich's engineers were so successful that the OCP engine runs with air-fuel ratios as lean as 80 to 1, according to Ken Johnsen, the chairman of Orbital's American operation. (Typical four-strokes can't run much leaner than 20 to 1.)

Such lean air-fuel ratios greatly help combustion efficiency. And with the benefits of the new injection system, and the two-stroke's lesser friction, the OCP engine is 12 percent more efficient than a comparable four-stroke, Johnsen says.

Sarich's engine is basically of a piston-port crankcase-scavenged design, with three cylinders and 1.2-liter displacement. Three is an appropriate number of cylinders for a two-stroke because the pressure pulsations in the exhaust system can be harnessed to push some of the scavenging air back into the cylinder as the exhaust port is closing. A variable exhaust port, like those found on some off-road motorcycles, helps spread these benefits throughout the rpm range.

Sarich's engine develops about 87 hp at 5500 rpm and 92 pound-feet of torque at 3500 rpm. Orbital figures this engine can replace a comparatively low-tech 1.6-liter four-cylinder four-stroke with about half the weight and half the size, and a 25-percent savings in manufacturing costs (about $200 per engine). The company

HOW THE TWO-STROKE WORKS

The two-stroke engine used in Trabants, dirt bikes, and chain saws is based on a concept patented in 1891 by the English inventor Joseph Day. This piston-ported, crankcase-scavenged design dispenses with poppet valves in favor of openings in the cylinder wall—called ports—that are covered and uncovered by the motion of the piston. The engine also uses the volume below the piston to pump the intake charge into the cylinder.

Each cylinder sits above a sealed section of the crankcase. As the piston rises, it creates a suction below, drawing in an air-fuel mixture from the intake manifold. At the same time, the rising piston is compressing the intake charge that is in the cylinder above the piston. (We'll explain in a minute how that intake charge got there.)

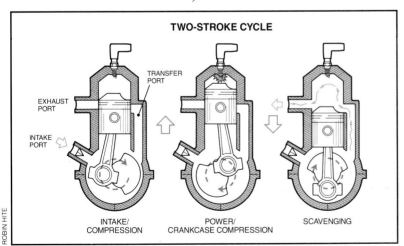

TWO-STROKE CYCLE

TRANSFER PORT

EXHAUST PORT

INTAKE PORT

INTAKE/ COMPRESSION

POWER/ CRANKCASE COMPRESSION

SCAVENGING

ROBIN HITE

Near the top of the piston stroke, the spark plug fires, initiating the combustion that drives the piston downward. The descending piston transfers power to the crankshaft and also slightly compresses the charge trapped in the crankcase. A one-way valve, called a reed valve, pre-vents any of this charge from flowing back into the intake manifold.

When the piston is about halfway down, it begins to uncover the exhaust port, basically a rectangular hole in the cylinder wall. The high-pressure exhaust gas rushes out into the exhaust manifold. As the piston descends further, it uncovers the transfer ports, several small passages that connect the cylinder to the crankcase.

Since the charge in the crankcase has been compressed by the descending piston, it rushes into the cylinder through the transfer ports and helps push the remaining exhaust gas out of the still-open exhaust port. This combination of intake and exhaust strokes is called scavenging.

The scavenging continues until the piston hits bottom and rises far enough to again cover both the transfer and the exhaust ports. The compression of the air-fuel mixture then begins, while the crankcase is again being refilled and the process continues.

Crankcase scavenging won't work with the oil splashing indigenous to a four-stroke-style pressure-fed, plain-bearing crankshaft. That's why two-stroke designs use roller-bearing crankshafts. Though relatively expensive, these bearings can survive with a light mist of oil injected into the intake port.

By shortening the compression and power strokes and essentially combining the intake and exhaust strokes, the two-stroke engine produces power *with every crankshaft revolution*—but at a price. A two-stroke's piston doesn't push on the crankshaft as hard as a four-stroke piston. Still, with twice as many power strokes, a two-stroke engine produces more power and torque than does a four-stroke, which is why it's virtually unbeatable in racing classes in which both compete at the same displacement. —CC also claims as much as a 30-percent fuel-economy improvement in a small car if full structural and aerodynamic advantages are taken of the engine's reduced size and weight.

If the question is why don't the carmakers just put Sarich's fuel injection on existing four-strokes and run them lean, the answer is emissions. Four-stroke engines depend on three-way catalysts to convert all three controlled pollutants—HC, carbon monoxide (CO), and oxides of nitrogen (NOx)—into less harmful substances. However, three-way catalysts only work if they are fed an exhaust stream that contains neither unburned fuel nor unburned air. That means that combustion must take place at a precise air-fuel ratio of 14.7 to 1. Maintaining this air-fuel ratio is the primary reason that most current engines have computer-controlled fuel-injection systems.

Two-strokes, on the other hand, can't use three-way catalysts, because they always pump some intake charge into the exhaust. And that means a lot more unburned air in the exhaust than a three-way catalyst can handle.

Fortunately, the OCP engine's lean operation produces inherently low HC and CO emissions. A two-way catalyst, which thrives on a lean-mixture exhaust, can easily reduce these emissions to the legal limits. These catalysts are also cheaper than the three-way kind because they don't contain any rhodium, which sells for about $66,000 a pound.

Lean operation also reduces NOx, but there's a more important factor that helps the two-stroke deal with this pollutant. NOx is formed during the highest temperatures of combustion. The higher the temperature and the longer it is sustained, the more NOx is produced. As it happens, the peak temperatures reached during two-stroke combustion are not very high for the same reasons that its power stroke is not as strong as a four-stroke's—the scavenging doesn't result in a full cylinder of fresh air-fuel mixture and the compression and power strokes are truncated. With a well-calibrated engine-management system, the OCP two-stroke can meet the NOx standards without catalytic assistance.

That means that to get what Sarich promises, you must go the two-stroke route. None of the carmakers we spoke with is fully sold on the claimed benefits of the OCP engine, but the carmakers recognize its potential enough to be actively pursuing two-stroke development.

GM has taken its Orbital-licensed technology and applied it to a slightly larger three-cylinder engine. Called the CDS2, it displaces 1.5 liters and develops 100 hp at 5500 rpm and 130 pound-feet of torque at 3000 rpm. A balance shaft quells the rocking motion produced by this large three-cylinder engine.

Paul Reinke, the GM staff engineer in charge of the program, does not at this stage of the game claim that the CDS2 is any more fuel efficient than a comparable state-of-the-art four-stroke, but he does suggest a 30-percent (70-pound) weight savings. This advantage would translate into about a 200-pound overall weight reduction in a vehicle designed expressly around the engine, with a lighter frame and suspension components. In a 2500-pound car, that's a 7-percent reduction, which translates almost directly into 7 percent better fuel economy.

Such talk is premature, though, until the emissions problems are solved. Reinke says that OCP engines meet the standards when new, but he confirms what Orbital's Johnsen reluctantly conceded—no engine has yet passed the 50,000-mile emissions durability test. Apparently the exhaust temperature of the two-stroke engine varies over a larger range than a four-stroke's. At full throttle, the temperature approaches the catalyst meltdown zone, but the real problem is too low a temperature at part throttle. The catalyst doesn't get so cool that it stops working, but a lukewarm catalyst doesn't cleanse itself of impurities very effectively. As a result, as the miles pile up, the catalyst's efficiency drops. An additional catalyst inserted directly in the exhaust manifold may solve the problem, but for now the durability issue remains the OCP engine's greatest identifiable stumbling block.

Ford also owns an Orbital license, but it is pursuing the engine's development in Europe rather than America. Europe still has less-strict emissions regulations and is more likely to accept a three-cylinder engine in a small car. Like GM, Ford is not convinced of the engine's efficiency advantage, but it is sold on the packaging and weight benefits.

Ian Macpherson, Ford's director of powertrain engineering, points out that although the basic engine is simple, it does employ some expensive technology. For example, while the three-cylinder pneumatic injection system is cheaper

Driving a Two-Stroke

The manufacturers we spoke with weren't prepared to let us drive off with their two-stroke prototypes. But we did get our hands on a car belonging to Orbital-Walbro—a Ford Fiesta we drove in Cass City, Michigan. The car is the firm's two-stroke injection-system demonstrator.

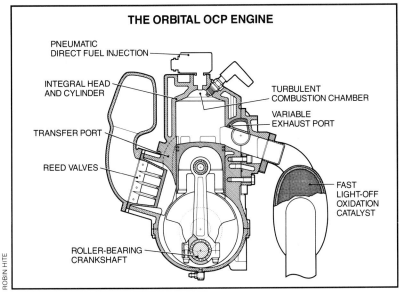

THE ORBITAL OCP ENGINE

PNEUMATIC DIRECT FUEL INJECTION

INTEGRAL HEAD AND CYLINDER

TRANSFER PORT

REED VALVES

TURBULENT COMBUSTION CHAMBER

VARIABLE EXHAUST PORT

FAST LIGHT-OFF OXIDATION CATALYST

ROLLER-BEARING CRANKSHAFT

ROBIN HITE

The 1.2-liter Orbital OCP engine appears lost in the Fiesta's engine compartment, even though nothing larger than a 1.6-liter four-cylinder four-stroke originally resided there. It's no wonder the stylists love this engine—the hood line could be lowered eight inches.

The engine spins to life easily, settling down to a smooth, solid 600-rpm idle. There's none of the crackling and popping of conventional two-strokes at idle, because the stratified charge ensures stable combustion, and there's no unburned fuel lighting off in the exhaust system. The catalytic converter and the conven-

tional automotive mufflers further suppress the exhaust sounds.

With three of us aboard, we pull away, and the OCP engine immediately shows its wide-band power. There's no need to wind this engine to its 5500-rpm redline to move smartly. Nor are there any sudden jumps in output. The variable exhaust port, the controlled combustion, and the electronic engine-control system work together to produce a smooth, even flow of power. The engine is so flexible that it pulls away clearly from 600 rpm in fifth gear.

There's no smoke either. The average fuel-to-oil ratio is said to be 125 to 1. Combined with the lean fuel flow, that means there isn't much oil going through the combustion process—so little that Orbital's Ken Johnsen claims that his engine uses less oil than a four-stroke when you count the latter's oil changes. And since the oil is only used once, it doesn't contain many of the additives needed in four-stroke oils.

Although the engine performs without a hint of temperament, there is a frantic quality to its sound. Without looking at the tachometer, one wants to shift at 3000 rpm—no doubt because the engine is producing the same number of power strokes that a four cylinder is making at 4500 rpm. A six-cylinder two-stroke would undoubtedly sound as turbine-like as most four-stroke twelves.

We won't draw many conclusions about the engine's smoothness, because this car had benefited from very little NVH (noise, vibration, and harshness) development. But based on this drive, we have no doubts that if the engine can be made to satisfy the EPA, it will have no problem satisfying American drivers.   —*CC*

than a diesel-type system, it will still cost as much as a sequential fuel-injection system for a conventional six-cylinder engine. The roller-bearing crankshaft is also pricier than a plain-bearing design, and its long-term durability is unproven in automotive applications.

When pressed, Macpherson suggests that an in-house test fleet of two-stroke Fiestas could hit the streets of Europe in a year or two. Production, however, is unlikely before mid-decade.

Chrysler is America's only big-time Orbital holdout. However, the automaker is pursuing its own line of two-stroke devel-

opment. Chrysler's prototype, seen in the Neon show car, displaces 1.1 liters in its three cylinders, develops about 100 hp, and weighs about 40 percent less than a comparable conventional engine.

Chrysler's engine departs from the Orbital concept in two significant ways. First, Chrysler is trying to develop a moderately priced diesel-type hydraulic pump developing over 1000 psi to provide direct-fuel injection. Second, the Chrysler engine uses an external blower to push fresh air into the cylinder rather than crankcase scavenging. A Roots-type supercharger, blowing through a number of

Toyota's S2 embodies the most complex elements of two- and four-stroke engines.

intake ports uncovered by the piston near the bottom of its stroke, forces the engine's exhaust out through an exhaust port as on the Orbital design.

This approach probably provides more thorough scavenging than a crankcase-scavenged design, and with the crankcase no longer used to pump air, it allows the use of a conventional, pressure-fed, plain-bearing crank. However, the blower costs money, weight, space, and the power needed to drive it. More power is sapped by the return of the oil-control rings on the pistons to keep the splashing lubricant out of the combustion chambers. Chrysler is also experimenting with a centrifugal blower, like the one used on a turbocharger, but such devices don't move much air at low rpm.

Richard Schaum, Chrysler's executive engineer in charge of alternative engines, likes the manufacturing familiarity and proven reliability of his engine's conventional bottom end. He also points out that a wet-sump engine can run for a long time without an oil change, while an oil-injected two-stroke promptly seizes if it runs out of oil. The absence of oil in the combustion process doesn't hurt catalyst durability either.

It remains to be seen whether the additional costs of the external blower and the mechanical fuel injection will offset the savings of Orbital's royalty (a rumored $38 per engine) and the benefits of a conventional crankshaft. But if the economics work out and the testing is successful, you might see a Chrysler two-stroke in limited production by 1996.

The externally scavenged approach may make more sense in a V-6 two-stroke for bigger cars because shoe-horning six

individual compartments into the crankcase of a V-6 is virtually impossible. Orbital has already put together such a powerplant—it weighs 200 pounds and develops 200 hp. It uses a centrifugal blower buried in the block that adds only about an inch to the length of the engine.

Elsewhere, Subaru has shown off a two-stroke, displacing only 1.6 liters. This powerplant uses a Roots blower in the middle of the V for scavenging and it also uses rotary valves in the exhaust ports to provide greater control over exhaust timing. Claimed output is 176 hp at 5400 rpm.

Toyota revealed a vastly more complex 3.0-liter two-stroke called the S2 at the 1989 Tokyo motor show. The engine looks just like a four-stroke in-line six with four valves per cylinder and a Roots blower. But its operation is classic two-stroke, with abbreviated compression and power strokes, and pressurized air scavenging when all the valves are open with the piston at the bottom of its stroke. For effective scavenging, the S2 apparently opens its exhaust valves before the piston is even halfway down the cylinder on the power stroke. That doesn't suggest very good fuel economy.

Toyota has revealed that its engine develops 235 hp at an extremely low 3600 rpm. Both this output and the Subaru's output suggest cylinder combustion pressures and temperatures that are clearly in the four-stroke range. And that implies four-stroke NOx production. However, with the oxygen-rich exhaust that effective scavenging generates, three-way catalysts won't operate. If Toyota or Subaru have some secret solution to this problem, they're not talking about it.

There's no question that two-strokes offer immense potential. It's hard to argue with the virtues of smaller, lighter, cheaper, more efficient, and more powerful. Still, the auto manufacturers will insist on absolute reliability and durability before they will risk their reputations—and bank balances—on the new technology. And with no two-stroke engine having successfully passed a 50,000-mile test—never mind the new 100,000-mile emissions durability test—talk of American sales within the next few years is nonsense.

Sarich has definitely started something here, but whether two-strokes will become the new standard or another novelty like the Wankel engine is anybody's guess for now.

PHOTOGRAPHY BY TOM DREW

NEW AGE CARS

By William Jeanes

Without reinventing the wheel, an accomplishment that any number of Washington, D.C., dimwits think can be done overnight for $53.19, may we remind you that the zealots in Washington believe that we must raise the Corporate Average Fuel Economy standard, presently 27.5 miles per gallon, to 40 mpg by the year 2001. CAFE, as this number is called by both government and industry, does not mean that *all* cars must deliver 40 mpg, only that all cars built by a manufacturer, big ones and small ones, must in combination achieve a fleet average of —in this instance—40 mpg.

We've thought this 40-mpg business over thoroughly and just can't see any fair way to do this unless each and every passenger and light commercial vehicle gets 40 mpg in highway driving. After all, fair is fair, and there are a number of cars that already get 40 mpg and beyond. What's more, if Congress thinks it's such a grand idea, why not do it now?

What would life be like if the government mandated 40 mpg overnight? Well, you say, a wise government wouldn't jerk its knee like that. We agree. Unfortunately, however, we are talking about *our* government, and if ever there was a group dedicated to trying to solve problems with the grand gesture, it's these gasbags.

Accordingly, we've prepared a number of scenarios that show us all driving cars that *already* get at least 40 mpg. (Well, sort of. We used the government's unadjusted highway numbers that are used for the actual CAFE calculations. They're a bit higher than those on the window sticker.) You'll see us all, including yourself: rich man, poor man, policeman, senator, even a normal American family . . . the unit that unfailingly takes it in the neck when government sets out to do good works.

As you peruse the following pages, please remember that the *cars* shown are innocent victims. They are good little machines, and their descent into the morass of satire is not their fault. Used as their builders intended, each of them is a worthy helpmate. Some are even fun. But here we see them pressed into service not for what they are, but because their achievement of 40 mpg makes them mandatory in our fantasy world.

VW JETTA GL DIESEL
Limousine

We caught silver-tongued, silver-haired Senator Sopwith Bentley, Democrat from a western state that has legal gambling, on the streets of our nation's capital. The senator has just stepped from his four-passenger diesel-powered Volkswagen Jetta GL limousine and paused to answer questions from nightly news correspondent Laura Lancet, whose inquiring mind has led her to ask, "Senator, just where do you stand on the issue of a higher gas tax to reduce oil consumption?"

The senator's answer: "We've passed a five-cent-per-gallon tax already, adding a burdensome $60 per year to the average household budget, and right there's your problem. Thanks to irresponsible spending by the Republicans, these household budgets just aren't as big as they ought to be. What we need is for the automakers to take all that technology they've been hiding and give the taxpayers the kind of cars they deserve . . . big, six-passenger cars that protect the family against 60-mile-per-hour crashes. Cars that get 60

STEVE WATZ, DON SCHROEDER, BUD ALLEN, JOELLE SHANDLER, PHIL BERG, TOM COSGROVE

miles per gallon. And cars that can go from 0 to 60. I call this my 180-degree-out-of-phase program."

It's clear, clearer than the senator's statement anyway, that the Jetta limo is just the ticket for the man about Washington. Senator Bentley can rush to lobbyists' offices on the Beltway at speeds as high as 88 mph, according to VW's capital spokesperson. We estimate that the figure will be slightly less if he brings aide Thurman Short (168 pounds) along and if the Jetta is driven by chauffeur Grumman

Maidstone (156 pounds). Highway mileage is a commendable 56 mpg according to government sources.

Vehicle type: front-engine, front-wheel-drive, 5-passenger, 4-door sedan
1992 base price: $12,040
Engine type: SOHC 4-in-line diesel, iron block and aluminum head, Bosch mechanical fuel injection
Displacement .... 97 cu in, 1588cc
Power (SAE net) .... 52 bhp @ 4800 rpm
Transmission 5-speed
Wheelbase .... 97.3 in
Length .... 172.6 in
Curb weight .... 2400 lb
EPA fuel economy, city driving .... 37 mpg

GEO METRO LSi

Sports Car

In this all-too-familiar setting, we find Vincent "Vinnie" Goodman III, son of Vincent P. Goodman Jr., owner of the largest chain of gourmet pet-food stores. Vinnie has the third-largest collection of gold neck chains in Cherry Hill, New Jersey, and once drove a Camaro Z28 with gold wheels and two phones.

Today, required to drive a 40-mpg car, Vinnie gets as many as 46 highway mpg, thanks to his peppy little Geo Metro LSi convertible with a 1992 base price of $10,254.

Despite his economical car, madcap Vinnie has still managed to exceed the 55-mph speed limit on the Interstate, incur-ring the wrath of Officer Marv Brimstone. Officer Brimstone, in the halcyon days he spent behind the wheel of a 1984 Crown Victoria, was often called "Leadfoot" by the jolly gang of ticket-writers back at headquarters. Not anymore.

Vehicle type: front-engine, front-wheel-drive, 2-passenger, 2-door convertible
1992 base price: $10,254
Engine type: SOHC 3-in-line, aluminum block and head, Suzuki engine-control system with port fuel injection
Displacement .... 61 cu in, 993cc
Power (SAE net) .... 55 bhp @ 5700 rpm
Transmission 5-speed
Wheelbase .... 89.2 in
Length .... 146.1 in
Curb weight .... 1800 lb
EPA fuel economy, city driving .... 41 mpg

CLIFF WEATHERS, BROCK YATES, JOHN ROE

HONDA CRX HF

Police Car

The Honda CRX HF you see here gets 67 CAFE highway mpg and might reach 100 mph downhill, quite enough in the New Age. Its 1991 base price was $9325. The CRX has been a favorite at *C/D* for many years. In its fastest version, it probably wouldn't make an altogether bad police car. Of course there's no room for hauling alleged perpetrators, but Marv Brimstone's partner, young Lee Harvey Czolgoz, has an answer for that minor inconvenience.

Vehicle type: front-engine, front-wheel-drive, 2-passenger, 3-door coupe

Base price: $9325

Engine type: SOHC 4-in-line, aluminum block and head, Honda engine-control system with port fuel injection

Displacement . . . . 91 cu in, 1493cc
Power (SAE net) . . . . 62 bhp @ 4500 rpm
Transmission 5-speed
Wheelbase . . . . 90.6 in
Length . . . . 148.5 in
Curb weight . . . . 1950 lb
EPA fuel economy, city driving . . . . 49 mpg

SUBARU JUSTY GL

Taxi

What's more fun than vacationing in the islands? A lot of things, according to Sal and Norma Dee Hepatica. We join the Hepaticas in the U.S. Virgin Islands, which, as a U.S. possession, has recently adopted the 40-mpg standard. Sal has hailed a taxi driven by retired herpetologist Fred Sheckter. Fred's cab is an economical Subaru Justy, a five-door hatchback that cost just $8299 in 1991, gets 41 mpg on the highway, and has room for four, counting Fred.

Fred does not think his Justy also has room for the Hepaticas' seven American Tourister three-suiters, largely because the Hepatica luggage weighs almost as much as the 2050-pound Subaru. Sal, a lab technician at the One Day Hernia Repair facility in Detroit, disagrees. So does Norma Dee. Fred, however, remains adamant and is sharing with Sal and Norma Dee his long-held belief that tourists should never carry more than they can run with. Fred's right, of course.

Vehicle type: front-engine, front/4-wheel-drive, 4-passenger, 5-door sedan
Base price: $8299
Engine type: SOHC 3-in-line, iron block and aluminum head, Subaru engine-control system with port fuel injection

Displacement	73 cu in, 1190cc
Power (SAE net)	73 bhp @ 5600 rpm
Transmission	5-speed
Wheelbase	90.0 in
Length	145.5 in
Curb weight	2050 lb
EPA fuel economy, city driving	29 mpg

RAY HUTTON, LAURA LABODA, STEVE SPENCE

FORD FESTIVA GL

Family Car

Here's the Packer family: Ferd, Martha, Oliver, Sissy, and their dog, Albert W. Underwood, an Irish setter, off to Six Flags Over Priced near Hibbing, Minnesota. Hibbing is a long way from the Packers's split-level in Anaheim, but with their trusty Ford Festiva GL (54 CAFE highway mpg), there'll be no shortage of on-the-road high jinks and fun for the vacationing Packers. Carrying the half-ton Packer payload—that's all their luggage and vacation gear, plus Albert W. Underwood and six boxes of Gainesburgers with cheese—the little Festiva may have its work cut out for it as the Packers cross the Rockies. Will the food hold out? Will Oliver grate on his parents by asking for one too many rest stops? Will Martha turn snappish at high altitude? Will Sissy get carsick? Is that Cool Whip or foam on Albert W. Underwood's snout? Happy trails, Packers!

Vehicle type: front-engine, front-wheel drive, 4-passenger, 3-door sedan
1992 base price: $8275
Engine type: SOHC 4-in-line, iron block and aluminum head, Ford/Nippondenso engine-control system with port fuel injection
Displacement .... 81 cu in, 1324cc
Power (SAE net) .... 63 bhp @ 5000 rpm
Transmission 5-speed
Wheelbase .... 90.2 in
Length .... 140.5 in
Curb weight .... 1850 lb
EPA fuel economy, city driving .... 35 mpg

ELNA GEORGE, LINDSAY LABODA, ED GEORGE, JEFFREY LABODA, AND ROXY, THE WONDER DOG (HE'S IN THERE SOMEWHERE)

GEO METRO XFi

Hearse

The management at Loomis Funeral Home of Dingo, Texas, never dreamed that big gas-guzzling hearses would be outlawed. They are bearing up nicely with their $7284 Geo Metro XFi three-door converted to a New Age funeral coach by the Addams Ambulance Co. of Bovis, Connecticut. It gets 59 CAFE mpg in processions, 75 on the highway.

Edgar Don Pickens is bearing up less well. Ed's in the box (the Junior Execu-tive Sleep of Peace model from Howting Vaults, Inc.), and wouldn't be there if he hadn't lost his temper when his wife Irene (third from left) let the steam iron burn through his bowling shirt while she answered a phone call from Shirl's Curls (Shirl is second from left) about her nail appointment. Ed threw his bowling ball at Irene and in the process lost his balance and fell off the treated-cypress deck into a Mulch Master DX wood chipper (Norm

Simmons, who owns the chipper, is at the far left). You can imagine the rest.

Will Ed take comfort in knowing that he's helping to save gasoline, right up to the end? Will Irene keep her next nail appointment? And what about Norm Simmons? Just what was he doing out there with his wood chipper at *just* the right moment?

Vehicle type: front-engine, front-wheel-drive, 2 + 2-passenger, 3-door coupe
1992 base price: $7284
Engine type: SOHC 3-in-line, aluminum block and head, Suzuki engine-control system with 1x1-bbl throttle-body fuel injection
Displacement .... 61 cu in, 993cc
Power (SAE net) .... 49 bhp @ 4700 rpm
Transmission 5-speed
Wheelbase .... 89.2 in
Length .... 146.1 in
Curb weight .... 1600 lb
EPA fuel economy, city driving .... 53 mpg

JOHN PHILLIPS III, SUSAN SMITH JEANES, JULI BURKE, TOM DREW, STEVE WATZ, JEFFREY DWORIN

HONDA
VTEC-E

LEAN-BURN ENGINES

By Frank Markus

When the government began poking its nose in the automotive industry's business back in the seventies by ordering fuel-economy and pollution-control standards, many enthusiasts feared that the end was near for high-performance vehicles. Fortunately, this was not the case, and today's cars are vastly superior to those of the preregulation era in virtually every way. So when people begin whining that the end is once again near with the prospect of 40-mpg CAFE regulations and ever-tightening emissions standards, those of us with our eyes on the technology remain optimistic.

We're all from Missouri, however, where amazing new cure-all engines are concerned. So now we train the editorial eye on the latest technological wonder, the lean-burn engine.

Honda's all-new Civic VX has returned the word "lean burn" to the automotive lexicon for the first time since Chrysler scrubbed its Electronic Lean Burn engines in 1979. The hitch with lean combustion then—and now—is that it improves fuel economy at a direct cost to emissions quality. To understand the different approaches manufacturers are taking to overcome this inherent challenge, a brief primer on combustion theory is required for those of you who didn't major in Engine Design.

Running an engine lean means that

there is less fuel in the cylinder than is needed to completely burn all of the available air. With gasoline, 14.7 pounds of air are required to burn 1 pound of fuel. This air-fuel ratio is referred to as "stoichiometric." In the bad old pre-smog days, all cars ran a bit lean, cruising at air-fuel ratios of 17:1 or 18:1 to save fuel. The old carburetors would then, during acceleration, go rich—more fuel than needed to burn all of the air—to an air-fuel ratio of about 13:1 to ensure that there was enough fuel to burn every last molecule of the available air (air being the limiting factor in engine power).

Fuel is saved while running lean by reducing the pumping effort the engine expends during the intake stroke. That's because increasing the amount of air in the cylinder for a given amount of fuel (and power output) requires that the throttle be opened wider. This reduction in vacuum makes it easier to draw the intake charge into the cylinder.

But as an engine begins to run lean, a few other things start to happen. The good news is that less carbon monoxide (CO) and unburned hydrocarbons (HC) are produced. Unfortunately, as the air-fuel ratio increases to around 17:1 or 18:1, peak combustion temperatures rise and emissions of oxides of nitrogen (NOx) increase. Running the engine even leaner, with more excess air, brings down the temperature and the NOx emissions with it, even to below stoichiometric levels. But such mixtures become difficult to ignite and are slow to burn. If the mixture doesn't ignite, you've got obvious problems, but slow combustion also works against fuel economy.

In a theoretically perfect (ideal) four-stroke engine, the spark plug would fire just as the piston completes its compression stroke, and all the fuel would burn instantaneously so that every little bit of pressure from the ensuing explosion would be extracted as usable power. Unfortunately, even stoichiometric mixtures take a finite time to ignite and a further interval to completely burn a cylinderful of air-fuel mixture, so the spark fires a bit earlier, while the piston is still moving upward. A slower-burning lean mixture requires that the ignition timing be further advanced, adding more counterproductive work to the compression stroke.

The goal for a lean-combustion engine is to run lean enough to slink under the federal 1.0-gram-per-mile NOx-emissions standard (soon to become 0.4 gpm and 0.2 gpm in California) without help from a catalyst, because today's three-way converters do not efficiently reduce NOx in the presence of excess oxygen. To do this, the engine must first be able consistently to light off the air-fuel mixture at a very lean ratio. It must also encourage this lean combustion to progress quickly enough to avoid the inefficiency of extreme spark advance.

Having thus made combustion theorists of the entire *Car and Driver* readership, we are now ready to examine the available hardware. Honda, Toyota, and Mitsubishi displayed production lean-burn engines at the Tokyo motor show, and Mazda, Nissan, and Daihatsu showed prototypes. Only Honda has met the challenges well enough to sell cars in 49 of our states, so it gets top billing.

HONDA CIVIC VX, VTEC-E 1.5-LITER SOHC SIXTEEN-VALVE 4-IN-LINE; 92 HP @ 5500, 97 LB-FT @ 4500

Just like in the old days, this engine is designed to run lean only during light-load acceleration and cruising below 2500 rpm—however, an ultra-lean 24:1 air-fuel ratio takes care of the emissions problem. During hard acceleration and at engine speeds of more than 2500 rpm, the engine runs at stoichiometric conditions and relies on a three-way catalyst to clean up the exhaust.

Variable-valve-timing-and-lift technology developed for Honda's high-performance engines provides the key to speeding combustion and delivering an ignitable mixture to the spark during lean operation in the VTEC-E. The system virtually shuts down one of each cylinder's two intake valves, forcing all of the air-fuel mixture in through the other. This causes the intake charge to swirl rapidly around the circumference of the cylinder and concentrates the fuel near the center, where the spark plug is located. This locally rich "stratified charge" ignites easily, and the swirl propagates the flame quickly through a compact combustion chamber designed to squish the outermost (farthest from the spark) thirteen percent of the mixture in toward the center as the piston approaches the top of its stroke.

This simplified VTEC works its magic by allowing each intake valve to be actuated by its own rocker arm following its own cam lobe during low-speed operation. The "closed" valve is opened slightly (0.65mm) to allow fuel that is injected

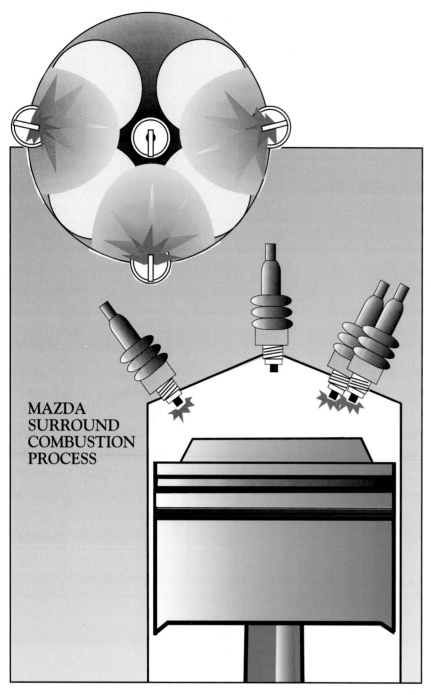

MAZDA
SURROUND
COMBUSTION
PROCESS

timing, allows this engine to run reliably at or near its lean limit.

The EPA rates the VTEC-E equipped Civic VX at 48 mpg city, 55 highway. Impressive figures for a car that goes from 0 to 60 in 9.4 seconds. Slick aerodynamics, low-rolling-resistance tires, low weight, and tall gearing all help, but to isolate the effect of running lean, just look at the California VX with the same VTEC-E engine, calibrated to run always at stoichiometry to meet that state's more rigid NOx standards. It's rated at 44/51, indicating that lean burn is worth an improvement of a little more than ten percent.

Honda is continuing to develop this engine in hopes of bringing it up to snuff for 50-state sale. Development of a lean NOx catalyst will be the most likely fix.

TOYOTA CARINA, 4A-ELU 1.6-LITER DOHC SIXTEEN-VALVE 4-IN-LINE 97 HP @ 5800, 98 LB-FT @ 3000

Toyota came to market in 1984 with an eight-valve, high-swirl lean-burn engine in its home-market Carina model, a sedan that would fit between our Corolla and Camry. In 1988, the 4A-ELU became a sixteen-valver. The major combustion dilemmas are confronted with the same basic approach used by Honda, except here swirl is induced by a "swirl control" flapper valve mounted upstream of the intake valve that shuts off the flow of air and fuel to one of the two intake runners below 2800 rpm. Another minor variation is that the swirl axis is angled slightly within the cylinder to provide better fuel atomization and increased turbulence.

Toyota had the first air-fuel sensor that —like Honda's—detects ratios between stoichiometric and 25:1 based on exhaust oxygen content. Using this sensor, the engine controller instructs the programmed independent fuel injection to maintain a 22.5:1 air-fuel ratio at cruise and to revert to 14.7:1 during acceleration.

In the European city fuel-economy cycle, the Carina delivers 30 mpg, and at a constant 56 mph it sips along at 44 mpg, as compared with the 2.0-liter non-lean Carina's 25 and 30 mpg. Not bad for a car the size and weight of a Saturn sedan, although the claimed 0-to-62-mph time of 10.2 seconds is nearly two ticks slower than the Saturn. But for the foreseeable future, that race will only exist on paper, because there are no plans to bring the 4A-ELU to our shores.

Toyota is playing another lean-burn

into both intake runners at all times to dribble into the cylinder. Above 2500 rpm, the rocker arms of both intake valves are locked together by a hydraulically actuated piston so that both open a full 8mm for high-speed breathing.

The final piece of technology that enables this engine to run lean reliably is a wide-range air-fuel-ratio sensor. Conventional exhaust oxygen sensors work like an on/off switch, sensing only the presence or absence of oxygen. The units can sense exhaust oxygen content to determine air-fuel ratios of up to 25:1. Such closed-loop electronic monitoring of the combustion process, when combined with precise fuel-injector and ignition

card very close to its chest. Its AXV-III concept car at the Tokyo show featured a 2.5-liter V-6 engine with continuously variable valve timing, a variable dual-exhaust system, combustion-pressure sensors, and a lean NOx catalyst. It is believed to run as lean as 30:1 with the help of a very high voltage ignition system. This one is probably way off in the future.

Mitsubishi Mirage, 4G15MPI-MVV 1.5-liter SOHC twelve-valve 4-in-line, 90 hp @ 6000, 90 lb-ft @ 3000

The next-generation Mirage (Colt/Eagle Summit) is available in Japan with the new Mitsubishi Vertical Vortex (MVV) lean-burn engine, in which the triple-diamond folks take Honda and Toyota's basically horizontal swirl idea and stand it on end. Each cylinder has two valves for intake and one for exhaust, with the spark plug located where we've grown accustomed to finding a second exhaust valve. The fuel is stratified by injecting it into only the intake runner that is pointed at the spark plug. The two vertical swirls, one of air and one of air and fuel, generate strong turbulence during the compression stroke with the fuel remaining concentrated near the plug, so the goals of reliable ignition and fast burn are met.

The MVV engine also uses a lean air-fuel sensor to run at up to 25:1 during cruise conditions. Compared with the standard 4G15MPI engine, the MVV has delivered twenty percent better fuel economy on the bench at virtually the same levels of power output. The three-door Mirage is ranked at 50 mpg on the Japanese city cycle (our current Mirage/Colt has an EPA city rating of 31 mpg). Once again, however, there are no plans to certify the MVV for U.S. sale.

Mazda Surround Combustion Process, 2.0-liter DOHC sixteen-valve 4-in-line, targeted performance: 123hp, 130lb-ft

In designing their lean-burn engine, Mazda engineers studied the Moslem parable of Mohammed and the mountain. Instead of worrying about bringing the ignitable air-fuel mixture to the spark plug, they bring the plug to the mixture, with four plugs in each cylinder. The engine operates on a single centrally located plug at idle, on three circumferentially placed plugs during cruise, and on all four plugs during heavy acceleration. The top of the piston has a dome feature that squishes the intake charge out toward the circumference, but the four valves operate just as they would in any sixteen-valve engine, because swirl is not the critical factor speeding combustion here. Temperatures remain uniform throughout the cylinder, which helps reduce knock despite the engine's high 12:1 compression ratio.

Lean operation is at 26:1. A standard three-way catalyst is planned, so there is probably a lean air-fuel sensor in the program, as well as stoichiometric operation under some conditions. There are currently no plans for production.

Others

Nissan has a lean-burn engine that utilizes a swirl-control valve, optimized intake-port configuration, and a lean air-fuel sensor to run in the 20:1–23:1 range, but its efforts are concentrated on development of a lean NOx catalyst. Daihatsu is working on a tiny 1.0-liter three-cylinder "twin-tumble" lean-burn engine similar to

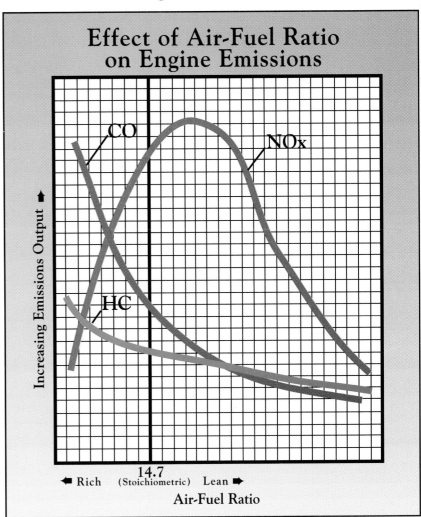

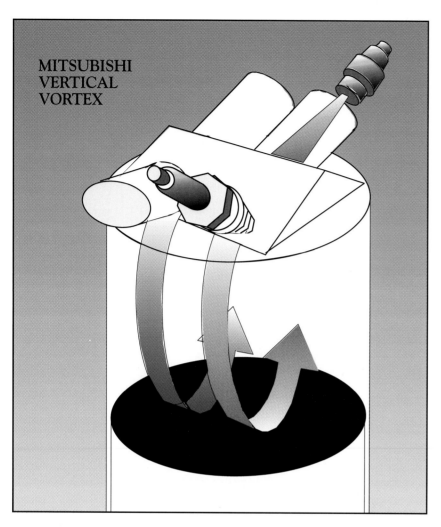

MITSUBISHI
VERTICAL
VORTEX

zeolite, which is currently used in some industrial applications to clean up emissions on stationary diesel powerplants. The good news is that zeolite costs far less than the noble metals employed in today's three-way catalysts, but Nissan reports that thermal durability at operating temperatures of between 1000 and 1400 degrees Fahrenheit in automotive applications is a problem. Zeolite also requires the presence of some unburned hydrocarbons to catalyze the NOx reduction, which are scarce in an efficient lean-burn engine. Still, there are many different formulas for zeolite, and with several companies researching them, it is probably just a matter of time.

Plasma ignition may raise an engine's lean limit substantially. The spark created by today's plugs is a tiny sphere of plasma, or ionized gas. *Ward's Engine Update* says researchers cashing in on some spin-off technology from the Star Wars defense program have developed a "rail plug" that can project a high-energy plasma arc into the cylinder, instantly igniting far more of the mixture than the tiny conventional spark. The combustion process is accelerated by reducing the distance the ensuing flame must travel, thereby raising the lean limit of a given cylinder.

Variable timing and lift of both the intake valves and the exhaust valves can better control combustion pressures and induce internal exhaust-gas recirculation, both of which reduce NOx. Camless hydraulic valve actuation, or "active valving," could do away with throttle plates and precisely adapt valve timing for all conditions to improve efficient lean operation further. And there are other exotic concepts out there, like variable compression ratio, variable stroke, and variable displacement, all of which are designed to improve combustion efficiency.

Is lean burn the panacea that will ensure carefree motoring for centuries to come? Not yet, but running lean has demonstrated fuel-economy savings of between ten and twenty percent for a given engine, with little or no cost to performance. Gains like that are appreciated by the motoring enthusiast. If a reliable, efficient lean NOx catalyst were available tomorrow, most modern multivalve engines would begin to run lean at 20:1–24:1 almost overnight. Truly exciting ultra-lean engines like Toyota's secret V-6 await the gestation of a few more key technologies, but these will come, and lean-burn engines will likely rise and conquer.

Mitsubishi's; it operates at between 16:1 and 23:1. Several manufacturers are also working on two-stroke engines, which also run lean and face many of the same problems.

The rest of the world appears to be either working on or awaiting the arrival of an efficient, durable lean NOx catalyst. Spokesmen at the Big Three indicate that with their current four-valve-per-cylinder technology, combustion-chamber dynamics, and available air-fuel-ratio sensors, many of their engines are capable of running lean. They are quick to point out, however, that U.S. standards are stated in grams of pollutants per mile, which is independent of vehicle size. So while a lean 1.5-liter 2100-pound car may be capable of squeaking by the NOx barrier, a 3.0-liter engine would have to be about twice as efficient, and operate much leaner, to meet the same emissions regulations in the type of car most Americans want.

FUTURE TECHNOLOGIES

All eyes are on the lean-catalyst front. So far, the most promising new material is

PEOPLE AND PAST

DAVID DEWHURST

Phil Remington Jon Olson AL BILL Carroll Shelby
JERRY TITUS Dick Smith Art DOWD Bob Johnson
Pete Brock Dan Gurney A.J. Foyt Ken Miles CHARLIE KEMP
ED HUGUS Bob Bondurant Chris Amon Phil Hill Ed Leslie
Hal Keck JERRY GRANT Tom Tony Spooler BILL STEELE Lew Spencer
Dave McDonald CARROLL SMITH Ray Geddes
RON RONNIE BUCKNUM
BUTLER Skip Hudson
Payton Cramer Spencer
RICHIE GINTHER George
ED Christianus Real
LOWTHER Ron Dykeman Dick
HAL FRACKEN Skelton
Sam Feinstein JACK SEARS

Carroll Shelby

HEART OF A GAMBLER

By Herb Shuldiner

Twenty-five years after he invented a popular Texas-style chili mix, Carroll Shelby can, at last, eat the stuff without suffering heartburn. He owes it to the young heart beating in his chest, which is half as old as he is.

It has been a remarkable medical success story for a man who was, just a month before that new heart was transplanted into his chest in June 1990, lying in a hospital bed certain that his legendary luck had finally run out, hanging on with a heart that had lost 86 percent of its ability to work.

And although the survival rate of heart transplants remains a dicey proposition—his surgeon says the success rate is about 75 percent these days—Shelby turned up less than a year later to drive the pace car—too fast, some said—at the 1991 Indy 500. Back at the Brickyard, Shelby seemed in better health than he had been in for a quarter-century. Certainly his Texan's way with words was salty as ever—asked to contrast how he felt before and after the operation, Shelby cracked: "It's like chicken shit and chicken salad.

"This time last year, when I thought I would be dead before the next Indy, I would have been perfectly happy just to dream that I could come back here on a cot and watch the race. But here I am driving the pace car," Shelby said with a sense of wonder in his voice. "You can imagine how thrilling this is to me."

Shelby, the working man's auto racer of the 1950s who drove in bib overalls and became a legendary designer of supercars bearing his name, was enjoying every moment of his "borrowed time." It was his second stint as pace-car driver at Indian-apolis, and to rehearse for it, the tall, white-haired Texan drove more than 1000 miles around the Brickyard in a Dodge Viper at what some passengers considered heart-stopping speeds.

Carroll Hall Shelby was one of 1700 persons in the United States who received a heart transplant last year. His remarkable road back has encouraged his surgeon to predict that Shelby will be "a long-term survivor."

At Indy, Shelby was operating at his old non-stop pace. "I can put in a good, honest eight-hour day, but I start getting tired after twelve or fourteen hours," he said.

That previous pace propelled Shelby through a storybook life. Born in the small town of Leesburg, Texas, on January 11, 1923, Shelby was the son of a rural mail carrier who liked to go fast. The elder Shelby delivered the mail in a 1928 Whippet. Young Carroll sometimes accompanied his dad, always urging him to go faster. Carroll has stayed on the fast track ever since. He has been a World War II bomber pilot, an oil-field roustabout, a chicken farmer, a big-game hunter and African safari leader, a tire distributor, and a chili tycoon.

But hardly mentioned during the last 30 years of his flamboyant life has been just how near the edge his faulty ticker had placed him, and the pain and apprehension he's lived with. He was stricken with a heart ailment at the age of seven. At 38, he cut short his racing career because of racking angina pain. The high point of Shelby's racing career came in 1959 when he became the second American (Phil Hill was the first) to win the grueling 24 Hours of Le Mans—achieved,

Shelby driving a Formula 1 Aston Martin in a vintage race at Long Beach.

unbeknownst to most, with the help of nitroglycerin tablets that were dissolving under his tongue during the race to control his chest pains. "I also won the U.S. national championship in 1960 taking nitro pills," Shelby said.

He has undergone fifteen major operations during a fifteen-year stretch to combat the ravages of heart disease and old racing injuries. Heart-bypass operations were performed in 1973 and 1978. Both of his carotid arteries had to be reamed out. (Shelby says, oddly enough, that his most painful hospital experience was the skin grafts he needed for burns after he dropped a sweet-potato pie fresh from the oven onto his foot.)

New medical technologies delayed the downward spiral of Shelby's heart disease, but they didn't stop it. Seven years ago, when he turned 63, Shelby was spending most of his days in bed. His cardiologist, Dr. Nicholas Diaco, told Shelby that if he was to continue living, he would need a new heart. His physician of 30 years, Dr. Rex Kennamer, concurred.

"I said I'm going to take a shot at this because I have a terrific desire to live," Shelby recalled. "I don't know whether that comes from owing so much money or my bankers keep me tweaked up." He also knew that transplant programs were far enough along so that he had a fairly good chance at a quality life. Shelby said emphatically, "I wouldn't want to live as an invalid."

Hearts available for transplants are scarce. Money alone can't buy one. The patient must qualify, and one of the requirements is to have sufficiently good health (the heart aside) to survive this radical surgery. "After thirty years of heart trouble, I didn't think I could pass the exams (to qualify)," Shelby said. He thinks his positive attitude helped to get him through a month-long battery of tests.

Despite his age, Shelby was accepted into the transplant program of Cedars Sinai Hospital in Los Angeles. Did his celebrity status help? Shelby doesn't think so. "I had to wait nine months for a heart and almost didn't make it." In this life-and-death line, the waiting is relieved only slightly by counseling programs. "They do a marvelous job in these transplant centers of preparing you for what life is going to be like," Shelby said. "They don't pull punches, and they don't tell you it's going to be a bed of roses."

After it was determined that Shelby was healthy enough to survive a transplant, he was issued an electronic beeper in November 1989. When a new heart was located, he would be signaled. "You have to be no more than an hour away from surgery all the time." Shelby was passed over several times in favor of patients in even worse condition than he was.

Christmas and New Year's passed, then February and March were gone. Shelby, too weak to work, spent up to 20 hours a day in bed in his Bel Air home. He was attended by a housekeeper, the Rev. Elmer Ponce, a Filipino who is also a Baptist minister. Shelby ate little and was too uncomfortable to have visitors. His lonely days were relieved only by visits from his sister, Anne Ellison, his children, and grandchildren. It seemed his beeper would forever remain silent.

By mid-May of 1990, there was considerable doubt Shelby would live long enough to see the operating room. "Finally I got down to about fourteen percent heart function," Shelby recalled. "My doctors told me I might live for only another few months." Late that month, Shelby, who was too weak to remain home any longer, was admitted to Cedars Sinai and placed on intravenous feeding. He is not a man to acknowledge or vocalize his fears, but one can imagine how he felt when two other heart-transplant candidates in nearby rooms died before hearts could be located.

"I wasn't worried about dying during the operation," he says. "Having gone through two bypass operations, I knew basically what the surgery consisted of. The odds are if you're in good shape, you're going to come through it." Shelby compares it to racing: "I never had any thought of crashing—you never start out in a race saying, 'What if I crash?' Your objective is to win the race and that's the way I approached this."

And then in June, a heart was located. The donor turned out to have something in common with Shelby: he was a gambler. While betting at a crap table in Las Vegas, the 34-year-old man suffered a cerebral hemorrhage and collapsed. He survived but never regained consciousness, and with irreversible damage, his family after nine days reluctantly made the decision to pull the plug and donate his organs.

Dr. Alfredo Trento, a veteran of 250 transplant operations, flew to Las Vegas to remove the heart himself. Knowing Shelby's history of bypass operations, Dr. Trento was careful to take enough of the connecting arteries so that he could replace Shelby's spliced vessels. Then the heart was rushed to Cedars Sinai, where the five-hour transplant operation went without a hitch.

But all was far from well when Shelby emerged from anesthesia. "I had pneumonia and my temperature was 104 degrees." He regards the critical hours following the transplant more as a success of the black arts than a triumph of medical science. Immunologists mixed up a batch of antibiotics that cured the pneumonia in just three hours. "That to me is a bigger miracle than the fact that they can transplant an organ now," Shelby said.

Thousands of cards poured in and Cedars Sinai's switchboard was flooded with calls, but only his daughter, Sharon Lavine, and sons Michael and Patrick were allowed to visit. The irrepressible Shelby had smuggled in a cellular phone to reassure a few associates, and he was using it the next day.

Just four weeks later, Shelby visited his vacation house at Lake Tahoe in the oxygen-thin High Sierra. In the twenty-five years he's owned the place, Shelby says he had never been able to climb the 67 steps from his boat house to the main house without stopping at least three times because of chest pains. "A month after the transplant operation, I walked up the steps *ten times*—I practically ran up, without getting angina pains." Shelby smiles at the memory. "It was the most exhilarating thing that's happened to me since the operation."

Some months after the operation, I sat with Shelby on the deck of his Bel Air home, high on a hill overlooking smoggy Los Angeles. He wore golf slacks and a polo shirt with the crest of the Bel Air Country Club, and there was a large ring on one of his fingers, a memento of having driven the pace car at the 1987 Indy 500. His face was tanned and he appeared remarkably relaxed as he sipped a glass of ice water while recounting the ordeal he has been through. His comments were matter-of-fact and almost entirely technical. He described his transplant as though he were talking about swapping a blown engine in a race car.

Shelby says he doesn't dwell on the transplant, nor does he feel as if there were a time bomb inside his chest waiting to explode. "I live from hour to hour, but I feel so lucky to be here and feeling as good as I am." He is, however, quick to acknowledge the fragile nature of his life. "I know I could drop dead at any minute, or I could reject within a couple of days," he says. "But I don't worry about that. I'm not going to worry about anything else for the rest of my life."

*Reunion at Palm Springs with
Phil Hill, Bob Bondurant,
Dan Gurney, Roy Salvadori, and
the late John Wyer.*

Dr. Trento, a graduate of the University of Padua in Italy who has been transplanting hearts for nearly a decade, says Shelby is highly motivated and that has made his recovery go faster. The surgeon says the longest heart transplant survivor lived for 19 years, only to be killed in a car accident. He won't predict how long Shelby will live, but he feels his patient can have a normal life with no restrictions except those imposed by age. Dr. Trento noted that Shelby is less subject to infections now, even though the old racer still takes cyclosporin, a strong drug that suppresses the immune system. "You learn how to protect yourself from common colds and infections," Shelby says.

Shelby walks on a treadmill daily for an hour. His only restriction is to keep his pulse rate below 120 beats a minute, which doesn't provide much latitude since his new heart, at rest, pumps 95 to 100 beats a minute, normal for persons with transplants. The reason for this is that the vagus nerve and other connecting nerves that control heart rhythms are severed when the donor organ is removed. The nerves cannot be reconnected. Thus, the heart beats by itself without any nerve controls. The good news is that those severed nerves are the reason Shelby can eat his own chili—the nerves used to send heartburn signals, but without them, he now can eat anything he wants.

After more than a year, biopsies conducted every two months on his new heart revealed no signs of rejection. The same technique used in angiograms is em-

ployed; doctors pinch little pieces from different locations on the heart and then analyze them for signs of rejection.

Shelby feels racing and car building have taken up too much of his life, and he has distanced himself from the ten businesses he owns. His main enterprises are a Goodyear racing-tire distributorship and Shelby Autos, the firm that built the original Cobra sports cars and modified sports cars for Ford and Chrysler. He leaves most of the daily administrative chores to longtime associates now, frequently escaping for holidays in Mexico with his grandchildren.

Shelby ventured into auto building in 1960 because he had a dream concept for a new kind of sports car. "I knew I wouldn't last very long as a driver because of my heart trouble," he says, "so I started making plans to build my own car." His idea wasn't unique: mate a powerful American V-8 engine with a lightweight European sports-car chassis. Such a car wouldn't weigh much more with an American V-8 because the European four-cylinder engines, originally designed for taxis and buses, were long and heavy. "A lot of people had the same idea," Shelby admits. "I just happened to get lucky."

About 1000 Cobras were assembled between '62 and '67. They sold at prices from $5900 to about $8000. Ironically, in light of current Cobra prices, it was the "stiff" stickers that eventually forced Shelby to shut down.

The men who made his luck were a pair of young Ford executives. Lee Iacocca, then Ford's sales manager, believed any success Shelby might have would rub off on Ford and boost his company's sales. Don Frey, then a deputy to Iacocca who went on to become chairman of Bell & Howell and a teacher at Northwestern University, persuaded Ford to back the ex-racer.

Later, Iacocca asked Shelby to do a sporty version of the Ford Mustang. "I didn't really want to do it," Shelby confesses, "because I didn't think I could make a decent car out of the Mustang." At Iacocca's urging, Shelby did some major reengineering—turning the Mustang into a taut-handling two-seater. The original GT350 that was equipped with the engine from the 289 Cobra was soon joined by big-block GT500s and convertible models. Some 14,000 Shelby Mustangs were built from '65 to '70. Prices for them today run in the $50,000 neighborhood.

Shelby says by the time his work on the Mustang ended in 1969, his heart trouble was getting worse. Shelby was keenly aware that both his parents died at early ages from heart disease. It convinced Shelby he needed to escape from business life and do what he really wanted to do with his remaining years.

But he would be enticed once more to return to the auto business when Iacocca became Chrysler's chairman. Iacocca believed that Chrysler, then near bankruptcy, could benefit from some of the Shelby magic. In all, Shelby modified six models and a pickup for Chrysler, building about 6000 vehicles.

Shelby's clear-cut favorite: the 1986 Omni GLHS. "It's fun to make a mule that'll outrun a race horse," Shelby says of the small turbocharged four-cylinder-powered $10,000 car. The GLHS represents Shelby's ideal—performance that's available to working-class people.

These days, Carroll Shelby is enjoying his new heart. "I want to do things that I haven't been able to do for thirty years physically," he says wistfully. And to underscore the point: "I've got to do them quickly or I'm going to be too darn old and suffer the other infirmities that will be setting in on me."

Shelby has always been full of surprises, and he pulled another one in August 1991, when he went to the wedding altar for the fourth time. His new wife is Lena Dahl, whom Shelby met in 1967 when she was only 18. The new Mrs. Shelby is a former Los Angeles Realtor and the mother of two teen-agers.

Shelby also raises money for organ-transplant programs and spreads the word that more donor organs are vitally needed to help all the people who are in dire need. "Half the people who are approved for new hearts never get them. Yet there are 25 times that number of cadavers buried with good organs," he adds. "There's no reason for any person in need not to get a new heart. You can give years of life by donating your organs," Shelby urges.

What would Carroll Shelby like to be remembered for?

"I don't care if I'm remembered or not," he says bluntly, adding that "fame is so fleeting that I'm not going to be remembered for anything—not for very long."

Shelby prefers to focus on the years remaining in his life. And work is one of the lowest of his priorities. "I don't want to be like Roger Penske (a close friend), who is the only man I know who's made $300 million working at minimum wage," Shelby says with a laugh. "I want to get well enough to travel where I want to go, instead of where I've had to travel. I never want to completely retire. I want to have something that keeps my interest. I want to have a reason for getting up in the morning. I don't want to ever say, 'What the hell am I going to do today?' "

Drivers Salvadori and Shelby with Wyer's Aston Martin DBR 1/300 that won Le Mans in 1959.

NO BASKET FOR THIS COBRA

By Rich Ceppos

Some time ago, we complained that Cobras have become so ridiculously valuable that they're now all "sealed in plastic and locked away in bank vaults."

A reader and Cobra owner, David Felstein of Terre Haute, wrote in to disassociate himself from those enthusiasts cloaked in investors' wool who rarely, if ever, drive their nest eggs. He put his mouth where his money is: "You can test mine any time you want." We happily accepted and inquired when we might expect to see his Cobra arrive all tarped-down on a flatbed trailer.

Naw, Felstein said, he'd just drive it up. What's 350 miles? What's money? Our kind of guy.

If you're familiar with Murphy's Law, you know what happened next. On the day he headed toward us, the sort of amusing Midwestern weather depicted in *The Wizard of Oz*—outrageously violent and simultaneous episodes of thunder, lightning, wind, and torrential rain—fell upon Felstein and his co-pilot, Hugh Crawford, as they neared Michigan.

This was especially bad because the top to Felstein's Cobra was leaky. Which is why he left the top at home.

And then the tornado touched down.

Now, picture a highway overpass, barely visible because the winds are whipping the wall of rain in unnatural directions, like a carwash whose powerful spray spigots have gone berserk, and parked there under that overpass—visible in flashes of lightning—are Felstein and Crawford, clutching a sheet of clear plastic around themselves, mummy-fashion, hunkered down in the quarter-million-dollar Cobra. But all Felstein was worried about was arriving late. "Hugh," he said, "looks like we're gonna miss dinner." Our kind of guy.

Later, about midnight, when it was finally still, like after a war, we heard the bellow of his Cobra rolling up our small-town Michigan street.

"Sorry we're late," said Felstein, who was apparently still alive. Peeling off his parka and tossing it into the drenched cockpit, he added, "We were held up by storms."

The Cobra's blood-red paint was streaked with mud. "See, I told you I drive it," Felstein said. "If I'd wanted a flowerpot, I'd have bought a flowerpot. I wanted a *car*, and cars are meant to be driven."

David Felstein's Cobra (serial-number CSX2229) was the 229th Cobra built. It was the original-recipe version, powered by the Ford 289-cubic-inch V-8. Cobra buffs refer to the early models as "small-block" or "leaf-spring" cars, distinguishing them from the more sought-after big-block 427-cubic-inch version, which rides on a much-modified coil-spring suspension. According to the Shelby American Automobile Club owner registry, the Cobra collectors' bible, just 1002 Cobras were assembled between start-up in early 1962 and the end of production in 1967. This includes all prototypes, European versions, and about 80 competition models. About 950 of them remain accounted for today.

About two-thirds of the Cobras are leaf-spring cars like Felstein's. Restored to like-new condition, a leaf-spring Cobra will fetch about $225,000. The rarer 427, with a thundering big-block V-8 under its hood, will punch a $400,000 hole in your investment portfolio. This is why most Cobras are sealed in plastic, and their owners reluctant to drive them in tornadoes.

But not Felstein. "I think mine might be the most-driven Cobra in the country," he said the next morning as he hand-washed the red car—using only clean towels and clear water. He spoke in a breezy drawl, more Southern than Midwestern. "I drive it maybe 5000 miles a year. I've driven it to every Shelby American convention that I've gone to—North Carolina, Pennsylvania, Charlotte, and three times to Detroit. I don't know how many miles it has on it —these things break speedometer cables all the time."

Felstein, 43, runs a chain of jewelry stores in Terre Haute, and he likes to play with his toys. He's a member of "Torque and Recoil," a group of spirited Terre Haute citizens who like to shoot machine guns and drive loud, fast cars. Torque and Recoil, you may recall, entered our *Save the Trabant!* contest in 1991 with a suggestion to use the Trabant for target practice during the group's annual machine-gun shoot.

Felstein put down his rag and recited the club's credo: "If it rolls, floats, flies, or shoots, runs on gasoline or gunpowder, goes fast, shoots a big bullet, and makes lots of noise, thus producing torque and recoil—it's cool. But if it's a ball, made out of leather or inflated with air, that's hit with a bat, racquet, or club, used in a game played on a course, green, or court by yuppies, Democrats, or liberals— *[bleep]* it."

Cobra owners fall neatly into two groups: those who covet leaf-spring cars and those who worship big-blocks. "I'm a small-block guy," Felstein said, dabbing his car's chrome wire wheels. "For me, the leaf-spring cars are Bo Dereks, the 427s are Dolly Partons. Besides, the entire Shelby American legend—the 'Hey Little Cobra' song, the Daytona Coupes, the FIA World Championship driven by Gurney and Bondurant—the whole shebang was done with small-block Cobras."

He has a point. Back in 1961, Cobra creator Carroll Shelby was a prematurely retired 38-year-old race driver attempting to invent a future for himself. Shelby had raced high-powered sports cars successfully in the United States and Europe, and in 1959 he won the 24 Hours of Le Mans in an Aston Martin.

He was on the way to becoming an American equivalent of Enzo Ferrari, building his own sports cars and racing them. "All I wanted to do," Shelby says, "was to go racing and have something to compete against the Corvettes with. I did expect the Cobra to be somewhat streetable—I didn't want to build something you couldn't register. But I thought, 'Hell, if I could sell 200 of these turkeys, that's all I'd ever build.'"

He eventually built five times that number of Cobras. However, very little of the car was truly of Shelby's creation. The Cobra was a marriage of a Ford V-8 engine and a British sports car, the AC Ace. Shelby cut a deal with AC Cars, Ltd., to supply modified versions of the Ace that would accept Ford's then-new, lightweight, 260-cubic-inch V-8. (The enlarged 289 version of that engine went in after the first 75 cars were built.) After the cars were shipped here, Shelby American installed the engine, the transmission, and some running gear.

The original-recipe version of the Cobra was powered by the Ford 289-cubic-inch V-8 engine. Its sound is illegal today.

The Ace had been around since 1954, and it was what Shelby was looking for. It was quite light—about 2200 pounds—thanks to a tube-frame chassis and aluminum bodywork. It was equipped with a fully independent suspension and disc brakes. And, most important, AC was happy to adapt its car to Shelby's specifications.

The first AC Cobra—sans engine—was delivered to Shelby American's California shop in February 1962. Soon it was stuffed full of American V-8 horsepower. That spring, car magazines raved about its sensational straight-line performance. The second Cobra was converted into a competition version for racing on the Sports Car Club of America circuit.

Shelby's timing was perfect. Ford was embarking on an ambitious international motorsports campaign that would see it win the Indianapolis 500 in 1965 and Le Mans the next year. Ford decided that Shelby was just the guy to lead an attack on the sports-car front, with factory support.

In its first race, at Riverside in the fall of 1962, the Cobra roadster was in the lead when it broke. By mid-1963, most of the mechanical gremlins had been exorcised, thanks to Shelby's competition director, British racing ace Ken Miles. The Cobra went on to win the SCCA's U.S. Road Racing Championship that year and again in '64. Meanwhile, Shelby was pursuing the FIA World Manufacturer's Championship for Grand Touring cars in Europe.

For the '64 season in Europe, an aerodynamic coupe body was fitted to the 289 roadster chassis—a legal modification under the rules—that gave the Cobra enough speed to duel with Ferrari's GTOs on the fast European tracks. The coupes helped Shelby finish second in the 1964 manufacturers' championship. That result prompted the cocky Texan to promise Enzo Ferrari: "Next year, yur ol' ass is mine!"

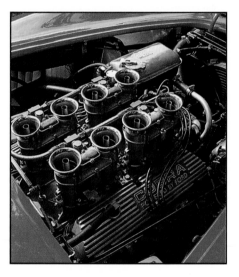

Backing it up in spades, the six Daytona Coupes (no more than four of which appeared in each race) won the European crown in '65. Shelby had planned to accomplish that feat with a new 427-cubic-inch model, but delays in production kept it from being certified by the FIA for the '65 racing season. A few 427s were eventually raced, but with little success.

It was the street performance of the 427 Cobra that catapulted it to stardom. For the time, it had enormous horsepower—485 hp (SAE gross). The 427 we tested in our November 1965 issue tore through the quarter-mile in 12.2 seconds at 118 mph. Twenty-six years later, the Ferrari F40 we got all weak-kneed over in the February 1991 issue of *Car and Driver* was only a tenth of a second quicker.

Way back then, we pointed out that the 427 Cobra was the quickest car in the world from 0-to-100 mph and back to 0. The Cobra we tested back in '65 managed that feat in just 14.5 seconds. Today's more accurate, computerized test gear would probably reveal that number as optimistic—but not by much.

Horsepower aside, the 427 Cobra

You sit low enough in the cockpit to hang an arm over the side and scrape your knuckles on the ground. An original Cobra emblem graces the hood of the real thing.

looked like a sex goddess (and most were plump in those days) who had taken out a membership at a gym. Shelby American hadn't simply dropped the big motor into the 289 roadster; the whole car was redesigned to improve its track performance (remember, the 427 was originally planned to carry the Cobra colors in racing). The 427 model ended up five inches wider and was outfitted with the latest unequal-length control-arm suspension and voluptuously swollen fenders that provided room for larger tires. It was a traffic stopper, which is why virtually every maker of Cobra replicas has chosen to duplicate the 427 body.

Still, when a Cobra—any Cobra—rolls into your life, it is reason enough to begin breathing heavily. Whether it's a 289 or a 427, it is a magnificent piece of sculpture. Felstein's 289 is as tight-waisted as a Miss America contestant and as slinky as a Vegas showgirl; the tops of its front fenders rise only to mid-thigh. The shape is from another era, but its purpose reaches across the decades to hit you in the solar plexus.

Felstein's Cobra has been thoroughly restored over the years. He purchased it in '81 for $38,000, and has rebuilt the engine, restored the bodywork, and reupholstered the interior. He's also added several factory options that weren't on the car when it was shipped to Jack Thrasher Ford in Terre Haute in January 1964. (It was blue when Felstein sat inside it in the showroom.)

The modifications—all of them available through Shelby American at one time or another—include a roll bar for the cockpit, front and rear anti-roll bars for the suspension, and a host of pieces for the engine: a Shelby "Le Mans" profile high-performance camshaft, a set of four two-barrel Weber carbs, and a pair of competition headers and side pipes, reworked with small internal mufflers and chromed for use on the street ("I did that for the noise," he says).

Felstein held out the keys and motioned to the driver's seat. The engine fired up like a stick of dynamite. Its sound is illegal today. The Ford V-8 and the Borg-Warner four-speed gearbox leave little space in the chassis for the occupants' feet. The transmission tunnel is so wide it forces the pedals far to the left; the throttle is about where you'd normally expect the brake pedal to be, and there's no comfortable resting place for your left foot.

The cockpit is intimate, tight at the hips and snug through the shoulders. The bodywork seeps under the windshield to form the top of the dash, then sweeps down into low-cut doors. The dash is a simple flat-faced panel. The stubby shifter is a seedling-sized version of what Ford used in its production cars at the time.

Driving the Cobra is a sensory delight. You sit low enough to hang an arm over the side and scrape your knuckles on the ground. You can lean out and see the front and rear wheels going up and down over the bumps. The exhaust note is pealing thunder. You sit upright behind a delicate windshield and the wind buffets you.

The view is spectacular. In many of today's sports cars, the windshield sweeps back so far that you feel hemmed in even when the top is down. In a Cobra you are *out there*—to the point of feeling vulnerable and just a little dangerous.

Cobras are supposed to be mean, nasty, and temperamental, but Felstein's is as cooperative as an altar boy. It shifts with two fingers, the clutch effort is manageable, and the manual steering only got stiff and

ornery when we tried to push hard in the corners, as if it were saying, "Hey, sucker, back off. I'm 26 years old." The ride was firm but far from teeth-rattling, and the Cobra was happy cruising down the highway at 75 or 80.

Just don't go out in this car if you want privacy. Every cruise is an event, and you are the celebrity-of-the-moment every mile of the way. "Oh, you look like you're in Europe," gushed a lady in a Honda as we sat at a stop sign. Exclaimed another passer-by, "Oh, it's so beautiful." We eased past a schoolyard, and the kids came running and waving. We even avoided a sure speeding ticket one night when a trooper suddenly appeared behind us (the Cobra's small mirror is nearly useless). We were doing 80, but all he did was pull alongside and give us a long look before accelerating into the darkness.

But is it fast? Is it mean? Is it temperamental? Well, this writer's pulse rate shot up every time the throttle went down. Driving CSX2229 was like being on a motorcycle powered by a loud V-8 engine. The wind whipped my skin, the pavement blurred, the exhaust barked like a Thompson submachine gun. The sound alone was worth the price of admission. There was plenty of torque and plenty of recoil, and it was all thoroughly exciting.

But the clocks indicated that Felstein's Cobra was probably ill—proving only that a sick Cobra is still bloody fast. It went 0 to 60 in just 5.8 seconds and performed the quarter-mile in 14.4 seconds at 96 mph. Given all of the high-performance equipment lashed onto the engine, however, we had expected more. The numbers we saw are most likely representative of what a dead-stock 289 could do in its day.

Our top-speed run was the giveaway. The engine peaked at only 6100 rpm and 117 mph; it should have reached 7000 rpm and about 135 mph. As if to confirm our suspicions, it swallowed a valve only a few miles after our test was concluded. This did not even perturb Felstein. "It's all part of the adventure," he said.

Still, our trip around the Chrysler proving grounds' high-speed oval in search of Mr. Top Speed should finally lay to rest the endless rumors and rampant speculation that AC Cobras—at least the leaf-spring variety—could attain astronomical velocities. Felstein's car was equipped with the stock 3.77:1 final-drive ratio, low enough to limit even a good-running 289 Cobra to less than 140 mph.

Vehicle type: front-engine, rear-wheel-drive, 2-passenger, 2-door roadster

Price as tested: $7000 (1964)

Options on test car: chrome wire wheels, wind wings, front and rear anti-roll bars, road-race oil pan, Weber carburetors, sun visors, Le Mans camshaft

Sound system: tube headers and side pipes

ENGINE
Type	V-8, iron block and heads
Bore x stroke	4.00 x 2.87 in, 101.6 x 72.9mm
Displacement	289 cu in, 4728cc
Compression ratio	10.5:1
Carburetion	4x2-bbl Weber 48IDA
Emissions controls	none
Valve gear	pushrods, solid lifters
Power (on a good day)	350 bhp @ 6500 rpm
Torque (on a good day)	330 lb-ft @ 5000 rpm

DRIVETRAIN
Transmission	4-speed
Final-drive ratio	3.77:1, limited slip

Gear	Ratio	Mph/1000 rpm	Max. test speed
I	2.36	8.2	53 mph (6500 rpm)
II	1.61	12.0	78 mph (6500 rpm)
III	1.20	16.1	104 mph (6500 rpm)
IV	1.00	19.3	117 mph (6100 rpm)

DIMENSIONS AND CAPACITIES
Wheelbase	90.0 in
Track, F/R	50.0/51.0 in
Length	153.0 in
Width	61.0 in
Height	48.0 in
Ground clearance	5.3 in
Curb weight	2266 lb
Weight distribution, F/R	49.2/50.8%
Fuel capacity	18.0 gal
Oil capacity	7.0 qt

CHASSIS/BODY
Type	tubular steel ladder frame
Body material	sheet and hand-beaten aluminum panels riveted to a lightweight steel tubular frame

SUSPENSION
F	ind, equal-length control arms integral with a transverse leaf spring, anti roll bar
R	ind, equal-length control arms integral with a transverse leaf spring, anti-roll bar

STEERING
Type	rack-and-pinion
Turns lock-to-lock	2.9
Turning circle curb-to-curb	33.3 ft

BRAKES
F	11.7 x 0.5-in disc
R	10.8 x 0.5-in disc
Power assist	none

WHEELS AND TIRES
Wheel size	6.0 x 15 in
Wheel type	Dunlop center-lock wire spoke
Tires	Yokohama A008, 215/60VR-15
Test inflation pressures, F/R	32/32 psi

CAR AND DRIVER TEST RESULTS

ACCELERATION
	Seconds
Zero to 30 mph	2.0
40 mph	3.1
50 mph	4.2
60 mph	5.8
70 mph	7.7
80 mph	9.7
90 mph	12.5
100 mph	16.3
Top-gear passing time, 30–50 mph	5.0
50–70 mph	3.8

Standing ¼-mile .... 14.4 sec @ 96 mph
Top speed .... 117 mph

BRAKING
70–0 mph @ impending lockup .... 196 ft
Modulation .... poor fair **good** excellent
Fade .... **none** moderate heavy
Front-rear balance .... poor **fair** good

HANDLING
Roadholding, 295-ft-dia skidpad .... 0.85 g
Understeer .... minimal **moderate** excessive

That's all the bubble-bursting we care to do. As far as we're concerned, nothing we learned during this outing gives us reason to chip any more granite off the Cobra legend. Twenty-eight years after it first hit the street, the 289 Cobra is still a very intense, exhilarating experience. And there's nothing wrong with that.

SHELBY CRIES, 'COUNTERFEIT!'

Carroll Shelby isn't perturbed that the car he built to sell for $7000 now goes for a half-million bucks.

"But it does bother me to see people selling Cobras that are made out of junk parts," he says. "They take this kind of brakes and that kind of suspension and then they take a fiberglass mold off the body and counterfeit the cars and call them Cobras."

Ford, which bought the Cobra name for a buck, did nothing to protect the Cobra trademark. This one's a replica.

PHOTO BY DON JOHNSTON

Shelby takes a dim view of Cobra knockoffs or replicars. "These people (makers of replicars) are trying to make a living out of things that drivers like Ken Miles gave their lives for," Shelby said recently. "It's not fair to his memory." Miles was a Shelby driver who collaborated on the development of the Cobra. He was killed testing a Ford GT at Riverside in 1966.

Shelby scoffs at claims that any of the knockoffs are made from original tooling, including those made by the current AC company. "If they're using original tooling, they're using our tooling," Shelby says. He concedes that AC might have "a little of the old tooling," but Shelby insists that the company does not make an authentic Cobra replica. "We just bought some parts from AC," Shelby adds.

Shelby sold the Cobra name to Ford in 1964 for one dollar. But Ford, he says, has never done anything to protect the trademark. That's why knockoffs are able to use the Cobra name.

There is hope, however, for a few more persons who lust after genuine Cobras. Shelby is toying with the notion of reconstructing as many as 43 partially assembled 427 competition models he's had kicking around since 1965. As Shelby tells it, "That's because we caught Mr. Ferrari lying on the number of 250LMs he had built (for homologation purposes)." The FIA required 100 completed examples for the car to be classified in the GT class, but when the FIA counted them, they found less than 60 completed 250LMs. The new 427 SC was Shelby's intended response to the LM, but the FIA found only 51 completed at the time of its inspection. Consequently, both Shelby and Ferrari used their 1964 cars in the 1965 GT season.

Although the records suggest that most of those originally uncompleted 427 SCs were ultimately completed as racing or street 427s, Shelby claims that he still has most of the original chassis and plans to refurbish them, using all original parts as necessary. What's more, Ford is planning to make new 427 side-oiler engines available soon. —*Herb Shuldiner*

A DEATH IN MODENA

By Brock Yates

The following is an excerpt from Enzo Ferrari: The Man, the Cars, the Races, *by Brock Yates.*

A bit of background: By the mid-1950s, Enzo Ferrari had become Italy's preeminent builder of exotic cars and championship racing machines. He had survived a mediocre career as a driver, had learned his trade with Alfa Romeo in the 1930s, had prospered during the war in the machine-tool business, and had hired brilliant engineers like Gioachino Colombo and Aurelio Lampredi in the late 1940s to create magnificent V-12 engines that were to become the heart and soul of his business. But it was Lampredi's little four-cylinder 500 that had carried Alberto Ascari to the World Championship in 1952 and '53 and had elevated Ferrari to "Grand Constructor" status.

Then came two disastrous years when his team was humiliated by the likes of Mercedes-Benz and Jaguar. He received a respite in 1956 with the acquisition— pennies from heaven—of the magnificent Lancia D50 Grand Prix cars and the hiring of Juan Manuel Fangio, who was to team with talented young Peter Collins and Eugenio Castellotti. The result was the Scuderia's third World Driving Championship.

But life was hardly tranquil for the man deferentially called "Commendatore." His marriage to Laura Garello Ferrari was a domestic battlefield, and he had the added responsibility of his mistress, Lina Lardi, and his eleven-year-old illegitimate son, Piero. Worse yet, Dino, his only legitimate son and heir to the empire, was mortally ill . . .

In June 1956, a drama was unfolding at the little apartment above the Scuderia Ferrari, on the edge of steamy, mosquito-cursed Modena. Alfredo "Dino" Ferrari, Enzo's 24-year-old son, lay on his deathbed. During the last weeks of the month, mechanics in the Scuderia workshop witnessed a new Ferrari, face contorted with grief, sobbing openly as he descended the steps from the apartment.

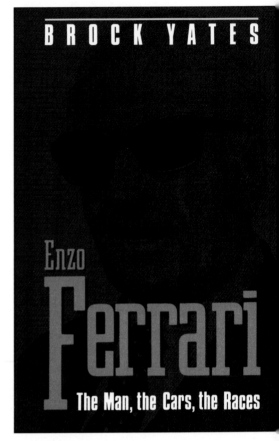

The end came on June 30, 1956, when the pleasant young man's kidneys failed and he slipped away. His father and mother were sick with grief. Romolo Tavoni, his close assistant, was with Ferrari the following afternoon when Eraldo Sculati, the team manager, called from Rheims to announce that Peter Collins had won the French Grand Prix. Tavoni attempted to hand the telephone to Ferrari, who tearfully waved it off, claiming that his interest in racing cars was forever dead.

A funeral cortege, numbering perhaps a thousand mourners, formed up outside the old Scuderia building on the Viale Trento e Trieste and snaked its way to the cemetery at San Cataldo. Ferrari, standing tall and proud, was in the vanguard, as was a thoroughly shaken, black-shrouded Laura Garello Ferrari, Dino's mother and Enzo's wife of 33 years. Chugging along in the midst of the marchers was a tiny Fiat sedan carrying Ferrari's mother Adalgisa, in her mid-eighties and unable to make the long trek in the drenching humidity.

What followed was a dirge of grief and posthumous glorification of Dino that bordered on the bestowal of secular sainthood. A massive Romanesque marble tomb was constructed in the cemetery at San Cataldo, financed in part with city of Modena funds, to serve as the family crypt. The remains of Dino and his grandfather were laid there, and places were reserved for Enzo, his mother and Laura as well.

The illness that killed Dino was to have a supreme influence on Ferrari and trigger a controversy that was to dog him to his grave. The exact nature of the sickness remains a mystery, and is the subject of lingering rumors.

Various biographers have claimed the illness to have been leukemia, multiple sclerosis, nephritis, and muscular dystrophy. The latter is most commonly mentioned, and Ferrari himself spoke of the "dystrophy" that afflicted both his son and his wife. He also said that a "nephritis virus" killed the boy, although no such ailment exists in medical annals. But the unspoken—the unspeakable—disease that may have finally brought down the likable young man, according to insiders, was the dreaded syphilis.

The story, which is entirely circumstantial yet so pervasive that it must be mentioned, goes like this: before she married Enzo in 1923, Laura Ferrari was reputed to be a *puttana* (prostitute), who transmitted the disease to the boy through her womb. Therefore it was not love but "guilt" that caused Ferrari to venerate his son, according to one senior member of his staff who worked at Maranello for twenty years. This story is endlessly repeated and confirmed by those who knew Enzo Ferrari best, although none wish to be quoted publicly. One man, whose acquaintanceship with Ferrari dated back to the 1930s, insists the story is true and that Laura had been a prostitute.

On the other side there are those, including longtime Ferrari associate, importer and sometime rival Luigi Chinetti, who claim that Laura Garello Ferrari was a decent, much-maligned lady who came from a family of small landowners south of Turin. Some credit her with helping finance the Maranello factory (probably untrue), a beneficence unlikely from a former streetwalker. Moreover, the comments of medical experts at the Cleveland Clinic and at Harvard University indicate that it is "extremely unlikely" that Dino died of syphilis and that the evidence is at best "circumstantial." Their reasoning: Among babies who contract the disease in the mother's womb, about 80 percent die within the first year of life. After that the death rate falls as time passes and it reaches a point where, after five years, mortality is only 10 percent. During the 1930s, when Dino was a child, the disease could often be cured by the administration of poisons like arsenic, bismuth and iodine. After the antibiotic drug penicillin came into widespread use after World War II, the cure rate for syphilis soared to nearly 100 percent, making it extremely unlikely that the boy would have died in the mid-1950s while under the care of what must be assumed to have been the best physicians available in Modena.

A major symptom of syphilis is neurological deterioration in the final or tertiary stage. Insanity, blindness and deafness are common symptoms that herald the end, but people who knew Dino in the final years of his life recall him as a cheerful young man who was perfectly normal except for being extremely thin and generally fatigued and having severe stiffness in his limbs. "Dino was a good guy, always smiling," recalls Carroll Shelby. "But his old man never spent any time with him and the kid didn't have much to do. I spent a lot of time with him in 1955, and the kid was left on his own. He just hung around the Scuderia, and the old man's claims that the kid did a lot of engineering is bullshit. But he was a helluva nice guy. He spoke good English. Aside from having trouble walking, he seemed normal."

If Dino was afflicted with muscular dystrophy, of which there are several types, it was probably the most common or Duchenne variety, which exclusively afflicts males aged three to ten and generally causes death in the late teens or early twenties. However, the final years of life usually bring complete debilitation, and it seems unlikely that Dino could have remained ambulatory—albeit with difficulty—up to the final months of his life if he had this disease.

It is known that Ferrari contributed generously to various muscular dystrophy causes following Dino's death, and one prominent American television producer and avid Ferrari collector recalls that he gained Ferrari's friendship only after he revealed that he had made a sympathetic documentary on the disease.

Yet Ferrari's explanation of the treatment of Dino's sickness only muddies the

Ferrari wrote to a friend, "After having lost my son, I did not have anything of greater value to give up."

waters. In *My Terrible Joys,* his first of several memoirs, Ferrari wrote: "I had deluded myself—a father always deludes himself—that we should be able to restore Dino to health. I was convinced that he was like one of my cars, one of my motors, and I had drawn up a table showing the calories of all the foodstuffs he could eat without detrimental effect on his kidneys, and so that I might keep watch on the trend of his illness, I daily brought up to date a graph indicating the degrees of albuminuria, the urinary specific gravity, the degree of atozemia, the diuresis, and so on."

According to medical experts, this chronicle is clearly related to kidney failure. Nephritis is, of course, a family of diseases involving inflammation of the kidneys, which can often be fatal. On the basis of Ferrari's personal recollections there can be little question that Dino finally died of kidney failure. But was it related to, or caused by, muscular dystrophy? That appears highly unlikely, according to medical experts. Was the nephritis related to syphilis? It is a possibility, but extremely rare. A plethora of questions remain: Could Dino have been cured by arsenic treatment in his youth which did fatal damage to his kidneys? Was the disease diagnosed too late and the treatment botched? Was he suffering from both muscular dystrophy and syphilis in the early stages of his life? Was his mother a proper middle-class woman or a *puttana?* Some in Modena close to the family claim that during the early 1920s Laura spent time in a private hospital for prostitutes in Turin, where she was administered the

cure for the disease, but no firm evidence exists.

Dino's death—whatever the cause—marked a pivotal change in Ferrari's life. From that point on he became more reclusive, more embittered, more cynical, more stoic about the other broken bodies that suddenly seemed to belittle his daily existence. If it was true that syphilis somehow played a part in the boy's early demise, then there is an obvious cause and effect. But if it was a purely vicious rumor, there can be little question that Ferrari—who was privy to every whisper of gossip—knew of the slander. This too could have prompted the man to shut himself off from the swirl of intrigues and politics that surrounded him.

For decades Ferrari would visit his son's grave as part of his morning routine, which, like clockwork, included a stop at the barbershop and a short session with his aging mother. All V-6 engines and the cars that carried them would be labeled "Dinos." The young man would be credited with creating the V-6 Formula 1 engine, but there is little doubt the basic engineering was done by such eminent engineers as Vittorio Jano and Aurelio Lampredi, among others. Ferrari's stark workplace at Maranello became more shrine than office, with a brooding picture of Dino facing his desk and acting as the cloying centerpiece of the room. For years he was to wear a black tie as a memorial to his only legitimate son and was to confer a number of awards and scholarships in his name and to donate substantial sums to various muscular-dystrophy causes (regardless of the actual illness that afflicted the young man).

Later that year the little trade school that had been started in the Abetone road stable was expanded into a formal technical school associated with the Corni Technical Institute under the auspices of the Italian Ministry of Education. Ferrari wanted the school named for his dead son, and due to his efforts it would be formally transformed into the Istituto Professionale Statale Alfredo Ferrari.

When Dino died, his father was 58 years old. Thanks to the aid of Fiat and Lancia and the largesse of numerous rich customers around the world, he was beginning to enjoy legitimate prosperity. He and Laura had, after years of a truly difficult marriage, operated at arm's length, linked only by a mutual interest in the business. But a kind of "entente cordiale" had been established, and they were accumulating real estate in Modena and environs and plans were afoot to expand the factory, which had produced 81 cars that year, and to convert the small stable across the road into a restaurant and a small inn. It was to be called the Cavallino —a hostelry that was to become almost as famous as the factory itself. But the loss of Dino overrode all else for a time. Ferrari repeatedly threatened to quit racing during the summer of 1956, and even those who had witnessed such theatrics before were inclined to believe him.

As is the case with many Italians, Ferrari wallowed in mourning with an intensity far greater than the attention he had given the boy in life. Death often brings the illusion of perfection, and so it was with Dino. His flaws were erased and the young man enjoyed the luxury of never having to again displease or disappoint his father. Ferrari, quite simply, could create a new and perfect Dino. His grief, prodigious as it was, evoked a measure of cynicism among those who knew him well. It was so protracted, so maudlin, so operatic, that associates began to question its motives. One former Ferrari engineer attributed Ferrari's grief to guilt. "The disease. He was guilty about the disease," he said. "Guilt was the source of Enzo Ferrari's mourning for his son."

With Dino gone but hardly forgotten, Ferrari still had a son to contend with. Piero had just turned eleven and was still living with his mother in Castelvetro. It is not known whether the two boys ever met or whether Dino even knew of his half-brother's existence, but there is no question that at some point in the late 1950s Laura Ferrari discovered her husband's second life. Her reaction could hardly be described as tranquil. She was clearly the loser. With her only son dead, Ferrari himself had seemingly hedged his bets by siring a second offspring—a substitute heir, as it were—who remained concealed to all but a few of Ferrari's closest associates.

Then death struck the family again, albeit obliquely, a little more than a month after Dino's death. Factory test driver Sergio Sighinolfi, who had been one of the pallbearers at the funeral, had been grief-stricken by the loss of his friend. The two young men had become extremely close as Dino's health had declined, and the hours spent with Sighinolfi had become increasingly pleasant diversions for Dino. Then came the news on August 9 that Sergio had lost control of the Ferrari he was

His marriage to Laura Garello was a domestic battlefield. And there was the question of her past.

testing in the Apennine hills and had been killed.

Enzo Ferrari was deeply affected by the loss. The young man's closeness to his son had transcended his simple employee's status. While Ferrari seldom blinked over the death of one of his drivers, he went to special lengths to comfort Sighinolfi's family. Money, the exact amount of which is unknown, was donated by Ferrari to help alleviate the suffering. This was a rare, if not unprecedented, act of generosity on his part.

This was a period of enormous tension for Ferrari, which only intensified his lament for the fallen Dino. He wrote to his friend Gino Rancati two weeks after the funeral, "In thinking deeply about the competition season I had decided to leave to others the task of defending the prestige of Italian automotive creation in other countries. In our lives we must learn to renounce some things which we value very highly and I believed that, after having lost my son, I did not have anything of greater value to give up."

This was but one of dozens of threats Ferrari made to retire from the sport that consumed him for his entire life—none of which he made good on until God finally removed this gritty old competitor from the field in the summer of 1988.

From the book ENZO FERRARI. *Copyright © 1991 by Brock Yates. All rights reserved. Published by permission of Doubleday.*

Dr. Trammell was only 31 when he faced the challenge of saving Danny Ongais's leg. Which he did. To date, he's performed some 30 operations on race-car drivers.

LOOKING FOR DR. GOODWRENCH

By Steve Spence

You would think that the surgeon most sought after by the rich and famous Indy-car crowd, the surgeon who has put bolts in the bones of Andretti and Sullivan and Unser and plates and screws in the old sidewinder Anthony J. Foyt, the doctor who saved Rick Mears's right foot from the operating-room parts bin, not to mention the doctor who installed a "jack" in the broken back of young Scott Pruett —you'd think a guy like that, a guy who's even got David Letterman bugging him about a sore neck, wouldn't have to deal with drunks anymore, but you would be mistaken.

It was a busted-up drunk, what is known in emergency-room lingo as "a Saturday-night special," that greeted Dr. Terry Trammell at dawn one day in late

February as he arrived at Indianapolis's Methodist Hospital.

By 9 a.m., Trammell had done what he could for the man and returned to his office. He wagged his head in disbelief. "You'll never see anything like that in an Indy-car wreck. The guy's not wearing a seatbelt, he's drunk, he hit something head-on at high speed, he went *through the windshield* and ended up *outside* the car. His face is all smashed up, all cut up, he's got multiple facial fractures. The guy's a mess."

Trammell, who is 41, has performed 30 surgeries on the best-known drivers in Indy-car racing, but on this day he is just a regular orthopedist "on call" at the hospital's emergency room. Break an arm today, and you get the most famous bone doctor in auto racing. He will be on duty for the next 24 hours, and if you were to walk into a room adjoining his office in the darkness of early morning, you'd find him asleep in his clothes on a bunk.

Trammell's still thinking about the drunk. "One of the things I'm always asked is: Do we apply the things we learn (in surgery on race-car drivers) on regular patients? It's the other way around—we apply the things we learn from everyday patients on the drivers. Everyday injuries are worse—"

He is interrupted by his chief aide, Diane Reed, who comes in and tells him what he's going to do next. It's her principal job to point the overextended Trammell, who will be in perpetual motion all day, to his next medical encounter.

Trammell gets up. "I've gotta go aspirate this guy's knee," he says, and he's gone. In a little while, I'll get to watch him ever-so-carefully amputate a construction worker's toes.

Boys growing up anywhere near Indianapolis—Trammell's hometown is Richmond, 70 miles to the east—take a chauvinistic pride in the May racing spectacle that has made Indianapolis famous the world over, and Trammell was no different.

The son of an electronics engineer, he grew up glued to the radio every Memorial Day, and later witnessed three or four races in person. He earned a degree in chemical engineering from Vanderbilt University in the early seventies. His area of interest had a medical application, and Trammell went on to medical school at Indiana University. (It was there he met his wife-to-be, Ludmila, who is also a physician; they have two children.)

In the spring of '73, Trammell took a fateful step that would lead to his current notoriety. He volunteered his medical services at practice sessions of the Indy 500.

"Practice was staffed by medical students. If you worked two or four sessions —I forget now—you got two tickets to the race and two box lunches."

Trammell describes the state of the art for crash victims at the time as "basically meat-wagon—pick 'em up, put 'em on a stretcher, take 'em to the hospital. Nothing happened between the scene of the crash and the hospital." As to the experience of medical students, Trammell chuckles. "We were woefully unqualified. If you had a wreck, you'd probably have

been better off getting help from a guy who knew first aid."

Trammell could not have volunteered for a more disastrous Indy 500. In '73, two drivers were killed (Swede Savage and Art Pollard), and an STP crew member (Armando Teran) was run over and killed by a fire truck. Rain caused the race to drag on for three days.

"I didn't have anything to do with the race. I was taking care of spectators. I think the gates opened at 5:30 in the morning, and within 30 minutes, I had three critically injured people: a motorcycle rider ran underneath a wire and clotheslined himself and crushed his trachea and was about to die from that, and there was a policeman who got run over by another bike rider and broke his back. And there was a woman who went into a diabetic seizure from drinking all night. I worked for three days in that rain and said, 'I don't want to do this anymore.'"

Trammell went back to the Brickyard, but thereafter he crimped a freelance photographer's credential.

After medical school and an orthopedic apprenticeship in Toronto—his specialty is the spine—Trammell returned to Indianapolis and went to work for what is now Orthopaedics Indianapolis, a private practice of eighteen physicians that occupies an entire floor of offices in a medical high-rise adjoining Methodist Hospital. One of the practice's founders, Dr. F. R. Brueckmann, was a pioneer in sports medicine, and he now watches over the Indiana Pacers basketball team.

The doctors in this practice take turns being "on call" to handle bone injuries at the nearby emergency room. In 1981, as the physician with the least seniority, Trammell got stuck with Memorial Day duty. And that's when he had a fateful rendezvous with one of the fiercest, most daring Indy-car drivers of the time, Danny Ongais.

Back in the office that February morning, an hour passes and no Trammell. When he does return, he gets off just two sentences before his assistant comes in and tells him where he is going next. "Linda's ready," she says.

Linda being Linda Vaughn, the voluptuous, magma mama of auto racing who has decorated more victory circles than all winners of the Indy 500. If you don't know who she is, you've never been to a race. If you've been to a race, you cannot have failed to have seen her.

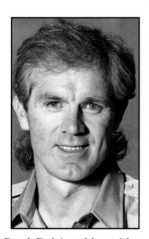

Derek Daly's ankle and leg may hold the record for hardware. Note the shaft running up the big bone in the leg, and the clean break at midpoint.

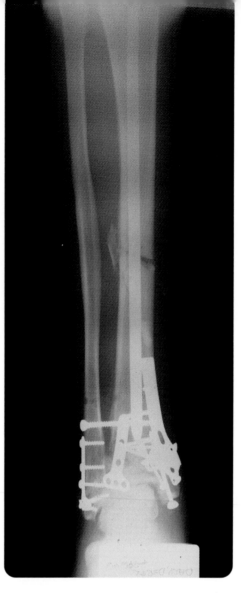

of crash surgeon to follow the circuit. That would happen later with a wave of the wand by CART founder Roger Penske after his number-one breadwinner, Rick Mears, almost lost a foot. There was always a physician on hand at the circuit, but it's reasonable to say the drivers got surgical potluck at emergency rooms on the racing tour, and when you realize that the youngest doctors normally get stuck with holiday and Sunday duty at the emergency rooms where mangled drivers are taken, it's a testament to macho that no driver complained.

Trammell was just 31 years old and in his first year of private practice when Ongais appeared at Methodist unconscious on a stretcher.

Among other injuries, Ongais's right tibia, the big leg bone, was shattered "from top to bottom—bones were sticking through his driver's suit," Trammell says. "He'd severed the artery and had no circulation in the leg. It looked like a china vase that had been broken in pieces. At that time, limb salvage was not something that was routinely done. Some places, he might have ended up with an amputation."

While Trammell struggled to put the pieces of the broken vase back together, using a kind of inside/outside Erector set and a toolbox full of pins and screws, a second surgeon redid the blood vessels. The next day, the repaired artery failed and a second surgery ensued. But Ongais's leg survived, and although he went on to have numerous surgeries, Trammell's reputation was born.

In a cubicle off the emergency room, a construction worker in his mid-forties lies languidly on a gurney, his eyelids at half-mast in gratitude to an industrial-strength painkiller. Something huge was dropped squarely on the toes of his right foot. Trammell peels back the gauze to look, but remains expressionless.

"I know you," the worker says with a slack smile. "I've heard about you."

A couple of the toes look like crushed grapes. Trammell makes it clear that he may wake up minus the tips of a couple of his toes, but reassuringly tells him their loss will have no effect on his ability to walk.

The worker shrugs. "Okay."

In September of '84, Rick Mears crashed in Canada. His left foot was severely crushed, but his right foot set some kind

While leaving the completed Daytona 500, Linda was involved in a traffic accident and injured her wrist. A doctor put a splint on it in Florida—the fracture did not require the scalpel, or any pins and bolts—but Linda being Linda, she wanted the best, flew up from Florida and insisted that the bone magician examine it.

Trammell had a look and informed Linda that the Florida physician had done a fine job.

Danny Ongais had started in the 27th position and taken the lead that day on the 60th lap, then slipped back when his car stalled in the pits, and was hell bent on regaining the lead when the car veered right entering Turn Three and met the wall. The car disintegrated in flames as it grated down the wall, and when the frame came to a stop, with Ongais fully exposed and limp as a rag doll, it seemed his luck had finally run out, permanently.

Racing's bosses, at the time, had yet to see the wisdom of hiring an orthopedist who specialized in racing injuries, a kind

of record—*every bone* in it was broken.

Trammell remembers the day: "I was on call here on a Friday afternoon. I got a phone call. They said Mears had been hurt and Roger's [Penske] plane was on its way to get me. I said I couldn't leave, I was on call. They said, 'Well, you tell that to Roger.' "

Trammell flew up to Montreal. "I took all these foot and ankle anatomy books on the plane up. I was going to put this foot back together. Mears had nosed the car under the guardrail, and it pushed his [exposed] feet back so they were pressed up all the way back on his legs, like flippers." The car continued on, with Mears's feet leading the way, slicing two guardrail posts off "like they were cut with a butter knife," Trammell recalls.

"I'd never seen anything like it. His right foot was so crushed it didn't look much like a foot at all. His feet were basically just bags of bones; it [the right foot] didn't look like there was anything left to fix, it was so trashed. His feet looked like they'd been burned—they were blackened, you could see imprints of the pedals on the soles of his feet, big black spots where they'd impacted.

"But the doctors there didn't want to amputate it without somebody coming up and taking a look."

After examining Mears, Trammell flew back—he was, remember, on call at the hospital that weekend—and then the plane returned to Montreal to bring Mears to Indianapolis.

"This was the most stressful operation I'd ever done," Trammell says. On the eve of the operation, "I sat up all night because I was sure he was going to lose his foot. I was very concerned that what we were going to do might not work."

During the four-hour operation, Trammell rigged a complex Hoffman External Fixator on the right foot. Long rods were run through the leg bone above the foot, then connected to an exterior Erector set that seeks to maintain the length of the foot. The broken bones were pushed back into place with long pins.

Later, a second operation was performed to screw together both shattered heel bones, and Mears went on to have skin grafts in San Francisco.

The operation was only part of the struggle. Trammell was concerned about infection, and the period after the operation was critical. "We were fighting to keep his foot alive. He was on all kinds of treatments to enhance the circulation, a drug to keep blood from clotting, and we had to turn up the temperature in his hospital room to 98 degrees to match his body temperature.

"He was in serious pain. I'd go in to lengthen the fixator every morning, and as soon as I'd leave he'd *un*-lengthen it."

This X-ray doesn't reveal the magnitude of the damage to Rick Mears's foot—every bone was broken, Trammell says. The bolts hold his shattered heel together. His left foot was crushed in a similar manner.

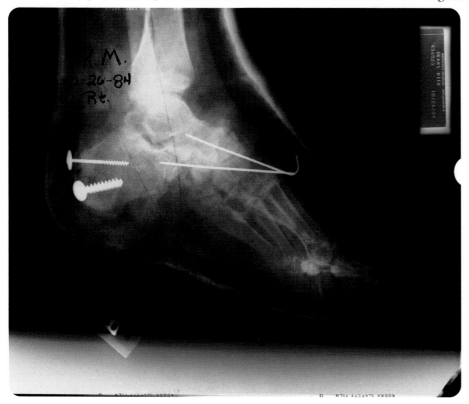

Today, Mears is back in business, even though an encore of his Canada crash could cost him a foot or two. "He couldn't take a hit like he took before and expect to keep his feet."

Mears had no thought of retiring. Of the accident, he says, "I know what happened and how it happened. If it was something I had no control over, something I didn't understand, maybe I'd think differently. I know now to avoid that situation—for one thing, there was a slower car lapping below me during that practice."

Asked why race drivers, unlike other sports stars, haven't demanded that highly specialized physicians be waiting in the wings, Mears replied: "I think my accident was the starting point [for those concerns]. It got a lot of people thinking in that direction. Trammell had a lot of experience, and that's why Roger [Penske] got him. Roger likes to surround himself with people with experience."

The amount of pain Mears has endured, with all the hardware bolted into his bones, is known only to Mears. "I can't explain it, I can't ever begin to describe it. I still have pain today, every day. It's something I live with. I hear guys around the tracks—everyone's got injuries—complaining how this and that hurts. I always feel like saying, 'Man, you oughta feel these.'"

There's a lot of chit-chat in the operating room, just like in *M*A*S*H*. The fellow assisting Trammell cannot believe that this team on TV last night had the lead *and the ball* with 30 seconds to go, and still lost.

"Unreal," he says.

"Tell me about it," says the anesthesiologist, agreeing.

The Beach Boys are pounding out "Graduation Day" on a tape deck.

A nurse and I cannot decipher the tattoo on the patient's slack right arm (he sleeps the sleep of the dead, and there's a plastic pipe the size of a garden hose inserted down his throat). The tattoo seems to be two cherries.

"I can't figure it out," the nurse says.

The anesthesiologist says, "It says, 'Here's mine, where's yours?'" Laughter.

Trammell does not even hear this. He is silent, locked in concentration on the construction worker's mangled toes. He moves around them, he studies them from different angles, he probes lightly with a scalpel to see beneath the surface. In the end, half of the little piggy that

stayed home and half of the little piggy that had none wind up in the parts bin.

In the hallway, he exhales. "It would have taken me 3000 hours to save those toes."

After Mears's accident, Roger Penske wanted Trammell to travel the entire CART tour. Trammell was given the title of Director of Medical Services for CART, and he attends about twelve races, while a colleague, Dr. Joseph Baele, covers the rest.

Trammell has performed surgery on Mario Andretti, Al Unser Jr., Gordon Johncock, Johnny Rutherford, Johnny Parsons, Derek Daly, Jim Crawford, John Paul Jr., Pancho Carter, and Kevin Cogan (twice). When Danny Sullivan broke an arm eight days before the '89 Indy 500, Trammell inserted a steel plate and seven screws, and Sullivan was off and running.

Knowing the huge amounts of money involved in racing, I guessed the CART folks were paying Trammell low six figures, maybe $200,000 a year.

"Until about two years ago, I wasn't paid anything. Then I got $400 for a race weekend. Now it's up to $1000 for a race. Unfortunately, it costs me $1200 a day to be away from my practice."

So why do it?

"I don't know."

By 1990, 29-year-old driver Scott Pruett seemed on the brink of success, like a fighter who had been brought carefully through the ranks. Since his first go-kart tour at age eight, Pruett had moved up with patient discipline: GTU, GTO (two championships), Trans-Am ('87 champion), GTP, the works. After his Indy 500 debut, he was named 1989 co-rookie of the year.

Pruett was a physical specimen, too—he ran five to ten miles daily and worked on the weights for two hours every other day.

On March 16 last year in Florida, while testing his Indy car, the brakes failed on a straightaway and Pruett hit the wall head-on at 140 mph. The car came down with such force that one of his vertebrae literally exploded. Meaning, he broke his back. Both kneecaps were shattered; both heelbones and one ankle were also broken. It took an hour and a half to cut him free of the car.

"It's just luck that he wasn't paralyzed," Trammell says.

"I was in Dallas, so Joe Baele did his

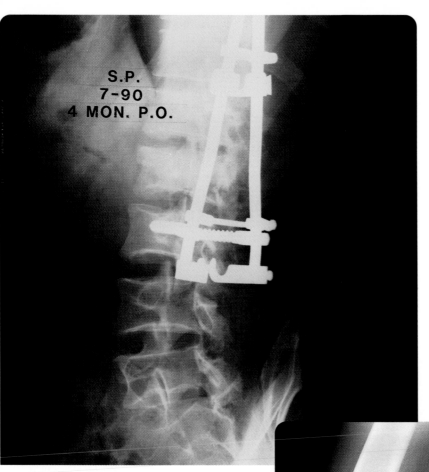

S.P.
7-90
4 MON. P.O.

This is the "jack" that was installed in Scott Pruett's back after he broke it in a Florida crash. Unlike most hardware, this jack will not be removed. Pruett's broken ankle required five screws during surgery.

ankles and knees [screws in one ankle, both knees wired to hold the kneecap pieces together]. Next day I did his spine." When the vertebrae exploded, bone was pushed into the spinal canal. With a network of rods, screws, and hooks, Trammell implanted what appears to be a jack. "It's just like jacking up a car, you have to expand the distance between the vertebrae, below and above."

The device, which Pruett says you can see when he bends to touch his toes, is permanent.

Pruett came to in the hospital to a state of depression. "It's a tough thing to swallow. We'd been doing so well, my rookie year was behind me, and then this happened. First I felt anger and then depression and then anger. The mood swings were amazing.

"I had to focus myself. My first goal was: How long until I can get in a wheelchair? Then it was: How long until I can start physical therapy? My only focus was getting back in that car.

"An accident like mine is going to make or break a driver. Either he becomes determined, or he's going to fade away."

Pruett's road back began in that bed with elastic bands. "Two weeks after the accident, I began physical therapy. At first it was all I could do just to flex the knees." Recovery became a full-time job. "For

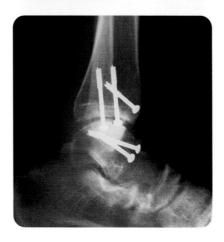

The pieces of Scott Pruett's shattered kneecap are held in place with a sizable length of wire. His right kneecap was similarly wired up. Five screws holding his ankle together (below) have been removed.

155

awhile, I was working eight or nine hours a day, seven days a week."

It was six months "before I was feeling pretty good." Pruett is fully recovered today and back on the CART tour. "Actually, my upper body is stronger.

"People ask me all the time if I worry about another one [crash]. It's actually less of a worry now than before the crash. Because I know what I can come back from, I know what I can go through. And I know I'm not going to have a crash worse than that one."

When A.J. Foyt lost his brakes at Elkhart Lake in September 1990, he instinctively headed off the track—at 180 mph—flew up and over an embankment, lost the nose of the car, and dug a ditch twelve feet long before coming to a stop. The car was planted in the earth like a garden spade.

"He was literally packed into the front of a car that was full of dirt," says Trammell. "Once we established that he was breathing and his heart was beating, I got down on my hands and knees and began digging his legs out of the dirt, like a dog.

"He was wide awake. I looked down and saw his knees, but the right foot was all the way over on the left side of the car. I thought his left foot was possibly severed."

Foyt being the charmer that he is, he started giving orders. "We told him what he needed to do, told him why, told him it was going to take a while. But it was taking too long. I told him, 'You're trapped, and if you move you're going to hurt something else.' So he got real shitty and said, 'Look, I can get myself out,' and he kept pushing me away. So finally I said, 'Okay, do it your way.' He got a couple of inches up and started screaming and sat back down, all pale in the face. And I said, 'Now, we're going to do it my way.' And that's what we did."

Foyt told a reporter later, "It's one of the few times I've been in an accident when I haven't been unconscious that I should have been. I had to get out of the car."

Trammell says, "We had a team of doctors for this one. [Dr.] Jim Steel and I did his tibia [Foyt's left leg bone was snapped cleanly in two]. A couple of doctors worked on his [right] foot—he had a crushed heel bone, the foot was dislocated, and he had a laceration down to the bone in his right leg. If this was just any 55-year-old guy, he'd probably never have walked again."

Foyt's X-rays are startling. The tibia was put back in place with a plate and *twelve* screws, and his ankle is likewise full of hardware. Oddly enough, the irascible Texan has been a model patient. "He's done exactly what I've told him to do. He's working out, sometimes six hours a day, at the Houston Oilers' training facility. He's strong again. I think a lot of it has to do with him wanting to show those young jocks what a macho 55-year-old driver can do."

For medical horror stories, Foyt's is hard to beat: the swelling of the foot was so extreme, Trammell says, that blood was seeping out through the skin like perspiration.

The list of horrifying accidents is lengthy. Jim Crawford crushed both taluses (the "cam" bone in the foot) in a crash. "Normally, that's a crippling injury, and he broke both of them—and he broke both legs besides," Trammell recalls. Crawford was clocked with a radar gun coming into a turn at 233 mph just seconds before the crash. "I was sitting on the grass right across from where he hit, and I knew it was going to be bad."

Trammell thinks Derek Daly might have been killed in a 1984 accident at Michigan International in which he hit the wall and was spinning toward it again, the car nothing but a frame with his legs and body dangling out of it, when another car T-boned him and spared him a second encounter with the wall. Daly's leg and foot injuries were horrendous.

Then there's Dennis Firestone. In 1986, he broke his foot at Indy. "We put him back in the car, and then he broke his neck." He is the only driver to record two breaks in a single month.

Moments after telling me that "Herm Johnson crashed and hit so hard it blew bones right out of his shoes," Trammell again insists that the worst accidents are found on the streets.

"There was this young woman. I still don't understand exactly how, but they said they found her outside the vehicle she'd had an accident in, and she'd gone *through the floor of the car*. They found her halfway in and halfway out of the car, and she'd shattered everything up to her hips.

"So Indy-car stuff's fairly predictable. People ask me if I tell (severely injured) drivers not to drive again. Really, statistically, they're more at risk in the family car than in an Indy car."

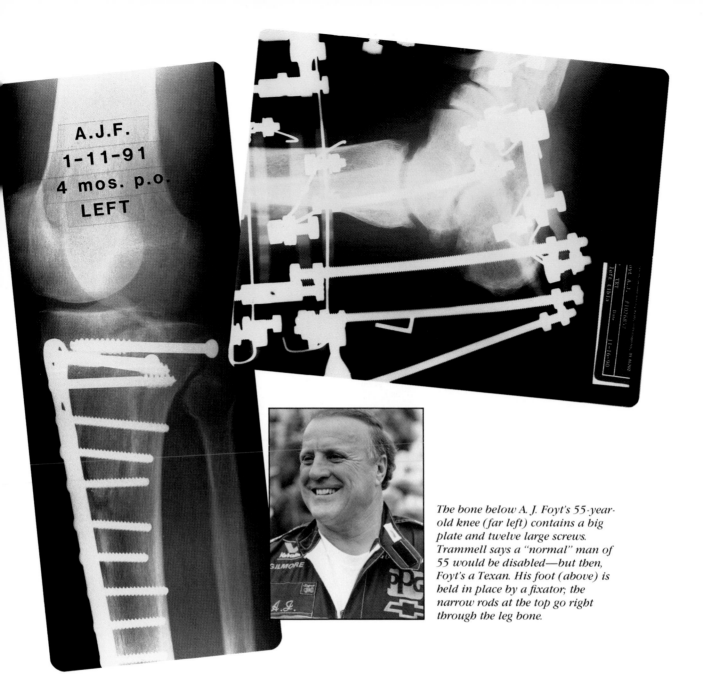

A.J.F.
1-11-91
4 mos. p.o.
LEFT

The bone below A. J. Foyt's 55-year-old knee (far left) contains a big plate and twelve large screws. Trammell says a "normal" man of 55 would be disabled—but then, Foyt's a Texan. His foot (above) is held in place by a fixator; the narrow rods at the top go right through the leg bone.

In 1985, Mario Andretti slammed into the wall at the Michigan 500, breaking his collarbone and fracturing his right hip. Trammell screwed together the big bone above Andretti's chest, and treated the hip. Andretti missed his next race—the first time he had failed to start in 21 years —but was back the week after at Pocono, where he finished seventh.

"There is no doubt in my mind," Andretti said, "without Dr. Trammell, I wouldn't have been ready for that race. Normal medical doctors would put us in wheelchairs. Trammell's surgical talents put drivers right back in action. He understands us.

"A lot of us," Andretti says, "have been touched by this man."

Trammell knows that in most cases it's a waste of breath to try to convince broken-up drivers to retire. "The real problem is some of these guys have a bad attitude—they think the body is like a car: if we break it, somebody can fix it. Somebody would say that to me directly, and I'd just go crazy."

Above: Artist Bill Neale. Left, top to bottom: Mazda MX-3, Corvette ZR-1, Acura Legend LS.

OUR MAN WITH THE BRUSH

By Phil Berg

Those of us who work at the *Car and Driver* editorial offices are the lucky ones. For more years than he cares to admit, Dallas-based Bill Neale has been contributing his paintings and drawings to *Car and Driver*'s "letters to the editor" column, among other feature stories. Our staff gets to see his original artwork full-size, in all its detail and impact. Readers, however, are likely to see reduced versions in the pages of the magazine.

Neale is listed in the Texas Auto Racing Hall of Fame along with Jim Hall, Carroll Shelby, and Lloyd Ruby. But he doesn't like the comparison. "I've been messing around with cars, but not enough to brag about," Neale says. At 66 ("Not near as old as Shelby") Neale is president of Point Communications, a Dallas advertising agency. "We're not big enough to scare J. Walter Thompson," he claims, adding "you've got to be nuts to be in advertising.

These pages provide a more comprehensive view of the work of contributing artist Bill Neale than our readers are normally given. Top to bottom: "Old Blue," Mazda RX-7, and Dodge Viper.

Painting and messing with cars keeps me from going nuts." He exhibits his paintings in galleries in New York, California, Europe, Mexico, and Japan. Most recently, he displayed his paintings at the Monterey, California, and Meadowbrook, Michigan, *concours de elegance* shows, the two most well-known car-people gatherings in the country. "I was flattered by the response," [from the crowds at the shows] he admits.

Neale used to race sports cars, including MGs, Porsches, Corvettes, and Cobras. That experience has given him insight into how to properly illustrate a car. Perhaps his knowledge of the sport is what makes his paintings stand above other ex-

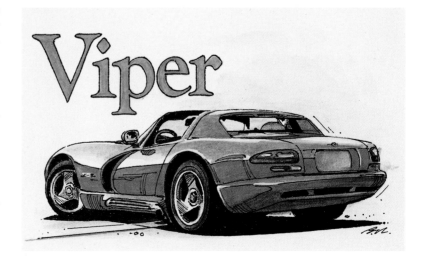

COBRA!

amples of car art. "I'm not one of those who likes to distort the image. When I paint a McLaren, I want you to know which one it is." About 90 percent of his painting is cars, and he uses mostly watercolor and acrylic mediums. "It's what I like best," he says, "I've just about gotten off of using oils." Portraits and paintings of aircraft make up the remainder of his work.

Neale also likes riding off-road motorcycles, but "not near as well as I used to," he reveals. He tries to go to as many car races each year as he can manage. But painting "keeps me off the streets," he jokes. Lucky for us.

Top: Bob Bondurant in Cobra #51 tries to catch a Daytona. The 427 Cobra (above) still sets pulses racing. Below, left to right: Mazda Miata and BMW 850i.

RACING

WHEN BIG BILL FRANCE MOVED ON MOTOWN

By William Jeanes

On a clear winter day in 1951, the late William Henry Getty France, best-known as Big Bill France, flew north from Florida, away from his world of dusty dirt tracks and a primitive entertainment called Grand National stock-car racing. He aimed his fragile single-engine plane toward Detroit, heart of the automobile industry and source of an intoxicating aroma: the scent of money.

The handsome, six-foot-five, 225-pound France, then 42, described himself as president of something called the National Association for Stock Car Auto Racing. NASCAR, formed only three years earlier, sanctioned races run mostly in the southeastern United States and usually on crude, dirt-surfaced ovals—the lone ex-

ception being the new paved "super-speedway" at Darlington, South Carolina, a venue emblematic of France's ambitions, though he had no part in its construction.

In 1951, stock-car racing was, well, rural. Certainly beneath the dignity of powerful, sophisticated, successful Detroit, hub of the American auto industry —whence came four of every five cars built in the world. Nine automakers shared turf today owned by Chrysler, Ford, and General Motors. The six that would disappear within the decade were Hudson, Kaiser-Frazer, Nash, Packard, Studebaker, and Willys. None, save Hudson, gave meaningful support to auto racing. None of the others wanted to hear Bill

France's reasons why they should go racing.

During 1951, Detroit would celebrate its 250th anniversary, a milestone that spawned a civic party unequaled in Detroit history. So big was the bash and so clout-heavy were Detroit city fathers that the 1951 baseball All-Star Game was moved from Philadelphia to Detroit.

A bald, sad-eyed newspaperman named Harry LeDuc, a devotee of auto racing who knew Big Bill France, suggested to Jim Chapman, a tall, courtly Southerner who was an established public-relations whiz, that nothing could be more fitting for the birthday blowout than an auto race—a race between cars that consumers could recognize. Stock cars.

Chapman, who had recently left the Ford Motor Company to open his own public-relations firm and had won the assignment of publicizing the 250th-anniversary events, didn't know much about stock-car racing. LeDuc, the sports editor of the *Detroit News,* did.

"Auto racing never had a better friend than Harry," Chapman recalled recently. "He had seat number one in the Indianapolis press box, and he'd covered stock-car races in the South."

LeDuc and Chapman sought support for the idea from industrialist Walter O. "Spike" Briggs, chairman of the anniver-sary committee, owner of the Detroit Tigers and of the stadium bearing his name. Briggs liked the idea. LeDuc next telephoned the man he knew to be capable of putting on a major stock-car race: William Henry Getty France—Big Bill to friends and admirers. Would he bring a race to Detroit?

"France had this little single-engine plane," says Chapman, "and he flew up to talk to us in February or March. When we finished telling him what we had in mind, he asked me if I could put together a

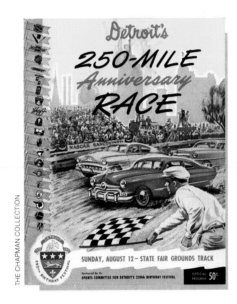

Left: Program cover showed Hudson Hornet in the lead— not the way things turned out. Below: The Packard pace car lurks behind the fence as 59 vintage-1950 NASCAR stock cars in full wallow dig up the Michigan Fairgrounds.

Looking like an illustration for the song "Wreck on the Highway," this photo reveals no seriously injured drivers. In fact, none were.

group to promote the race. I checked with Spike Briggs and the committee to see if this might be a conflict of interest, but they said no, it wasn't. So I went ahead with it." Chapman assembled a group of six "promoters" from among his Motor City friends and acquaintances and set about learning the arcane skill of auto-race promotion. In May, Spike Briggs announced that a 250-mile stock-car race would be held on August 12—the length harmonizing with the city's 250th anniversary.

The race would run on a one-mile horse-racing oval at the Michigan State Fairgrounds. Big Bill France would conduct the race; Chapman and his group would sell it. NASCAR's Grand National series was about to make its first incursion into big-city Yankee country.

France brought a colorful contingent of Southern drivers to Detroit. Some would become NASCAR legends: lean Red Byron of Atlanta, winner of the first NASCAR championship; hard-eyed Lee Petty from Level Cross, North Carolina; the fierce, fiery Flock brothers, Tim, Bob, and Fonty (whose sister, Reo, was named after a truck); brothers Bobby and Billy Myers; Frank "Rebel" Mundy; and the hard-driving, harder-drinking Curtis Turner.

From the Midwest came track-toughened midget and big-car drivers: 1949 Indianapolis 500 winner Bill Holland; the Rathmann brothers, Dick and Jim; Pat

Flaherty (Flaherty would win Indy in 1956 and Jim Rathmann in 1960); and Michigan cycle and midget racer Iggy Katona. And from Los Angeles, Johnny "Mad Man" Mantz, veteran of three Indy 500s.

Chapman strained to establish the event's respectability by rounding up as much high-level support as possible, an activity to which he was uniquely suited. "Every time anybody at Ford got the chairmanship of some civic committee," Chapman says, "he'd call me in to do the public relations. Because of that, I knew the Detroit establishment, including executives at the other car companies." One of those Chapman invited to his race was Harley J. Earl, the nattily dressed GM stylist who was the first of his profession to achieve star status.

"I remember calling Harley," Chapman says, "and he said, 'A damn stock-car race? You've got to be kidding! Now if you want to have a sports-car race, that's a different thing.'" Whether motivated by curiosity or by Chapman's entreaties, Harley Earl would show up.

Another Chapman effort turned out Packard's top executives. The race program contained a Packard ad showing a yellow 1951 convertible and noted that it had been selected as the pace car for the Detroit race. Indeed it had—for a fee.

"I got Packard to furnish the pace car and to pay $5000 for the privilege, plus give the car to the winner, which was unheard of at the time," Chapman recalls. "Also we got Speedway to be the official gasoline, in return for $3000 and fuel."

Another fuel company, the Pure Oil Company—now Unocal—would provide prizes at a race for the first time, giving the winner two cases of motor oil (25 cents a quart in 1951). Dick Dolan of Pure Oil's advertising department, an eager Notre Dame graduate in his first job, loaded a pickup truck with the oil and drove 300 humid miles from Chicago to award it.

Stoking the publicity fires, Big Bill announced, "This race undoubtedly will be the biggest ever held in the country." By the opening of qualifying, 107 entries had been filed, among them a raft of Fords, Oldsmobiles, Plymouths, Hudsons, Nashes, and Studebakers. There were three Packards, two Chevrolets, two Mercurys, one Henry J, one Cadillac, and one Pontiac. With typical hyperbole, France noted that the field could swell to 125 cars. All the cars were to be absolutely stock, as available in the showroom (including tires), with no modifications.

Qualifying for the 250-mile race began on Saturday, August 4, nine days before the race. Marshall Teague, 30, a paunchy, taciturn Floridian who had won five Grand National races that year, put his 1951 blue-and-gold Hudson Hornet on the pole at 69.92 mph, a hair ahead of Gober Sosebee's 69.89 mph in a black 1950 Cadillac.

On Sunday, NASCAR officials yanked Teague off the pole after discovering that his engine was fitted with twin carburetors, an arrangement as yet unseen in Hudson parts catalogs.

The next day, bald, bulb-nosed E. G. "Cannonball" Baker, one-time cross-country record-setter and motorcycle racer and now—at 79—figurehead commissioner of France's fledgling organization, investigated the carburetor affair. Hudson public-relations director Tom Rhoades told Baker that the twin carburetors ("Twin H-Power") were a new Hudson option. On Tuesday, Baker restored Teague to the pole position.

On Wednesday, Baker reversed himself again and took the pole away from the beleaguered Marshall Teague. Baker did this after Rhoades admitted that his company had filed the new specifications with the Automobile Manufacturers Association barely a month before, on July 2, and had made them public only three days before qualifying began.

"That (the carburetor option) may be," railed an indignant Cannonball Baker, "but the kit is not yet available to the man on the street." He was right; Teague had the only set, though Rhoades told Baker that Hudson could supply other Hornets with the kit.

Tom Rhoades, who is now 84 and lives in Indianapolis, recalls the events with amusement. "The man that came up with that carburetor setup was one of our engineers at Hudson, Vince Piggins. And Smokey Yunick did work for us, too. Being a PR man, I was somewhat in the dark about what the engineers were up to."

Rhoades recalls clearly how Teague gained Hudson's help. "That winter, I got a call from Bill France. He asked if I knew that Marshall Teague had won the beach race at Daytona in a Hudson Hornet. At that time I had never heard of Bill France or Marshall Teague, let alone a beach race."

Rhoades telephoned Teague, who—like Bill France before him—operated a service station and garage in Daytona Beach (and was also a Pure Oil distributor). Rhoades was so impressed with Teague's manner that he brought him to Detroit for a press conference. In turn, Hudson president A. E. Barit so liked the publicity that he approved a car and parts, but no money, for Teague—one of stock-car racing's earliest "factory deals."

On Thursday, August 9, Teague requalified his Hornet—now fueled by a single carburetor—and shaved more than a second off his original time. But the pole position remained in the hands of Gober Sosebee, whose car sported a Confederate flag painted on its left front fender. At the conclusion of qualifying, Bill France announced that 52 cars would start the race, pre-qualifying hype having turned out to be just that.

Pre-race hype continued unabated, stoked by enthusiastic local writers who applauded stock cars but had little sympathy for the expensive, purpose-built racing cars that ran at Indianapolis.

Nor did Cannonball Baker have kind words for Indy "specials." Baker ground the anti-Indy axe with populist vigor, saying, "Racing, those special cars, that is, is a dead duck. Stock-car racing is the successor to those rich man's toys."

Harry LeDuc, in the race program, wrote, "Stock-car racing died some 40 years ago when the makers withdrew their support; and they withdrew because

Aftermath of "a phenomenal crash" on lap 94: Indy 500 winner Bill Holland's Cadillac.

too many were building special racing motors, special chassis, special everything."

Writer Carl R. Green, identified only as a "national authority," summed up the case for stock-car racing: "Races between strictly stock cars are filling the grandstands. Now that nearly everyone owns a car, each owner is interested in seeing races between regular cars of the type or style he drives himself." Green then tainted this prescient assessment of stock-car racing's popularity by adding, "He is also interested in learning the tricks of turning a street corner on two wheels and making the tires squeal."

LeDuc, wrapping the sport in the flag, added, "Stock-car racing appears to be reviving because those who like to race and can't afford $25,000 for a special job have the free American right to buy a car from any dealer (at something under $5000) and race it under rules that let him improve the car's performance if he does not change its parts."

Dust, dirt, discomfort, and destruction figured prominently in the vivid pre-race writings of at least one newspaper reporter. Describing the "50 heavy stock cars" that would start the race, he wrote, "They'll rip ruts so deep it will look as if excavators have been at work. Before the 200-mile mark is reached they'll be laboring hub-deep as if in a freshly plowed field." Dust clouds would rise 30 feet in the air, he warned, and the destruction he foresaw would compare to "the angriest part of a dust bowl devastation."

France, quoted in the same article, calmly said, "No, you're wrong. We've run these races on the dirt many times. Sure, some dirt will fly, but nothing like you imagine." Of the predicted dust clouds, he said, "We're using 45 tons of calcium chloride on the track, 15 tons for trials and the rest just before the race."

Chapman recalls, "Our biggest expense was calcium chloride to keep the dust down. I remember that Bill brought his son Billy with him, who would have been seventeen or eighteen, I guess, and he helped spread the calcium chloride."

No sooner had the dust settled than it began to rise. Race day Sunday dawned hot and humid. A capacity crowd estimated at 16,352 crammed the grandstand and infield. In the crowd was a young New Jersey racing writer who had hitchhiked to the race—Chris Economaki. "The place was jammed," Economaki says, "the promoters had done a great job."

Tickets ranged from $2.50 for infield standing room to $12 for the best seats. Atop the grandstand, in the race course's 56-seat clubhouse, Jim Chapman assembled a number of the city's high rollers at the astronomical price of $18 each.

"It was very hot and very dusty," Chapman says. "Nothing in those days was air-conditioned except a few theaters. We did have windows that we could open in the clubhouse. And we had food, drinks, everything. Even padded seats. Imagine all that today for eighteen dollars."

Following ceremonies during which the city's "festival empress" presented medallions to the drivers and renditions of "Michigan, My Michigan" and the "Star-Spangled Banner" were sung, the cars lined up two abreast. Just after 2 p.m., with track dust already rising, the Packard pace car pulled off the track, the starter showed the green flag, and 59 cars, each with muffler firmly in place, whooshed away in a shower of dirt.

"One of the things that stands out in my mind," says Economaki, "was the physical suffering of the crowd in the heat."

The crowd watched happily as a herd of bulbous cars, none with roll cages (and few if any with seatbelts), on standard suspensions and ordinary tires, wallowed around a one-mile track, lashed on their way by a bunch of grimy madmen who asked and gave no quarter. For four hours and 21 minutes, in intense heat and steaming humidity, the multitude cheered—and were dampened by perspiration and covered with layer upon layer of beige dust.

Long as it was, the race was anything but humdrum. Economaki recalls details of one of the three spectacular crashes: "It was at the head of the backstretch, and I could see Bill Holland's white Cadillac going end over end. It was a phenomenal crash. "That crash, on lap 94, damaged seven cars, one of them Lee Petty's number-42 Plymouth. Petty rolled his car but drove the wrinkled result to thirteenth.

A five-car pileup enlivened lap 131, leaving Curtis Turner's Oldsmobile 88 in the lead, followed by Tommy Thompson in a Chrysler. Thompson, a relative newcomer to stock cars, found himself jousting with legend-in-the-making Curtis Turner, the Virginian who said he liked racing with a hangover because "you feel so bad you don't care what happens to you."

Turner held the lead until lap 212, when Thompson took it. Turner regained it on lap 216. On lap 225, Thompson fought back into first. On the next lap, the inevitable happened: the two cars tangled coming out of turn two. When the dust cleared, the crowd saw that both had smacked the wall and were stopped on the track. Thompson's Chrysler was relatively unscathed, but Turner had mashed his Olds's left front fender and had punctured his radiator, leaving the win to Thompson.

Harry LeDuc described the race in the *Detroit News:* "Five leaders—with the lead changing twelve times. One seven-car smashup. Another five-car crash. Solo accidents with machines rolling over, plunging into fences, throwing wheels, blowing tires, boiling over. Spectators alternately aghast and cheering. Infield fans rushing hither and thither to scenes of destruction with police a-horse and on motorcycles checking the concentrations. All preceded by bombs and balloons, songs, band music, an old-and-new-car parade, a flag raising. And climaxed by the victory of a personable young man who definitely defeated 57 [sic] other drivers, all of whom came through without a scratch of any kind."

That personable young man was Howard W. "Tommy" Thompson, 29, of Louisville, Kentucky. Thompson averaged 57.37 mph for the race's four hours, 21 minutes, 38 seconds and won $5000, plus the Packard pace car. Thirty-seven sec-

NASCAR commissioner E. G. "Cannonball" Baker (at wheel) confers with Big Bill France.

onds behind Thompson came Joe Eubanks in an Oldsmobile, followed by Johnny Mantz in a battered Nash Ambassador. Red Byron was fourth in a Ford. A young driver named Hershel McGriff, winner of the 1950 Mexican Road Race, crashed early and wound up 54th. Marshall Teague's Hudson Hornet departed with cooling problems after 136 miles. He won $10.

The crowd went home fully entertained, Chapman and his associates went home with $7500 each, and Big Bill France went home having made new friends. Useful friends.

The race ran in 1952 as the Motor City 250, for which Jim Chapman assembled an "advisory board" that included "Engine Charlie" Wilson, head of GM, and Ford executive vice president Ernie Breech. More new friends for Bill France.

After the 1951 race, "Bill France finally had his foot in Detroit's door," says Chapman. "From that time on, he got his phone calls returned and he could get in to see people. That's all it took for him. He was a very persuasive man."

The compelling, soft-voiced France expanded his friendship with Harley Earl and Spike Briggs. Both became investors in his dream project: the 2.5-mile, high-banked Daytona International Speedway.

A VIP skybox at the Daytona track is, as it has been since 1959, called the Harley Earl Suite.

Jim Chapman remains head of his public-relations firm. Erect, silver-haired, and still courtly at 76, he oversees PPG's interests as sponsor of the CART PPG Indy-Car World Series.

Tommy Thompson, winner of the afternoon-long 250-Mile Anniversary Race, accepts his trophy. Big Bill France, right, in white cap and loud shirt, beams appreciatively.

The Hudson name disappeared from America's showrooms in 1957.

Vince Piggins died in 1985, following a long and distinguished career as head of Chevrolet's racing program.

Tommy Thompson never won another NASCAR Grand National (now Winston Cup) race.

In 1959, Marshall Teague sailed over the west banking at the new Daytona superspeedway—in the Sumar Special, the tired car he had driven to seventh place at the 1957 Indianapolis 500. He was killed instantly.

Curtis Turner died at the controls of his plane in 1970.

Lee Petty went on to win three NASCAR championships. His son Richard has won seven.

Hershel McGriff, at 65, still competes in NASCAR races.

Hitchhiker Chris Economaki's tabloid *National Speed Sports News* is considered to be auto racing's American bible, and he is the dean of racing telecasters.

Pure Oil pickup driver Dick Dolan is manager of automotive events and public relations at Unocal. Unocal is NASCAR's official racing gasoline.

Big Bill's son, Bill Jr., one-time calcium-chloride spreader, now 59, heads the empire created from his father's dreams, including NASCAR and the International Speedway Corporation. ISC built the superspeedways at Daytona and Talladega (Alabama) and now owns the historic Darlington track. It also operates the road course at Watkins Glen, New York.

NASCAR's Winston Cup racers now come to Michigan twice a year. Last year, the two races at Michigan International Speedway drew 175,000 fans. Five million fans saw the races on television.

All 29 of the NASCAR Winston Cup series races are televised, reaching an estimated 100 million viewers each year.

Estimates of today's manufacturer and sponsor involvement in NASCAR Winston Cup racing range as high as $600 million.

The person seeking to locate more than a handful of stock parts on a modern Winston Cup car will not succeed.

NASCAR Winston Cup racing has been called the only major new spectator sport of the twentieth century.

Big Bill France died of Alzheimer's disease at the age of 82, in the summer of 1992 in Daytona Beach. Two weeks after his death, his son and successor, Bill Jr., viewed the top NASCAR drivers in an exhibition race at Indianapolis Motor Speedway, yet another inroad made by the stock cars where they were previously banned. If Big Bill France could have lived to see the stockers race at Indianapolis, it would have made complete his life as the most enterprising force behind American motorsports.

STEWART'S SECRETS

By Patrick Bedard

Modern engineering is very good at making fast cars. But there's only a foggy understanding of what makes a fast driver. How could we find out more?

What if we got the world's best driver and strapped him into an instrumented car? Could we see what the best driver does differently from drivers who are merely good? And if so, could we then inject his technique into the good drivers to make them clones of the best? These questions are simply too logical to be dismissed.

Jackie Stewart, the three-time Formula 1 world champion, is certainly among the best drivers ever to have grabbed a steering wheel. Since his retirement from racing at the end of the 1973 season, he's

been a nonstop advocate for advancing driver skills, and he's been unfailingly generous in sharing his insights.

For some years, Stewart has been a consultant to the Ford Motor Company. Ford was interested enough in our driving questions to make him and the company's Dearborn proving grounds available for our tests.

The Dearborn handling circuit is, in many ways, ideal for this inquiry. Stewart has frequently driven on it over the years and so have our staffers, which meant that only a few laps of refresher time would be required. Moreover, the circuit is flat, with lots of run-off room, so the drivers could concentrate on getting around the track quickly without worrying about the

The wee Scot lectures the Car and Driver *brain trust: from left to right, Csaba Csere, Rich Ceppos, Jackie Stewart, and Patrick Bedard.*

consequences—other than embarrassment—of a mistake. The seven turns in its slightly more than one-mile length are mostly long, predictable, constant-radius bends on which we could easily approach the limits of the tires. These bends are connected by very short straights. Therefore most of the time is spent in corners, or transitioning into and out of them, which is exactly where differences in drivers should show up. All of the turns require some slowing on entry but only two require braking. That gives us a chance to examine two distinctly different kinds of turn entry. Speeds for a quick road car range from a low of about 50 mph to a high of 85.

Originally we planned to rely on a g-Analyst (Valentine Research, Inc., $379) to reveal each driver's methods. This is an on-board, three-axis accelerometer, corrected for body roll, that records and displays acceleration in the plane of the road. But unbeknownst to us, Ford has installed a vehicle-dynamics measuring system at the Dearborn proving grounds that goes beyond anything we'd dreamed of. In effect, it's a land-bound equivalent of that part of the military's Star Wars system that locates faraway enemy missiles so accurately they can be shot down while they're still far away. This system tracks the position of the car on the circuit with an accuracy of plus or minus one inch in real time. Computer processing of that data can reveal more than we can think to ask. Ford even has transducers that show slip angle of the tires. Fortunately, the system's maestro, Dan Hagan, is a merciful man: he didn't bury us in more plotter paper than we could understand.

For the record, he did provide times for each lap and for five individual segments that make up each lap, a speed plot

After a few laps in the test car, a bright-red Thunderbird Super Coupe, all the drivers were using third gear only.

around each lap, a lateral-acceleration plot and a longitudinal-acceleration plot for each lap, a steering-angle plot, and an instantaneous turn-radius plot that is so esoteric that we won't mention it again.

The test car was a bright-red Thunderbird Super Coupe with a five-speed transmission. After a few laps, all the drivers were using third gear only.

Our drivers were Rich Ceppos and Csaba Csere. For years, both have done as much amateur road racing as their time and budgets would allow, and though neither is actively racing now, neither has declared his retirement. They live in readiness. Think of them as highly practiced, needing only a dose of Stewart magic to have a shot at the bigs.

Stewart, as a part of his consulting, regularly drives in tire tests. Consequently his sensitivity to tires is acute. He warned that tire wear and tire temperature were variables too large to let go uncontrolled. Cold tires are faster, he said. And no less important, tires with substantial shoulder wear behave much differently than original-contour tires. If we just passed the same set from one driver to the next, as we originally intended, he warned that the drivers would always be responding to the distressed tires they'd inherited rather than to the car and the course.

As a solution, all three drivers did their familiarization round on a shared set of tires. After that, each had his personal set of Firestone Firehawk SVX 225/60ZR-16s that were reinstalled for his laps and removed to cool in the interim.

Before taking his turn, Stewart nodded toward the Star Wars plotter and called it "the bad-news" machine. For truly, such instrumentation gives the driver no place to hide. He might just as well check his ego at the door, because his driving will be laid bare for all to see.

In the first official five-lap round, Stewart was fastest, followed three-quarters of a second back on average by Ceppos, and about two seconds back by Csere. Speed differences, of course, were to be expected. But isolating the essence of Stewart's method is more complicated than looking at a few plots and saying "aha!"

Because the Ford system shows the line through turns, that was the easiest variable to compare. In most cases the differences were minor, except in the first turn where Csere had his own unique solution that amounted to hugging the inside through Turn One in order to have the best shot at the left-hander that followed.

Since Stewart's speed plot showed better speed through both turns, Csere quickly concluded that he'd originated a lose-lose compromise.

From the beginning, this investigation sought differences in driver methods, not differences in the lines they chose through turns. Still, the methods would surely be obscured by different lines. So it was important that all three drivers were in substantial agreement on the fast line after the first round.

One other discovery, very surprising, was apparent from a scan of g-Analyst printouts. Logic suggests that a properly done corner should show constant lateral acceleration at the peak of tire adhesion from beginning to end. The shape should be like a Montana mesa—a steep up slope on entry, then flat on top, finally changing to a steep down slope on exit. But Stewart's curves didn't look like that. The flat tops actually showed a slight down slope right from the beginning. He was systematically reducing lateral force as he progressed through the turn, by about a tenth of a g, more or less, from beginning to end.

Ceppos's formations tended to be flat on top, as we would have expected of a good driver, and Csere's tended to rise as he progressed through the turn.

Although Stewart's driving had surely been analyzed on other days with other instruments, he seemed as surprised by this discovery as we were. Because a g-Analyst print shows lateral and longitudinal acceleration traces side by side, it's very easy to see what the driver is doing with power as he moves through the turn. Early in the turn, Stewart was working the throttle—a cycle or two of feeling for power and then easing out while he established the balance he wanted—then he would taper up to full power. The tapering wasn't always constant, but there were never any major lifts once he began to press on the gas.

Stewart agreed with these observations, yet the big clue to his method didn't come until the next session. Both Ceppos and Stewart dropped a few tenths then, mostly because outside temperatures had increased. Csere, on a better line, improved his average by about 1.2 seconds. Clearly, though, Csere's method and Stewart's were quite different. Csere's tire squeal got louder and louder as he progressed through the fast turn adjacent to our observation point, and it usually peaked just before he straightened the

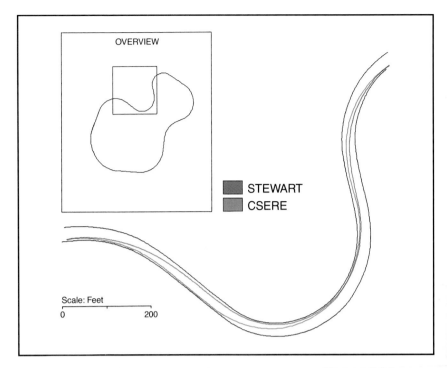

OVERVIEW

STEWART
CSERE

Scale: Feet
0   200

wheel for the following straightaway. Stewart's tire noise grew quieter as he passed through the second half of the turn.

Steward uses animal metaphors. "Imagine a horse with the bit in his mouth. He's trying to go and you're pulling the reins tight. You have to give him his head. Let him go. The same for the car. You're working under understeer. You want to open it out, give it air."

Stewart was setting up a trajectory through corners that allowed him to begin unwinding the steering well before the end of the turn. And that unwinding produced the gradual falloff in cornering force that we had observed earlier. Csere, on the other hand, held more of a constant arc through the turn, and as he increased power toward the exit, the outside front tire protested louder and louder. That sort of high tire loading, Stewart said, would rapidly increase temperature and cause a reduction in grip in succeeding laps.

By the way, Stewart's claim that cold tires have the best grip seems to be supported by his lap times. His first or second lap of a session was always his quickest, with a small but unmistakable drop-off in the subsequent laps. Our drivers had too much scatter in their times for this drop-off to be apparent.

The notion of quickly distilling off Stewart's method and injecting it into our guys simply wasn't possible. High-perfor-

A radar-tracking system shows the drivers' lines. Stewart's line through Turn One was nearly half a second quicker than Csere's. Without the high-tech device, it might have taken an hour's discussion and several laps to uncover the driver's problem.

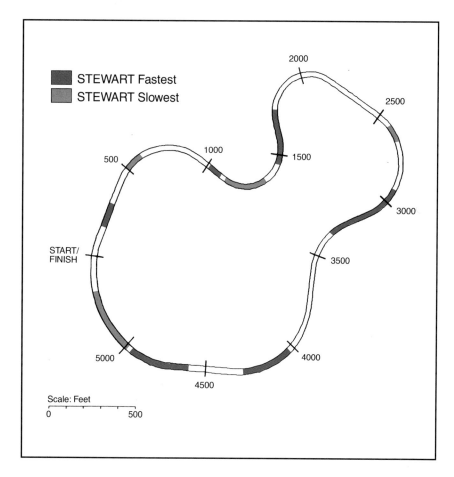

STEWART Fastest
STEWART Slowest

2000
2500
500
1000
1500
START/
FINISH
3000
3500
5000
4000
4500

Scale: Feet
0   500

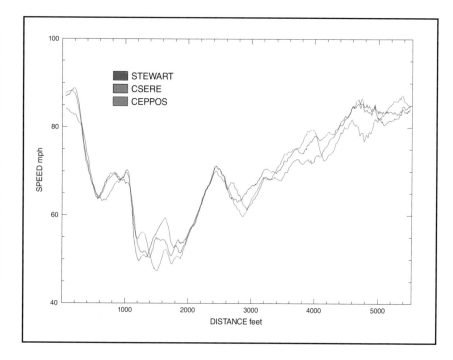

STEWART
CSERE
CEPPOS

SPEED mph
100
80
60
40

1000   2000   3000   4000   5000
DISTANCE feet

mance driving throws up too many details to analyze in only a few hours. Still, Ford's plot of speed around the track was provocative. There were places where Stewart was slower than both of our guys. And they were followed by longer stretches where Stewart was faster. Stewart spoke of "staying ahead of the car, settling yourself down before you find yourself in a dilemma you can't control."

Csere observed, "If you carry too much speed in some places, it looks like you have to give it all back, plus interest, later."

In the final session, Ceppos tried very hard for smoothness and overcompensated, leaving himself about a second behind Stewart. Csere produced commendably consistent laps, on average a half-second behind Stewart.

Although the third session finished our allotted time for driving, it was only the beginning of our learning. We then rode with Stewart to watch what he did. And we devoted several days to studying the plots provided by the Ford and g-Analyst data. From all of these sources, we draw the following conclusions about how Jackie Stewart drives.

1. Stewart's always ahead of the car. His speed at any given point on the track is determined by what he wants to do next, not what the car is capable of now. Too much speed in the wrong place makes it impossible to execute the next move on time. Ford's plots of speed around that track show that Stewart is consistently slower than our guys in the early part of turns. He apparently gets more of his turning done in that slow part, then accelerates out of the turn on a slightly straighter line, usually carrying more speed on to the following straight.

By the way of explanation, Stewart went on to say, "I try to get my steering lock off as soon as possible."

2. Smoothness doesn't mean limp driver inputs. Ford's steering-angle plots show that Stewart makes more steering inputs, and larger ones, than our guys. And his timing is different. His big inputs are earlier in the turns. He looks smooth on the track because the car goes exactly where he intends, not because he's steering less.

3. He's the master of braking. The plots show that Stewart maintains his speed in the straights slightly longer than our guys, yet very quickly thereafter he's the slowest guy in the turn. Once he applies the brakes, he gets up to peak deceleration

quicker than our guys. His maximum deceleration rate also tends to be higher, but not greatly higher. The result is more area under the braking curve, an observation confirmed by the speed plots.

Such a description of braking implies a certain violence of motion that is absolutely not there. To a passenger, the braking is very smooth: no slam at the onset and no detectable end of the braking phase. The latter is explainable by the give and take of trail-braking. As the driver trails out of the brakes, he simultaneously increases steering; since Stewart is doing a lot of steering relatively early in the turn—and since steering scrubs off speed—his steering-induced deceleration probably masks the end of braking. This is our theory anyway.

We also have a theory for his smooth onset of braking: it's magic.

4. He makes his straightaways longer. He appears to start braking later and to hold a straight path slightly longer on entry to turns. For sure, he exits the typical turn on a slightly straighter path. Together, these straightenings add up to more time at full power.

5. He is extraordinarily aware of his tires. "Squeal is the only way tires have to talk to you. And beyond squeal is grunt. Those sounds mean too much slip angle."

Too much slip angle both slows the car and heats the tires.

As if to summarize his method, Stewart said, "You must control your belief that you have to be on the power all the time. Most people over-drive. They feel obligated to get that throttle to the floor. They get too much speed to suit conditions. They fall behind the car. Then they have to give speed back, and that puts them behind on the watch."

He pointed to several sections on the Ford track where too much speed going in puts the car off line for the series of turns that follow. This piece of analysis is not exactly news, but it can't be dismissed either.

Surely Csere answered for all motivated drivers when he laughed and told Stewart, "I buy into that, but I guess I never buy into it enough."

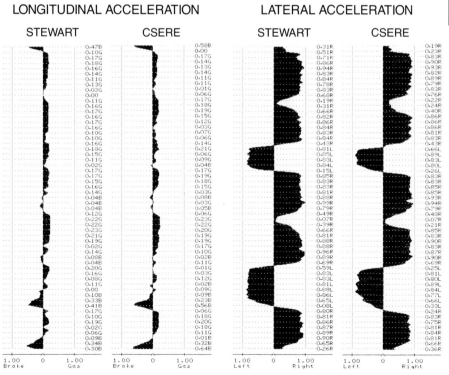

LONGITUDINAL ACCELERATION

STEWART   CSERE

LATERAL ACCELERATION

STEWART   CSERE

These g-Analyst traces, with time proceeding from bottom to top, show that Stewart reaches peak acceleration right after turning; he unwinds his steering slightly through the corner. Csere turns in more gingerly and doesn't reach peak until well into the corner; his lateral acceleration fluctuates through the corner. Csere shows much more fluctuation in longitudinal acceleration, and he's backing off the throttle to keep the Thunderbird's tail in line. Stewart, on the other hand, relies more on steering to balance the car.

The High-Tech BS Filter

Listening to drivers dissecting the laps they've just run is like listening to tele-preachers bragging about their fund-raising exploits. The drivers sound like this:

"I was seeing 5700 at the end of the straight...You mean you're not taking Turn Three flat?...That apex is way too late, you want to be well on the power by then."

Road racers are probably the most blatant BSers on the planet. If all of them are driving so well and are so knowledgeable about what they've done, why do the same few guys always seem to win?

Ford's new instrumentation provides the answers. This hardware not only traces a car's position and speed, but it can also monitor virtually any control or vehicle parameter that could possibly interest a driver. And you can't argue with the system because it presents the results in black and white.

For example, when we overlaid Stewart's line around the course over mine, I found that we took turns one and two totally differently. Without the instruments, it could have taken an hour of discussion and track walking to identify and explain this difference. With the printout, I assimilated the information in a matter of minutes. Adopting Stewart's line in the next session was worth nearly half a second per lap.

Few of the other differences were as obvious, but as we pored over the data, we learned more and more. Stewart tended to go slower into corners and faster out of them than we did. His lateral acceleration traces were smoother than Rich's and mine, which was no surprise, and so were his throttle movements. However, his motions at the steering wheel were not. At Stewart speed, apparently, you do whatever you have to do to keep the car moving smoothly.

We could have used a few more days to dissect and drive the data. But then none of us, including Stewart or Dan Hagan, Ford's instrumentation expert, had any experience using such information for driver education. But in the hands of a Bob Bondurant, a Jim Russell, or a John Powell, this instrument could eliminate the BS and become the most powerful driver's teaching aid since the blackboard. —*Csaba Csere*

How To Take It From Here

You probably can't get Jackie Stewart as a tutor, and you've little chance of duplicating Ford's Precision Location Vehicle Dynamics Test System. But there are other ways to clean up your track act.

Finding the fast line through the turns is essential, but that's not as mysterious as it seems. In almost every case, the best line is the one that produces the fastest exit speed. Get in the habit of noting a speedometer or tachometer reading at the end of each turn. Then experiment with lines until you're found the highest exit speed.

Probably the biggest barrier to fast laps is your own mind. Every driver on the track is dead solid certain he's operating at the hairy edge all the time. "Why, hell, Leroy, I spun out three times that lap." Yes, that's three trips over the limit, but what about the rest of the time?

If you can face cold, electronic evidence of your shortcomings, the g-Analyst is a helpful tool. I wish it had been available when I was racing. At the very least, it helps with cockpit quality control. Stewart not only does the right thing, but he does it almost exactly the same every lap. The g-Analyst lets you study your quality control in the quiet time after you get out of the cockpit. Are you cornering as hard in the fast turns as in the slow ones? Do you really have the power full on through the esses? Is your braking up fully to the tires' limit? Every turn? Every lap? Fast driving is the sum of a lot of details, all done exactly right.

The g-Analyst, because of its simplistic display, is cryptic in the way it reveals its findings. Only when paired with a computer—we downloaded to a Toshiba T1000 laptop (about $600) running g-Logger 2.0 software ($95, including special cable)—does it rise to its full potential. Then you can examine up to 30 minutes of track time with just a few keystrokes. Different laps—or different drivers—can be compared side by side. We can even do friction-circle plots. For hard copy, a Diconix 150 portable inkjet (about $260) will print anything you can see on the screen.

Stewart, it must be said, managed to capture three Formula 1 World Championships without any of this electrickery. The rest of us need all the help we can get.

—*PB*

FREQUENT FLIERS

By John Phillips III

At the 330-foot mark, Gary Ormsby knew he was in trouble. He just didn't know how much.

"I was saying to myself, 'God, this thing is hooked up. A hell of a pass.' Then I thought, 'You know, the nose is awful floaty. I hope I don't have to get out of it [lift the throttle].' It wasn't until 660 feet that my brain really processed the data. That's when I noticed my eyes weren't pointed at the track anymore. I said, 'Uh-oh.' I was looking at the Arizona horizon. Somehow I had the presence of mind to pull my foot out of the stirrup [a strap that keeps the driver's foot on the throttle], because I was afraid if I crashed that my leg would slam down on the pedal and zing the motor. I had time to do that, because the car was just floating through the sky for 200 feet or so. I was still going maybe 230, 240 mph. Then it went vertical and blew out every single body panel —ripped them into confetti. That's when

I said, 'This is definitely not good. I'm going over.'"

Ormsby's dragster shredded a $42,000 chassis and shed another $30,000 or so in attendant pieces, but it managed to make it through the timing lights in a hail of debris at 6.05 seconds/170.4 mph. *Backwards.*

Ormsby's wild and potentially fatal ride was his first experience with what drivers in the NHRA's Top Fuel division call a "blowover," a new phenomenon now common to dragsters that would have been on their way to sub-five-second passes. The recipe for this curious catastrophe is simple: an imbalance between front and rear wings, aggravated by traction and torque so incomprehensibly immense that, in drag parlance, "the pinion climbs the ring gear." At which point, the 25-foot-long dragster becomes a lever, and the car's nose describes a 180-degree arc—finishing its journey upside down

and facing the starting lights. With the driver on his head.

Ormsby, who owns Toyota and Subaru dealerships in Auburn, California, has been racing Top Fuel cars since 1964. In 1989, he became the NHRA's Top Fuel champion. He has clocked the quarter-mile run in 4.88 seconds at 296 mph. When the people at the NHRA were asked who would score the first 300-mph run—an ominous prophesy that unnerves the drivers and the sanctioning body alike—they either changed the subject or said: "It won't happen this year. Probably. Unless you mean Ormsby. Gary could do it."

But only if he can keep his car ten or fifteen feet closer to Mother Earth.

To grasp the blowover phenomenon, consider first the complicated, stupefying forces at work in Top Fuel racing.

When Ormsby's car is "really hooked up," it leaves the starting lights with 5.5 g's of acceleration—the same face-flattening jolt experienced by a pilot in a Navy A-6E Intruder catapulted off a carrier's deck. After a particularly good holeshot, Ormsby's dragster will hit 100 mph in *one second* of mind-warping noise, smoke, and fury. Put another way, a perfectly launched Top Fueler can accelerate from standstill to 100 mph in 79 feet—just three times its own length.

Think for a moment of a truly fast street car—a Corvette ZR-1, for example—which can travel from 0 to 60 mph in 4.9 seconds. Impressive? A strong Top Fuel car manages 60 mph in three-quarters of *one* second, and while the ZR-1 is putzing around attaining 60 mph, Ormsby has attained 296 mph 0.02 second *sooner.*

When it is launched, the dragster's tractive force is so great that Ormsby's right foot, as noted earlier, is lashed to the throttle pedal. As the dragster approaches the timing lights—at, say, 287 mph and climbing—its on-board computer has noted that the vehicle is still accelerating with as much as 1.2 g's. That is an accelerative force greater than a Porsche 911 Turbo can pull in *first* gear.

Stand within 50 feet of the starting line and you quickly learn that if you don't turn your head as if you were watching a tennis match, a Top Fuel dragster can remove itself from your field of vision. It's like watching a film that jumps its sprockets. Your mind has no reference, no prior experience with a 25-foot-long object that moves so far in a single second.

How much horsepower does it require to effect such colossal disappearing acts? Until recently, nobody knew. Even if there exists a dynamometer that can measure a 500-cubic-inch Top Fuel engine's output, there is certainly no dyno that can be programmed to present the engine with a facsimile of the bizarre load it sees in a five-second pass down the quarter-mile. And simply getting a dyno up and measuring is a process too lengthy to accommodate the engine's life expectancy at full throttle: 60 seconds.

That's why Patrick Hale, of Racing Systems Analysis in Phoenix, began experimenting with computer simulations. By calculating everything from atmospheric conditions to the asphalt's "traction index," Hale can estimate horsepower (at least in 1100-hp Pro Stock engines) to an accuracy of one percent. After examining all the bits and bytes he could pull from the data-gathering computer in the pencil

nose of Ormsby's dragster, Hale reported confidently that, at 6800 rpm, Ormsby's Top Fuel engine produces—grab your asbestos Jockeys—4221 pound-feet of torque and *5465 horsepower.* That's 14.6 times the output of a Corvette ZR-1, all of it harnessed to a vehicle that weighs 1925 pounds.

Forcing a reciprocating engine—even a supercharged (to 34 psi) godzilla motor—to produce 5465 horsepower is both difficult and dangerous. "It's like plunging your toilet with a Claymore mine," says one engine builder. "It will probably work, but it's hard on the toilet."

You start with the most explosive fuel you can find: nitromethane. If you're serious, you buy it (at roughly $950 per 50-gallon drum, and you'll need two and a half drums per weekend) from a refinery in Beijing, where they swear their juice is 97-percent pure. Then pour fifteen gallons of the stuff, which was used in the 1940s as a rocket propellant and remains today an industrial explosive, *undiluted* into the baffled fuel tank in the dragster's nose.

The engine (sometimes called an "ignorant nitro-burning flywheel") will gulp eight gallons of nitromethane just idling for two minutes. During its five-second full-power run, the dragster will squirt through its 32 injectors another *five to seven* gallons—a minimum of a gallon per second. That is 7.5 times the rate at which fuel flows from the self-serve nozzle at our local Mobil station. In five seconds, that is more fuel than you could *spill* by overturning seven one-gallon buckets. The dragster's custom-built fuel pumps are each fed by a fuel line with an unusually large inside diameter—think about this for a moment—of 1.5 inches.

Not only is the engine insatiably thirsty, but all that nitro must be delivered under frightening pressure: 120 psi is good for a start, 170 is better.

Sky-high fuel pressure, as it happens, is one of the secrets of instantaneous engine response—essential to a low ET. "At the starting line, a Top Fuel dragster idles around 2150 rpm," explains Ormsby's crew chief, Dana Kimmel. "When the light turns green, I want the revs to climb to peak efficiency [6500 rpm or more] in exactly the time it takes Gary to fully depress the throttle." In an engine with a reciprocating mass roughly that of a Coney Island ferris wheel, this seems utterly impossible. It isn't. To rev from idle to 6500 rpm, Ormsby's monster motor requires just over a tenth of a second.

What happens next, curiously enough, has nothing to do with Ormsby's skill as a driver. Instead, it depends on the skill of team manager Lee Beard, who looks like a young Bruce Dern and has nearly the same cunning and malevolent intensity.

It is Beard who decides how all 5465 horsepower is put to the pavement. "The best route," he says, "is not all at once." The weak link in Top Fuel cars is not power, but traction.

The answer? Traction control. Well, it *was* the answer until Ormsby and Beard used electronic traction control to win three times in 1989. Which prompted the NHRA to rule that while on-board data-gathering computers were legal, electronic engine-management or traction-control computers were not.

Ever resourceful, Beard and other team managers invented a "clutch-management system" that works as a primitive form of traction control. Primitive, but Goldbergian in its complexity.

In a box in front of the driver's feet are eleven mechanical timers, each connected to a nightmarish spaghetti-tangle of pressurized air lines leading to the clutch and the engine's sewer-size fuel lines. The guts of the box look like a tidy fuse panel for a municipal power plant. Beard sets each timer to "detonate" at a precise moment along the quarter-mile. Five of the timers regulate the pressure in a pneumatic cylinder that controls the engagement of the centrifugal clutch. As they progressively bleed pressure from the cylinder, more and more of the clutch's fifteen fingers grab the friction plates, allowing more and more horsepower to find its way to the 17.5-inch-wide slicks. The managed slippage means that the clutch is sometimes dissipating more than 2000 hp as heat. Not surpris-

dense the air is. But it's a decision based on history—based on the previous run—rather than a decision made in real time, which is what traction control on street cars can do. If I guess right, I can make this thing hold four g's [of acceleration] for two seconds. More than two seconds and you'll see 300 mph."

What the clutch-management system means is that Ormsby is mostly along for the ride. After the clutch-finger timers are armed, the driver's job is simply to mash the accelerator when the light turns green, then aim. If the tires go up in smoke at any point along the quarter-mile, the run is aborted. It is Lee Beard's fault, not the driver's.

"This sport is 70 percent mechanical, 30 percent driving," says Beard. Hearing this, Ormsby shakes his head and, for a moment, appears offended. "More like 90 percent mechanical," he says.

Beard's black magic with the clutch timers isn't performed entirely in the dark. He learns much from the dragster's on-board data-gathering system. (Because the NHRA is always suspicious that these computers may occasionally be directing true traction-control systems, tech inspectors show up unexpectedly—usually in the staging lanes—and force teams to make one pass sans computer.) Beard's computer records engine rpm, driveshaft speed, fuel pressure, exhaust temperature, manifold temperature, linear movement and pressure of the throwout bearing, positive and negative g's, distance traveled, and miles per hour.

Following one of Ormsby's strong 4.99-second/287-mph passes, the computer tells Beard that, at 1.0 second into the run, the engine was spinning at 6360 rpm but the driveshaft was turning only 2564 rpm. The clutch and its magic fingers have responded exactly as Beard programmed them, allowing only 40 percent of the engine's horrific potential to find its way to the slicks. At that point on the track, Beard knows there isn't enough grip for the tires to accommodate anything more. Incredibly, it isn't until 4.75 seconds into the run—a mere two-tenths of a second from the finish—that engine speed and driveshaft speed match exactly at 6980 rpm, indicating full lockup. Only then is the 500-cubic-inch engine truly uncorked.

After the run, Beard agonizes over the figures. If he had detonated one or two clutch fingers a quarter-second earlier, would Ormsby have gone through the

Team manager Lee Beard directs his cunning at arming the nightmarish timers, which "detonate" at precise moments during a pass. If Beard guesses right, his reward may be a 300-mph pass. If he guesses wrong, Gary Ormsby's weekend is toast.

ingly, the clutch is replaced after every run.

As each clutch finger engages, the engine encounters a new load, and its appetite for nitro fluctuates. Too much fuel at the wrong millisecond is the mechanical equivalent of Buster Douglas on angel dust. That's because liquid cannot be compressed, and if it "pools" in a cylinder . . . well, Dana Kimmel recalls a whole cylinder head that was bent in half as it lifted itself free of *thirteen* head bolts and set off in the general direction of Marin County. Thus, to keep internal pieces in peace, another set of pneumatic hoses activates plungers that alter fuel flow as the engine bogs or races.

Setting the clutch timers involves guesswork born of experience. Says Beard: "I look at how old the track is, its surface temp, how much oil is on it, how

lights at 300 mph? Or would the tires have gone up in smoke? Or would the whole dragster have clawed its way skyward in a 280-mph blowover that would have put paid to Ormsby's day and maybe his life?

It is Beard's job to find out—on the car's next pass. It is easy to see why he can go through an entire race weekend without smiling.

Of course, most of what the on-board computer tells the crew is less ominous. Often it saves them money. It reveals, for example, that at 4.0 seconds into one run, cylinder number four lost 86 degrees of exhaust temperature in just a tenth of a second. Sure enough as the seventeen-minute engine teardown proceeds, a crew member finds a delicate crack—barely visible to the eye—in a valve-spring damper. When he removes the spring and compresses it, it snaps in two.

During his heart-stopping blowover, Gary Ormsby was, ironically, saved from grievous injury—like five other drivers during their own blowovers—because his car landed squarely atop what may well have triggered the flight through Arizona airspace in the first place: the 7.5-foot-tall carbon-fiber rear wing. Ormsby refers to that car's last moments of existence—a car, by the way, that had a grand total of three runs under its belt—as "my Scud-missile run."

Ormsby and his colleagues prefer *guided*-missile runs, so they rely increasingly on the advice of aerodynamicists: people like Mike Magiera, who forged his reputation designing slippery "funny car" bodies for Trans-Am Fords, Chevys, and Oldsmobiles.

Magiera has designed a carbon-fiber ground-effects package for Joe Amato, the reigning Top Fuel champ. The lash-up consists of what Magiera calls "tire wipers or mud flaps"—essentially fairings in front of the rear wheels—and a venturi-shaped belly pan that extends beneath the engine and exits into an enormous diffuser tunnel.

The goal is to dispense with the Wilt Chamberlain-tall rear wing, yet retain the same 6200 pounds of downforce it can generate. (That wing works so well, creating such a vacuum directly beneath it, that it must be vented or it will explode!) Magiera chases ground-effects downforce for traction alone and not to clean up the dragster's inherently dirty Cd of 0.70, twice as bad as the average passenger

car's. In fact, dragsters are aptly named, creating so much drag that, according to Magiera, "at 250 mph, you need 2500 horsepower just to pull them through the air."

Once the huge dual-element airfoil is out of the equation, the car responds less like a teeter-totter when its front and rear wings are at improper angles of attack. "If you suck the car down from below, rather than mash it down from above," adds Magiera, "you might eliminate blowovers. Also, you know, when a dragster's nose gets four or five feet in the air, a funny thing happens: You can't steer anymore."

It sounds like an easy fix, but development of Magiera's $25,000 undertray has been a decade in the making. Part of the problem—if a team runs the ground-effects package on every pass during a perfect weekend—is that the braintrust gets exactly 40 seconds of experience with it. And part of the problem is that ground-effects systems work best with a fixed, *low* ride height. Unfortunately, a dragster has no suspension, relying instead on its 25-foot-long frame to flex. And flex it does, changing ride height a little as the car "arches its back" and changing ride height a *lot* (as much as seven inches) as the rear tires grow.

At the conclusion of each quarter-mile run—presuming his car crosses the line nose-first—Ormsby yanks a hand lever to his right to activate the $7000 composite disc brakes, the same type used in F-16 Falcon fighters. The brakes alone—which Ormsby says are capable of locking the rear wheels at any speed he has yet attained—supply 3.5 g's of deceleration. Which is peanuts compared with the 5.5 to 6.0 g's Ormsby experiences when he pulls the hand lever to his left, popping the twin parachutes. Those negative g's are sufficiently intense to hurl the remaining fuel forward so violently that the engine starves. It works as an unintended kill switch.

Even though Ormsby's arms are strapped in place, slowing a human body so quickly is similarly violent. "If I have enough shutdown area, I pop only one chute," he says. "Open them both and you compress into the belts like you hit a brick wall. I still feel it on Monday."

If Ormsby is occasionally uncomfortable, so, too, is NHRA founder Wally Parks. Parks frets about the companies who insure his events: "You know, 300 mph is a

Top Fuel champ Joe Amato runs his ground-effects car —with fairings, a venturi-shaped belly pan, and a diffuser tunnel— he installs this tiny rear wing.

red flag to them, and so we've tried to slow the cars. We've mandated a 3.20:1 final-drive ratio, which acts as a rudimentary kind of rev limiter. Spec tires are required. And the way we now compute speed is to begin measuring it 66 feet *prior* to the [finish] lights." Which means that at least five Top Fuelers have—as they crossed the finish line—already achieved 300 mph, but neither the spectators nor the underwriters have been told about it! *[Editor's note: Finally, in March 1992, Kenny Bernstein's Budweiser King Top Fueler showed an official speed of 301.7 mph in Gainesville, Florida.]*

"What I can't do is legislate what these guys spend," adds Parks. "If they want 300 miles per hour bad enough, they'll develop stuff like four-valve engines that rev to 10,000 rpm. The only thing that keeps them under 300 right now is that it's still elapsed time that wins races, not speed."

Parks is right about the dollars. Top Fuel teams rarely flinch when it comes to disbursing wads of cash. A single chassis and engine is worth $87,000. Crankshafts and connecting rods are junked after twenty runs, presuming an engine doesn't have what the team euphemistically calls "a rod event." Transmissions live for 75 seconds. After every pass, the $7000 clutch's four discs and three floater plates are garbage. The differential lasts four runs. Joe Amato's crew installs a fresh $3500 supercharger for every pass. And depending on a track's relative "stick," tires are good for only 20 seconds before they are banished to the no-smoking lounge.

Ormsby has six engines ready for assembly, each worth $45,000, but only one at a time is ever up and running. The reason is simple. After every single run, the team dismantles the engine to the bare block. Kimmel reads pistons and engine bearings in the same casual way most racers read spark plugs. "We learn what to do next by examining damage," he says. "You know, if we didn't squash a main bearing really hard, then we know to add more boost."

Beard calculates that every time his green dragster makes one five-second pass down the quarter-mile, it costs $5000 to $7500. A minimum of $1000 per second—money spent on hardware alone.

What has all this got to do with the world of motoring? "Not much," says smiling Joe Silver, a marketing consultant, who, like so many Top Fuel crewmen, looks and talks like he could be working for Roger Penske. "Top Fuel cars are to passenger cars what kangaroos are to white mice. They're related, but it was a long time ago. The appeal, I think, is that nobody else is so perpetually on the ragged edge. If Sam Peckinpah were in charge of worldwide motorsports, he'd put Ayrton Senna in a dragster. It's barely controlled violence, the perfect American entertainment: five seconds of action, then a pause—like pro football. Minimum attention span. A kind of fiery, high-speed sound bite. And they come in droves to see those kangaroos, man, because those babies hop and jump down the track, and occasionally one just up and kicks your damned face in."

DRIVING

BOYS. AGAIN.

By Steve Spence

Top: Learning to drive looks faster from inside the Bondurant Formula Ford race cars. Bottom: Students' first experience with high-performance driving comes in production-based Ford Mustangs.

He was a heart surgeon pushing 60, his hair turning wispy and white. A lifetime of stress in the operating room had rewarded him with a florid complexion and an awareness of his own mortality. Coffee was offered. "I don't drink coffee," he said. "It's not one of my vices."

Coffee's dangerous, huh? Soon, this doctor was going to drive 80 miles an hour, which was about 50 miles an hour faster than he was used to, into a ridiculous left-hand turn—but coffee, well, that's risky. I hear this, and look at my cigarette like it has just grown ears. But I don't put it out, not me. I'm about to be a boy again.

This happened at the Bob Bondurant School of High Performance Driving. In Phoenix, Arizona.

In all, thirteen of us—no women—signed up at about $500 a day for the three-day course. Most of us were at that age when gray is insidiously becoming the dominant color of the hair, but we clung to the dress code of the sixties—jeans and sneakers and sweatshirts and jackets with words and messages on them. When I was a boy, heart surgeons did not wear washed-out denim jackets—farmers did.

Youth was represented by a twentyish producer (Of what? Rock music? Films? Commercials?) from Los Angeles. He wore basketball high-tops and a colorful Indian vest and sported the ponytail favored by show-biz folks on their way up. When he arrives up there, if indeed he does, the ponytail will come off, the Armani suit will go on, and he'll put ink to the Porsche lease. Thanks to Bob Bondurant, he will know how to drive it.

There was a father and his teen-aged son from Yosemite. A kind of role reversal was going on: it was the father slouched down in his classroom seat like a lump of laundry, the way we did in high school, and the kid who was all grown up. In a tone of voice beyond his years, he said he hoped the experience "will help me be a better driver in the snow." (I about fell over. No, no, kid, with any kind of luck this experience will make you popular with girls!)

Boys and would-be boys. About to be taught driving techniques, certainly, but knowing that sooner or later we'd be let loose on a road course in some plenty-fast 5.0-liter Mustangs. After all of the grown-up classroom instruction—all the talk of oversteer and trail-braking and weight transfer—they were going to let us drive

just as fast as the kid in each of us wanted to go. Boys again!

In the bright classroom, we performed group chants on oversteer and understeer. On a magic-marker blackboard, the instructor made his finger crash into the imaginary wall, and then he'd cue us: "What's happening when this happens?"

We replied: *"OH-vur-steer!"* Like multiplication tables.

That first day they put us on an asphalt patch the size of a K-mart lot. Up and down we went in our Mustangs, getting the feel of the gear progressions, the brakes. Then we ran through emergency lane-changes and took turns sliding around in a squirrely skid car, a jacked-up Taurus as dicey as a pig on ice.

There was a coned handling course of tight turns. The idea was to get through it quick as you could. Timed runs, with one-second penalties for every cone knocked over. The instructors mentioned that 60-second times "are right up there." I ran a couple in 63 seconds. Then 62, then 61, then 60.8, then a horrible 64 caused by overrunning my ability. Then I knocked over two cones. Then I began swearing.

Is this what it's like to be a race-car driver—obsessed, crazy, pissed, talking to yourself? Probably. But there *does* come a moment, amid all the flailing and foot-stabbing and teeth clenching, when you get the tiniest sense of the great variety of skills, the fanatic's concentration, that it takes to be even a good racer.

I got out of the car, frustrated, and discovered steel threads like wild hairs poking out of my left front tire. With new tires, I got below 60 seconds and began rehearsing my acceptance speech for the awards banquet. And then Youth—the ponytail—aced me by a quarter-second. Ambition is a terrible thing, but there's worse stuff—the aging process, for one.

On the last day, we were issued helmets and racing suits. When the zipper of the suit reaches your neck, profound changes come over the psyche.

The instructor drove us each through the course, hard. Heel and toe. You must keep your eyes up ahead, you must keep the revs up, and you must turn the wheel this way or that way in a spin.

You must, you must, you must. For my part, I recall Stirling Moss's admonition: "It is better to go into a corner slow and come out fast than to go into a corner fast and come out dead."

Once on my own, it was "laps." Round and round, seeking to learn the nuances of each corner, building speed in fugue-like repetitions, each squeal of the tires sending its message. And coming out of that last S-chute and into the straightaway, there's one breathless moment as you shift into high: you become the car, its voice is yours, you are it—and then it starts all over again, brand-new, with each lap: brake, heel-and-toe, give it gas, double-clutch and downshift, push it up high, no, no, get back down, look ahead. Do it again, do it again, faster, faster.

A couple of guys lose it and go spinning off the asphalt and into the infield, raising big roostertails of dirt as they lurch wildly to a halt. Like a kid, you grin. Does Dale Earnhardt?

Passing has begun. You haunt the guy in front of you. You see puffs of exhaust fumes when he shifts. And coming out of the chute you veer sharply to his right, the engine screams near the redline, *Whooom!* you're in fourth, and oh, did they see that in the stands, did they *see* that?

Finally, school's out. It's ·been chilly, but removing the suit, I'm startled to find I'm sopped. Out on the highway, headed to the hotel with my graduation plaque and my official Bondurant stickers and pins and patches, I shift a gear and feel a sting in the palm of my hand. There's a big broken blister, the size of a half-dollar, where I had shifted the Mustang, over and over. A blister caused by intensity.

The next day, the torn skin had turned pink and shiny and hard. A few days later, there was no trace of it, just the memory, just something that happened when I was a boy. Again.

Sunny Firebird Raceway near Phoenix has safe facilities for students to learn driving skills. Bottom: As skills develop, students take to the track in Formula Ford race cars.

IN MEAT WE LEAD— OTHERS FOLLOW

By John Phillips III

At 1 a.m., near Vinita, Oklahoma, a woman on the radio is howling. I have been on the road for fifteen hours, and if a Holiday Inn doesn't hove into view soon, I'll begin aiming the car at all these twelve-foot spiders and hitchhikers who look exactly like James Dean. Fortunately, the radio howler is doing a better job of keeping me awake than the coffee I bought 30 minutes ago at the Union 76. The woman is railing about "nick witties." I have never heard of them, but they sound like some kind of savings plan.

"It's our *nick witties* that's keeping us from prosperity," she bellows. Junk bonds? New IRAs? They are evidently per-

nicious things that have bankrupted her. The mystery lingers another ten minutes, then it's clear. The screamer is the host of "The Baptist Bible Hour," and she is divulging her own devilish *iniquities.*

On cross-country trips, I take no cassettes and follow a single self-imposed rule: When a radio station begins to fade, I punch the seek button once. Just once. Using this technique, I have learned when corn is tasseling, where to get oversize permits, and which body parts are on sale at Dwyer Auto's Scrap Metal Division. I know that the Shamrock Lounge's motto is "Always rum for one more," that Joe Don Hyde· is selling his 351-cubic-inch

Cleveland-head V-8, that Texas feed lots are cutting back on their slaughter hours, and that, in exchange for a truckful of alfalfa, I can acquired two Model A tires on spoked rims in Socorro, New Mexico.

An Indiana weatherman on a barely audible AM station says that tomorrow's winds "will be stronger than Jane Russell's bra." This is followed by a funereal advertisement for the American Will Kit. You fill out the will at home, presumably just before your stroke. It sells "for $12.95 plus shipping." Shipping? A plain pine box? Are embalming tools part of the package?

Between Joplin and Tulsa, I latch onto a deejay explaining his station's latest promotion, "The Start-to-Finish Baby Race." Babies in carriages, pushed at reckless speeds by their mothers? No. Worse. Much worse. The winner of this contest will be the woman who conceives and delivers a human being in the briefest period. The baby rockets down the birth canal and presumably receives not a smack on the fanny but the wave of a checkered flag. My first question: Who determines the, ah, moment of conception? I envision solemn-faced notary publics standing discreetly in dark corners of the bedroom, now and then politely averting their eyes and softly clearing their throats. Although this aspect of the Baby Race is never made clear, the grand prize is: an all-expenses-paid lark in Dallas. For the mother. The father and the high-velocity offspring evidently stay in Tulsa.

A stab at the seek button delivers "Our Heifer Sale," a trade-'n-swap show on KTJS, in Elk City. A woman caller says, "I have two diamond dinner rings and will sell one and swap the other for a console TV and a crocheted yellow bedspread made of yellow Luster-Sheen yarn." Think about that. I did for 75 miles.

In Hobart (pronounced "HO-bert"), the AM News Bureau of Oklahoma describes the robber of a nearby convenience store: "He wore a ski mask that completely covered his head and gloves." This news is brought to me by Blue and Gold Sausage.

Which is fitting. By the time I reach New Mexico, food has become the dominant topic of AM radio. Near Los Lunas, a local chiropractor promotes Patient Appreciation Day: "We've got a food bar and refreshments," he explains. "Come in and meet the doctor personally. Free chiropractic services. You can eat."

You can eat.

A few minutes later, in Belen, I learn the proud and memorable motto of Adam's Market on South Main Street: "In meat we lead—others follow."

It is snowing gently as I approach Show Low, Arizona ("Named by the turn of a card," says a sign at the city limits), where I lock on to a call-in show. Today's topic: the budget deficit. One by one, listeners bleat about $600 toilet seats, Stealth bombers, the S&L fiasco.

"Hello, you're on the air," says the host as the fifth listener connects.

"Ah, is this Jim?" the caller asks. "Am I on the air?"

"Yessir. Go ahead. What have you got for us today?"

"Well, Jim, I've got a cow I'm selling for $45 and some carpet for $2 a square foot and . . ."

Click.

"Hello, you're on the air," blurts Jim to the sixth caller.

At the California border, I expect the airwaves to become slick, professional, predictable. Deejays who never stutter and hourly syndicated news broadcasts featuring Paul Harvey. Instead, in Joshua Tree, I fasten onto 95.7 FM, where the morning deejay exhorts: "I'd like to remind one of you—and *you* know who *you* are—to call Gail and return the turkey you stole, no questions asked. It was not a meal. It was a pet."

And then there's the "L.A. Breakfast Show" on 920 AM. Nancy, who operates a mobile flu-vaccine van, calls to report her location. Proximity to an actual public-service message catapults the deejay into full Willard Scott mode: "Flu shots, that's good!" he offers. "A fellow from the Muppets died of flu. No. It was pneumonia. Are you giving pneumonia shots?"

Nancy is sufficiently dumbfounded that she is thereafter unwilling to divulge the location of the flu-mobile.

Back when Garrison Keillor narrated "A Prairie Home Companion," I always wondered where he got his material. Not whether it was true or not. Just where he got it and how he got so much. Here's how: He occasionally drives from Ann Arbor to Seal Beach.

As an AM radio station faded, the author (above) would push the seek button just once. In that way he learned that two original Model A tires were worth a truckload of alfalfa, and a diamond dinner ring was worth a console TV and a yellow Luster-Sheer yarn bedspread.

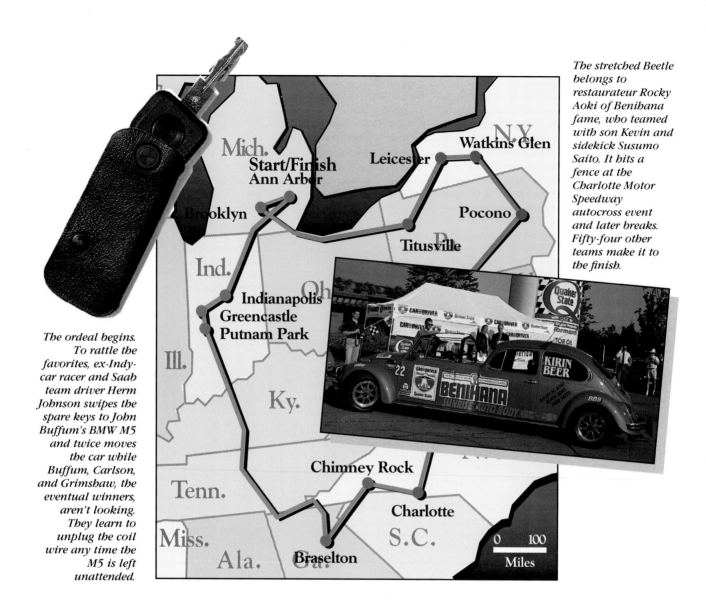

The ordeal begins. To rattle the favorites, ex-Indy-car racer and Saab team driver Herm Johnson swipes the spare keys to John Buffum's BMW M5 and twice moves the car while Buffum, Carlson, and Grimshaw, the eventual winners, aren't looking. They learn to unplug the coil wire any time the M5 is left unattended.

ONE LAP OF AMERICA

By Phil Berg

Everybody thinks it's a flat-out race across the country," says Stephen Jones from behind the wheel of his police-friendly Consulier.

"People have never heard of One Lap," says Corvette driver Steven Meitz, "but they know all about the Cannonball and Burt Reynolds."

Which is what One Lap isn't. What it is: Our own Brock Yates's latest *Car and Driver* One Lap of America rally. Think of it as a baseball game with each inning played at a different stadium. Covering 2800 miles in June, 57 teams flogged a variety of machines at five racetracks, ran a bracket drag race, and slid around at a three-mile time-speed-distance rally and hillclimb. It took four days. It began in Ann Arbor, Michigan, ran west to Indianapolis, then south to Atlanta, north through Charlotte, then to Pocono, Pennsylvania, and Watkins Glen, New York, finishing back in Ann Arbor. John Buffum, Tom Grimshaw, and Satch Carlson won in a BMW M5. Ten-time U.S. rally champ Buffum and navigator Grimshaw have now won four One Laps. They didn't get any tickets, either.

◄ Ancient Dodge Challenger at left, which finished second in the 1972 Cannonball and third in the 1975 race, lines up at the Indianapolis Raceway Park bracket race. Driven to 39th place by Brock Yates Jr. and Mike Roberts, the car had been sitting in storage for seventeen years.

►
After waxing Buffum on a wet autocross course at Charlotte, Billy Edwards displays attitudinal index finger. "We were fast, but we were pretty boring," says Edwards, who drove a white Galant. Buffum came in third behind a team of Canadians—Jeff Boyce, Gary Magwood, and Bob Vilas—in a Subaru wagon.

◄ At Road Atlanta, driver Dave Jahns launches his Spirit R/T, which comes down quite spiritedly on its nose, triggering the air bag, and then does a swell flip and rolls to the tire wall. Lunch time! Team gets style points for showing up at the Michigan International Speedway autocrosses with a spare car. (Co-drivers Joe Leonard and Richard Ehrenberg finished second last year in a Dodge Omni GLH.)

▲ At Watkins Glen, Steven Meitz's Corvette is thirteenth in single-lap times, but he eventually wins the Sports/GT1 class and finishes third overall. Meitz, 36, read about the Cannonball Run in his youth and saw the movie. Co-driver Kurt Gifford gets bagged by Ohio trooper. Despite these accomplishments, both have yet to meet Burt Reynolds. Slick BMW wagon at right finishes third in class behind a pair of Subaru wagons.

◄ At Charlotte, Yates Jr., foreground at left, watches co-driver Mike Roberts put the '72 Challenger off the speedway track. Roberts had taken the wheel after complaining that his teammate had muddied the car after ditching at both the Putnam Park and the Road Atlanta tracks. A day after the One Lap ends, Brock the Younger carries on the Cannonball tradition, driving an IROC-Z to California from Ann Arbor in 31 hours, averaging something less than Gurney's memorable time.

▲ *Spectators ask, "What kind of kit car is that?" It's not—it's a real 1933 Buick Victoria. One minor modification: it's got a Corvette drivetrain. The two-door was entered by driver/builder Glen Dodd, who won the bracket drag race at Indianapolis Raceway Park and went 102 mph on this Watkins Glen straight.*

Al DeBoni's crew, above, performs shut-eye maneuver in Motel Spirit R/T. Elsewhere, Grimshaw and Carlson get five hours sleep in Charlotte, later develop interesting routine of registering for hotel rooms while Buffum runs the speed events. Rest doesn't increase alertness: Grimshaw says team went off course while being engaged by Carlson stories.

At top, C/D's Tom Cosgrove remembers mom's directive about oral hygiene. Above, Don Lee and Michael Hickman's bitchin' 1981 Camaro was almost as cool as the 1962 Ford Falcon wagon driven by Bob Edens, Peter Neal, and Dennis Thomas of—where else?—Lodi, California.

THE OFFICIAL RESULTS

CLASS WINNERS

Sports/GT Cars over $30,000: Steven Meitz/Kurt Gifford, 1991 Chevrolet Corvette

Sports/GT Cars under $30,000: Phil Berg/Don Schroeder/Everett Smith, 1990 Mitsubishi Eclipse GSX

Special Sports: Ron Daly/Steve Blomme, 1973 Datsun 240Z

Luxury Sedans: John Buffum/Satch Carlson/Tom Grimshaw, 1992 BMW M5

Sedans: Billy Edwards/Ralph Beckman/Britt Ponder, 1992 Mitsubishi Galant VR4

Station Wagons: Jeff Boyce/Gary Magwood/Bob Vilas, 1992 Subaru Legacy Touring Wagon

Pickup Trucks: Edward Dow/Daniel Dow, 1991 GMC Syclone

Economy Sedans: Eric Grubelich/Mark Grubelich/Robert Kane, 1985 Plymouth Horizon

EVENT WINNERS

Venue: Indianapolis Raceway Park
Event: Bracket drag race
Winner: Dodd/Fant/Stein
Car: 1933 Buick Victoria

Venue: Putnam Park
Event: Autocross
Winner: Buffum/Carlson/Grimshaw
Car: 1992 BMW M5

Venue: Road Atlanta
Event: Autocross
Winner: Buffum/Carlson/Grimshaw
Car: 1992 BMW M5

Venue: Chimney Rock, N.C.
Event: TSD Hillclimb
Winner: Teal/Teal/Briody
Car: 1992 Olds Ninety Eight Touring Sedan

Venue: Charlotte Motor Speedway
Event: Autocross
Winner: Edwards/Beckman/Ponder
Car: 1992 Mitsubishi Galant VR4

Venue: Pocono
Event: Autocross (canceled)

Venue: Watkins Glen
Event: Autocross
Winner: Buffum/Carlson/Grimshaw
Car: 1992 BMW M5

Venue: Michigan International Speedway
Event: Autocross 1
Winner: Those guys again
Car: You know

Venue: Michigan International Speedway
Event: Autocross 2
Winner: Same
Car: Same

Rare Falcon wagon from Lodi spins in turn one at Road Atlanta and hits inside guardrail. Driver Bob Edens promptly chains the fender to the guardrail and, shifting into reverse, pulls the fender and the bumper neatly away from the front tire.

Contrary to rumors, Buffum's winning M5 did not use Atlas Amigos, opting instead for fancy rally tires. Rules said cars had to use the same tires for the entire event.

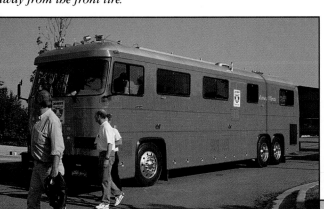

◄

Where's Brock Yates in all of this? At the wheel of a red Newell bus, where he belongs. A blue Prelude runs into it on Interstate 81. Miraculously, Yates survives, and begins planning explanation to owner Larry Minor. This is not at all like being on the set with Burt. Below, left to right, winners Carlson, Buffum, and Grimshaw discuss who's buying tonight with heavy hitter in suit, C/D Editor William Jeanes. (Continued next page)

OVERALL RESULTS

THE TEN BEST: 1. John Buffum, Satch Carlson, Tom Grimshaw, 1992 BMW M5. **2.** Billy Edwards, Ralph Beckman, Britt Ponder, 1992 Mitsubishi Galant VR4. **3.** Steven Meitz, Kurt Gifford, 1991 Chevrolet Corvette. **4.** Stephen Jones, Rick Reizen, 1990 Consulier GTP Sport. **5.** James Smith, Stephen Wynne, 1992 Mitsubishi 3000GT VR4. **6.** David Anderson, William Knepper, 1990 Nissan 300ZX Turbo. **7.** Phil Berg, Don Schroeder, Everett Smith, 1990 Mitsubishi Eclipse GSX. **8.** Dan Schaut, Stan Milam, 1990 Nissan 300ZX Turbo **9.** Jeff Boyce, Gary Magwood, Bob Vilas, 1992 Subaru Legacy Touring Wagon. **10.** Dan Corcoran, Robert Thomson, Howard Kelly, 1993 Audi Quattro S4.

ALL THE REST: 11. Geoffrey Thornton, Donald Metz, 1989 Ford Mustang LX. 12. Tim Winker, Herm Johnson, Ann Gelehrter, 1992 Saab 9000 Turbo. 13. Albert DeBoni, Robert Boutin, Albert Chan, 1991 Dodge Spirit R/T. 14. Claire Lilly, Bob Lilly, Michael Nellis, 1992 Dodge Daytona ROC-Z. 15. Fay Teal, David Teal, James Briody, 1992

Oldsmobile Ninety Eight Touring Sedan. 16. Gordon Medenica, Scott Hughes, Lance White, 1991 BMW M3. 17. Stu Ballantyne, Tom Hnatiw, Al Ayre, 1992 Subaru Legacy Touring Wagon. 18. Edward Dow, Daniel Dow, 1991 GMC Syclone. 19. Bob Gibson, Steve Bray, Ed Luce, 1992 Pontiac Grand Prix GT. 20. William Cook, Don Hubbard, 1985 Nissan 300ZX Turbo. 21. John Keller, John Rose, Fred Mis, Roy Hopkins, 1992 Oldsmobile Achieva. 22. John Raymond, Sten Eric Carlson, Kapriyel Ferah, 1993 Audi Quattro S4. 23. Mark Gasser, William Pintaric, 1990 Mitsubishi Eclipse GSX. 24. John Russo, John Calabro, 1990 Chevrolet Corvette ZR-1. 25. Brad Smith, Teresa Smith, 1988 Chevrolet Cavalier Z24. 26. Joseph Russo, Robert Dossinger, 1990 Chevrolet Corvette ZR-1. 27. Allan Dick Jr., Norman Dick, Allan Dick, 1992 Chevrolet Lumina Euro 3.4. 28. John Beutell, William Beutell, Scott Ceyzyk, 1989 Merkur XR4Ti. 29. Ron Daly, Steve Blomme, 1973 Datsun 240Z. 30. Donald Lee, Michael Hickman, 1981 Chevrolet Camaro Z-28. 31. Tony Bruno, Mike Bruno, Steve Bruno, 1989 Ford Taurus SHO. 32. Ted Cureton, Joy Cureton, 1991 Porsche 911 Carrera 4. 33. Steven Pusker, David Pusker, 1991 Nissan 300ZX Turbo. 34. Mike Kane, Barry Suntrup, Ray Gulson, 1993 BMW 535i Touring. 35. Glen Dodd, Reese Fant, Mike Stein, 1933 Buick Victoria. 36. Richard Ehrenberg, Joseph Leonard, David Jahns, 1991

Dodge Spirit R/T. 37. Bob Edens, Peter Neal, Dennis Thomas, 1962 Ford Falcon wagon. 38. Eric Grubelich, Mark Grubelich, Robert Kane, 1985 Plymouth Horizon. 39. Brock Yates Jr., Mike Roberts, 1972 Dodge Challenger. 40. Michael Hanley, Harry Neiman, 1979 Jaguar XJS. 41. Michael Graves, Glenn Skala, James Zizelman, Al Klossner, 1993 GMC Jimmy SLE 42. Michael Winter, Richard Frank, 1988 Honda CRX Si. 43. Richard Roberts, Bart Baxter, 1989 Pontiac Firebird Formula. 44. Gary Dickson, Scott Dickson, Mariel Dickson, 1992 SAAC Mk I. 45. Alister Bell, Alan Manessy, Scott Yon, 1993 Land Rover Defender 110. 46. Russell Estes, Maurice Cozzo, 1991 Volkswagen GTI. 47. Ray Windle, Larry Gulledge, Mark Mancini, 1967 Ford Custom 500 police car. 48. Bruce McNaughton, William Hopkins, 1984 Jaguar XJS 3.6. 49. Juli "Reno" Burke, Jacqueline "Vegas" Macy, 1992 Audi 100CS Quattro wagon. 50. Chris Sarkisian, Tom Sarkisian, 1985 Ferrari 308GTSi Quattrovalvole. 51. Kurt Gossen, Chuck Thompson, 1991 Lincoln Town Car. 52. John Joiner, Terry McLeod, 1991 Ford Mustang GT. 53. Tom Cosgrove, Marty Padgett, 1993 Nissan King Cab. 54. John Vanier, Dan Witol, Robert Klimas, 1986 Volvo 740 Turbo. 55. Jamie Schneider, Jason Yost, Brad Boender, 1991 GMC Sierra. **56.** Rocky Aoki, Susumo Saito, Kevin Aoki, 1971 Volkswagen Beetle limousine. **57.** Paul Porteous, Paul Whittrock, 1988 BMW M3.

("One Lap," continued)

◄

At left center, the stylish Kurt Gossen, driver of the "Lincoln from Hell," gives rally tips while baring King Richard-quality pearlies to C/D's Juli Burke and alleged Duke graduate Marty Padgett. Burke finishes 49th; Padgett 53rd. Lackluster showing attributed to low sugar count. Gossen also upsets Yates, announcing in official tones after the crashes at Road Atlanta that the event will be delayed an hour. Petty is absent from ordeal, and therefore not offended.

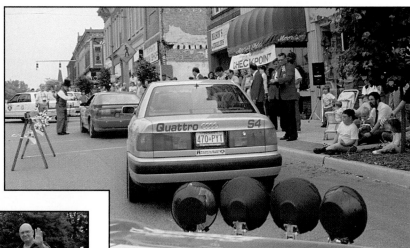

Above, team of Stephen Jones and Rick Reizen discover the Consulier's serious defroster weakness during a rainy-day autocrosss run at Charlotte. Side windows are then removed, soaking everything inside the car. Team vows to return next year—with another Consulier. Why? Composite-chassis car turns out to be somehow police-friendly. Although caught in six instant-on traps, cops inexplicably don't pull it over.

▲

C/D's Burke and co-driver Jacqueline Macy broadcast racy novel VOX over CB radio at 4 a.m., keeping most competitors awake. Not true they charged $5 for the first mile, and $2 for every mile after that. Rain-shy photogs fail to capture heavy use of Rain-X by Glen Dodd's 1933 Buick and the Land Rover team after their wipers break down. Dodd testifies: "The faster you go, the better it works."

At left, typical delirious fans along the course go nuclear upon seeing One-Lappers. Above, we're in Greencastle, Indiana, where the mayor's name is a politician's dream—Mike Harmless. He informs teams, "Go ahead and burn out. There'll be no tickets today." Canadian-entered "Lincoln from Hell" cracks up crowd as occupants perform amazingly bad Richard Petty impressions over the PA. Leaving town, John Keller's Achieva hits a 60-pound bag of laundry that had fallen off a truck.

TEN BEST USED CAR SIGNS

By John Phillips III

Used-car lots, like meteorites and Gerald Ford, are evidently likely to fall just about anywhere. In Franklinville, New York, for instance. That's where buyers are dying to test-drive the 1991 dirt-tracker that is parked on the front lawn of the Babbitt & Easton Funeral Home.

Is the recession killing used-car sales? Not that we can tell. Not as long as we've got imaginative used-car salesmen. And we do.

Business is booming at Consignments 'R' Us/Pawn Cars & Fashion Wear. Buyers are bullish on Bob Carey's Cars and Cattle Company. The vehicular cream is rising to the top at Hoppy's Used Cars and Dairy Dream. In Indiana, Roach's Auto Sales and Ceramics is out for the kiln. Harold Robbins fans are flocking to Fort Gudim Paperbacks and Auto Sales in Minnesota. No one is getting fleeced at Cars and Carpets in Wisconsin. And North Carolinians couldn't be happier about getting sheared at Jack's Car Corner and Barber Stylist.

Okay, okay. Not everybody is rolling in black ink. Guys like Swindle Auto Sales in Kentucky, Dearth Motors in Wisconsin, and Lemmen Used Cars in Michigan. But those are clear marketing faux pas. The owners ought to get some pointers from the showroom manager at Too Fun Auto Sales. Or from Hubbard Auto and Cemetery Monuments in North Carolina. Hubbard's motto: "Walk-ins welcome."

▼
Jane acquired much of her vehicular inventory during the very early stages of divorce proceedings.

Chris Stephens
New Bern, North Carolina

▲
Metrocrest Motors, open every third Thursday, 1 to 2 p.m.

John Meyer
Carrollton, Texas

▶
Perfect one-stop shopping if only they also sold liquor and X-rated videos.

Dan Whitman
Lansing, Michigan

◀
Boone's Import Cars: "Inventory Control Our Specialty."

Ralph Paxton
Boone, North Carolina

◀
Truth-in-advertising winner. You can't beat Beater's neat four-seaters.

Steffew Hagen
Parksville, British Columbia

(Continued next page)

191

► At E&E Auto Sales, spiraling inflation and the winds of fortune had a clear effect on overhead.

George A. Carson
Sturgeon Bay, Wisconsin

◄ They're clean. They're used. It doesn't say anything about bent, okay?

Janet Woodward
Denver, Colorado

▼ As a parking valet, James was inattentive, sometimes clumsy.

Ted Harris
Chandler, Arizona

▲ Lose your pawn ticket, lose your Edsel.

Mi Ae Lipe
La Crosse, Wisconsin

► Specializing in Barracudas and Marlins—where prospective buyers need not ask, "Is the tank full?"

Joe Dockery
Naperville, Illinois

192

ROYAL PALMS IN FAHKAHATCHEE STRAND

A FRESH-WATER SAWGRASS MARSH IN THE EVERGLADES

A MANGROVE TREE GROWING ON A FLORIDA BAY SANDBAR

A FIRE RAGING ON A PINELAND RIDGE

EGRETS, HERONS AND OTHER EVERGLADES BIRDS

A JUMBLE OF SEA SHELLS ON A CAPE SABLE BEACH

A NEST OF BABY ANHINGAS IN A MOSS-HUNG CYPRESS

VERDANT KEYS SCATTERED ACROSS BISCAYNE BAY

THE EVERGLADES

THE AMERICAN WILDERNESS/TIME-LIFE BOOKS/NEW YORK

BY ARCHIE CARR
AND THE EDITORS OF TIME-LIFE BOOKS

TIME-LIFE BOOKS
———————————

FOUNDER: Henry R. Luce 1898-1967

Editor-in-Chief: Hedley Donovan
Chairman of the Board: Andrew Heiskell
President: James R. Shepley
Chairman, Executive Committee: James A. Linen
Group Vice President: Rhett Austell

Vice Chairman: Roy E. Larsen
———————————

MANAGING EDITOR: Jerry Korn
Assistant Managing Editors: David Maness,
Martin Mann, A. B. C. Whipple
Planning Director: Oliver E. Allen
Art Director: Sheldon Cotler
Chief of Research: Beatrice T. Dobie
Director of Photography: Melvin L. Scott
Senior Text Editor: Diana Hirsh
Assistant Art Director: Arnold C. Holeywell

PUBLISHER: Joan D. Manley
General Manager: John D. McSweeney
Business Manager: John Steven Maxwell
Sales Director: Carl G. Jaeger
Promotion Director: Paul R. Stewart
Public Relations Director: Nicholas Benton

THE AMERICAN WILDERNESS
SERIES EDITOR: Charles Osborne
Editorial Staff for *The Everglades:*
Picture Editor: Iris Friedlander
Designer: Charles Mikolaycak
Staff Writers: Gerald Simons,
Harvey B. Loomis, Simone D. Gossner,
Anne Horan
Chief Researcher: Martha T. Goolrick
Researchers: Doris Coffin, Rhea Finkelstein,
John Hamlin, Beatrice Hsia, Carol I. Clingan,
Ruth Silva
Design Assistant: Vincent Lewis

Editorial Production
Production Editor: Douglas B. Graham
Assistant Production Editor: Gennaro C. Esposito
Quality Director: Robert L. Young
Assistant Quality Director: James J. Cox
Copy Staff: Rosalind Stubenberg (chief),
Eleanore W. Karsten, Barbara Quarmby,
Florence Keith
Picture Department: Dolores A. Littles,
Joan Lynch
Traffic: Feliciano Madrid

Valuable assistance was given by the
following departments and individuals of
Time Inc.: Editorial Production, Norman
Airey; Library, Benjamin Lightman; Picture
Collection, Doris O'Neil; Photographic
Laboratory, George Karas; TIME-LIFE News
Service, Murray J. Gart; Correspondents
Margot Hapgood (London), Ruth Annan and
Jane Rieker (Miami).

The Author: Archie Carr is a graduate research professor in the zoology department of the University of Florida, where he has taught since 1937. An internationally known biologist, he is the author of nine books, including *The Reptiles* and *The Land and Wildlife of Africa* in the LIFE Nature Library. He has also written numerous scientific papers and several short stories, one of which won the O. Henry Award in 1956. Dr. Carr has also received the John Burroughs medal for exemplary nature writing and the Daniel Giraud Elliott medal for preeminence in zoology.

The Consultant: William B. Robertson Jr. is a research biologist on the staff of Everglades National Park, and a specialist in animal populations. For his Ph.D. degree at the University of Illinois (in 1955), he wrote his doctoral dissertation on the land birds of southern Florida. After a stint on the Illinois Natural History Survey, he returned to Florida in 1956. One of his current interests is a study of the endangered bald-eagle population of the park.

The Cover: A southern Florida creek, framed by the fronds of a cabbage palm and bordered by a red mangrove at right, laps the edge of a plain of sawgrass, the ubiquitous ground cover of the Everglades. A clump of cabbage palms partially obscures a "tree island" of hardwoods on the horizon.

Contents

A Low-lying, Watery Wilderness

The Everglades region of southern Florida (green rectangle above) includes some 13,000 square miles of wilderness, shown in shades of green in the detailed relief map at right. The predominant terrain is marshy grassland, represented by dotted green areas. Wooded tracts are shown in darker green; urban areas in yellow.

The entire region is low and flat, making for poor drainage. The interior, drenched by 50 to 60 inches of annual rainfall, remains largely under water most of the year. However, the land tilts slightly downward from the region north of Lake Okeechobee (map on page 22); this natural declivity keeps the peninsula draining southward at a rate that has been accelerated by the digging of canals (straight green lines south of Lake Okeechobee and blue lines north of the lake).

Black squares indicate points of special interest; a line of blue dots at bottom left traces the Wilderness Waterway, a 100-mile-long route for small boats. Red lines mark boundaries of parks and wildlife refuges. Black lines mark older roads, including the Janes road (at left) and Loop Road (center) traveled by the author.

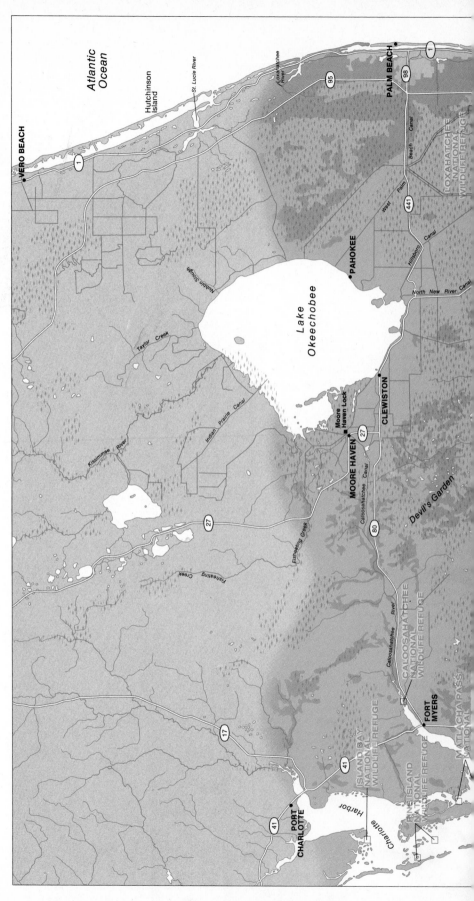

1/ The River and the Plain

Here are no lofty peaks seeking the sky, no mighty glaciers or rushing streams.... Here is land, tranquil in its quiet beauty, serving not as the source of water but as the last receiver of it.

HARRY S. TRUMAN/ *ADDRESS AT DEDICATION OF EVERGLADES NATIONAL PARK*

Not long ago my wife and I spent a day cruising a network of roads in central Florida near the city of Orlando. We were looking for the beginnings of the Everglades. It might seem an odd place to be searching for the beginning of a wilderness. Traffic whizzed past; Walt Disney World was nearby; and strictly speaking, the Everglades were away down south of Lake Okeechobee, a hundred miles from where we were.

But ecologically the Everglades are linked with a long series of lakes and streams that begins halfway up the interior of peninsular Florida, on the southernmost slopes of the high mid-section of the state known as the Central Ridge. From there this hydrologic system fans out southward through much of the lower half of the peninsula, extending down the Kissimmee River Valley, into Lake Okeechobee and then out across a vast, gently sloping plain covered with sawgrass (a sedge up to 12 feet tall, with leaves set with fine sharp teeth along the midrib and edges). This enormous spread of grass, punctuated with little clumps of hardwood trees—known as tree islands—extends to the bottom of the peninsula, to the coastal mangrove fringe, the sandy storm dunes, and the brackish estuaries of Florida Bay and the Gulf of Mexico.

The southwesternmost corner of this region is the 2,020-square-mile Everglades National Park, the third largest national park in the country. Though it seems horizon-wide when you look out across it, the area it covers is actually only a corner of the whole Everglades, which spread back northeast to Lake Okeechobee and beyond, for 125 miles. To the north and west of the park lies Big Cypress Swamp, 2,400 square miles of complex landscape so closely linked with the Everglades that in places it is hard to tell where one begins and the other leaves off.

Though the sawgrass plain is the heart of the Everglades and though millions of people have visited the Glades—as Floridians call them —queer notions about the place persist. Perhaps influenced by what they have heard about Big Cypress, visitors still arrive expecting to see a dim, mysterious swamp-forest full of reptiles, exotic birds and eerie noises, a sort of Hollywood jungle set in which boa constrictors or a band of apes would not come as a total surprise. This probably accounts for the let-down look park rangers see in the faces of some newcomers as they gaze out over the sawgrass plain for the first time.

But the Everglades are unique: they have no counterpart anywhere on earth. Although the region is almost perfectly flat, few landscapes anywhere have a more intricate interplay of physical and biological factors. The plain is old sea bottom—or, more accurately, new sea bottom, since the whole sawgrass region was exposed only a few thousand years ago by the last retreat of the sea during an ice-age buildup. No folding or warping of the sea bottom was involved. The water simply drained off as the ice at the North and South Poles built up, and the limestone bottom came out as flat as a table top. The land it made tilts barely enough to keep water flowing across it, when there is any water there and when no man-made obstacles intervene. It is this flow that integrates the southern tip of Florida with Lake Okeechobee and the Kissimmee Valley into one vast ecological entity.

If one has the time, the best way to appreciate this unified structure is to follow the drainage gradient—the excruciatingly slow descent of the land from the southern end of the Central Ridge to the Gulf of Mexico on the west, to Florida Bay on the south and to the Atlantic on the east. I had decided to trace out as much of the drainage system as I could without swimming through any culverts, and that is what my wife and I were doing southwest of Orlando that day I mentioned.

We had spent hours searching, and by late afternoon had moved so near the origins of the system that going farther was really superfluous; but the maps we had with us carried the headwaters farther still, and the gap was a challenge. The drainage of this stretch of country, however, was only vaguely shown, and it is risky to indulge a sudden whim to leave the freeway there to see where some creek comes from.

After three hours of combing the area, dodging traffic and denouncing absent map makers for their discordant views of Orange County geography, we finally fixed on a body of water called Turkey Lake as what we were looking for—as the real beginning of the Everglades. The lake was clearly in the Shingle Creek drainage system that we knew flowed southward into Lake Tohopekaliga, the northernmost of the big lakes in the Kissimmee Valley chain. But even after we decided that Turkey Lake was what we were after, we could find no access to the lake shore from any of the roads around it. None, that is, except by vague two-track trails that faded out in the woods around the shore. Finally, in desperation, I turned off into one of these trails, and we quickly found ourselves blocked by a garbage dump that spread for acres through what had once been a fine live-oak hammock. We parked and went on from there on foot, and after walking a hundred yards or so, came out suddenly at the edge of Turkey Lake.

It was a good lake; you could see that at once. Somehow, it had escaped the fate of the woods around it. The water was clean, fish were striking, and somewhere a kingfisher rattled. I took off my shoes and waded out through a narrow zone of marshy shore to open water, flushing a banded water snake along the way. There were patches of applesnail eggs on the cattail stems. Farther down the shoreline a Louisiana heron rose, and up the other way in a cypress tree a snakebird was preening. Though it was a fair, warm Sunday afternoon, there was only one boat on the lake, with a man in it quietly casting for bass. I wondered what curious quirk in the trend of the times had saved a good lake like that from the usual fate of suburban waters. Finding it there added joy to our pilgrimage to the upper limits of the Everglades, and I hoped this augured well for the future of the region.

Looking down into the water around my feet, I saw a posse of gambusias, six little mosquito fish an inch or so long—pusselguts, they call them in northern Florida. There were two males in the school and four females. One of the males was lording it over the other fish, and I fell to musing that back before Florida got into the hands of developers and engineers an able little fish like that, if charged with supernatural drive, might have made his way from Turkey Lake clear down to wherever salt water stopped him at the end of the Everglades. And even today, I thought, if he followed the man-made changes in the route he still might complete the journey. Anyway, he could do it with much less trouble than I could; and the thought came to me that I ought to let him try. There in Turkey Lake, far up inside Florida, the fish was still

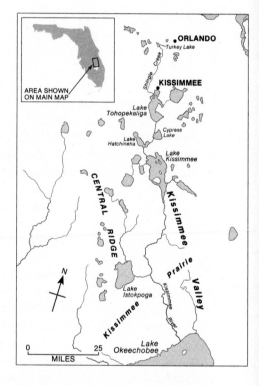

The area shown on this map, which supplements the map on pages 18-19, is a vital part of the ecological system of the Everglades, although it lies to the north of Lake Okeechobee—usually considered the northern boundary of the Glades. The waters that feed the Everglades originate just south of Orlando in the Kissimmee Valley and collect in Lake Okeechobee, before beginning their slow southward journey to the tip of the peninsula.

within the Everglades basin, and in his minuscule way was a working part of its ecology. The slow flow of water bound together all the varied biological communities of southern Florida: the Kissimmee Valley, Lake Okeechobee, Big Cypress Swamp, the sawgrass Glades, the coastal mangrove forest, and even the adjacent waters of Florida Bay and the Gulf of Mexico. All these geographical features were, in a very real way, parts of a single ecologically organized unit.

It was this thought that started me tracing the little gambusia's downstream journey in my mind. I imagined him puttering about the edges of Turkey Lake searching for the outlet, locating it at last, then working his way down ditches, through culverts and across ponds, into Shingle Creek, the first sizable stream of the Everglades basin. From there on, the trail was plain, downstream to the western edge of Lake Tohopekaliga. From here southward there would be some lake hopping to do down the upper Kissimmee Valley. In the days before the way was strewn with levees, locks and dams, fish surely traveled from lake to lake by simply moving when flood times came. Nowadays the route from Tohopekaliga goes through three other big lakes—Cypress, Hatchineha, and Kissimmee—that are connected by canals.

I became intimately acquainted with the route down the chain of lakes one cold, rainy November day a few years ago when I was invited to go on a duck census there. We traveled in an airboat, one of the various gasoline-powered inventions of the devil. For chasing poachers and monitoring duck populations, airboats are useful, I suppose, but they are terrible vehicles all the same—uncomfortable, intrusive and noisy. Anyway, we took an airboat all the way down the chain of lakes and back, on a trip to count the local colony of the mottled duck, a resident mallard and the only duck that nests in peninsular Florida.

The trip began at the city of Kissimmee, on the northern end of Lake Tohopekaliga. We blasted away from the boat ramp at the edge of town and raced down the right-hand shore of the lake, keeping just inside the shoreline vegetation. I noticed that a lot of new flat shore had been exposed since my last visit. For nearly a hundred years the whole Kissimmee Valley has been subjected to drainage operations of one kind or another. The latest, carried out only recently, was a drastic drawdown of Toho's waters, aimed at exposing bottom deposits to oxidation, with the hope of lessening the lake's overenrichment with nutrients from sewage and fertilizers. Part of this pollution comes from the city of Kissimmee; but some also comes from far up the little tributaries of Shingle Creek, even including some near Orlando. The Tohopekaliga water, in turn, pouring southward through the valley, was polluting the lakes farther down the chain and even exacerbating the problems of Lake Okeechobee itself. Thus Orlando dishwater goads Okeechobee algae into intemperate growth—proof that the flow of water integrates the whole Everglades basin into one ecosystem.

All the way down through the chain of lakes, the airboat pilot kept us just inside the fringe of shoreline plants. Where these were rushes or maiden cane we flushed few waterfowl; but wherever the grass gave way to patches of pickerelweed, or to open fields of water lilies, ducks appeared in abundance. Mottled ducks were few and scattered, but there were hundreds of wood ducks, blue-winged teal in thousands, a lot of ringnecks, shovelers and widgeon, and even a few little bunches of greenhead mallards, which one doesn't see often in Florida, or I don't. In some places teal and coot were so thick and so loath to leave that we charged into the splash of their rising. That horizontal rain, added to what came down from the sky, kept us soaking wet. We had lunch in a warm little restaurant beside the lock and dam at the head of the Kissimmee River, then made the whole ranting journey back in a steady rain. The round trip was 150 miles, the mottled duck count was 300. And I had seen for myself that, given long life and a driving wanderlust, a pusselgut could very well travel from the delta of Shingle Creek in western Lake Toho to the head of the Kissimmee River.

The Kissimmee River is the chief tributary of Lake Okeechobee and the master stream for a vast complex of landscapes linked to the Everglades system—prairies, marshes, sloughs, hammocks and pine flatwoods. Parts of the Kissimmee Valley look very much like the Everglades—so much so that some of it, the sawgrass and wet prairies in the valley's southern and western sections, is sometimes called the Little Everglades. Before the Kissimmee River was channelized, when it meandered through a hundred miles of meadows, its valley was much wetter than it now is. Nevertheless, early visitors recognized it as promising cattle country, and soon after the Seminole wars—in the 1830s and '40s—the region began to go into ranches. As these spread, artificial drainage increased, and the water table went down markedly. But it is still good country, and parts of it have hardly changed at all.

The flatlands of the Kissimmee basin, including the region loosely known as Kissimmee Prairie, are a part of the coastal lowlands, the series of sandy marine terrace plains that extend down both sides of pen-

A pair of mosquito fish—the two-inch-long female is much larger than the male—scout the water for a meal. Scientifically known as Gambusia, the fish was nicknamed for its main food: an adult can daily consume up to its own weight in mosquito larvae.

insular Florida and meet northwest of Lake Okeechobee. In the north these terraces are mainly covered with pine flatwoods of several different kinds. In the south they merge with the sawgrass Everglades below Lake Okeechobee and with the tree swamps, glade lands and pine flatwoods of Big Cypress Swamp.

In Florida the word prairie is applied to two different landscapes, neither of which, except in flatness, resembles the dry Western country the term usually brings to mind. In northern Florida where I live, prairies are solution basins—that is, marshy lakes filled with emergent and floating herbaceous plants, and subject to abrupt drying up when water levels drop and the water drains through holes in the limestone bottoms. One season you may fish from a boat in one of these places; the next season you may walk across dry ground there. These northern Florida prairies are similar in general appearance to what are known as wet prairies in the Everglades, where they are one of the landscape variants in the sawgrass plain.

Prairie means something different in the expanse of lowlands above Lake Okeechobee. The prairies here are low, flat, tremendous meadows, set with stands of saw palmettos, copses of live oaks, groves of cabbage palms or mixed hammocks of various temperate and tropical hardwood trees.

The dry prairie is the characteristic country of the Kissimmee Valley region; nowhere on earth is there a terrain just like those short grass and saw-palmetto savannas. A place it brings to mind is the grassy savanna land of eastern Africa. Kissimmee Prairie all but cries out for antelope, but lacking those, it has made do with white-tailed deer, wild Kissimmee ponies and box turtles. It is a land where long-legged birds stalk the uncluttered ground, or walk from pond to pond, and where once I saw wild turkeys, sandhill cranes and wood storks standing together on a burn. The storks were just at the edge of a drying pond, the turkeys and cranes not 50 feet away on fire-blackened grass.

Like most of Florida, the original prairie was almost surely a landscape shaped by fire. As in the sawgrass Everglades—and in most of the big savanna lands of the world—fire is constantly in the background here; although its role is confused by other factors that help to keep the land as grassland. Periodic drought and periodic flooding, for instance, are both involved. Some of the original aspect of Kissimmee Prairie was no doubt due to seasonal soaking and a high water table and some to seasonal drought and baking of the surface. But the most fundamental factor that kept short-grass savanna here was probably the fires that intermittently or regularly crept or swept across the land and prevented the growth of broad-leaved trees except where some special local condition allowed patches of hardwood and palm to develop.

Before the white ranchers came, the prairie was Indian country. The Seminoles loved to burn the land—to flush out game, to kill ticks and rattlesnakes, or to make new grazing land for their cattle and ponies. When white men moved in they did the same, only worse, because they were more uneasy than the Indians about snakes, ticks and the black wolves that howled in the night. But the question is, how prevalent was fire before people of any kind came to the prairie? The answer obviously depends on how often you think lightning hit tinder at times when dry fuel lay on the land. It seems to me that this must have been often, and that you see a sign of it in the avid way each new generation of prairie birds quickly learns to crowd onto newly burned ground to eat the cooked animals there, especially the big grasshoppers that seem too dim-witted to flee from fire.

Two characteristic birds of the prairie community are especially fond of cooked victuals. One of these is Audubon's caracara; another is the Florida sandhill crane. There are two distinct subspecies of this crane in the state. One is migratory; it nests in Michigan and spends the winter in the South. The other is a year-round Florida resident, and its chief remaining stronghold is Kissimmee Prairie. Its feeding habits obviously evolved in a prairie environment, and its predilection for burned ground suggests a long association with fire. Anyway, back in the days when fires were more prevalent than they are today, if you wanted to find cranes the best thing to do was to ride a horse out to where a big smoke had been rising for a day or so.

When you got out to such a burn you nearly always found Audubon's caracara there. The caracara is as intrinsic a part of this landscape as the saw palmetto. Though it doesn't exactly look the part, the caracara is a kind of long-legged hawk. The name caracara is supposed to suggest the creature's voice, a peculiar grating croak that is uttered as the bird tilts its head back between its shoulders.

The third member of the avian triumvirate of Kissimmee Prairie is the burrowing owl. A small bird, standing about nine inches tall, it too has very long legs for its body. While this amiable owl is a characteristic occupant of Kissimmee Prairie, it also turns up in other parts of the peninsula that have a proper prairie look. Much of Florida has recently been put into short-grass savanna, in the form of pastures, golf courses and airports; and these are the habitats the little owls have colonized. Their settling at Miami International Airport stirred the Florida Audubon Society to have the airport designated a wildlife preserve.

Burrowing owls are gregarious, and if you come across one anywhere it is likely to be a member of a colony. The burrows are tunnels that, in Florida at least, usually seem to be scratched out by the owls themselves. They are about three inches high and five wide, and go down at a slant for several feet, the final depth often being determined by the top of the water table. The burrow serves as refuge, dormitory and nesting place. During leisure times outside, the owls stand about on little raised places, and bob up and down engagingly when approached.

Because the prairie landscape in its original form was unusually well suited to human needs, the man-made changes there seem a little less drastic than in other Florida terrain. The whole region is certainly much drier now than it was when the wolves and Indians left it, because of the increased drainage that came with the growth of the human population and the spread of the ranches. At the same time, the frequency of wildfire has been reduced. While this is clearly a blessing for snakes, quail, mice and box turtles, it is bad for cranes and caracaras, depriving them of the grasshopper bakes that brightened the days of their fathers. Both of these birds are as stimulated by the disaster of fire as storks are by the disaster of fish-stranding drought. It may be because of this change that cranes and caracaras are less numerous now in Kissimmee Prairie than, say, back in the 1930s when burning was practically a ceremonial practice among tenant farmers.

But I ought to return to tracking the little mosquito fish in his travels southward. We left him in Lake Tohopekaliga. From there he would continue his trip via the Kissimmee River, which flows out of Toho's southern edge. The descent of the river, now that the canal has sliced across all the bends and meanderings, is a great deal shorter than it used to be. A fish would find it all steady swimming today, with the flowing stream cut into placid segments by six locks. I wonder whether the gambusia swims fast enough, once inside the lock, to leave it in company with the same boat he had to await to enter it. But no matter; just imagine him cruising on down through the cut-up river into 65E, the last Kissimmee lock, and out into Lake Okeechobee, the "Big Water."

Okeechobee is 750 square miles of water—roughly 35 miles long and 30 miles wide, and next to Lake Michigan the biggest fresh-water lake wholly within the contiguous United States. It has an average depth of only 14 or 15 feet. Its most important tributary, after the Kissimmee

River, is Fisheating Creek to the northwest, the name of which is a translation of the Seminole word *thlothlopopkahatchee*—changed, presumably, because it was hard to pronounce.

The lake has no natural outlet. Originally it just flooded out over its southern rim and spread into the Everglades. The southern shore used to be densely forested with a magnificent swamp of buttressed custard-apple trees standing on a deep deposit of peat. So in the old days an itinerant fish could have crossed the lake to its southern shore, waited for the wet season, and then wended its way out through any of a thousand little waterways into the custard-apple swamp. At that time these waterways served as small floodgates, holding back high water in the lake, rationing out the excess, and thus prolonging the productive wet stage of the Everglades' annual cycle of drought and flood.

Our latter-day gambusia, however, would find no downstream way out of Okeechobee anywhere except through man-made structures. After two disastrous hurricanes, one in 1926 and the other in 1928, dikes were built to protect the rich farmlands south of the lake. Water now leaves only under human control: westward to the Gulf of Mexico by way of the Caloosahatchee River, eastward or southward through canals to the Atlantic or into vast artificially impounded reservoirs —water Conservation Area Nos. 1, 2 and 3. These occupy most of the upper two thirds of the old sawgrass Everglades that has not yet been drained and converted into farmland.

The fish could leave Okeechobee at its southeastern edge by way of the Hillsboro Canal, enter Conservation Area No. 1, and from there proceed south through Area Nos. 2 and 3. But a route closer to the primeval drainage pattern would be from the southernmost shore of the lake into the Miami Canal, across the muck farms to Levee No. 5, then out through a culvert into Conservation Area No. 3. This impoundment adjoins the Shark River Slough and Everglades National Park, and delivers to the park whatever ration of overland flow it gets.

The gambusia is now nearing the heart of the Everglades—Pahayokee, as the Seminoles knew it, or the River of Grass, as Marjory Stoneman Douglas called it in her book of that name. The sawgrass spreads over a mat of peat resting on a limestone plain elevated no more than 15 feet above the sea in which it formed. In places the surface of the stone floor is fantastically pitted and craggy, but you see this only when the covering of peat has burned off or been blown away. This is a country so flat that no streams form on it. When heavy local showers come, the

Nearly four feet tall, a pair of wary sandhill cranes—the male's head is the brighter red—survey their nesting area.

rain water collects in low humps and trickles outward through the saw-grass that covers the plain. The dip of the land is so gentle that you almost have to accept on faith that there is any flow at all. No matter how hard you look down into the clear, warm water you see no movement in it, or see only the tiny surge from the waving sawgrass stems. So there is no real current to speed the gambusia as he threads southward through forests of sawgrass, and more open stands of picker-elweed, skirting the scattered tree islands and pausing to consort with others of his kind under lily pads in alligator holes.

Despite the distance he has come, there are few things out here in the sawgrass to surprise or offend a gambusia. It is bigger country than he knew back at Turkey Lake, and warmer, and more densely grown over with grass; but the familiar array of food is reassuring—the teeming tiny crustaceans and insect larvae that keep him constantly fed along the way. It is the talent of gambusias to take the world as they find it anyway. They inhabit big lakes, little ponds, brackish ditches or the water-filled tops of old cypress stumps. They eat any nourishing object they can swallow or break apart, and they bear living young that are able at birth to fend for themselves. And they reinforce this survival pattern with an extraordinary ability to spread about the country. It seems wholly impossible to account for their presence in some of the places where you find them. In fact, gambusia is one of the fish that cause people to speak of fish raining down, or of their traveling in mud on the feet of birds. It has never been proved that gambusias do either, but their ubiquitousness tempts one to think of such exciting ways for fish to travel. In any case, this mosquito fish whose journey we have traced all the way from Orange County into the sawgrass Everglades has faced no serious hardships anywhere along the way. And now, out in the River of Grass, he is in a classic gambusia landscape —or will be when he moves on down to the lower end of Conservation Area No. 3, goes out through one of the spillways that run under the Tamiami Trail, and swims through the willows and cattails into the sawgrass of Shark River Slough and Everglades National Park.

Out there he will have come a long way from Turkey Lake—200 miles or more, as the crow flies—but nowhere along the way has he been in alien surroundings. A 30-pound channel catfish in Lake Okeechobee may have surprised him, to be sure, but mostly he took with aplomb the new faces he met. Had he been a real fish, instead of an imaginary one, he would long before have stopped in some sedge-rimmed pool or bladderwort patch where his kind of hunting was good—where the little crustaceans called *Cyclops* danced like gnats in the amber water; where young gatorfleas frolicked among hanging duckweed roots; where tender beetle larvae slithered along the rush stems, and pink worms cowered in the silt. All down the line he would have been kept alert by the ever-present chance that he himself might be eaten, but always the danger would have been a known one—a warmouth bass charging through the sheltering weeds of water milfoil, a tiger beetle lurching at him, a dragonfly larva groping hopefully up from the bottom, a diving-bell spider plunging down from his hunting stand on a stem of pickerelweed.

Such threats are only the way of the world to a gambusia. So our traveler could have stopped off anywhere along the way and no doubt have lived happily there; but because he exists only in my mind's eye anyway, I will move him on down toward the zone where the sawgrass begins to feel the nearness of the sea, and the creeping flow of water begins to ravel out into a maze of mangrove-bordered creeks and estuaries. When finally the little fish stops, it is in a place 85 miles downstream from Lake Okeechobee. Out in the northwest lies Big Cypress Swamp. Tarpon Bay is due west, and from there the Shark River flows on to the Gulf of Mexico. To the south, through mangroves and hammocks, are the coastal prairie and the shores of Florida Bay.

There, in the last alligator hole that never turns too salty for his taste, where the first few mangrove trees begin to mingle with the thinning sawgrass and the last of the cypresses, the itinerant gambusia falls in with a band of his fellows and stops. The pool in which he ends his voyage was derived from different sources. Part of it was local rain; part came out of Big Cypress Swamp. The tinge of salt in the pool washed up from downstream during storm times. And another part of the water came in from the farthest reaches of the River of Grass, and all those distant places beyond, where the fish, too, began his journey.

Portraits of the Land

PHOTOGRAPHS BY RUSSELL MUNSON

Observed casually from a plane, the 4.3 million acres of southern Florida that includes the Everglades appears to be an endless green and brown sprawl of flat terrain. The only perceptible movements in this vast, generally watery tract are the ripple of trees and grasses in the wind, the shifting of cloud shadows over the earth and the glint of sun on water.

But an attentive eye can detect the subtle clues that identify differences among the region's landscapes. The aerial photographs on the following pages, taken from a low-flying plane at the start of the summer rainy season, comprise a gallery of portraits of the land that bring out these differences separately and precisely.

The five distinct but dovetailing regions shown, and located by dots on the maps accompanying the photographs, are typical of the watery parts of the Everglades and their environs. Starting with the area below Lake Okeechobee, they stretch 100 miles south to Florida Bay. Southwest of the lake lies Big Cypress Swamp, where green domes of pond cypress dominate paler ranks of dwarf cypress (right). The water that is visible from the air hints at the swamp's soggy nature; it is flooded most of the year.

Adjoining Big Cypress is the region of the Shark River Slough (pages 34-35). Though from above it seems a continuation of the swamp, the land is more open. The green bulges are not cypress domes but irregularly contoured islands of relatively fragile coco plums and other hardwood trees. The tan carpet surrounding them is sawgrass, the sturdy sedge marking the true Everglades; and the sawgrass is underlaid and nurtured by a barely moving sheet of shallow fresh water.

In the third region, at the headwaters of the Shark River (pages 36-37), the land from a height looks like an arid steppe. In reality, it is a lush concentration of sawgrass, cut by creeks that have begun to channel the fresh waters from the Shark River Slough on their seaward journey.

Sawgrass plains yield to mangrove jungles and fresh water to salt water in the last two landscapes shown. The Shark River estuary and the Ten Thousand Islands (pages 38-39) are areas of ceaseless give-and-take between sea and land, each trying to withstand the encroachment of the other. In the region of Florida Bay (pages 40-41), with its mangrove-fringed keys, or islands, the open sea prevails over the land at last.

Like verdant craters, domes of pond cypress thrust up from Big Cypress Swamp, surrounded by dwarf cypress. The marl soil of the swamp is often less than a foot above bedrock. But in some places the porous limestone base has crumbled, leaving shallow depressions with rich, soggy soil in which cypresses can root and grow as high as 100 feet —more than 20 times that of their stunted neighbors. The "ponds" in the center of the cypress domes are caused by deeper sinkholes in the limestone.

Dense hammocks of tropical hardwood trees punctuate a plain of sawgrass and spike rush on the south side of Shark River Slough. The fresh water of the slough collects in this basin and slows almost to a standstill, enabling seedlings that gained footholds here to evolve into well-defined, roughly circular islands.

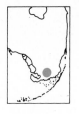 

An island of coco-plum trees stands in the mainstream of the Shark River Slough, where the waters —unlike those at the slough's periphery —move at a slow but sure rate. Their erosive power is clearly revealed in the teardrop shape of the island, tapered to a point at its downstream end.

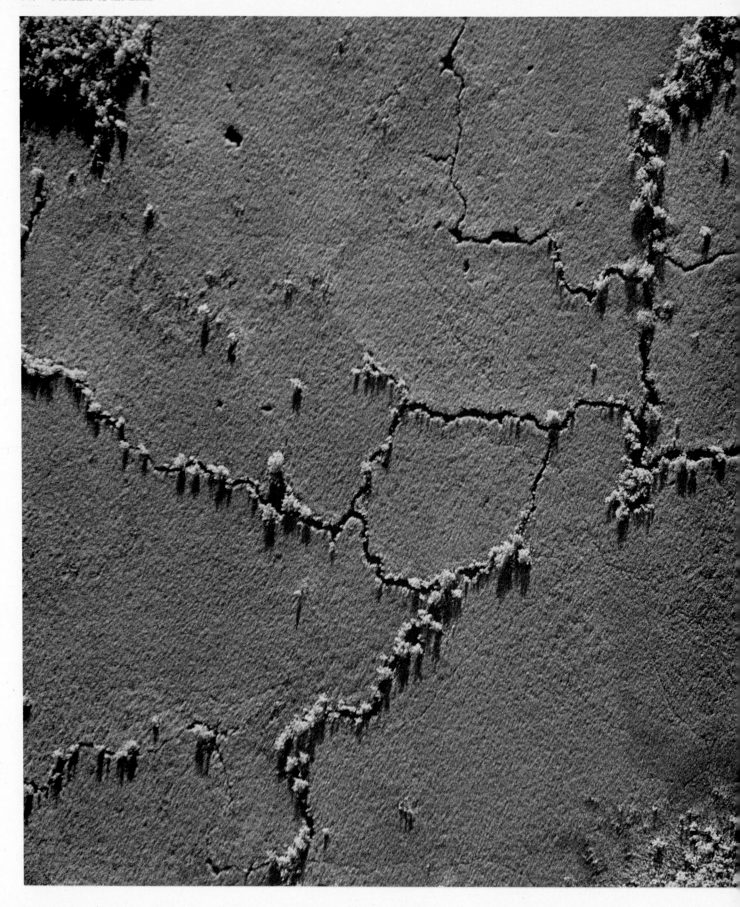

A field of 12-foot-tall sawgrass, so tough it takes a hurricane to lay it flat, flourishes at the headwaters of the Shark River. What appear to be fissures are creeks, issuing from the slough to the northeast; fringing them are mangroves that have invaded from the south. For aquatic creatures to survive, the creeks must be cleared of the mangroves' clogging roots. Here, the prime flow engineer is the alligator, which uses its snout to dredge the channels, tearing away the mangrove roots with its teeth.

Sunlit waters in the estuary of the Shark River meander in a mangrove maze as they mix with sea water on their way to the nearby Gulf of Mexico. The mangroves here—some as high as 80 feet—are able to resist the inroads of the sea on outposts of land their roots have gathered and continue to hold together.

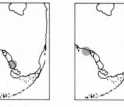

More vulnerable to violent storms, the Ten Thousand Islands off the Florida coast in the shallows are actually elongated shell bars, some only four feet wide. But despite the sea's recurrent attempts to reclaim these spits of land, their mangrove forests tenaciously hold—and even increase—their acreage.

Remnants of a drier epoch, these keys in the shallow waters of Florida Bay mark the last outposts of the Everglades lands. Once hammocks set in a prehistoric swamp, they have struggled against the rising sea over the past 5,000 years, protected against total destruction by the mangroves on their perimeters. The trees continually collect soil and build up a barricade secure against all but the most severe hurricane tides.

2/ The Big Cypress Swamp

Deer...led us through a dream world of gray cypresses and silent Spanish moss and soft knee-deep watery sloughs.... I stood and stared and could not believe that I held orchids in my hands.   MARJORIE KINNAN RAWLINGS/ CROSS CREEK

It is a habit of mine to file away, more or less retrievably in my memory, recollections of small bits of landscape I have seen—not just big, grand things like mountain views but perfect little fragments of country that I can think back to with a surge of the pleasure the first sight of them brought. One of these places lies within Big Cypress Swamp in southwestern Florida. It is a particular bayhead that I recall—a low evergreen swamp made up chiefly of bay, pop-ash and custard-apple trees—and though it covered only a minute part of the million and a half acres of Big Cypress, it gave me my first real taste of the magic that the entire region holds.

The memory of this bayhead comes down from the time when the Tamiami Trail was new and still sparsely traveled, and a drive across the edge of Big Cypress on a June day was constant excitement. Turtles and young alligators basked along the banks of the canal that parallels the road, and a half acre of herons, egrets and ibises might be spread over any little prairie that you passed. There were lots of snakes along the road shoulders in those days, and at the mouths of the little rills that frothed into the canals after a shower rowdy gangs of short-nosed garfish and soft-shelled turtles crowded, thrashing and squabbling over flotsam that washed in from the Everglades.

This particular bayhead hovered over a dark little stream that crossed the trail somewhere between the towns of Ochopee and Marco. I stopped my car and got out because a speckled six-foot king snake was lying in the road. After communing with him awhile I goaded him into gliding off into the canal and swimming across it into a patch of bushes. I then turned idly to peer down into the sparkling water that was sucking into the culvert at its upstream end. It was clear black like Costa Rican coffee, and I could make out the dim front half of a big snook and a lot of garfish stacked like cordwood, all lurking together in the shadows. I had a casting rod in the car, but I knew that an old, cynical roadside snook would put no stock in my little shiny spoon, or in any other bait short of maybe a big live golden shiner. So I dismissed all thoughts of catching the fish in the culvert. I looked upstream to where the water flowed out of a tunnel in the fringe of moonvines at the edge of the bayhead. Through the tunnel I could see open space back inside under the overhanging trees, and though the water in there was shaded, here and there its surface glistened with quick flashes of gold light. I knew the look of baby tarpon rolling in black swamp water, and I went back to the car and got my rod.

The stream was the only way into the place, so I waded out into it waist deep and walked up through the low opening in the vine tangle. Under the arched ceiling of ash, maple and pond-cypress trees only little rays of sunlight came in, and gleamed green gold and amber on the leaves and glossy water. I could see that if I followed the channel upstream I would pass from one such vaulted chamber to another, all connected by tunnels through the tangled vines over the deeper runs. The little tarpon stopped their frolic as I entered. My rod was useless in there; it was too crowded to cast a spoon. But I didn't care much, because the place was cool and dreamlike and different from any place I had ever been. And besides its look and feel, the scent of ghost orchids in bloom filled the water-floored room like a greenhouse at Easter time. The ghost orchid is a leafless species, with a big waxy white flower that looks, as the botanist Donovan Correll has said, "like a snow-white frog suspended in midair." The flowers are borne on short spikes rising directly from speckled roots that snake about on the trunks of trees, especially pop-ash trees.

There were other things that I recall: a green tree frog sleeping on a vanilla-orchid leaf; a lot of slender striped anole lizards stalking and bobbing on moonvine stems; and a thin rough green snake that rested weightless, motionless and elegant across the tips of a wax-myrtle bough. All these, too, keep that place clear in my memory.

The last time I stopped by that little bayhead a bulldozer had gone through it, and the creek ran milky with silt under a confusion of cat briers. Still later—after droughts and more draining—the country around Ochopee and Marco dried out badly, and a fire roared through the bayhead, and a small but singular and important part of the world had gone. So I cling to that first June day to think back to.

Actually there are a great many such places left in Big Cypress country, even in these lean days. Maybe none with young tarpon flashing silver gold in amber water under ghost-orchid flowers. Perhaps that special juxtaposition required some primeval water pattern that now is gone for good. But if you don't mind wading, there are other vignettes to be stored away in your memory: a troop of young otters roistering in the water under a hanging garden, or a snowy egret standing incandescent in the midday twilight by a black swamp pool in air so still there is never a ripple in the thin lace of its plumes. A person would have to be very shut-minded or badly afraid of snakes not to enjoy wading navel deep through a Big Cypress bayhead. The dim light and moist cool air, the clear black water, the profusion of orchids and other plants growing perched in the trees cast a spell that is at once bizarre and tranquil. And mainly because of the diversity of these plants, no two bayheads are ever just alike.

As a whole, Big Cypress Swamp presents an immensely varied landscape spreading west of the Okeechobee-Everglades basin between the sawgrass plain and the slightly elevated sand ridges of the Gulf Coast. Despite its name, which refers not to the size of its trees but to its great expanse, it is by no means all tree swamp. Its 2,400 square miles include many strikingly different kinds of country: wet prairies and marshes of spike rush or sawgrass; broad savannas set picturesquely with clumps of cabbage palm; and, on the low outcrops of limestone, islands of pine or hammocks of mixed tropical and continental trees. The tree swamps themselves may contain various combinations of trees —ash, custard apple, red maple, willow or oak in addition to the bald cypress and pond cypress, and even these two related kinds of trees make very different-looking kinds of country.

The bald cypress—a deciduous conifer that gets its name from its bare look in winter, after its leaves are shed—thrives best in places with the more lasting water supplies, and with a soil of muck, clay or fine sand. In Big Cypress such places are mainly the sloughs. In local parlance, the word slough is applied to a shallow trough in the limestone floor of the region where drainage concentrates and forms a relatively permanent body of water. The mature bald-cypress tree usually rises out of a buttress near its base, a swelling that may be eight to 10 feet in diameter. This helps the shallow root system support the tree in unstable ground. The roots develop conical offshoots, called knees, that stick up out of the water; these were once thought to serve as respiratory organs, and this is still believed by some botanists, though apparently nobody really understands the function of these knees.

A slow grower, the bald cypress can reach enormous age—some as many as 600 years old have been found—and regularly attains heights of over a hundred feet. The bands of cypress timber that grow in the sloughs are, as in much of the southeastern United States, known as strands. Since the region was first settled in the 1870s, the strands were hungrily contemplated by lumbermen. Logging in a swamp is understandably troublesome, and it was only the great cost and difficulty of timbering in Big Cypress that postponed the ruin of the strands for so long. But by the time of the building boom of the late 1940s the price of cypress lumber, a long-lived wood widely used for roofs, boats, coffins, stadium seats and pickle barrels, had risen spectacularly; the demand warranted the enormous logistic effort and expense required to get it out of the swamps. It has been estimated that 36,000 trainloads of cypress logs were taken out of the Big Cypress area in the 1940s and early 1950s. Many of the trees that were cut down were over a hundred feet high, up to eight feet in diameter above the buttress, and 400, 500 or 600 years old. Practically all of the big bald-cypress timber of Big Cypress Swamp was cut.

Another variety of cypress that has fared better is the pond cypress. Smaller and more widespread than the bald cypress, pond cypress may crowd in tight stands, or scatter over open savannas. It forms the original marginal vegetation of many ponds and streams, and its stands sometimes mix with slash pine.

One striking contribution of pond cypress to the landscape is the cypress dome. This is a roughly circular, dense stand of trees that forms a dome-shaped canopy against the skyline, with the trees tall in the center and evenly decreasing in height toward the edges. It makes a remarkably symmetrical and convex silhouette, and a lot of the domes scattered around, separated by prairie or cleared pineland, give the impression of artifacts of some kind—as if somebody had planted them there with some esoteric sylvicultural plan in mind.

Among the most bizarre landscapes of southern Florida are the dwarf-cypress savannas, tracts of drastically stunted pond-cypress trees growing with sawgrass at the brackish edges of the Everglades. Here the cypresses may be no more than three or four feet tall; afflicted by fluctuating water levels and poor soil, they seem to be growing under almost intolerable conditions. What the dwarf cypresses look like, really, is bonsai trees, growing under the care of some clever Japanese family that every few years comes by and does occult things that keep the trees tiny though big-buttressed and twisted with age. Some people, when they view these little trees, make the mistake of thinking they are cypress saplings, but the spread of their bases tells the true story. In most cases they are much older than the big, ebullient trees that grow tall and dense on better cypress land.

Pond cypresses are far more favored than bald cypresses as a host for the epiphytes, plants that grow perched on the limb of a tree or clinging to its trunk. The ghost orchids I mentioned in my favorite bayhead are one kind of epiphyte, as are many other species of orchid. Many of them produce colorful, fragrant blossoms. Contrary to popular belief, all air plants are not parasites; most kinds get only support and a place in the sun from the host tree. One kind, however, the strangler fig, is a relentless killer of even very large trees. Often it starts with a tiny seed dropped into a tree by a passing bird. As it sprouts, the little plant fastens itself to the tree and then sends down long roots that take hold in the ground and wrap tightly around the host tree as they gradually strengthen and multiply. Eventually the host is crushed to death, while the strangler fig grows in its place.

The dominant epiphytes in the bayheads and swamps of Big Cypress are types of air plants called bromeliads. As you drive through the region, one of the eye-catching landscapes you will see from the road is a stand of pond cypresses with their trunks bristling with stiff-leaved air plants, which are spectacular when in bloom. If you travel out from Naples toward Fort Lauderdale on Highway 84, called Alligator Alley, you may see the car ahead screech to a perilous stop next to one of these cypress-and-air-plant communities, and somebody in the car will more than likely yell, "Look at the orchids!" The plants they see are not orchids, however. They are bromeliads; the name is derived from their botanical family name, *Bromeliaceae*.

Bromeliads grow mainly in tropical America, and most of them on host trees, although a few varieties grow on the ground. The pineapple is the best-known bromeliad and that is why the epiphytic members of the family are sometimes called wild pines. The Spanish moss that is

Butterfly orchids, so called because the delicate petals at the center resemble butterfly wings, seem suspended in the forest air—and they almost are. As epiphytes, or air plants, they attach their roots to pond cypress and other trees for support, but they take their nourishment entirely from air, moisture and sunlight.

so widespread through the Southeastern coastal plain is another member of this group; in general appearance it is the least characteristic of the lot. In the United States you don't get into real bromeliad country until you reach southern Florida. Some of the swamps, heads and domes of Big Cypress offer the best examples of epiphytes to be seen in the North Temperate Zone, and for sheer abundance the bromeliads there are as impressive as can be found anywhere.

The nearest thing to a bromeliad census in Big Cypress that I have heard of was a casual estimate made by three botanist colleagues of mine from the University of Florida: Dan Ward, John Beckner and John Carmichael. A few years ago they spent a morning wading around in the Fahkahatchee Strand. At noontime the three men stopped for lunch in one of the watery Gothic antechambers of the place, and as they stood there belly deep, eating sandwiches, unable to find a stump to sit on, they fell to cogitating on how many epiphytes there really were up there on the trunks and limbs of the six big trees that formed the dome of the room they were in. The thought took hold, and they decided to try to make some sort of an estimate. Each of them made spot counts of selected cubes of space, then multiplied these by figures they thought approximated the total epiphyte-covered area on the ceiling and walls of the pool-floored room. It was not a very precise exercise, obviously, but it was a useful thing to do all the same. When Ward, Beckner and Carmichael pooled their counts, the totals ranged from 1,000 to 10,000 orchids, and from 10,000 to 100,000 bromeliads—all in that one small corner of the Fahkahatchee Strand.

The bromeliads do more, however, than give an exciting look to the landscape. The leaves of many of the species are broad and cupped at the bases, and collectively these make a rain-water reservoir that may last through a normal dry season. Besides tiding the air plants themselves over periods of drought, these tanks are lifesavers at such times for a great many kinds of small animals, which keep from drying out by living in the plants. Various kinds of frogs, salamanders, snakes, snails and lizards, and a whole host of insects, spiders and scorpions make use of this refuge. For many such creatures, the moisture trapped in the leaves of bromeliads is a nutritious soup comprising rain water, dust, rotting leaf matter, animal droppings, the juices of plants and the decomposing remains of various insects. Some of the bromeliads that do not store water nevertheless make excellent hiding places for insects, and thus provide full-time foraging for such insectivorous birds as the blue-gray gnatcatcher and the yellow-throated warbler.

The heartland of Big Cypress—nowadays, at least—is the Fahkahatchee Strand. The name is a word from the language of the Miccosukee, one of the remaining tribes of the Florida Indians; it means forked river, though the two branches the Indians had in mind are no longer easy to locate. The Fahkahatchee, a 100,000-acre strip of wilderness some 25 miles long and seven miles wide, includes samples of almost every landscape to be found anywhere in Big Cypress Swamp. The Strand is a self-contained drainage basin that collects and distributes the rainfall of a great area. There are permanent lagoons and ponds in its interior, and during the wet season these spread out into a shallow, slow-moving watercourse that delivers vital fresh water to the mangrove estuaries of the Gulf Coast.

The deeper central parts of the Fahkahatchee once contained the best of Big Cypress timber. In the 1940s and '50s, however, a complex system of timbering trails and railroad lines was run out into all but a few small scraps of the tract, and wherever these reached, the mature timber was all removed.

The timbering of the Fahkahatchee prompted an all-is-lost attitude among most conservationists, and until lately this has hidden the fact that the place is still a treasure house of wild country. Much of the Strand has been drastically modified by man, but the place has not by any means been irrevocably ruined. It is still a vital asylum for harried wildlife and the home of such endangered species as the Everglades mink, the wood stork and the Florida panther. It also exerts a stabilizing hydrologic influence on the whole surrounding region.

I can remember my own feeling when they cut down the big timber in the Strand. I did just what I am complaining about in other people: I wrote the place off and for years made no effort to visit it again. But one day not long ago I drove out the Janes Road, the old timber road that runs northwest from Copeland, and I met a black bear and saw the royal-palm strand, and I realized how simple-minded it is to think that only virgin landscapes are worth saving.

It was the palm strand I was mainly looking for that day. I had spent the afternoon before in a little Cessna airplane flying over and up and down it. I was astonished at what I saw and decided I had to see what the strand looked like from the ground.

I had grown up believing that the only native royal palms in Florida were the seven or so that used to stand in Royal Palm State Park—now part of Collier Seminole State Park, near the western end of the Tamiami Trail—and a few others down on Paradise Key in Everglades National Park. Even those few palms, I had heard it said, had probably been planted by Indians. I knew vaguely that in the late-18th Century there were royal-palm groves in Florida as far north as the Saint Johns River, but I thought they had all fallen before some cold wave. So the royal palm had always seemed to me an exotic kind of tree, imported mainly, I supposed, by Thomas Edison and his friends to ornament Fort Myers, his winter home for half a century. Actually, as it turned out, most of the royal palms that have been used to decorate city parks and streets came from native Florida stock.

The royal palm—which no doubt got its name from its magisterial form and bearing—is one of the handsomest of all palm trees. It is stately to the point of stylization, and hardly seems to be a genuine vegetable. The trunk is like a concrete column, gray white, clean and unswervingly erect for up to a hundred feet. It holds up a heavy crown of long, feathery, gracefully curved dark green leaves, and in fruiting time a ponderous cluster of little nuts hangs just below the crown.

In southern Florida, the royal palm has been severely diminished in recent years because of the draining of its natural habitats. Those groves that withstood the frenetic draining and burning of the land have been steadily raided for young trees for nurseries and urban landscapes. For all that, the fact never got noised about that there were still hundreds of big royal palms and thousands of seedlings and young trees standing in the heart of the Fahkahatchee. Although local people and some outside deer, turkey and orchid hunters have known all along of the existence of the palm strand, I myself did not learn until lately that the remains of one of the most extraordinary plant communities in North America—a hammock swamp of bald cypress and royal palm —could still be seen there. It is perhaps the only undisturbed remnant of an association of the two kinds of trees that used to cover miles of the Fahkahatchee Strand.

The day I went out to see the place it was cloudy. Having no compass, I spent a couple of hours scaring myself by wading out into the swamp until I began to feel uneasy about which way would take me back out to the narrow road. I never had much sense of direction anyway, and the thought of how far it was through the strand to any other way home kept turning me back toward the road. But in spite of this I got far enough in from the road to see the big palms stringing out in both directions. Since then I have returned and worked my way farther back inside at several points. You have to wade to get in, and there is tangled country to claw through for a while before you reach the grove, but it is worth the trouble. If you keep looking up through the breaks among the crowns of the young cypress trees, you can make out the huge tops of the majestic palms towering high over the rest of the forest, and this way you can stay in the grove.

The whole interior is wet during most of the year. The water is mostly ankle deep to calf deep, though if you blunder into the pools and gator holes you can soak yourself to the ears. But this is a small price to pay for a walk among Florida royal palms. There are places in the strand that probably have no equal for their abundance of ghost orchids, swamp lilies, and bird's-nest ferns. Wherever the forest opens over pools and ponds, the limbs and trunks of the surrounding trees are wholly hidden by epiphytes. The buttressed stumps of the old big cypresses have moldered and crumbled into mounds of moist punk, covered over with great clumps of royal ferns. Here and there the grotesque basketwork of a strangler fig still squeezes the disintegrating body of an ancient cypress that was shattered by the falling of its fellows in the timbering days. Vanilla orchids, grass ferns and low-spreading peperomias make parts of the palm forest resemble much more tropical areas, reminding me particularly of the Caribbean.

The old royal palms are thinly spaced, but by searching out their tops through the occasional breaks in the cypress canopy you can get an idea of the density of the stand. Seedlings and young palms occur all through the forest; the older palms evidently suffered no ecological setback when the bald cypresses with which they shared the ground were taken out by the lumbermen. There are no old relict trees left standing as there usually are in cleared cypress swamps. When the Fahkahatchee was timbered, the logs were snaked out at high speed by cable, and even the old hollow or crooked cypresses—useless for logs —were cut down to clear the way. But the smaller cypresses and saplings that survived the violence are 30 years older now, and you can see what the place will be when, in time to come, their crowns have climbed up level with the crowns of the royal palms.

I also mentioned seeing a black bear in the Fahkahatchee Strand. He was just standing there in the road when I saw him; but bears are scarce nowadays in southern Florida, and you can travel through a lot of back country without seeing one. Besides, running into one that day was a curious coincidence, because I was looking for panther tracks at the time. After leaving the royal-palm strand, I had driven on out the

Leafless in dry seasons, dwarf-cypress trees support clusters of stiff-leaved wild-pine—an air plant related to the pineapple.

Janes Road to where it was blocked by the outermost canal of a ghastly gridwork of ditches that real-estate developers have dug out there in the wilderness. I stopped at the new gash, sat on the excavated limestone bank, and watched the clean, dark water washing out westward toward the sea, racing away like blood out of a big cut artery. I thought of the futility of the Fahkahatchee trying to heal itself in the face of such hemorrhaging, and got depressed beyond description at the sight. Having just come out of the royal-palm strand, where the regeneration of an incomparable landscape depends on a steady water cycle, I was forcibly struck by the senselessness of the canal; it seemed not just a lesion in the body of the land, but a public tragedy.

I got up off the rocks, still heavy-hearted, and stayed that way for a while as I drove back down the lonely little road. But then I saw some buzzards circling low over a shrunken water hole on the marl and remembered that I had intended to look around for panther tracks. The palm strand was the main reason I was out there, but I also wanted to try to find where a panther had walked. Practically all of the panthers left in the eastern United States are in southern Florida, not far from where I was, a short way to the northeast, or down in sections of Everglades National Park, where abundant deer and coons provide food and poachers are few. But panthers wander; I had heard that a deer hunter had seen one along a trail just off the Janes Road only a few weeks before. Though I have lived in Florida practically forever, I had never seen a panther here. What made this worse was that my wife, who grew up on the edge of Big Cypress Swamp, once saw one in the road behind her house. That made the gap in my life list of Florida beasts a very serious thing indeed.

It was the dry season. The pools and ditches were mostly just bare marl and muck and the ground was in good shape to take footprints. So when I reached a big spread of wet prairie I spent an hour or so walking out across it and on into the swamp beyond, looking hopefully about the marl for big cat tracks. Though it was pretty much a needle-in-a-haystack search, panthers are restless and leave a lot of tracks in a night's prospecting; if one has been around, and there is bare mud where he passed, you are likely to see his sign. But this time, in an hour of searching in the swamp, I found no big, round, clawless tracks at all. There were opossum prints galore, and coons had walked all over the place. There was also a lot of armadillo sign—triangular prints with a tail mark between them, like the spoor of some little kind of leftover dinosaur; and there were places where alligators and turtles had crawled over the mud from one shrinking pool to another. Herons had made cuneiform inscriptions at the edges of most of the ponds, and around one dried-down hole that was dismal with dead and bloated garfish, buzzards and an otter had turned the marl into a regular Rosetta stone of marks and scratches.

But no panther had been there anywhere. After a while I gave up the search and walked out to the dim timbering trail I had clung close to after leaving the prairie. It was there that I saw the bear. It was in the trail, looking the other way, and I quickly stepped behind a bush before it saw me. It shuffled back and forth beside a shrunken water hole in the lime rock, walked out into the water briefly, then went back into the trail and paced back and forth a few more times. It seemed undecided about something. That was about all I could gather, watching it —that it was probably worried about something. Then all of a sudden it loped straight into the brush and disappeared; I heard a stick snap as the willows took it in.

I walked to the car and drove to the Copeland fire tower to talk with the foresters about bears and panthers. They said both were out there, and that a few of each were seen every deer season, but there was no way to find either one on call. They said I ought to feel pretty good over just having seen a bear. And I was happy about it, of course; though you see so many bears in national parks that it somewhat dims the exhilaration of seeing one, even where bears are rare.

If the Fahkahatchee Strand is a good example of a partly sullied wilderness that is still well worth saving, Corkscrew Swamp, up in the northwest corner of Big Cypress, is the most important remaining fragment of virgin full-sized bald-cypress forest in southern Florida—a superb specimen of an almost lost kind of terrain. It ought to be seen by anyone who dreams of the world as it was before the arrival of man.

Corkscrew is now a sanctuary managed by the National Audubon Society. The features that attracted the support necessary to save such a place were mainly two: the stand of gigantic bald-cypress trees and the biggest wood stork rookery left in Florida. Both common egrets and wood storks have nested there in considerable numbers since early times. As long ago as 1912, when almost all the plume birds had been shot out of Florida, the National Audubon Society hired a warden to guard the Corkscrew rookery. The first land parcel in the series that produced the present sanctuary was acquired in 1954, after concerted efforts were made by various people and organizations, with the whole-

Air plants obscure the branches of pond cypresses and other host trees in the Fahkahatchee Strand. The giant wild-pines—those that look like pineapples—are the largest of the Everglades air plants; they grow up to four feet wide and six feet high.

hearted cooperation of the owners of the tract. Today the protected area, including its buffer zones of prairie and pineland, comprises about 11,000 acres. Development of Corkscrew Swamp Sanctuary must certainly be counted among the more outstanding achievements in the field of conservation.

You can walk out into the heart of Corkscrew on a 5,800-foot boardwalk, carefully laid out to take an observer through the different biological communities in the tract. Before reaching the swamp you go through a marginal zone of virgin slash pine, which is itself an extraordinary relic. This is kept free of encroaching hardwoods by controlled burning, and has the nostalgic look of a southern Florida landscape that was once widespread but now has almost completely disappeared. It is also the winter home of goldfinches, red-cockaded woodpeckers and brown-headed nuthatches. From the zone of slash pine the boardwalk cuts across a wet prairie and goes through a dense stand of pond-cypress trees bristling with epiphytes. After passing some little ponds, the walk enters the bald-cypress forest, with its understory of custard apple, pop ash, coastal-plain willow, swamp fern and fire flags. It finally ends, more than a mile from its beginning, in a broad central marsh around which most of the numerous nesting groups that make up Corkscrew's wood stork colony usually locate.

By all odds the most awesome of the Corkscrew communities is the stand of immense bald-cypress trees rising up out of gleaming black water. Some of the trees are more than 700 years old, and their massive trunks hold up heavy, flat crowns. The trees appear too short for their great girth, often as much as 25 feet—no doubt they were truncated by Hurricane Donna in 1960, or by earlier and even more fiendish hurricanes that all old southern Florida trees have weathered. What must be another sign that this is a hurricane community is the wide spacing of the cypress crowns. The sunshine that streams in among them has generated a prolific lower story of custard apple, pop ash, oak and maple trees, and beneath these is a welter of ferns and water plants. Though bald cypress is a less attractive host to epiphytes than pond cypress, big wild pines perch in crotches of the old trees, and butterfly and night-blooming orchids are numerous. Some of the cypresses are strapped and bound with strangler fig.

In this big-timber section of the sanctuary you may be disappointed to find no constant slithering and sloshing of wild creatures. As in most heavy woods, the inhabitants stay strangely quiet or out of sight. But you can be sure they are there, awaiting the right time of day or season, or a quieter and more patient watcher. Meanwhile, the botanical architecture of the place is a stupendous thing to see.

The value of an asset such as the Corkscrew Sanctuary is beyond calculation. Material values can be assigned to some of its aspects, but there can be no adequate assessment of the ultimate worth that is generated when, say, a lot of people just down from Michigan or Connecticut stand in the middle of a virgin cypress swamp on a winter day and hear an alligator bellow.

I saw that happen not long ago. It was a cold February day turned suddenly fair after high winds and rain the night before. The heavy cypress tops were thrashing under a gusty northwest wind that came in from the Gulf. Here inside the swamp it was too cold for the comfort of reptiles, and the people I met as I went along the boardwalk were mostly trying to name warblers, or just standing and pondering the Mesozoic look of the woods.

Then I came to a place where the boardwalk emerged from the swamp and cut across a small body of open water known as Lettuce Lake—a black-water pond carpeted with water lettuce, floating ferns and duckweed, and ringed about with willow, ash, and custard-apple trees. Out on the walk, in the sun-flooded midsection of the pond, some two dozen people stood. They were in three separate groups, and were gazing or pointing cameras at three different denizens of the swamp that were out there making the most of the morning sunshine. One was an alligator, an adolescent just under four feet long. Its head and shoulders were raised high above the floating lettuce, and though the rest of it was hidden, it obviously was standing on a submerged snag that gave support to its effort to rise as high as it could toward the comfort of the sun on a chilly day. This was an unusual pose for an alligator—a melodramatic one, in fact. Most of the viewers weren't necessarily aware of that, but they did volubly appreciate the large amount of this alligator that was out in view.

Another group of people were leaning anxiously over the rail on the other side of the boardwalk. Most of them held cameras or binoculars hopefully poised. All were looking down into a brushy tangle on a raft of root-laced bottom muck that had floated to the surface and now supported growing plants. I walked over and looked the way they were looking and gradually made out the dark brown, speckled, almost wholly camouflaged form of a limpkin, a long-legged, long-billed wading bird that is one of the essential creatures of the Florida swamps. Oblivious of its audience, it was standing on the raft and industriously probing for snails in the vegetation along the edges. For a while it poked around there, nearly hidden among the lizard tail and Indian turnip plants. Then suddenly it moved out from behind the screening leaves and the people could see it clearly in the viewfinders of their cameras; they all started furiously snapping pictures of the limpkin in case it should go away again.

I was only sorry it did no shouting. The voice of the limpkin—an unsettling sort of wailing cry—is wild and strange, and is bound to confirm an outlander's oddest notions about tropical swamps. But the limpkin is great to see even when it is quiet.

The people in the third group on the boardwalk over Lettuce Lake were watching the antics of an anhinga, or snakebird, a mature male in exemplary black-and-silver plumage that he was busily preening back into shape after the wind and wet of the night before. His wings were akimbo, his tail jutted to one side, his serpentine neck was curved in a long loop that brought his beak to bear on some spot of disorder between his shoulder blades. He looked like a product of somebody's first lesson in taxidermy.

Anhingas are weird, anyway. They are nearly three feet long from bill tip to tail tip, and are very thin. They have inadequate oil glands, and so have to spend a lot of time drying out after wettings, with their wings spread like an emblem in heraldry. In the water a snakebird will swim around under the surface stalking fish, once in a while slipping a foot of neck out above the surface and cruising about like a needle-nosed snake—or, if the fishing is good, coming up with a quarter-pound bream and juggling and tossing it in the air until it gets the headfirst grip it needs for swallowing. But an anhinga doesn't need to be hungry to go for a swim. When a snakebird tires of a perch it will as often as not just crash headlong into the water and disappear, perhaps showing up again far across the pond. When it has got so wet it can't fly, it will plunge out of the water like a sea lion and claw and chin its way up a post or tree trunk and hang itself out to dry in the sun.

The snakebird is really strange. It looks peculiar and acts the same. It can soar like a buzzard, and its voice—reserved mainly for the expression of resentment—is a coarse *buzz-buzz-buzz-buzz*, like a rotating rattle with gaps in it. And it seems to me that snakebird nestlings must be about the ugliest of animals.

The snakebird at Lettuce Lake was perched on a low limb, no more than eight feet above and a little to one side of the walk where the people were. So, being exotically photogenic anyway, and cavorting out there in the full 11 o'clock sunlight, he brought gratification to the aspiring wildlife photographers in the crowd. A dozen or more cameras were turned on him—from unassuming automatics to an elegant instrument with just the right telephoto lens to fill a 35-mm. slide with the blood-red eye of a breeding male snakebird. There was even a lady sitting out there in the middle of the walk with a short tripod in front of her and a tiny camera attached to an expensive and powerful miniature telescope. She couldn't have been more than 30 feet away from her subject. I judge she must now have some excellent portraits of the kind of feather lice that snakebirds have.

So it was a pretty satisfactory situation out there on the Corkscrew boardwalk; and all of a sudden it got astonishingly better. There was a rumble of blasting from some construction work far out in the northeast somewhere, and instantly an alligator answered it with a belly-deep roar from a patch of little willows not 20 yards from the walk. I looked that way and behind the willow switches I could see the old beast sloshing into a new position in six inches of water and mud. As I watched, it stopped and swelled and roared again.

Then I noticed that 20 or 30 baby alligators were swarming around and over the big one, and I realized it was a female, probably roaring defiance because she took the noise of the blasting for a neighbor that might have a mind to move into her nursery. Anyway she roared back at the now quiet dynamite six times in all, so close that the boards of the walk trembled beneath our feet. Before she stopped making that incredible noise, I lost all decent restraint and, to my sons' embarrassment, started rushing up and down the boardwalk, pleading with the puzzled tourists to appreciate how blessed they were.

3/ Gator Holes and Fish Jubilees

*The whole system was like a set of scales on which
the sun and the rains, the winds, the hurricanes, and the
dewfalls, were balanced so that the life of
the vast grass and all its...forms were kept secure.*

MARJORY STONEMAN DOUGLAS/ *THE EVERGLADES*

Although the Everglades are fundamentally watery, the most relentless factor there is drought. Each year legions of small animals, and others not so small, dry up or suffocate during the winter dry season. Little rain falls in southern Florida from November to April, and the dying off is so widespread at this time it is sometimes hard to see how the animal life will revive with the May-October wet season. Some of the more wide-ranging animals—birds, mammals and flying insects—escape death by leaving the Everglades. Others go into a more or less torpid state called estivation, after walling themselves off in chambers or capsules that stay damp under the crust of sun-baked muck or marl. One salamander, the long, two-armed siren, makes a spherical chamber in the hardening mud and lines it with slime; here it can outlast drought that is not too protracted. In the cracked bottoms of vanished pools I have found congo eels—another type of long salamander—as well as live bullfrogs and four kinds of hard-shelled turtles.

Some creatures are able to find refuge in scattered ponds, holes and depressions that retain water even after the River of Grass has dried up in its bed. Crayfish and alligators dig their own water holes, and in the dry times these come to be occupied by a great variety of refugees from the drought. Crayfish burrows sometimes go down two feet or more, and many smaller animals join the crayfish in the moist gloom of their depths. Alligators gnash and slosh out pools—called gator holes —in the muck or marl, and these regularly turn into teeming little microcosms, where most of the aquatic creatures of the region find asylum. Besides these gator holes, alligators often make water-filled dens or dig caves back into the side of their gator holes, and in these they can sometimes survive baking drought even if the gator holes dry up. I know of one 10-foot live alligator that was dug from a mud-covered den in which it had apparently been lying for months after the bayhead it inhabited was drained.

But alligators do much more for the Everglades than just preserve themselves underground through times of drought. The area around the little ponds in which they pursue their more active existence serves an immensely important use for other creatures. In May or June, the female alligators build their nests—mounds of plant debris mixed with mud, and perhaps three or four feet high and six to eight feet long—usually located near a gator hole. Over the years the dredging up of muck and trash out of the ponds and the heaping up of nest mounds have combined to produce a unique feature of the terrain: a deep little pool flanked by a curved mound on which willow, buttonbush, myrtle and other small trees can grow. These mounds are often the highest ground for hundreds of acres around. Turtles lay their eggs on them, swamp rabbits and raccoons bivouac there, and birds nest in the trees and bushes. In the pools themselves representatives of most kinds of aquatic animals of the Everglades survive each year, and from these the River of Grass is repopulated when the spring and summer rains restore it. So a gator hole is far more than merely an asylum for the alligator that builds it; it is a major factor in keeping the Everglades environment both stable and diverse.

When the rainy season arrives in late spring the refugees in gator holes, crayfish burrows, or holes and cracks in the bedrock move out again into the newly flooded plain. Those that passed the dry time estivating underground push up out of the newly softened mud. Bacteria, protozoa and tiny crustaceans come out of their drought-resistant eggs or cysts; teeming new green algae begin their production of sugar to fuel the complex food chains of the reviving community. As fast as these smaller forms of life regain their abundance, the flying aquatic insects return, and the little fish appear, at first in small posses and then in bigger schools. Snails, glass shrimp, crayfish, turtles, garfish, mud eels and catfish venture forth from their various shelters. Aquatic plants sprout and grow. Bullfrogs and tree frogs sing, mate and lay eggs that quickly produce tadpoles. Half a dozen kinds of turtles climb out onto the few high places and leave their eggs to hatch wherever the marl or peat rises above the lap of the River of Grass. Even the bass and bream come back—from where it is hard to tell, since they are among the first to die and float belly up when water levels fall in winter. The alligators reestablish their territorial patterns, bellow, breed and build new nests. The water birds disperse throughout the reviving landscape. It is an essential pattern, and probably has been since the Ice Ages.

Although drought has always brought recurrent stress to the Everglades, nowadays the normal peril is increased by a growing water famine. Ever since the first canals were dug over a half century ago—in order to drain the water off the incredibly rich muckland soil and realize the golden promise of winter vegetables for the New York market —water levels in the Everglades have been falling. The dry seasons have become longer and more pronounced, and catastrophic drought and the fires that follow occur more frequently. On the other hand, not all the ecological problems of southern Florida are caused by a scarcity of water. There can be too much water, when successive hurricanes bring unusually heavy or unseasonal rains, or when the managers of the impounded conservation areas try to relieve their own flood problems by opening sluice gates and sending vast and sudden surges of water into the downstream Glades when they are already saturated.

The essential point, in short, is that the health of the region suffers when any phase of the annual wet-dry cycle—the seasonal balance of drought and flood—gets out of gear, for whatever reason. The original animals and plants of southern Florida were there not simply because the place was wet, and certainly not because it was dry, but because a productive high-water period regularly alternated with a time of drying down. This annual cycle has shaped the whole ecological organization of the region, and it molds the life cycle of every animal there.

There is no more graphic example of this balance than that of the reproductive cycle of the wood ibis, or wood stork, known among old Floridians as the ironhead. By any name, this bird epitomizes primeval Florida to me. As far as I am concerned ironheads are esthetically indispensable. They fairly exude atmosphere. The most vivid recollection I have of my first trip to the Everglades, years ago, is of six of them standing in serious caucus in a little glade set with clumps of slender palms that were silhouetted against the mist of an early morning. Ever since, the Everglades have been an enchanted place for me.

A mounded alligator nest—about eight feet across and two to three feet high —conceals a clutch of 30 to 60 eggs under its sawgrass cover. When the young are ready to hatch after nine weeks' incubation, they signal by grunting, and their mother, waiting nearby, rips off the cover of the nest so they can come out (overleaf).

Ironheads are white and black and half as tall as a man. They have long meatless legs, a bald knob of a head, bare cheeks and a bill 10 inches long, three inches deep at the base and a little curved at the tip. It is the bald head and broad base of the beak from which the "iron" in the local name derives. The birds clap their beaks at you, and the way they use them in their fishing is a marvel. Ironheads eat small fish. They hunt by moving along in shallow water, crouched over forward, touching the tips of their partly open beaks against the bottom. As they walk they usually hold one wing nervously stretched out to the side—to scare up prey, perhaps—and they shuffle along that way, pushing first one foot and then the other jerkily forward as if to muddy the water and herd small forms of life into the trap of their beaks. Wood storks hunt by touch rather than by sight, no doubt because the touch reflex is faster than the interplay between eye, brain and beak muscles that visual hunting requires. You rarely see a stork visually spotting and selecting an individual victim to grab. Instead, it gropes blindly along in the shallows with its beak partly open, snapping reflexively when it makes contact with a fish. The snap reflex is incredibly fast. In tests with a captive stork, the zoologist Philip Kahl measured the time between a touch and the closing of the beak and found it to be only about 1/25,000 of a second. He also proved experimentally that successful snaps do not depend on sight; when he covered the stork's eyes with blackened halves of Ping-Pong balls, its ability to fish was not impaired.

For all its remarkable fishing skill, this bird is perilously close to extinction. The whole future of the species may depend on what happens to the few protected nesting colonies that remain in Florida. You sometimes hear people say what the hell—there are plenty of wood storks in Mexico; but the last time I looked there I saw a disheartening number of them smoked and stacked for sale in the Veracruz market. From what I see and hear, there is no real comfort to be found anywhere in the ironhead situation. Certainly, throughout southern Florida, it hangs in critical balance.

One factor in the decline of wood-stork populations has been man's manipulation of drainage and the interruption of overland flow of water by dams and dikes; this interference retards multiplication of the little animals the birds feed on. Another factor is the disruption of the balanced alternation of high-water levels that produce food supplies with the low levels that concentrate food during normal dry seasons. Ironheads are so sensitive to this balance that whenever the wet-dry

An alligator hatchling—only minutes old and about nine inches long—crawls over its still unhatched siblings' eggs in search of its mother.

cycle is upset, for whatever reason, their reproduction is imperiled.

Ironheads in the Everglades begin their breeding in November and December, early in the dry season. One recent November day I visited Corkscrew Swamp Sanctuary to see ironheads nesting there. Directly over a section of the boardwalk in the interior bald-cypress forest there was a cluster of 30 or more nests among the branches of the big trees. Some of the nests were still under construction, and others no doubt had eggs in them. There was no sign of young, but there were a lot of wood storks sitting up there, perched hunched-shouldered and quiet or fussing over nests or clapping their bills at the people staring up at them. Out around the edges of the broad Central Marsh there were more clusters of white in the cypress tops, where other sections of the colony had lodged. A ranger I met told me that there were still other nesting groups, and that an aerial survey the day before had tallied about 4,000 pairs.

Two weeks later I went back to see how the rookery was getting along. I expected to see a lot of nestlings by then. To my surprise I found the nests over the boardwalk completely untended, with no storks to be seen anywhere. I scanned nest after nest through my binoculars and finally made out a patch of white where one lone bird was setting. But the colony had obviously been abandoned. Even out around Central Marsh, the six or eight nesting colonies that had been there two weeks before had disappeared. Wherever any spot of white showed, it was only one lonesome-looking bird.

The change was dramatic and puzzling. I had long been accustomed to associating the ecological troubles of southern Florida with lack of water. Though the rainy season just past had been a little drier than normal, it had been no worse than others in which up to 6,000 pairs of storks had nested in the sanctuary. I asked a ranger what had happened.

"Rain," he said.

"What do you mean, rain?" I said, hung up on the idea that Everglades troubles come from *lack* of rain.

"Sure," the ranger said. "Too damn much. It rained so much the storks figured they better not try to breed after all."

The ranger's remark made no sense at the time. But later, when I thought about it, the reason for the Corkscrew catastrophe became clear. I remembered what I had read about the dependence of storks' nesting success on the normal wet-dry cycle in Kahl's paper on the food requirements of the wood stork in Florida. According to Kahl, the bird usually nests at the outset of the dry season for two closely interrelated reasons: first, the recent wet season has brought populations of the small food fish that are preferred by the stork to their yearly peaks; second, with the falling water levels of the dry season, the forage fish are crowded closely together in diminishing ponds and pools, and the storks can catch them in the great numbers needed for feeding nestlings. The shrinking of the ponds and the consequent concentration of the food supply apparently generate the decision to nest. Florida ironheads, and perhaps ironheads everywhere, have developed an ability to judge when water has fallen low enough that nestlings can be amply fed. If the proper lowering of levels fails to materialize, the storks simply refuse to breed. Occasionally, if breeding has already begun and an unseasonal rainfall occurs, the rain will abort the breeding. That is what happened in the case of the nesting failure in the Corkscrew rookery. The storks evidently abandoned their nests because they had been discouraged by a few days of heavy rain in what was normally the dry season.

For a bird that fishes by random groping and touch, anything that reduces the density of the fish supply—as rising waters do—is a setback. At nesting time, when wood storks require a prodigious amount of food, it is a calamity. Kahl estimates that a family of storks, including two young ones, needs about 440 pounds of fish to sustain itself during the four months of the breeding season. Over that period a colony of 6,000 pairs—roughly the average population of the Corkscrew ironhead colony—would require more than two and one half million pounds to get by. And most of this food comes in small packages. While the stork catches many different kinds of small fish and even some lizards, snakes and frogs, its most frequent prey is the mosquito fish.

Compounding the problem is the particular way in which storks handle their parental duties. According to Kahl: "Both parents feed the young. Food is carried in the throat or stomach of the parent and regurgitated on the nest floor, where it is picked up by the nestlings. Up until the age of three or four weeks, nestling storks are seldom left unattended; one parent remains at the nest at all times while the other parent forages. . . . By three or four weeks of age the nestlings are able to defend themselves and both parents begin to forage at the same time. The period before the young are left alone is especially critical since the increasing food demands of the nestlings must be supplied by the fishing efforts of one parent."

Obviously, storks have to work hard to meet these demands. To locate fishing holes, as well as to extend the limits of their daily hunting travels, they augment their own powers of flight by using rising currents of warm air—as many birds of prey do. If on a clear, calm morning you find yourself anywhere near an ironhead rookery, you will almost surely see storks spiraling over the nesting trees, climbing in the updrafts that the morning sun generates when it heats the land. By riding these thermals, a bird can climb high without spending much energy, and in that way can vastly extend both its field of search and its foraging range. If their nesting period is to be successful wood storks are compelled to make daily trips in search of some densely populated, drought-shrunken pool. What determines a good hunting ground for them is not fish per square mile, but fish per heavily crowded cubic foot of water. Because they depend upon prey randomly colliding with their beaks, and because the dependence is obviously most urgent when young are waiting to be fed, they may have to travel farther than they can fly under their own power to find the right kind of fishing hole.

So if you go to a southern Florida wood-stork rookery on a morning when a ravenous new generation of nestlings has emerged, you will surely see the parent birds flapping from the tops of the mangroves or cypresses in which they are nesting. They will rise in growing circles as they move out over the sawgrass; then, climbing as high as the buzzards, they will either move across country with the updraft or glide out to a good gator hole they already know, or perhaps to a new one they have spotted from their high vantage point.

In front of my home in northern Florida there is a 10-acre pond. Every decade or so the bottom drops out of a sinkhole at one end of the pond bed and the place goes nearly dry. Although the pond is hidden by trees and is five miles from any regular ironhead haunt, it takes no time for the storks to learn of the low water and gather at the pond for the easy fishing. But five miles is no distance for the storks to travel in their search for food. Kahl has found that storks sometimes commute as far as 30 miles each way between the Corkscrew rookeries and fishing holes up around Lake Okeechobee.

For most Everglades creatures, the periodic drought that is essential to the nesting and breeding pattern of the wood stork requires the single most important adjustment of their lives. There are two aspects to that adjustment. One is the capacity to resist suffocation and total dehydration in the dry season; the other is the ability to spread rapidly and recolonize new expanses of water as soon as the wet season returns.

Two wood storks wade in a shallow Florida pond to stir up mud and bring an ample supply of small fish within easy reach of their bills.

Gambusias and their various relatives in the killifish family—which includes some of the smallest fish in North America—are specialists in both skills. Some of their feats in withstanding the ordeal of the dry season—living for days almost without oxygen, packed together by thousands—seem nothing short of black magic. The last time I was in the Everglades during a dry April I walked out on a marl prairie south of Alligator Alley to a shallow prairie lake that had dried down. A water hole, no more than 20 feet across, was all that remained. The outermost rim of the pool was ringed with the corpses of bluegill bream, warmouth bass and largemouth bass. These were being picked over by buzzards. On the moist mud inside this ring there was a mosaic of dead garfish and smaller fish of a number of kinds. At the innermost center of the pond, where the water was still in a semifluid state, there was a closely packed mass of very small fish—all killifish: flagfish, golden top minnows, least mosquito fish, a few lucanias and myriad gambusias. Although nearly immobilized by crowding in their diminishing puddle, many of them were still alive.

I couldn't tell how long it had taken the pond to shrink to that size. But it must have been at least three or four days earlier that the bass and bream had died from suffocation, at a time when the area of water was many times greater than at this final melancholy stage. So for at least three days the fish I found still alive had managed to survive in a teeming body of noxious warm water that was surely devoid of oxygen. I remember thinking at the time that this represented some kind of paradox; the visual evidence in the pool simply did not add up. The fish still alive in that dismal soup were kinds that have no known means of supplementing their aquatic respiration by taking in air, as some species do. What, then, had kept them from expiring long before, when the last oxygen in the awful little place disappeared?

It was a real puzzle, and one with obvious bearing on the machinery of Everglades ecology. Later I came across what may be an answer. It appeared in a paper by William Lewis Jr. of the University of Georgia dealing with the ability of killifishes—both the live-bearing and the egg-laying kinds—to survive in oxygen-deficient waters. Dr. Lewis concluded that the tilted mouths and flat heads of these species enable them to tolerate such conditions by taking oxygen from the inexhaustible reservoir of dissolved gases up in the thin surface layer of water where it is in contact with the air.

I am ashamed that this reasoning never occurred to me. I had spent quite a lot of time pondering the question of how flagfish, golden top minnows and gambusias—all similarly tilt-mouthed and flat-headed —are so marvelously able to survive drought long enough to be found wiggling in a hatful of wet mud, when this is all that remains of a 20-acre pond. Everybody has seen fish "gasping for air" at the surface of an undersized pool or container. Until I read Lewis' paper it was never really clear to me that the uppermost surface layer in any body of water, no matter how polluted—an aquarium, a bucket of bait or an Everglades water hole—is never completely exhausted of oxygen. In this layer oxygen is moving in from the air as fast as it is absorbed by the body of the water below. It is this thin stratum that crowded fish gasp after. But the heads of bass and bream are high, their mouths are placed at the front of their heads; to keep their mouths at the surface they would have to swim around tilted at an angle of 45° or more. The upturned mouths of killifish, on the other hand, allow them to stay in a natural horizontal position while they systematically suck in the oxygen-rich upper layer of their habitat. Lewis believes that this adaptation could account for a great part of the extraordinary drought resistance of the mosquito fish and its relatives. If so, I suggest that it accounts for a large part of the ecological organization of the Everglades.

But obviously, the ability of a small fish to live through the dry season in an isolated, oxygenless water hole will not in itself contribute much to the ecological productivity of the River of Grass. It is just as important that the forage fish have the ability to recolonize their wet season habitat when it is restored by the coming of the rains. When the wet season returns it may last only a few months. If the expanse of new water is to support new populations of larger animals, the little fish they eat must be able to spread as fast as the water spreads.

When a period of drought in the Everglades is ended by rains, and residual pools join together to form shallow lakes, it is a marvel to see how fast the new habitats are repopulated. Some animals, such as birds and aquatic insects, simply fly in. Some come up out of estivation in the crusted-over mud, or hatch out of drought-resistant eggs or cysts left by progenitors before the dry season. But most Everglades fish have to swim to the revived country, and it is remarkable how promptly they return to it. The principal pioneer species, gambusia and its kin, are to some degree omnivorous; so presumably they have no trouble finding food in newly flooded territory. But what are the goads and signals that set them swimming out into new habitat and that tell them which direction to go in? They get about too promptly merely to be wandering aimlessly.

An important aspect of the pioneering ability of Florida pond fish and other kinds of aquatic animals may be their occasional custom of leaving quiet water and making mass upcurrent migrations when drought is ended suddenly by heavy rain. At these times you often can see fish, aquatic amphibians and crayfish that have gathered by hundreds, even thousands, in pools below stretches of fast water or other obstructions in temporary or swollen streams—at the downstream ends of culverts, for instance. At the University of Florida we have borrowed the term jubilee for these gatherings, taking it from the famous springtime congregations in Mobile Bay of salt-water fish and crustaceans, which are pushed by a layer of oxygen-depleted water toward the beach, where most of them die. The jubilees of peninsular Florida apparently have nothing to do with oxygen-depletion, and their goal is not death on the shore but new uncrowded space to live in. The only way I can account for these fantastic conclaves is to suppose that the individual members of these assemblages have been stimulated by a rain-generated current to use it as a road to a new habitat upstream somewhere. And obviously they are right—the current is a way to survival; any flow that comes into a crowded, dried-down water hole is a pathway to a new life for its inhabitants.

This jubilee behavior seems inconsistent at first because the fish, amphibians and invertebrates most frequently and abundantly involved are not current-loving species at all but inhabitants of quiet water. But when the new water flows into ponds and pools cramped by drought, the jubilee creatures suddenly become current seekers, presumably reacting to the flow because it bears the exciting taste of renewed opportunity upstream somewhere.

When you find one of these sporadic upstream migrations in progress, gambusias are nearly always involved, sometimes by tens of thousands in volumes of only a few cubic feet. In their numbers and density, gambusias are accomplished pioneers. They are also willing to eat almost anything nourishing, and they produce live young. In the mosquito fish, fertilization is internal. The female gives birth to a few fully formed offspring, which the moment they appear seem ready and eager to take up adult responsibilities. Thus, for the small creatures of the Everglades, disaster is built into the normal yearly cycle. But not being prone to anxiety they flourish, holding on in the gator holes during the dry time, going off on jubilees when the first spring floods come, and in summer scrambling back out through the reborn River of Grass.

If the wet season brings plenty of rain, the numbers of small fish that will crowd into the shrunken ponds and water holes when another dry season comes will be cause for celebration and conviviality among the larger animals of the Everglades—not just the ironhead storks but most of the other fish-eating creatures as well. A hundred years ago, an Everglades gator hole in the early dry season must have been a spectacular bit of landscape—not the equal of a good water hole in Tanzania, because the Everglades creatures are mostly smaller than those of Serengeti, though sometimes every bit as feverishly active. Even today, although the populations of most of the larger Everglades species are less numerous than they used to be, a gator hole in the early days of a dry season brings together in fantastic juxtaposition a wonderful array of predators and prey. When the River of Grass dries up, alligators and otters are crowded with their own kind, and with unusual concentrations of raccoons, herons, garfish, snakes and soft-shelled turtles. You can still sometimes see two dozen water snakes at once around the edges of a fish-filled gator hole, and maybe 10 kinds of wading birds will be there stumbling over the snakes.

So in the Everglades, each year brings a time of dwindling and bare survival followed by a time of spreading and explosive reproduction. Millions of individual animals die in the rhythmic disaster of winter drought; but the species to which they belong are adapted to disaster and will certainly revive again when the rains return, if man will only curb his abuses of the landscape they live in. Extinction has no natural place in Pahayokee. There is only an endless round of decimation and spectacular renewal.

The Ordeal of Drought

In the Everglades, the pendulum of the seasons swings in a wide arc between flood and drought, producing alternating periods of fecundity and barrenness. From early spring well into autumn, the Glades are usually kept flushed by ample rainfall, annually averaging about 50 inches. But by November the last drenching tropical storm of the year has gone, and its passage signals the start of the dry season, a time of trial for the creatures of the Glades.

The seasonal change takes effect slowly, after weeks of little or no rainfall. As the water level is lowered by evaporation and runoff, the higher terrain drains and the low, muddy areas dry in a maze of cracks (right). The isolated ponds that remain in small depressions trap great numbers of fish in their dwindling waters. In the desiccated areas, the shallow-rooted grasses and weeds gradually turn brown and die off, providing fuel for the ground fires that normally burn out large tracts of vegetation. In years of extreme drought, even the wide sloughs have dried out completely or shrunk to streams too narrow to serve as effective firebreaks.

By late January as a rule, the lack of water and the related threat of famine confront the creatures of the Glades with a deepening crisis. Each species meets this challenge in its own way. Many birds fly off to wetter habitats. Many land animals—deer, raccoons, opossums, panthers and various small rodents—hold on, though they are forced to spend their days roaming the dried-out marshes in search of water.

Some species, unable to sustain normal activity, retreat into estivation, a torpid state similar to hibernation but not as deep or persistent. Estivating tree snails conserve their bodily moisture by attaching the openings of their shells to the bark with an airtight mucous seal. Apple snails, frogs and turtles dig into the moist undersoil and there lapse into a self-preserving lethargy. During especially severe droughts, even alligators will estivate in damp dens beside their shrunken water holes.

Sometime in May, usually, the first abundant rainfall in months begins to quicken the pace of life in the Glades. By then, the drought has served a grim but essential purpose. Many creatures of every species have died of thirst and hunger; and this natural check on their proliferation helps to ensure a stable, balanced population in the Glades.

Cracked soil and withered sawgrass testify to the drying out of water sources along the Shark River Slough. The slough itself, up to 40 miles wide during the rainy season, normally shrinks to a few narrow streams during the November-to-April dry season.

Dry Times in a Shallow Pond

As the water level recedes in the low, flat Glades, a few feet of elevation can make the difference between life and death for innumerable fish during the dry season. Many of those trapped in dwindling pools have little chance to survive. Yet as ever in nature, nothing is wasted. A fish that dies will make a meal for a ravenous raccoon, and the subsoil beneath even a desiccated pond will retain enough moisture to save the life of an estivating turtle.

In general, the first casualties in a shrinking pond are its largest fish, such as bass and bream. Sunfish and other medium-sized species are the next to perish.

As evaporation and overcrowding progressively reduce the oxygen supply in the pond, these fish cannot breathe; their mouths are too big and clumsy to utilize the last resource—a fragile film of relatively oxygen-rich water at the surface.

Some fish survive through special adaptations. The tiny mosquito fish has an uptilted mouth that enables it to take in oxygen while remaining horizontal in a mere trickle of water. The large garfish is equipped with a primitive air-breathing lung that sustains it up to a point—even out of water. And, the bowfin, similarly equipped with a lung, can burrow into the bottom of a completely waterless pond and breathe the meager air that filters through a thin layer of mud.

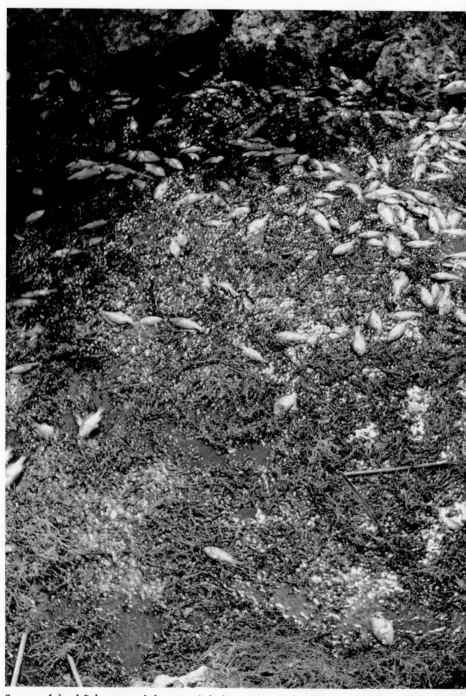

Scores of dead fish, most of them sunfish, lie victim to the shrinking of their shallow pond

Predator or scavenger depending on opportunity, a coon devours a dead fish.

ish in deeper rivers and sloughs usually survive drought.

Preparing to estivate, a slider turtle digs into the moist soil under a dried pond.

Drying footprints trace an alligator's search for water.

The Gator Hole: Peaceful Refuge

Of the Everglades' many debts to the alligator, none is more important than the benefits that accrue from its relentless search for water in the dry season. Moving across the arid flats, the great reptile keeps its heavy body elevated to make maximum speed, thus leaving no belly marks between its footprints *(left)*. Sooner or later, instinct and persistence lead the alligator to water, or to a low place where the water table lies close to the surface.

The alligator then sets to work either to deepen and enlarge the existing water hole or to excavate a new one, breaking the caked earth with its powerful tail and shoveling away the debris with its broad snout. During the worst droughts, alligators have been known to dig their way down through four feet of compacted mud and peat before water has oozed up from the porous bedrock.

Such gator holes, found throughout the parched Glades, attract many thirsty creatures ranging from otters to herons, and soon become biological microcosms of the whole region. The alligators, conserving energy and living on their own fat, largely ignore the intruders; the refugees sustain life on the gator hole's remaining fish, insect life and vegetation, and live side by side in a relative state of truce. When the rains finally return, it is from these oases that the various species go forth to repopulate the Glades.

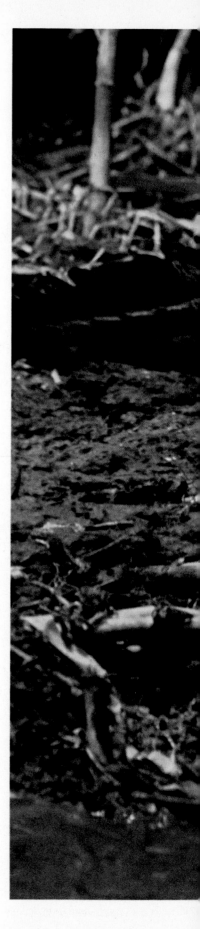

An alligator relaxes on the mudbank near its watery den. Several alligators—and many smaller animals—may occupy one gator hole.

4/ Sanctuary in the Park

The flooded forest, combining...the forces of earth and water, was a common ground where all creatures moved in quiet, with respect. PETER MATTHIESSEN/ AT PLAY IN THE FIELDS OF THE LORD

The squall had moved out of the drenched land an hour before and now was lingering offshore in the Gulf, its thunder dwindled to sullen rumbling in the night air. I had walked along the prairie road west of the Everglades National Park buildings at Flamingo, hoping the mosquitoes would stay hidden for a while. My flashlight revealed a little water snake on the road, and the eyes of a raccoon and two marsh rabbits. The thin trill of a cone-headed cricket came from somewhere in the grass, and along the shore a squawking great blue heron flew off into the darkness. At least I supposed it was a great blue. Cape Sable has great white herons too, and I wondered idly whether I was hearing one of them. Then a lightning flash printed a spread-winged image of the heron against the sky, and I saw it was a great blue after all.

In the quiet after the heron had gone I heard a lonesome-sounding frog chorus far off across the prairie. It was almost too far for me to sort out the voices in it, but I gradually made out the piteous *ma-a-anh* of narrow-mouthed toads, the yelping *erp-erp-erp* of the green tree frog, and a rasping chant that could have been either the *ark-ark-ark* of the Cuban tree frog or the flatter *ack-ack-ack* of the rain frog.

I was sleepy and didn't feel like sloshing across the wet marl to see for certain what other frog was singing with the green tree frogs and narrow-mouthed toads. But the singing frogs reminded me of the much bigger chorus I had heard up at Taylor Slough the night before and I thought, as I have many times, how neglected frog songs are. Not scientifically neglected—herpetologists spend quite a lot of time taping frog calls—but esthetically neglected. Frogs do for the night what birds do for the day: they give it a voice. And the voice is a varied and stirring one that ought to be better known. Ever since the days of the first talking pictures, Hollywood movie-makers have used recordings of the voice of the Pacific tree frog as background sound for scenes anywhere from New Guinea to the Carolinas. That they have been getting away with this decade after decade suggests to me that there has been a melancholy decline in the sensibilities of Americans. Frog songs are distinctive; every kind of frog has its own voice. You can learn to recognize frog songs as readily as the songs of warblers. Although frogs are fewer in species than birds, Florida is blessed with a great many kinds, and because they sing mainly at night when most birds are quiet they give the wet places much of their incomparable nighttime atmosphere. Perhaps the reason frog songs are not generally appreciated is that they are sung in places where mosquitoes and snakes live.

I still treasure the memory of a night when I stood by a pond with a little swamp at either end, and heard 14 different kinds of frogs singing all at once. That happened in northern Florida, where frogs are more diverse than anywhere else. You may never hear quite that many kinds in the Everglades, but you can easily find choruses of six or eight species in good frog weather. I recall a June night when the frogs drowned out the bellowing of an alligator I was trying to listen to.

Although frog-song is mostly confined to the night, it often breaks out on cloudy days, when the barometric pressure and the relative humidity are propitious. Two kinds of frogs can be heard in warm weather in the Glades on all but the brightest, driest days. One is the little cricket frog *Acris,* whose *ik-ik* is the most ubiquitous amphibian voice of the region. The other voice is the baritone *urr-urr* of *Rana grylio,* the southern bullfrog, which also is known as sulfur-belly, and pig frog. I have never liked the name pig frog, not because I have anything against pigs, but because *grylio* doesn't sound like one. The grunt of a pig has a nasal quality, a French *on*-sound; and it is usually two-toned, rising in pitch or else trailing off into a similarly Gallic *in*-sound. There is nothing nasal about the sulfur-belly's voice, nor is it two-toned. It is a deep, short, resonant, staccato trill, as if the *urr-urr* were being said by a person from some part of Spain, where "rr's" are reverently rolled.

The big bullfrog, *Rana catesbeiana,* lives in southern Florida too; but because it is partial to wooded ponds and tree swamps, its ponderous *jug-a-rum* is rarely heard in the Everglades where *grylio* holds forth. There is, however, another sort of bullfrog out there—if by bullfrog one means any member of the genus *Rana*. This is the slim, far-jumping southern leopard frog, which has a less authoritative voice than the other two. Its voice quavers or jerkily scratches out its song like a dry hand dragging across a tight-blown rubber balloon. The leopard frog is a superior animal, alert, sharp-faced, great at hurdling across broken country; but because its voice is both seasonal and quavery, and not too different from that of New England and Wisconsin leopard frogs, I lean toward the sulfur-belly as the true cantor of the River of Grass.

The Everglades are the sulfur-belly's kind of country. It is indispensable in Everglades ecology, harvesting tons of crayfish, aquatic insects and snails, and itself providing a staple food for reptiles, birds and bass. It zealously guards its territory. The drum-roll sound of its *urr-urr* is believed to serve as a signal for proclaiming its territorial rights.

The sulfur-belly has suffered grievously from market hunting. Along with the alligator and the plume birds, it stands out among the creatures that have borne the brunt of man's effort to force a living from the Everglades wilderness. The sulfur-belly is the main market frog of southern Florida, and when airboats began to ply the Everglades in the 1930s frog hunting quickly became a specialized calling. The biologist Frank Ligas has estimated that the best frog hunters used to get up to 400 pounds of legs in a two-night hunting trip. They can't match that today. Sulfur-bellies feed heavily on crayfish. The dry times have become too hard and long to keep crayfish abundant in the River of Grass. And the frog hunters themselves destroyed a lot of bullfrog habitat by hunting alligators, legally and illegally, on the side. As they killed out the gators, the gator holes and water trails grew over with vegetation, driving the frogs away. But down in the heart of the Everglades National Park, where all hunting is prohibited, the frogs are coming back.

As anyone would expect from looking at a map, the animals and plants that have colonized the relatively new land at the tip of the Florida peninsula are a mixture of temperate-American and tropical kinds. As also might be expected, species derived from the continent predominate, simply because salt water separates Florida and the West Indies, and most creatures have a hard time crossing salt water.

The animals and plants of new land that appears above the sea don't spring full-blown from the ground. They have to move in from other places. How they move and where they come from is the specialty of

A nimble climber, this green tree frog owes its agility to specialized feet, which have large toe pads that grip like suction cups.

biogeographers. Up in northern Florida, where I live, the land is maybe 15 million years old, and the animals and vegetation of northeastern North America have had plenty of time to colonize. But down in southern Florida some of the land was being formed only about 3,000 years ago. Because the dry ground there is separated from the nearby West Indies by salt water, and from the continent to the north by broad expanses of glades and prairie that vary from bone-dry to watery in a normal year, you would expect the fauna to have been built up out of the more vagile—the more biogeographically footloose—kinds of animals. And so they have been. The region is heavy in birds, for instance. In fact its crown jewels are its birds—tropical forms such as the black cuckoo-like ani, the white-crowned pigeon and the roseate spoonbill; the wide variety of resident species derived from the temperate zone; and the hosts of migratory warblers, thrushes, vireos, ducks and shore birds that stop over in their travels. Many wingless creatures that live with special sets of ecologic conditions—as earthworms, salamanders and upland fishes do—may have found it impossible to reach whatever small tracts of suitable habitat may exist in southern Florida.

The land platform on which Florida rests is very old, and though there have been repeated floodings and withdrawals of the sea during the last million years, there was land in central and northern Florida most of the time, and terrestrial life persisted there. It is from there that much of the fauna and flora of southern Florida was derived.

Nonaerial animals vary markedly in their ability to get across salt water. Lizards are good at island-hopping; salamanders are quite unventuresome. The capacity to colonize new range is not directly related to locomotor ability. Frogs, though able hoppers, are easily foiled by the barrier of salt water. One reason for this is the dual nature of their life cycle. As tadpoles, frogs resemble fish; when they mature they are terrestrial but scaleless, and prone to desiccation and salt-pickling. No frogs have come into southern Florida from the West Indies by natural means. The two tropical kinds that do occur—the Cuban tree frog and a tiny sweet-voiced greenhouse frog with the generic name *Eleutherodactylus*—were almost surely introduced accidentally by man.

The most conspicuous tropical element in southern Florida is botanical and it is not hard to see why. Most of the West Indian plants that occur there have fruits, seeds, or other reproductive bodies that are susceptible to distribution by storm winds or ocean currents. Some of these may have been brought in by birds. More than a hundred of the tropical southern Florida trees have small fruits that birds eat regularly. Anyone who has parked his car where migratory robins roosted after raiding a cherry-laurel tree will know what sowers of seeds a flock of birds can be. There is no doubt that within southern Florida birds carry the fruits of pigeon plum, saffron plum, coco plum, satin-leaf, mastic, Jamaica dogwood, silver palm and a host of others, and set up new stands wherever the seedlings are able to take hold. So perhaps some tropical plants were brought to southern Florida by birds.

Whatever the origin of the Everglades flora and fauna, they have managed to adapt to a rigorous environment. At first glance the tip of peninsular Florida might seem like an easy place to get along in—jutting down almost into the tropics, nudging into a curve of the Gulf Stream, with freezing temperatures rare, and with up to 60 inches of rain a year. It sounds like lush, lazy country, in which any creature able to get there would surely find a way to live. But despite the absence of tumbling streams or grinding ice, the Everglades Basin animals and plants have developed under stress: drought, flooding, fire, the winds and driving water of hurricanes, even sporadic killing frosts. These factors—some regular and predictable, some operating only once in a decade or so—have surely kept out many potential colonists. The species that have successfully pioneered are, in one way or another, adapted to absorb the recurrent shocks and then recoup.

The most dramatic trials they face are the hurricanes. In 1960 Hurricane Donna drove tons of salt mud across the prairie, tore up ancient forests of mangroves, and left 200-pound loggerhead sea turtles slogging about in the marl far inland. After the hurricane of 1935 we went looking for crocodiles at Madeira Bay and found enormous masses of reinforced concrete, chunks weighing 10 tons or more, in the edge of the mangroves; they had been part of the Lower Matecumbe ferry slip, 30-odd miles across Florida Bay.

For all the ecological vagaries, the Everglades provide a refuge that may be vital to the survival of a number of kinds of animals that are declining seriously outside southern Florida. Most of the endangered or declining species are birds. It was in what now is the Everglades National Park that the most important episode in the hairbreadth rescue of the plume-birds occurred. The spirit that accomplished that unprecedented feat was of unreckoned significance in the evolution of human concern for natural species.

Few people are aware that in spite of the environmental disruptions of the past few decades, you can now see more herons and egrets in a day's drive through southern Florida than you would have seen in a whole year back in 1905. The change came about mainly through suppression of the feather trade. The tales of the killing that took place at the rookeries to adorn ladies' hats sound today like nightmares.

It was the establishment of the Audubon Societies and the courage of their early wardens that started the trend against this slaughter. The murder of an Audubon warden, Guy Bradley, by poachers at Flamingo in 1905 focused the indignant attention of the world on the bird plume industry, and soon thereafter the fad for the feathers began to languish. Since then there has been a creeping decline, even in the rural southeastern United States, in the idle shooting of herons. There has also been a blessed disappearance of the kind of hunter who would petulantly shoot any bird that came within range. Today, finally, such people are being looked on with more disgust and less indulgence. The culprits still exist, but nowadays increasing numbers of their fellows regard them as misfits, and this gets to them harder than any laws.

The outlook for other depleted species may be improving, or at least less dismal than seemed the case a little while ago. Take the roseate spoonbill, the most generally eye-catching of all the native wading birds of Florida. Somehow, the spoonbill has held on in southern Florida though for decades its numbers there were almost vanishingly small. I spent 30 years in the state thinking of spoonbills as virtually legendary, and when I finally saw my first one it was down in Honduras. Now, however, you can see spoonbills almost any day at low tide on the mud flats around Flamingo.

Some people believe that the flamingo is even more spectacular than the spoonbill, and I agree. The flamingo is probably the most spectacular bird in the world. Few sights in the bird world can equal the fields of pink flame that feeding flocks of flamingos make, or the incredible spectacle of the nesting colonies, with acres of rose-colored birds, each perched on a stumpy clay mound.

Unhappily, however, flamingos don't nest in Florida. The captive flock at the Hialeah Race Track near Miami has somehow been wheedled into breeding there, but there are no natural nesting colonies in the state—and perhaps there never were. Nobody can say why, but predation was probably the reason. In Florida a big conspicuous edible bird, with the strange habit of nesting on a short thick pedestal on a mud flat, has far more potential enemies than there are in the West Indies. The abundant raccoons of Florida could, alone, account for the ab-

An Everglade kite prepares to devour an apple snail, the only food it eats. The dwindling snail supply threatens this bird's extinction.

sence of wild flamingo breeding colonies. Some flocks used to come over from the Bahamas at molting time, when they were particularly vulnerable to predation.

Those that turn up here and there in Florida nowadays are thought to be birds that escaped from captivity—particularly from Hialeah, where they were established 40-odd years ago. A flock of 19 birds escaped from Hialeah in 1931—their custodian had neglected to clip their wings or pinion them—and smaller groups have subsequently been lost there and at other tourist attractions, though some unpinioned birds have been persuaded to remain. We will have to get along without this admirable bird as a true resident, though, and that is a real deprivation.

The story of the great white heron is more encouraging—if encouraging is the right word to describe the consolidation of as tiny a range as that of the great white. The total United States population of this tall, raucous-voiced bird is confined to southernmost Florida, from southern Biscayne Bay down the Keys, out into Florida Bay, and up around the west coast to Everglades City. According to Alexander Sprunt IV, research director of the National Audubon Society, the great white heron is "in fine shape." He is speaking comparatively. He estimates that there are probably about 2,500 to 2,800 birds in existence, and is pleased with the number because it used to be a whole lot smaller. One peculiar attribute of the great white heron that, in view of the dismal influx of people into its range on the Florida Keys, may be necessary equipment for survival is its willingness to fraternize with man. It often ventures into waterside human neighborhoods. Down in the lower Keys, where the Great White Heron National Wildlife Refuge has been created, the birds sometimes stroll about from backyard to backyard in the new subdivisions, accepting spare victuals from the residents. A few days ago I saw one standing beside a man on a dock, hopefully watching him clean a fish. The great white heron has come a long way since my first visit to Florida Bay in 1931, and it may live on.

The prospects of the reddish egret are less comforting. The first of these rare birds that I ever saw was, like my first spoonbill, not in Florida but on a shallow-water marl flat on Great Inagua Island, toward the southern end of the Bahamas. What I beheld there seemed to my casual and unexpert eye to be an ordinary heron of some kind, probably a young little blue. It was foraging in ankle-deep water in company with a sprinkling of mature little blues and a thin stand of roseate spoonbills. Suddenly what I assumed to be a young little blue began cavorting as I had never seen a heron cavort before, dashing around the shallows, abruptly stopping once in a while to stab at the water, and then gulping down some small creature. This behavior was without precedent in my heron lore, but there was a bird man with me and he said casually, "that's a reddish egret out there," and I vaguely recollected two things I had heard about this species: that they are not red but come in white and dark phases; and that their foraging behavior is peculiar.

Actually, the behavior goes far beyond the merely peculiar. In fact, watching the one on the Inagua flat that day it was hard for me to understand why the other normal-acting herons and spoonbills out there put up with such clowning. It bordered on the antisocial, or seemed to. Later, however, I read some papers on heron behavior by Andrew Meyerriecks, a zoologist at the University of South Florida, and learned that the reddish egret's eccentric feeding habits are probably an adaptive device that allows the species to avoid competition with other herons. According to Meyerriecks, if wading birds of different species all fed in the same way, they would spend more time threatening each other and squabbling over morsels of food than actually feeding.

Wading birds are not the only kinds of birds that are in trouble. Perhaps the most seriously threatened of all the Everglades birds is the Everglade kite, or snail kite. It qualifies as endangered by any definition. The range of the subspecies it belongs to is small—it is confined to southern Florida. Its total population is minuscule, probably not having been more than 150 birds in recent years. And its numbers are clearly declining. According to Paul Sykes of the U.S. Fish and Wildlife Service, the colony was down to probably no more than 20 to 30 birds in 1972, and these had been scattered by drought and fire into places far out of their usual range. There is no clear rescue plan in sight.

The chief cause of the snail kite's trouble is the decimation of Everglades snail populations by combined natural drought and human mismanagement of the water system. This species of kite is the most specialized bird of prey in North America. Its diet consists solely of a single species of fresh-water mollusk, the apple snail. The apple snail, which is about the size of a golf ball, is one of the group that wall themselves off in their shell by means of an operculum—a sort of door —common to many other snails. Unlike most operculate snails, however, the apple snail has a lung, and comes to the surface to breathe. This is the habit that brings it within reach of the snail kite. The bird pries off the operculum and with the long tip of the upper beak severs the muscle that holds the snail in its shell. Then it picks out and swallows the snail in chunks. The ranges of the two animals coincide closely. The survival of the kite population in Florida will depend on what can be quickly done to stabilize the apple-snail population.

Except for the masses of apple-snail eggs that conspicuously decorate the stems of emergent water plants, fresh-water mollusks go mostly unobserved in the Everglades. There is little evidence of the many-faceted ecologic role played by snails, mussels, pea-clams and the tiny limpets that huddle like wan barnacles against any smooth submerged surface. But the mollusks are down there in millions, filtering plankton, scraping algae, and industriously building themselves into food for larger creatures. Not many Everglades animals are strongly specialized eaters of mollusks, but various reptiles, amphibians, fishes and mammals eat snails, mussels or both, and if more were known about the flow of energy in the Everglades, snails would probably prove to be one of the most important links in the food chains there. Bullfrogs eat them regularly, and so do turtles, young alligators and many fishes.

Otters like snails too. At least our pet otter was avid about them. His idea of a pleasant outing was to be driven to a little pond that was full of coontail moss and ram's-horn snails. There he would porpoise about in the weed-choked water for an hour or more, crunching the snails so loudly we could hear him from where we used to sit in the pondside shade. Not long ago my wife and I saw a young wild otter in some kind of altercation with a limpkin. It was down on the Pinecrest Road, at the south edge of the Big Cypress, during a hard rain. From some distance away we noticed in the middle of the road two live, dark forms of about the same size but very different shapes. They appeared to be tilting at each other, and when we drove up close we saw that a half-grown otter and a limpkin were contending over some round black object. When I stopped the car and walked toward them, the limpkin flew off and the otter loped into the ditch beside the road. I walked over to the object of their strife. It was a big apple snail, still alive. The otter had not had a chance to take the snail in its mouth for crunching, nor had the limpkin gotten close enough to grab the snail with its beak. The snail, its operculum tightly closed, did not have a mark on it.

The feeding habits of the limpkin and two other mollusk-eaters, the Everglade kites and the boat-tailed grackles, have been the subject of an exhaustive study done by Noel and Helen Snyder. Their examination of this one section of a wetland feeding web shows how three very different species of animals can converge upon a food resource without harmful confrontation, and so illustrates an important principle of evo-

Two adult crocodiles bask on an Everglades mudbank. A narrower, pointed snout distinguishes them from the more numerous alligators.

lutionary ecology. The only open conflict the Snyders recorded among the three mollusk-eaters occurred between grackles and kites, or between grackles and limpkins. It usually was instigated by the grackles. Boat-tailed grackles—glossy, dark-plumed relatives of the blackbird—are omnivorous and versatile feeders. Through most of their extensive geographic range they are by no means dependent on or even especially partial to mollusks as food, but in parts of the Everglades apple snails predominate in their diet. They either catch the snails themselves or steal them from limpkins. Between limpkins and kites the Snyders observed no conflict, presumably because the two hunt in different ways. The kites cruise on the wing, flying at low levels over open, deep water. When they sight a snail near the surface of the water they drop fast and seize it in one extended foot. Limpkins avoid the open places, hunting usually in dense aquatic vegetation; because they move on foot they stay away from deep water. Wherever the Snyders found grackles feeding heavily on apple snails, the birds were hunting in shallow water like the limpkin. The grackles would search purposefully, sometimes leaning to lift a lily pad and inspect its undersurface.

Although the three birds' sharing of a particular food source in a particular area would appear on the surface to be ecological competition, it is not. To be competitors in a strict sense, they would have to feed in a way that decreased the common food supply, and this happens negligibly, if at all. Their predation causes only slight fluctuations in the snail population. Far greater effects on the numbers of snails are produced by the recurrent disasters of drought and fire, which kill the snails, drive limpkins out of their haunts, and in 1971 scattered the Everglades colony of snail kites as far north as Georgia.

Along with endangered birds, southern Florida and Everglades National Park serve as a refuge for other animals whose future seems uncertain. Two of these have become widely known test cases. One is the manatee or sea cow; the other is the American crocodile.

Although nearly all the early Florida explorers used to take home exciting tales of alligators, it was not till after the Civil War that the presence of crocodiles in the region became generally known. This seems strange, because the two are not really very much alike. The snout of the crocodile tapers much more sharply, it has the big ostentatious teeth in its jaws arranged in a different way, and in habits and temperament it is not at all like an alligator. Nevertheless it took a long time for Floridians to become aware there were crocodiles among them.

Once this was known, it took a lot less time for them to reduce the crocodile population to a tiny colony. In the early 1870s the range of the crocodile extended from Palm Beach on the Atlantic Coast to Key West, and up the Gulf Coast to Charlotte Harbor. Today nearly all of the few remaining crocodiles live in the northeastern corner of Florida Bay.

As with most of the other animals that are in danger of disappearing from Florida, the loss of the crocodile would not automatically mean the extinction of the species. It is pan-Caribbean in distribution and still survives in Cuba and Jamaica, along the mainland Caribbean coasts from Mexico into Central America. But little comfort can be taken from this wide range, because practically everywhere outside Everglades National Park crocodiles are under fearful pressure. The pressure comes from both hide hunters and the puerile "sportsmen" who get themselves guided out to a safe, shady place from which they can comfortably shoot a basking crocodile with a deer rifle.

From the time Everglades National Park was established in 1947 it was pretty clearly the only hope for saving the crocodile in the United States. For a while the hope was feeble, but now there seems some chance that it may be realized.

I recently went with park biologist John Ogden and ranger Stan Robbins to look at crocodile nests in the southeast section of the park. We saw five nests. Any clear expanse of shore appeared acceptable as a nesting ground. Some of the nests were in marl, some in friable shell sand. One had been dug down from beach level while the others had been excavated in mounds piled up by the crocodiles during several pre-nesting visits. One of these was 5 feet high and 20 feet across.

Since the recent spread of efforts to raise alligators on farms and ranches, quite a lot has been learned about the nest-building activities of the female alligator. Practically nothing has been known about the habits of the crocodile, however. In Central America the species makes its nests on seaside beaches or in the sand of river bars. A young friend of mine in Costa Rica got chased by a big female that built her nest at one end of a beach at Tortuguero. Until then, I had never known whether female crocodiles show the extraordinary parental concern for their nests and young that so distinguishes female alligators among reptiles. John Ogden's observations now show that they probably do.

Censuses that Ogden has taken suggest that the Florida crocodile colony has stabilized, and may possibly even be slowly growing. He estimates that there are probably 300 to 400 crocodiles now in the park, and that about 20 females nest there each year.

Submerged in salt water, a manatee, or sea cow, forages for aquatic plants. A one-ton adult eats about 200 pounds of vegetation a day.

The crocodile's position has no doubt been strengthened by the severe penalties for alligator hunting. Poaching is harder to get away with than it used to be. Certainly few people go out cold-bloodedly nowadays to hunt crocodiles for their hides. So the drain on the adult crocodile population comes mainly from inadvertent entanglement in the nets of mullet fishermen. Catching a crocodile in a mullet net is a fairly traumatic occurrence, for the fisherman as it is for the crocodile. Only a sawfish can make a worse mess of a net. In days gone by, the task of removing a croc from net webbing was performed with little or no sense of stewardship for the endangered species. But now, John Ogden tells me, some fishermen who used to kill the crocodiles they caught "to thin them out" actually cut them free.

The other chief cause of loss in the crocodile colony is nest robbery. Crocodiles nest in the marl or shell of beaches along the shores of eastern Florida Bay and upper Key Largo. Since most of the nests are mounded, they are easy to locate. Every year Ogden finds some of them destroyed by human predators, partly, he thinks, out of vandalism, but in some cases to get eggs from which to hatch little crocodiles for illegal sale. On the strength of this information the park management has recently closed three creeks in the prime nesting corner of the Bay shore to all but authorized persons. So the crocodile population of the park is probably the best protected colony of the species anywhere, and at the rate at which wilderness is being invaded in the tropics, it is a main hope for the survival of the species.

Another Florida animal whose future almost surely depends heavily on the protection it gets in the park—not as a year-round refuge, perhaps, but as a seasonal migration station—is the manatee or sea cow. There are parallels between its case and that of the crocodile. Though sea cows are more widespread than crocodiles in Florida, the total population in the state is probably not much bigger; and the two animals have somewhat similar distribution outside United States waters.

One could argue that the case of the manatee is the most important survival problem the Everglades National Park is involved in. I realize that it is risky to speak of degrees of importance where extinction is threatened. Obviously, all creatures are equal in the sight of the Lord. But I suggest that sea cows rank higher than most creatures as candidates for human solicitude. My criteria are their steady depletion during the last century; their present perilously low population level; the uniqueness of the order to which they belong; their enormous size

—they weigh up to 1,500 pounds—and their astonishing appearance. But all the reason anybody really needs for saving manatees is that they are fabulously outlandish and lovable beasts. Not every visitor to the Everglades National Park may have the privilege of seeing a sea cow; but everyone who does is bound to be glad there is such a place for such a beguiling creature.

Manatees belong to the Sirenia, an order of mammals of which the dugongs of the tropical Indo-Pacific area are the only other surviving members. Although they are derived from a common terrestrial ancestor, and are distantly related to elephants, manatees are strongly modified for aquatic life. A sea cow's body, while tremendous, is wholly streamlined. The front limbs are paddles, the back limbs have completely disappeared, and there is a broad, horizontally oriented tail flipper. The upper lip is a short, thick, snoutlike implement used in grazing on submarine vegetation. The face is whiskered and wrinkled.

There is a persistent tradition—reflected in its scientific name—that the manatee was the mermaid of the early mariners. If so, then one can only pity those chaps. Manatees are splendid, amiable animals, but they are ugly as sin, and one wonders how their one ladylike attribute—a pair of pectorally placed teats—could have so bemused the wistful old sailors as to evoke the mermaid legend.

The most encouraging development in the survival outlook of the Florida sea cow—aside from the establishment of Everglades National Park—has been the reappearance of a good-sized winter colony in the headwaters of Crystal River in Citrus County. According to a careful study of the herd there by Daniel S. Hartman, the sea cows turn up in the river regularly after the first cold spell of winter, apparently attracted by the warm spring water at the source of the river. Most of the adult manatees have numerous propeller scars on their backs. Dr. Hartman has made ingenious use of this phenomenon. By identifying the different scar patterns of 50 individual manatees, the way an ornithologist bands birds, he has been able to track them during two seasons and thereby study their movements and behavior.

This reappearance of manatees in the big springs of the peninsula seems almost incredible. I have known Crystal River well since the 1930s and never saw a sea cow there until 1967. No doubt the resurgence was produced partly by improved law enforcement against poachers and partly by a marked increase in submerged river vegetation. Suburban development around the headwater springs has grievously overenriched the river, and the burgeoning water plants seriously interfere with boat traffic. Manatees graze on the plants, and that makes them welcome visitors. Dr. Hartman's important data are now being used by Friends of the Earth as the basis for an effort to have the Citrus County springs declared a manatee sanctuary.

Another factor in the increase of manatees in the midpeninsular springs may be the slowly improving protection the sea cows are getting far to the south when they move on to Everglades National Park. The Crystal River manatees are there only in winter; when spring comes they disappear. Since this is when they most often are seen in southern Florida, the assumption is that a seasonal migration occurs. If this is a fact, then success in saving the Crystal River sea-cow herd will depend on protection in its more southerly summer range.

Fortunately, the most important part of that range appears to be within the limits of the Everglades National Park, in the labyrinthine mangrove country east and north of Whitewater Bay, and the Cape Sable area. Park pilot Ralph Miele sees them often there, and recently located a herd of 20 or more. They are often seen with calves there in spring and summer. They also are regularly reported by people traveling among the Ten Thousand Islands south of Everglades City. If these are the same manatees that turn up in November or December in Crystal River—and if the proposed Citrus County sanctuary becomes a reality—then the whole Gulf Coast manatee colony might be saved.

In 1885, in his book *Life and Adventures in South Florida,* Andrew Canova had a dire prediction for the Whitewater Bay manatees: "In days long gone by, the Seminoles living . . . near Cape Sable killed the manatee, jerked the flesh and sold it to the Spaniards at a good price, and ten years ago the meat could be bought at fifty cents a pound. Of course the animals are becoming far too scarce to admit of its being sold at all. There is no doubt that the manatee is fast becoming an extinct animal. . . . The sea cow will pass out of existence . . . and the only remaining trace of its former existence will be a few old bones."

Canova wrote that almost nine decades ago. The sea cows are not yet gone. It is clear that only great vigilance is going to save them, however, and that the main hope for achieving this is the calving ground in the mangrove bays and mazes of Everglades National Park.

An Audubon Sampler

Apart from the alligator, no creatures are more symbolic of the Everglades and their environs than the curious and beautiful birds that live there. And no one has done more to dramatize them—and bring them to the consciousness of the public —than the 19th Century painter-naturalist John James Audubon.

As in his wildlife studies in other regions of the United States, Audubon's superb visual record of the birds of the far south benefited from a method he devised to ensure true, lifelike representations. Because a bird's colors fade soon after death, Audubon used freshly killed models; by passing a sharpened flexible wire through the model, he was able to bend it into a pose characteristic of the living bird.

Produced in the 1820s and '30s, these paintings served as the basis for the engravings in Audubon's monumental work, *The Birds of America*. In time most of the original watercolors were acquired by the New-York Historical Society, which has exhibited them only intermittently to protect them from fading. It was from these originals that the photographs on the following pages were made. The studies of the anhinga *(page 104)* and the common egret *(page 107)* are here published for the first time anywhere; later paintings of the same birds were chosen for *The Birds of America*. In their freshness and vitality, all nine studies capture Audubon's intense feeling for nature—a feeling, he recorded in his journal, "bordering on phrenzy."

Audubon was deeply disturbed by the senseless slaughter of birds for the plume trade, which nearly resulted in the extinction of the common egret and the snowy egret, among other birds. The artist's revulsion at such wastage helped spur a demand for legislation, first passed in 1910, that prohibited the sale of plumage for ornamental use. But Audubon's unique contribution to the birds he loved remains his gift for tireless observation, expressed not only in his art but in his writings. Though not scientifically trained, he became a great ornithologist and a meticulous compiler of information, and was well aware of his contributions. "What a treat for me," he once wrote his publisher, "to disclose things unknown to all the world before me. . . . The truths and facts contained in my writings and in my figures of Birds will become more apparent to every student of nature."

Far more common in America today than its endangered cousin the brown pelican, the white pelican is one of South Florida's largest birds, with a wingspread up to nine feet. As Audubon painted it, the bird appears to be standing on a shoreline at dusk, holding its catch in its large pouch after a fishing expedition in offshore waters.

Amply endowed with soft, fluffy white feathers ideal for adorning hats and fans, the snowy egret was once a prime target for Florida hunters. Almost extinct 50 years ago, the bird has made an impressive comeback; at nesting time in spring, snowy egrets now safely congregate by the thousands.

The roseate spoonbill, one of the Everglades' most spectacular wading birds, is named for its spatulate bill, some six to seven inches long. Audubon noted "a considerable degree of elegance" in the way the bird uses its bill, swinging it from side to side as it munches insects or small shellfish.

The green heron abounds in Florida,
but its protective coloring makes it
hard to detect. As the painting shows,
this shy bird, smallest of American
herons, easily blends with the marshy
vegetation growing in the shallows
through which it wades in search of its
staple diet of insects and small fish.

Another heron, the reddish egret, is
never red, but most often gray, with a
rusty brown head and neck; some
are white (Audubon mistook this for
the mark of an immature bird). But all
reddish egrets have flesh-colored,
black-tipped bills and a clownish walk;
sometimes they lurch as if drunk.

A bird of diverse talents, the anhinga goes by three aliases: snakebird, for its serpentine neck; American darter, for its jerky movements; and water turkey, for the way its tail spreads in flight. It is as adept in the water as in the air, swimming either entirely under water or with head and neck showing.

The limpkin's name derives from its jerky gait as it prowls its marshy habitat hunting for the fresh-water snails that provide its main food. But the limpkin does not always limp. As Audubon noticed, its feet are so broad that it can walk easily in mud—and even on the leaves of aquatic plants.

About four feet tall, the great blue heron is one of the largest wading birds in North America. It may spend its entire life in Florida, building what amounts to a permanent home in its nesting areas near Everglades waterways; it will occupy the same bowl-shaped nest of sticks and grass year after year, renovating and adding to it with each passing season.

The mating-season plumage of the common egret—50 delicate long white aigrettes that grow between its shoulder bones and extend beyond its tail—was nearly its undoing in the 19th Century heyday of feather-decorated millinery. Now multiplying in many parts of Florida, this most beautiful of the herons has become a remarkably friendly, easily approached bird.

5/ Rock, Snakes and Snails

*The whole world of the pines and
of the rocks hums and glistens and stings with life.*

MARJORY STONEMAN DOUGLAS/ *THE EVERGLADES*

In 1838, during the Seminole War, a U.S. Army surgeon named Jacob Rhett Motte accompanied Colonel William S. Harney's Second Dragoons on an expedition to hunt down the elusive Chief Abiaka, also known as Sam Jones, as he retreated inland from Fort Dallas, the present site of Miami. Dr. Motte, a South Carolinian, was an articulate reporter, and his account of crossing the limestone pinelands of southern Florida enhances one's admiration for the Indians who traveled that country ahead of the U.S. Army—and for the Army too, in spite of the fool's errand they were on. It was an extraordinary and somewhat forbidding landscape, as Dr. Motte's impressions make plain:

"We pursued our way through a pine-barren, the ground being formed of coral-rocks jutting out in sharp points like oyster beds, which caused us great suffering by cutting through our boots and lacerating our feet at every step . . . as if we were walking over . . . a thick crop of sharply pointed knives. The whole of this part of Florida seemed to present this coral formation protruding through the surface of the earth, and which rendered it impracticable for horses and almost impracticable for men unless well shod. We were puzzled . . . how the moccasined Indians got over such a rough surface until we subsequently ascertained that they protected their feet . . . by moccasins of alligator hide when in this part of Florida. . . . It was certainly the most dreary and pandemonium-like region . . . where no grateful verdure quickened, and no generous plant took root—where the only herbage . . . was stinted and the shrubbery was bare, where the hot steaming atmosphere constantly quivered over the parched and cracked land —without shade—without water—it was intolerable—excruciating."

And with all that they never caught Sam Jones.

It is easy to understand why these flatwoods, visited in the bleakness of the dry season, should have distressed a homesick and poetic doctor accustomed to the magnolia and live-oak groves of Charleston. But a lot depends on one's point of view, and some people react differently to the rocky pine country. I used to go down there every chance I got, and though it was mainly reptiles I was after, other things there made memories too. One of these was just the look and sound of the pines, with their trunks a little more twisty and gnarled of limb than the pines I knew farther north, and with their sprays of thin needles singing in a special way against the particular blue of a southern Florida sky. The pines eke out sustenance and a water ration by spreading their roots widely over the honeycombed rock and invading every depression in it. To see what a plant is up against in this region you ought to look at a pine tree that has been pushed over by a bulldozer—at the upturned disk of desperate roots that in their sculpturing reflect every irregularity in the crazy stone surface they had grown on. Nevertheless, some of the pines used to reach heights of 80 or 90 feet.

These woods have undergone more widespread destruction by man than any other landscape in southern Florida. The pine timber, once a prime resource, has been repeatedly cut everywhere except in some of the Everglades National Park lands on Long Pine Key. Moreover, fire has been kept under better control in recent years and, in fire-free areas, broad-leaved hammock vegetation is invading the old domain of the pines. More relentless than either of those factors has been the spread of the cities of the lower east coast, which have engulfed most of the landscape. So the limestone pinelands are mostly gone now; and if the National Park had not preserved some sizable samples, in more or less mint condition, this fascinating landscape would only be read about or seen in a few old photographs, mostly bad.

Actually, there is no landscape like this one anywhere in the world except in the Bahamas. It is an open forest of slash pine growing on a limestone ridge known variously as the Atlantic Coastal Ridge, Rockland Ridge, Pineland Ridge or Rock Rim. This slightly elevated region is a series of outcrops of Miami oolite, a limestone formation—not an old coral reef, as Dr. Motte thought—that extends intermittently southward along the east coast for more than 50 miles, from north of Fort Lauderdale down to Florida City. There it curves westward into Everglades National Park and ends far out in the Glades on the pine island called Long Pine Key. The Rock Rim varies in elevation from 20 feet above sea level at the northern edges of Miami to less than two feet near its westernmost extreme in the park.

The surface of the ridge is thinly covered with sand or completely bare. Much of it is so fantastically eroded, pitted and perforated, and in the dry season seems so inhospitable, that one wonders how plants or animals could ever have found life ecologically feasible there. But the place is almost free of winter, and each dry season is sure to end with rain, because most of the ridge is located near the Gulf Stream downcurrent from tropical Cuba and in the same moist storm track as Cuba. Besides that, the ridge is not only the highest but also the oldest land in southern Florida, part of it having stood above the seas that covered the land around it for tens of thousands of years. There has therefore been a respectable span of time for any tropical plants that could get to the place, and could put up with its rigors, to establish themselves.

To botanists the limestone pinelands are in some ways the most exciting landscape in Florida. Though pines, palms and palmettos predominate, the ridge communities also include a great variety of small tropical trees and shrubs and herbaceous plants. The strong tropical contingent, which occurs all through the pine-wood understory, beneath the main canopy of the forest, is mixed with numerous representatives of the Temperate Zone flora.

Among these plants are the partridge pea, which has bright yellow flowers and leaves that fold up when touched—perhaps reacting to the pressure and heat of the hand's contact; and fire grass, which thrives in the aftermath of fire, with flower stalks eight feet tall. Another is the coontie, a kind of arrowroot with a bulbous root and bright orange-red fruit. The Indians gave it its name, and made flour out of the starch in its root. The plant, growing in plenty throughout the pinelands, was their staple source of carbohydrate food, and it was one of the factors that made the Seminole War the most frustrating the United States ever got into, until we went to Vietnam; the elusive Indians, pursued by white troops, might abandon their stores of coonties, but there was always plenty more to be gathered.

Of the tropical species in the pinelands, one of the most striking is the gumbo-limbo. In Honduras and Nicaragua the tree is called the naked Indian, because of the smooth, brightly copper-colored bark that peels away in thin curls like birch bark, only thinner. Other widespread tropical species of the pinelands are poisonwood, a relative of poison ivy with a similarly rash-raising juice, and blolly, a shrubby, scaly barked member of the plant family known as four o'clock, for their way of closing their flowers during the afternoon.

Whatever their origin, nearly all the plants of the pinelands show some kind of adjustment to fire. The slash pine itself, for example, germinates best in the mineral soil produced when a ground fire burns off the duff. Though vulnerable as a seedling, it quickly becomes insulated by heat-resistant bark, and tight rosettes of terminal needles protect its growing points. Some pinewoods plants, like the coontie, resist fire by storing much of their substance in bulbous stem bases or roots that will support quick regeneration when the fire has gone by. Most of the plants of the community are either clothed in fibrous, nonflammable bark or leaf bases, or, like the grasses and pines, protect their buds with tight clusters of twig-tip leaves that burn partly away while the bud remains unhurt.

The other principal vegetation of the limestone ridge is the tropical hammock, an elevated isolated forest that occurs only where fire has been excluded. Like the hammocks of northern and central Florida, these tropical hammocks are composed mainly of broad-leaved trees, but in other ways they are very different. The southern Florida hammocks are usually somewhat lower, and botanically they are usually more diverse. The most striking difference is that in southern Florida trees in the hammocks are mainly of West Indian origin.

These West Indian trees and shrubs are the most conspicuous tropical element in southern Florida. Some hammocks are exotic-looking stands of almost wholly Antillean trees with marvelous names like strangler fig, pigeon plum, Madeira, bustic, torchwood, fiddlewood, nakedwood and paradise tree. In other hammocks, various combinations of these mix with live oaks, red bay, mulberry, hackberry or any of a dozen members of the hammock flora of northern Florida.

Like the pinewoods, the tropical hammocks of the Rock Rim show the tragic effects of man's spread. In Dade County alone, according to an estimate by John K. Small, there were once 500 separate hammocks. A single hammock five miles long and half a mile wide used to run along the shore of Biscayne Bay where Miami now stands, occupying the highest section of the Rock Rim. Most of it became real estate years ago, but a fragment of it is preserved more or less intact in Simpson

Park. This is well worth walking in, though it almost makes old naturalists weep to do so.

With the widespread destruction of the hammocks, the scientific —and esthetic—interest in those that remain is more intense than ever. Some fundamental questions about them remain to be solved. How, for example, are the sparse, limestone pinewoods replaced by a hammock forest with a closed canopy and a moist, dimly lighted interior? And what maintains hammocks once they are established? At least part of the answer to the second question seems to be that they shade out pine seedlings, and that the higher humidity in normal years helps to keep out fire, which can quickly destroy hammock vegetation. The more difficult problem is to explain how hammocks begin in the first place—how the shade and interior moisture they require are achieved before fire bats down the incipient hammock growth. Most botanists agree that the live oak is often involved in the earliest stages of the development of a hammock. Charles Torrey Simpson suggested that some of the Rock Rim hammocks probably began with a single live oak tree. Lodging as an acorn derived from who knows where, the tree sprouted, managed to get through several years without succumbing to the ground fires that swept the surrounding pinewoods, and gradually covered the ground with its own hard little fire-resistant leaves that in time provided moisture-hoarding shade.

What then keeps the fire away from the pioneer oak when it is very small is not easy to say. Often the site is the edge of a pothole or sink where water has already humidified the surroundings; or in some cases the rock surface of a site is so bare and so jumbled that ground fire dies without entering it. In any case, the oak gradually creates a little zone of fire resistance, and other hardwoods soon begin to exploit this. The berries and small fruits of increasing numbers of shade-tolerant, fire-tender tropical species are, over the passing decades, fortuitously blown or carried there by birds. Finally a diverse, clean-floored forest is formed, and this creates its own moist internal climate, and holds out all fires except the driving holocausts that come in the most drastically drought-ridden years.

As time passes, the tropical composition of the woods continues to increase. The tropical species that arrive, though vulnerable to fire, are all of kinds accustomed to competitive life in tight stands. Their roots outfight the roots of the pioneers and the deepening shade kills the seedlings of the first comers. Dr. Simpson noticed that a live-oak seedling is

Slash pines—which are locally known as Dade County pines—stand among bushy neighbors of saw palmetto. Burn resistant because of their moist bark, the pines and palmettos are sturdy and thriving despite charring by a ground fire. Occasional and limited fire actually helps the pinelands, killing the seedlings of competing hardwoods that move in from nearby hammocks.

seldom found in one of the more diverse tropical hammocks, even though old live oaks may persist there. He also pointed out that the old trees themselves become the special prey of the strangler fig. In any old hammock in which live oaks persist, many of them can be seen, as Simpson says, "enfolded in the stifling embrace of this terrible *Ficus.*"

Next to the plants, the most conspicuously tropical living things in southern Florida are butterflies. No more convincing evidence of the nearness of the tropics is needed than the beautiful zebra butterfly, a member of a group as characteristic of the American tropics as spider monkeys and tapirs are. The larva of the zebra feeds only on the leaves of the passionflower, a woody vine with a showy flower of which parts were once thought by the Spanish to resemble aspects of Christ's Crucifixion. Though the zebra is not confined to southernmost Florida, it is most abundant there, and seems clearly at home drifting about the quiet hammocks under the naked-Indian trees on its long thin wings of gold and velvet black.

Hammocks are the best butterfly habitat in southern Florida, but you can see more of them in the open vistas of the pinelands. On any clear warm morning the viceroys, swallowtails, hairstreaks, blues, sulphurs, and a bewildering host of other species spread out over the saw palmettos beneath the pines, floating or dancing about according to their kind, hovering over wild crotons or tarflowers and gathering in mixed bouquets at the blazing butterfly weeds.

A few southern Florida butterflies have almost died out during the past few decades. The most famous case is Schaus's swallowtail, a drab brownish species that is now one of the rarest of North American butterflies. The beautiful atala, marked with brilliant iridescent blue-green, has also been reduced almost to extinction. Between 1925 and 1927 it disappeared from view; then, in 1959 a small new colony was discovered in the pinelands and by transplanting larvae from that population, an effort has been made to establish the species in Everglades National Park.

The tropical aura supplied by the butterflies was but one of the attractions of the Rock Rim country for me; another feature that particularly appealed to me, as a north Florida zoologist with a predilection for reptiles, was the presence of snakes slightly different from those I knew at home. For example, the snake known in the north as the blue racer is slate gray in the south; there, the yellow rings of the northern Florida king snake break up into a pattern of yellow specks, one on each scale; in tropical Florida a marvelous confusion of pinkish rat snakes replaces the red-blotched corn snake and brown-striped rat snake of the north.

As everywhere, collecting reptiles in the limestone flatwoods involves one in an orgy of turning over logs. In fact, other than random search, rolling logs is about the only known snake-catching technique. I have turned over a great many southern Florida logs in my time, and have found quite a few snakes that way. My liveliest memories of those ventures, however, are not of snakes at all, but of the array of scorpions and centipedes that live under Dade County logs.

Of scorpions there seem to be three kinds that a nonspecialist comes upon. One of these, whimsically called the slender scorpion, is a broad, redoubtable beast as long as your finger. To turn over a log and come upon a big female of this species, almost completely hidden in a swarm of newly hatched young, is a stirring experience; but not so stirring as stumbling upon a certain species of Dade County centipede. It is six inches long and a half inch wide, and has an astounding redundance of active legs. This particular species of centipede is to me the most unsettling animal in Florida, one of the very few creatures whose mere appearance completely undermines my professional zoologist's objectivity. I attribute this to having been crawled on by one as a child when camping in West Texas. Another creature you find under the Rock Rim logs is a kind of millipede, as long as the centipede and with even more legs, but a lot less demoralizing—for me, at any rate.

There are more engaging, though not necessarily more interesting, animals in the limestone pinelands of Everglades National Park, and some are prime examples of the versatility of the region as a refuge for wide-ranging species. The most hopeful place to look for a panther south of the Big Cypress Swamp, for instance, is said to be the edges of the pinelands bordering the Glades at the southwestern end of Long Pine Key. It is in these woods, also, that extraordinary aggregations of young bald eagles occur. According to park biologist William Robertson, up to 50 eagles or more, mostly two or three years old and not yet breeding, assemble to roost in the tallest trees of the park pineland.

Few of the mammals that turn up in tropical hammocks are indigenous; most of them are species that also occur in the rest of peninsular Florida. One of the inconspicuous mammal inhabitants of the tropical hammocks is the wood rat, a close relative of the pack rat of the western states. Not long ago, in the dense low hammock on upper Key Largo, I came upon a wood rat's nest—or lodge—that looked just like the work of a small, somewhat inept beaver. It was a stack of twigs and billets piled waist-high against a gumbo-limbo tree.

The reptiles and amphibians of the hammock are also largely representative of the fauna of the Florida peninsula as a whole, although the tropics are represented by two little geckos and by a couple of lizards of the genus *Anolis,* called chameleons because of their ability to change color. True chameleons belong to a different family. Hammock reptiles, like most deep-woods animals, stay mainly out of sight. Still, you may come upon a surreptitious blue-tailed skink, and if you look closely you may see a tiny ground skink scrambling away in the leaf mold. With luck you will find a graceful rough green snake, a rat snake, a yellow-speckled kingsnake, or a poisonous, gleaming banded coral snake. Out near the hammock edge, you will more than likely come upon one of the gray racers peculiar to the region. Back in the days when hammocks were more widespread and people fewer, you were likely to come face to face with the indigo snake. This big, shining blue and personable animal reaches lengths of nine or 10 feet, and vies with the coachwhip, the horn snake, and possibly the diamondback rattlesnake as Florida's longest serpent. And speaking of rattlesnakes, if you leave a hammock trail, it is well to walk with extreme care, because drought, fire and famine in the pinewoods, or flood in the sawgrass, often bring diamondbacks into the hammocks to forage for rats, deer mice or swamp rabbits.

The list of tropical animals in the hammocks will very likely lengthen when entomologists have done more field work. Nearly every entomologist who collects in Everglades National Park finds new species of insects or specimens of hitherto unrecorded West Indian kinds. That strange insects remain hidden in the hammocks is suggested by the elusive character of the Margarodes, or "ground pearls," that have been found there two or three times. These glistening objects resemble pearls of irregular shapes but all about the same size; they have been discovered buried in tiny caches in rock crevices or around the bases of hammock trees. Nacreous little lumps of natural jewelry, they are actually the waxy shells formed by a kind of scale insect; in some West Indian islands, where they occur more regularly, they are strung as beads. Ground pearls evoke the wonder and admiration of all who see them.

It is the same with tree snails. If there is a single species in which the essence of tropical Florida seems to be packed, it is that of the lovely, painted tree snails of the genus *Liguus*—the ligs, as they are known to

Exquisitely varied in their banded color patterns, six tree snails of the species Liguus fasciatus browse on microscopic fungi and algae that grow on the bark of the hardwood trees in their homes in the Everglades hammocks. The two-inch-long snails owe their great range of coloration to longtime isolation. The treeless wetlands around the hammocks restrict the tree-snail populations to their own native habitats; after innumerable generations of inbreeding, the snails in some hammocks have evolved into local sub-subspecies. Fully 52 color variants have been found, and others may exist in unexplored hammocks.

collectors. And they are as baffling as they are alluring. The ligs have excited—and confused—scientists for over half a century.

The Florida tree snails live almost secretly, and only in hammocks; their appeal to zoologists is based on the explosive microevolution they have undergone in these isolated tracts of hammock habitat. They are hardy, and able to withstand long periods of drought by sealing the openings of their shells to any smooth surface. But they feed, breed and flourish only where there is a steady supply of the microscopic fungi and algae that they scrape from the smooth trunks and limbs of such trees as Jamaica dogwood and wild tamarind. Good grazing occurs only in the moist shade of the tropical hammocks, and it is for this reason that these woods are the sole habitat of Florida *Liguus*. A lig in a hammock is often quite as isolated from contact with outside relatives as if it lived on an island in the sea. The snails' evolutionary response to this situation has produced a microzoogeographic classic.

Tree snails of the genus *Liguus* are known only in Cuba, Hispaniola and Florida. Those in Florida are obviously derived from Cuban ancestors. None is the exact equivalent of any Cuban form, however. In their classification of Florida *Liguus*, William Clench and G. B. Fairchild recognized four subspecies of a single species, *Liguus fasciatus*. It seems likely that each of them represents the separate landing of a Cuban snail somewhere in southern Florida. It is easy to see how the snails could be transported by either hurricane-blown debris or ocean currents, because once they have stuck to a limb and sealed themselves shut they will stay alive, though dormant, for months. Besides the four subspecies that reflect separate arrivals from Cuba, there are more than 50 named color variants in the southern Florida hammocks, many of them also showing slight differences in the texture or shape of the shell. Nearly every snail-bearing hammock has its own form or its own combinations of forms of lig. While all the 50 color variants occur as pure separate colonies, they are also subject to all sorts of hybridization and merging.

Even if the tree snails were merely animals in black and white they would excite biologists. But they are much more than that. Naturally ensconced in their habitat, they are among the most exquisitely beautiful of creatures. They are about two inches long and are colored in nearly any way that you might imagine. Some are clear white, or white with a pink spire, or with thin green lines around the spiral of the shell. Others are marked with combinations of yellow, orange, green, blue or various shades of brown. Some look like objects in porcelain; some seem carved out of the most highly variegated tortoise shell. Laid out in rows in a tray, tree snails are spectacular enough. To find one hanging in the forest twilight from the smooth limb of a wild tamarind tree is an unforgettable event.

The tree snails long ago stimulated the development of a cult—a polyglot, fanatic set of people who, though utterly diverse in background, shared a language most of us couldn't understand. They had a minute knowledge of the southern Florida terrain that, in the days before the advent of helicopters and Glades buggies, was truly extraordinary. Membership in this loose but rabid fraternity ranged from eminent scientists to commercial shell tradesmen and out-and-out snail hogs. No matter what the angle of their approach, these people were all similarly inflamed by the gemlike beauty of the snails, and shared the same fervor for hunting out secret virgin hammocks.

If the numbers of these lig collectors had grown at the rate at which Miami grew, there would be not one painted snail left hanging like a gem from a single dogwood limb in all of Broward, Dade, Monroe and Collier counties—except in the Everglades National Park. Everywhere outside the park the hammocks are disappearing, and with every lost hammock a colony of tree snails is destroyed. If people were turned loose in the few remaining hammocks to Easter-egg-hunt the tree snails as people gather shells on beaches, the rate of extinction would immeasurably swiften.

But a lot of snails are being saved in the park; and recently its personnel have embarked on a project to establish pure strains of all the threatened forms in hammocks within the park boundaries that now have no tree snails, and so to save these strains from extinction. Some people may feel uneasy over the introduction of outside snails into the park, on the grounds that any man-made change in the natural distribution of animals is deplorable. But in this case, with the creature involved so lovely and so clearly innocuous as *Liguus* is, and as sure to stay each in its own assigned little woods—in such a special case, with each planting purposeful, meticulously recorded and monitored, why not let the park go ahead and save the snails any way it can?

NATURE WALK **/ A Visit to Paradise Key**

PHOTOGRAPHS BY ROBERT WALCH

From a distance Paradise Key is a dark green wall of tropical hardwood trees rising sharply from the flatness of the surrounding sawgrass plain. In Florida parlance Paradise Key is a "hammock" (a word possibly a variant of "hummock"), but in the same vernacular it is also called a key. Isolated amid a great sea of grass, it is no less an island than those more famous keys that curve out across the turquoise waters off the Florida mainland 20 miles to the southeast.

This tree island got its name back around 1900, when it was known only as a fabled place of unusual size and beauty somewhere out there in the uncharted Glades southwest of Homestead. Since then Paradise has been pinpointed. It is one of the biggest hammocks in the Glades, measuring a mile by a mile and a half, and it lies along the western edge of Taylor Slough (pronounced "slew") near the main headquarters of Everglades National Park at Homestead. Since the watery expanse of the slough provides a natural firebreak, the hammock has been relatively free from fire damage over the years—at least at its southern end, where it has also largely escaped human damage. The vegetation there is as close to being unspoiled as that in any tree island in the Glades.

Paradise Key is an ideal setting in which to absorb the peculiar enchantment of a tropical hardwood hammock. It is a cool, dry-footed oasis in a steaming wet landscape, a quiet woodsy place where the limitless scale of the Glades becomes comfortably man-sized. Though it is much frequented, with a Park Service building and even some paved walkways, there are parts in its interior where almost no one ever goes, and where no man has left any trace of his presence.

On a warm June day a faint rank of cumulus off to the south threatened a rainy afternoon to come; but for the moment the midday sun shone serenely on the approach to the key, glinting off the white trunks of a few twisted buttonwoods sticking up here and there above the sawgrass. Scrubby encroachers like the red mangrove, the buttonwoods' presence was a sure sign that something—perhaps the gradual lowering of the Glades' mean water level —had disturbed the equilibrium of the moist sawgrass community. Given time, the intrusive buttonwoods might even take over the wetlands here, but for now the sawgrass was in charge, and alive with the buzzing and chirring of countless insects.

Close inspection of the sawgrass revealed that some of the plants were in early bloom. The sawgrass near the key was not showy: the teeth that give it its name were much easier to feel than to discern, and its reddish-brown blossoms, subdued in

SAWGRASS IN BLOOM

this season, went almost unnoticed. But the few scattered flowers provided a subtle counterpoint to the sunlit green of the marsh.

The sawgrass is not part of the hammock, but merely defines its limits. It was a relief to leave the glare of the road and plunge into the cool, dim greenness of Paradise Key's wooded interior. The first impression was of an overwhelming variety

SAWGRASS, BUTTONWOODS AND (BACKGROUND) PARADISE KEY

DUCKWEED AFLOAT IN A SOLUTION HOLE

of vegetation—trees, shrubs, ferns, bushes everywhere seemed to crowd one another for growing room. The first stop along the path, however, was at a break in the vegetation—a large shady pond called a solution hole or a sinkhole—that offered a telling look at the hammock's eroding rocky underpinning.

A Porous Foundation

Cropping out around the edges of the pond was the jagged, pitted limestone called Miami oolite, the hammock's foundation, seldom more than two or three feet below the organic peat that serves Paradise Key as soil. The sinkhole, about 25 feet wide, is carved into this bedrock. It has been formed over the ages by rain water, charged with carbon dioxide and carbonic acid, that drops off the leaves and trickles down through the porous limestone, dissolving it and carrying it away in solution. The resulting hole, some 20 feet deep, is filled with clear, coffee-colored water that silently rises and falls with the changing water level of the Glades outside.

There was an air of magic about this lush, cool grotto and somehow the dappled light conjured visions of elves and fairies. Most elfin of all was the tiny duckweed that decorated the pond surface with a yellow-green appliqué design. Duckweed is one of the world's smallest flowering plants, and it floats unattached to the pond bottom, buoyed by leaves that measure no more than a quarter of an inch in diameter.

Spreading its branches across the water was a large pond-apple tree, a

AN UNRIPE CUSTARD APPLE

A SHY BOX TURTLE

A LUSH GROWTH OF FERNS

tropical species that would have nothing to do with the comparatively dry hammock were it not for the moisture provided by the sinkhole. The tree is also known as a custard apple, perhaps because its fruit, when ripe, has the consistency of blancmange. It is considered a delicacy by turtles. Now in late spring, though, the fruit was bright green and hard as any other unripe apple; one hanging from the leafy roof of this little Eden was comely, but untempting to the palate.

A rustle in the damp shade near the pond announced a common box turtle cautiously exploring for lunch. At the approach of human danger it pulled its head inside its shell and waited patiently. Despite the elegance of its black and yellow shell, which looked as if it had just been lacquered, the turtle was a prosaic note in this exotic place. It would not have seemed out of place poking around a maple woods in Illinois or a birch grove in Vermont, as some of its cousins do.

Many of the ferns around the pond also would look familiar in northern woods, but here they are bigger and much more prolific. The dark, narrow sword fern and the broader shield fern are the two most numerous plants in the hammock. They thrive wherever the ground is moist, in shade or brilliant sunlight, and are the leitmotiv of Paradise Key.

From the pond, the way led toward the key's interior, where the path was uncertain and the light even more subdued, but still capable of magical effects: the bark of a small gumbo-limbo tree had peeled away from the slender trunk and, backlit by a vagrant sunbeam, was glowing like a firebrand. The show lasted only a few moments—the sun moved and the fire went out. But even without dramatic lighting the gumbo-limbo, with its variegated pa-

SUNSTRUCK GUMBO-LIMBO BARK

pery bark, is one of the most distinct and recognizable trees in the hammock. It is a native of the tropics, and the origin of its name is obscure. Some people believe it comes from the Spanish-Dutch combination *gom elemiboom*, signifying "gum-resin tree," and was bestowed on the tree by West Indian colonists who recognized its major significance to the islands' natives: they collected its ar-

A STRANGLER FIG AND ITS FALLEN HOST

omatic resin to meet many of their needs, including solvents, medical ointments and even incense.

Beneath the peeling bark—the mark of an immature tree—the wood is soft and workable, and that is why many a gumbo-limbo ended up, back in more ingenuous times, spinning in circles as a merry-go-round horse.

A Bizarre Killer

There was nothing so whimsical about the strangler-fig tree that suddenly loomed in the path, its roots wound like a tangle of boa constrictors around a huge old live-oak trunk, which, toppled and dead, now belied its name. Certainly the fig is a bizarre plant. Though a true tree, it often spends years of its life growing like a vine until its roots spread down the trunk of its host, and finally dig into the ground. Though not a true parasite—taking neither nourishment nor moisture from its host —it nevertheless dooms the tree it grows on to inevitable slow death by constriction.

This specimen, however, had apparently not killed the oak it was entwining, but was simply using it as a prop—the oak had probably been felled years ago by a hurricane. The oak was the biggest tree encountered yet, and even dead was an impressive representative of one of the hammock's three foremost tree species (gumbo-limbo and strangler fig are the other two). Unlike them, the live oak hails from the temperate zone, no different from those serene old giants that grace the lawns and driveways of plantation houses all through the South.

BUTTONWOOD

WAX MYRTLE

WILD COFFEE

SATINLEAF

Scrambling over the rough-barked old hulk was no problem, but beyond it the going got slower. Now the undergrowth was much more dense, a bewildering disorder of different kinds of plants presenting an even more bewildering similarity of appearance. All the shrubs and young trees that grew here seemed to have smallish, dark green leaves with pointed tips and a smooth, waxy surface. This may not be a coincidence: many botanists believe their tipped design is an adaptation that allows heavy tropical rainfall to flow easily off the leaves. Such a leaf structure is useful for the plants but confusing to an untrained eye trying to tell one species from another.

A more careful inspection, however, revealed distinctions among the array of similar-looking plants. Within the compass of one glance was a scrub buttonwood bush, like the ones in the marsh outside, sporting little fruit like miniature hand grenades; wax myrtle, also called southern bayberry, and cousin to the northern variety, whose waxy berries make sweet-smelling candles; the vivid, deeply veined leaf of wild coffee, related to the domestic plant, but of no use in the kitchen; the satinleaf, which has a dark, oval leaf with a delicate russet underside; and various other plants whose names sound an exotic botanical litany —poisonwood, pigeon plum, lancewood, Jamaica dogwood, paradise tree, medicine vine, bullbrier, tetrazygia and dozens more.

Suddenly the dense tangles of undergrowth opened out into a place

A MATURE TROPICAL HARDWOOD FOREST

of dense vegetation took over. The fire burned itself out, however, before it could ravage the southerly part of the key, and here the old growth of trees, tall and straight, has spread a leafy canopy aloft that largely keeps out the sun and eliminates all but the most shade-tolerant plants. Among them are the ubiquitous ferns and a few coonties—a low shrubby vegetable with a tuberous starchy root that was once a favorite food of the Indians.

In this mature forest the aggressive growth that pervades other parts of the key gave way to a sense of stillness and peace. Dead leaves provided a comfortable cushion. One of the six large live oaks that dominate the place made a fine backrest. The minutes passed serenely in that lovely place, and the steamy, teeming Glades, which edge up to the key less than half a mile away, seemed part of another world.

But there was more to see and do,

where there was very little brush at all: a mature forest of lofty trees, a shadowed harmony of muted brown and yellow-green.

As in so many other places in the Everglades, the reason for the abrupt change of scene is fire. In 1945, a year of great drought in the Glades, even Taylor Slough went dry, and wind-swept flames raged across it to engulf the northern part of Paradise Key. In the fire's wake a new growth

A GOLDEN ORB WEAVER AND HER PREY

A LUBBER GRASSHOPPER

CORN-LEAVED TRIPSACUM NEAR A LICHEN-SPLOTCHED TREE

and the way led north and west, toward the rim of the hammock and another change of scene. Now, no longer screened out by the forest canopy, sunlight flooded in and exposed some of the creatures of the key. At eye level, a large, marvelously constructed spider web fractured the sunlight with exquisite symmetry. It was the work of a female golden orb weaver, whose silk is stronger and finer than a silkworm's and whose instinct for design is spectacular. This spider's web was at least three feet across and she sat dead center, suspended five feet off the ground, waiting. A sudden twitch of the web galvanized her into swift attack on a hapless beetle that had blundered into the trap; just as quickly she was back at her place again, the beetle clasped in her jaws.

A Defensive Reaction

Above her a huge, armor-plated lubber grasshopper crept along a tetrazygia branch, munching whatever leaves it encountered—and then, when it was picked up, spitting them all out again in a defensive brown stream of fragments.

A cardinal flashed brilliant red and a faint breeze stirred the slender leaves of several tripsacum plants (which at some point in evolutionary history had shared an ancestor with golden bantam corn). Behind them stood a tree trunk that appeared splashed with white paint —which turned out to be a splotch of lichen decorating a lisoloma tree. Lichens of all textures and colors embellish tree trunks everywhere in the hammock, making many types of

A YOUNG GIANT WILD-PINE AND RESURRECTION FERN GROWING ON A LIVE OAK

trees unrecognizable. The air plants create the same baffling effect.

No hardwood hammock is without air plants—also called epiphytes —and in some hammocks they grow in more abundance than anywhere else in southern Florida except Big Cypress Swamp. They have no use for roots in the ground, getting all they need for life from sunlight, air and rain. They perch everywhere, high and low, on trees, stumps, rocks, roots and twigs. In this part of Paradise Key the air plants' favorite hosts are the live oaks, whose rough bark gives them a good foothold. Sometimes they completely reclothe the tree trunks in green.

The most abundant air plants in southern Florida are the bromeliads, whose most conspicuous species, the

A STIFF-LEAVED WILD-PINE

stiff-leaved wild-pine, looks enough like its relative the pineapple to account for its similar name. Another cousin, the giant wild-pine, is the largest of the bromeliads, sometimes achieving a height of almost six feet. The resurrection fern, also an epiphyte and a member of a more ancient family of plants, curls up and shows only its brown undersides in dry times, then uncurls and appears bright green after a life-giving rain.

All these, plus an assortment of other epiphytes, including a variety of orchids not yet in bloom, were seen garnishing a single big live oak; they managed to give the tree the look of an overdressed dowager draped in her bright costume jewelry and green feather boas.

The most vivid aspect of this part

A GREEN DARNER DRAGONFLY

A RAIN FROG

of the key was the greenness of everything, whether high in the oaks, or at ankle level, where a saw palmetto shone like an emerald sunburst. Beneath its leaves, each of which spread out evenly from a central stem, was a tiny green rain frog, crouching on a leaf in ceramic immobility. It could easily have been a porcelain figurine but for the almost imperceptible pulse that beat in its throat. One of several kinds of frogs with adhesive toe pads that enable the animals to plaster themselves to Florida windows, it gets its name from the fact that its regular, throaty song is often heard after a summer rain shower.

A Swarm of Mosquitoes

From the look of the sky at that moment, it appeared that the rain frog would soon have something to sing about. The softly piled cumulus that had seemed so far away earlier in the day was now poised directly over Paradise Key. Solid shelter was more than a mile away, and a wetting seemed inevitable, but there was a more disconcerting and immediate problem. Perhaps it was the sudden atmospheric change announcing the storm that brought out a merciless swarm of mosquitoes from hiding. The mosquitoes were in their prime at this wet time late in the spring season, but fortunately some dragonflies were in evidence, avidly doing their best to keep the mosquito population down. The most prevalent dragonfly was one known locally as a green darner, with a twig-shaped body two to three inches long and two pairs of transparent wings.

SAW-PALMETTO FANS

Their name derives from the darning motion made by the female's body when she lays eggs, and by the male's during copulation; but neither sex seemed interested at that moment in anything except eating, for they were purposefully darting and whizzing about in search of food. One finally settled down on a thin branch and immediately became nearly invisible; its body blended almost perfectly with the background and only its delicate fairy wings caught and shaped the sunlight.

After a minute of resting or digesting, the darner buzzed off again. A few minutes later the sun went too, and the rain came down.

It made no difference, really. A big gumbo-limbo provided shelter of sorts, and it was a treat to watch the bark turn dark red, like dyed tissue paper, as it got wet. All the small, tipped leaves shed water efficiently and indiscriminately; within minutes everything in the hammock had been

A RAIN-BEJEWELED TREE SNAIL

thoroughly and satisfyingly soaked.

The rain was a good one, hard and noisy, with a few thundercracks to give it authority. This is what late spring in the Glades is all about: rain to make things grow, rain to fill up the marshes so the animals can spread out across the Glades to start a new life cycle. Rain is life itself in the Glades, and no creature there minds getting a little wet.

The shower lasted about 15 minutes and then, in the way of tropical rains, stopped suddenly, leaving the woods dripping and the ground soggy. The noise of the rainstorm yielded to the typical quiet of Paradise Key, in which the voices of the hammock's creatures were increasingly audible. Most distinctive of all was the slow, deliberate *ack-ack-ack* of rain frogs celebrating the wetting. Mingled with their song in sudden cacophony were the harsh scream of a great blue heron, the cardinal's persistent *what-cheer-cheer-cheer,* and occasionally the percussive *tonk-a-tonk-a-tonk* of a pileated woodpecker attacking a dead tree.

The Spectacle of a Snail

It proved to be a lucky rain, becase no walk in a tropical hardwood hammock is complete without a tree snail, and now here, just above eye level, was a lovely specimen with brown and white and yellow stripes. These highly polished bands

A LITTLE BLUE HERON ON THE HUNT

WATER-SHIELD PADS AFTER A RAIN

of color, following the whorled contours of the mollusks' shells, are the marks that identify each snail's variety—in this case *Liguus fasciatus walkeri*. Many another tree island, smaller and more isolated than Paradise Key, supports only a single and unique variety of tree snail and holds the strain to a color evolution all its own. But *walkeri* is only one of the varieties found in such a large hammock as Paradise Key, and a common one for all that. Yet, whatever the snail lacked in exclusiveness, it more than made up for in the brilliance of its shell, enhanced by a molten crystal drop the rain had left gleaming at its tip.

When interrupted by the rain the snail had been working its way along a tree branch, browsing on the fungus and algae growing there, leaving a tiny furrow behind it. Now it moved again, the raindrop fell and the snail resumed its grazing.

A few squishy steps led to the end of the path and the edge of the open Glades. A low bank marked the rim of the hammock. Beyond it, pads of water-shield plants cupped the rain in their water-repellent leaves like pools of mercury. Out in the sawgrass a little blue heron posed elegantly and solemnly, its piercing eye peeled for a fish dinner. And beyond that the great marsh stretched out to the low green line of another hardwood hammock in the distance. The rain cloud rolled on to the north, leaving the water level in the Glades a tiny but vital bit higher. Behind, from a fig tree in Paradise Key, a vireo sang its evening song.

THE VIEW FROM THE EDGE OF THE HAMMOCK

6/ The Tropical Borderland

*Green, grateful mangroves where the
sand-beach shines—/Long lissome coast that in and
outward swerves.*   SIDNEY LANIER/ A FLORIDA SUNDAY

One sign that the tip of the Florida peninsula is edging down close to
the tropics is its coastal fringe of mangrove swamp. The Florida mangroves are among the most luxuriant in the world. Mangrove forest
straggles north to Cedar Key on the Gulf Coast and to St. Augustine on
the Atlantic side of Florida, but the farther south you go the finer the
trees look, and along the southernmost edges of the mainland the mangroves are the equal in density of any to be found anywhere.

The word mangrove is apparently a contraction of *manglegrove*, derived from the Spanish name for the tree, *mangle*, combined with the
English *grove*. Strictly speaking, the name mangrove refers to the 60-
odd species of maritime shrubs and trees that belong to a single
botanical family, *Rhizophoraceae;* the red mangrove (*Rhizophora mangle)* is the only Florida species. But the term is more loosely given to
other, unrelated trees that grow in tidal habitat in the tropics, and the
name also applies collectively to the various types of swamp and forest
vegetation that these trees build. A common way of life at the edges of
the land has molded them into similar habits and structure.

Although *Rhizophora* is the only true mangrove in Florida, the mangrove forest there includes three other salt-tolerant shore zone trees,
two of which also bear the name mangrove. One is *Laguncularia ra-
cemosa,* the white mangrove; the other is the black mangrove *Avicennia
germinans,* which produces the strange-looking breather roots known

as pneumatophores that stick up out of the mud beneath the trees like a multitude of quills or little cypress knees. White mangroves sometimes have these too, but theirs are much smaller and more sparse. The black mangrove is the most cold tolerant of the mangrove-forest trees, extending farther northward along the coast than the others. Its flowers produce a honey that is well thought of by some people.

The other salt-forest tree is the buttonwood, which gets its name from its groups of little spherical fruit and flowers. Buttonwood usually grows farther inland than the others, often mixing with terrestrial hardwoods. Mahogany and buttonwood often grow together, for example, especially in the once-famous mahogany country of the northern shore of Florida Bay. In some of the woods near there you can see live oak, mahogany and buttonwood growing in mixed stands. Buttonwood bark is favored by epiphytes as a surface to grow on. The trees apparently live a long time, because you often see big ones, repeatedly blown over by hurricanes, lying recumbent and looping off across the ground from one set of roots to another, or even doubling back across their own trunks before slanting up toward the sun again. The wood of this species used to be the favorite fuel of people on the Keys. Expeditions to burn buttonwood charcoal and cut mahogany brought some of the earliest settlers to the remote northwest coast of Florida Bay.

In Florida the shore zone is usually dominated by red mangrove, chiefly young plants growing on ground that is periodically under water. Turtle grass and manatee grass are often associated with red mangrove, and there may also be patches of the marsh grass *Spartina*, and a sprinkling of seedlings of black and white mangroves. In meeting the ecologic challenge of life in the difficult, storm-wracked unstable zone where tidal salt water laps the edge of the land, the red mangrove has evolved into one of the most bizarre of all vegetables. Because the ecologic demands of the various kinds of seaside environments are very different, this species varies markedly in form. Some red mangroves are tall and straight-trunked; some are low-crowned domes standing on thin stilts; some spread out horizontally, and repeatedly re-root as they go, like vegetable centipedes.

Two of the fundamental adaptations that fit the red mangrove for its perilous life at the edge of the sea are salt tolerance and an ability to cling to unstable ground. A third adaptive achievement is a reproductive device that allows the species to disperse widely and colonize new habitat. Red mangroves have little yellow, waxy flowers; the seeds that these produce germinate before they leave the tree, generating a cigar-shaped seedling 6 to 12 inches long. When these seedlings fall, some may lodge and take root beneath the parent tree and become part of a growing forest there, but most of them drift away with tides and currents and may travel for hundreds or even thousands of miles before they strand or die. When a seedling strands in shallow water it quickly grows roots, and these pull the little stem erect. A few leaves appear, and in a short while a new little mangrove stands in the shallows. As it grows, thin aerial roots arch out of the trunk or drop from the spreading limbs. As each of these touches the bottom it frays out into thin claws that seize the mud to anchor the young tree against the waves, tide-wash, and winds of seaside storms. The roots multiply, the stem rises until it is lost in the growing crown, and eventually the tree may stand only on its multiple prop roots. The roots have several special functions: they bring up sap; they raise the short trunk above the water; they serve as breathing organs to furnish oxygen that is not available down in the mud; they make a system of props and braces that holds the tree erect in unstable ground; and finally they reduce wave-wash and current flow, and so promote the accumulation of silt and detritus, and consolidate the hold of the tree on the unstable edge of the land. A single, well-grown, tidal-zone red mangrove standing high on its thin legs is a strange-looking plant. A forest of such trees is one of the most offbeat kinds of vegetation to be found anywhere.

Although there is some tendency for the different kinds of mangrove-forest trees to segregate according to the salinity of the water, this is not nearly so marked in Florida as it apparently is in other parts of the world. The outermost pioneering rank is nearly always composed of red mangrove, and buttonwood is the most prevalent on drier land; but otherwise, the species mix unpredictably. The red mangrove is even able to survive in fresh water, though it seems unhappy there. One of the more striking landscapes to be seen along the road through Everglades National Park to Flamingo is a stand of dwarf cypresses that meets a stunted outlier of the red-mangrove fringe growing with the fresh-water sawgrass, under what appear to be almost intolerable ecological conditions. The tiny, many-legged, widely spaced mangroves probably grew from seedlings blown there by hurricanes, and they seem barely able to survive in the scanty soil that covers the limestone bedrock. Some of them are only a couple of feet high, but they are obviously not young trees; the botanist Frank Craighead thinks some of them may have been there for a hundred years or more.

Contrast those spidery growths with the trees of the original mangrove forests of Florida, before the tan-bark crews got to them to strip off the bark that was widely used in tanning and dyeing, and before the forests were lashed by the disastrous hurricane of 1935, then by Donna in 1960, and finally by Betsy in 1965. What must have been one of the finest of the Florida mangrove forests evidently grew about the mouth of Little River, between Fort Lauderdale and Miami. There, according to Charles Torrey Simpson, "Some of (the trees) were braced by air roots fully eighteen inches in diameter that sprung from a height of twenty-five feet above the ground, and in other cases slender roots dropped from the branches fully thirty-five feet above the soil. . . . These trees easily ranked among the most wonderful vegetable growths of the State of Florida."

Though most of the mangrove forest that remains is typically composed of lowish, round-topped trees sprawling over tidal shallows along the shores of brackish bays and estuaries, the trees rise high and straight-stemmed when they find themselves on slightly higher or deeper or more stimulating soil. I don't know what the top heights of such mangroves are around the world, but people who speak of the forests of some parts of Southeast Asia often mention 100 feet, and the same figure has been repeatedly mentioned as the maximum height of the red mangroves of Florida.

An old forest of red mangroves growing on slightly elevated solid ground can be walked through as you would walk through any dense woods. To walk through mangroves in tide-covered ground, or to wade or swim through them, is next to impossible. By far the best way to go, if this should ever be really necessary, is to scramble and brachiate —that is, swing by the arms from one hold to another—through the interlocking branches, well above the shell-encrusted basketwork made by the arching and interlacing prop roots.

Throughout the tropics, mangroves are of utmost importance in the ecology of marine estuaries, the bays or river mouths in which the sea meets the fresh water running off the land. So long as estuaries remain untouched, the fresh water they receive and the nutrients that this brings in are mixed and mellowed in an orderly way with the tidal sea water, producing what have belatedly come to be recognized as some of the richest environments in the world. Besides supporting a diverse fauna of their own, estuaries provide a breeding place and nursery ground for a great many kinds of marine animals, and they are a way station in the migratory travel of many others. The recent growth of public interest in human ecology has called attention to the widespread destruction of natural tidal-shore environments. Until lately tidal swamps and marshes have been thought of as dismal half-worlds that ought to be dredged, filled and bulk-headed to make clean-shored waterfront real estate. Florida has suffered grievously from this compulsive destruction of shoreline environments, and because the state has so much shoreline and is growing so fast, the damage has been appalling.

Mangroves make a vital contribution to the estuarine environments of southern Florida, protecting them against the hydraulic power of hurricanes. Of all living organisms the mangroves are best able to stay in place during the earth-moving exercises of a 200-mile wind and the attendant seas. Without mangroves the big storms would continually reshape the coast in the hurricane belt. There is no telling what southern Florida would look like if mangroves had never flourished there.

The staying power of tide-zone mangroves has saved people as well as coastline. In the days when hurricane warning systems were poor —when, for instance, Florida depended heavily on bulletins cabled by a priest at a Catholic college in Havana—the deadly big hurricanes often came by surprise; and a main recourse of people who got caught was to take refuge in their boats, which they anchored firmly in narrow creeks in mangrove swamps. I have heard old conchs, as the Keys people used to call themselves, say repeatedly that the mangroves were the place to be when hurricanes came.

Besides their role in steadying the interplay between fresh waters and the sea, mangroves contribute directly to the nutrient cycles of coastal regions. The leaves of red mangroves are an important food for various insects, including several kinds of butterflies. The larva of the common mangrove skipper, for example, favors these leaves, and the larva of a species of moth lives in the reproductive seedlings. Mangrove leaves have been found in the stomachs of sea turtles, both the hawksbill and the green turtle. The stomach of a Honduras hawksbill that I once examined was tightly filled with pieces of mangrove seedlings that had been bitten off in sections about an inch long. Back in the days when green turtles were held for long periods awaiting the schooners to take them to market, they were kept in crawls—water-filled palisaded pens —frequently located on mangrove shores. The turtles were sometimes fed on red-mangrove leaves. Nobody seems to know how important mangrove detritus may be as a natural travel ration of the Atlantic green turtles, whose periodic migrations take them through regions in

The air-absorbing roots of a black mangrove rise from the water in dense array. Called pneumatophores, these solid structures—about a half inch thick—grow up from the plant's submerged lateral roots and supply the tree with enough oxygen to prevent it from drowning in sea water or smothering in mud. The leafy shoot at center is an encroaching red mangrove.

which the submarine vegetation they prefer is lacking, and where fallen mangrove leaves are probably the only plant food they see. But the detritus would seem to be more than an emergency ration. You often see green turtles in mangrove creeks. During a short cruise only a few weeks ago I counted six half-grown ones in the mangrove estuaries around the mouths of the Shark and Little Shark Rivers.

Although land animals are not at all conspicuous in the Florida red-mangrove forests and swamps, a great many kinds of birds come and go in them. Gray squirrels occasionally live there at fruiting season, and fox squirrels are sometimes seen in the Collier County mangroves, which to a northern Floridian seems incomprehensibly out of character, because fox squirrels belong in long-leaved pines. Raccoons are abundant in even the most chaotically jumbled mangrove forest; wildcats and panthers travel in it to get back and forth between hunting places; and even antlered deer are able to negotiate it with ease.

I don't know how a deer can possibly get through a mangrove swamp. A tidal mangrove forest is a place of such monumental disorder that you would swear it had been designed by a demented maker of children's Junglegyms, or by a computer programed to keep out everything but snakes. Yet deer do somehow get through; and the raccoons pass without apparent hindrance. But pity the poor coonhound when the coon takes to the mangroves. Back in the days before television superseded coon hunting as the evening pastime of rural Floridians, there was much suffering by hounds whose masters hunted too near the mangrove swamp. Coons systematically head straight for the mangroves when dogs are after them, knowing better than the dogs appear to know that dogs can't travel there. I knew a coon hunter on the east coast who spent a whole night fighting his way through mangroves to where his dog had hung itself up in a tree.

You sometimes see rat snakes prowling in mangrove trees, and once in a blue moon you come upon a tree frog. In Chapter 4, I mentioned the intolerance of frogs for salt water. This applies mainly to direct contact, however. A frog can't be born in a mangrove swamp—it has to move there from a fresh-water pond or ditch somewhere; but sometimes you find mature frogs that have wandered far out into saline vegetation to reap some special harvest. On a recent visit to Everglades National Park I came upon a gangling, slim-legged, green tree frog in a tidal stand of young red mangroves on the shore of Florida Bay. The frog was a handsome one, with an ivory stripe down each side and with gold flecks scattered on its green silk back. It was industriously catching mosquitoes. One usually sees such frogs hunting on window screens at night. You rarely find one hunting in the daytime, and even more rarely in a mangrove tree. But this one was in a perfect frenzy of mosquito-catching. It was a drizzly day and there were so many mosquitoes it was hard to breathe, yet I noticed that not one of them sat on the naked frog. It seemed totally immune to the hordes, as if shielded from them by some personal secretion of bug repellent. On straw-thin hopping legs it dangled and swung from twig to twig, snapping at the inexhaustible store of prey on the glossy leaves, as seemingly at home in mangroves as if they had been willows or buttonbush trees. On the bigger Keys and all through the mainland mangrove fringe, mosquitoes are not only a seasonal nuisance but also a fundamental part of the energy cycle of the region. It would be hard to overestimate the importance of mangrove mosquitoes as a source of food for the Everglades' animals, ranging from the little fishes that catch the larvae to the bats, frogs and lizards that prey on the mature mosquitoes.

All sorts of marine creatures, both large and small, favor mangrove-bordered water. Manatees are partial to such places. Alligators and crocodiles used to come together there and still perhaps do, once in a while, in the small patch of country in which crocodiles remain. A number of kinds of fishes prefer mangrove-bordered streams and bays. Most of the numerous fishermen that cruise through the mangrove country are going after tarpon, snook, mangrove snappers or redfish; the rest of them are simply lost.

There are many kinds of crabs in the mangroves, ranging in size from the fiddlers that teem on mud flats at the edges of the forest to big blue land crabs in the higher tracts of swamp. Where the mangroves border bays or estuaries the mangrove terrapin—a southern relative of the northern diamondback terrapin cherished by gourmets—may be found. Low tide in the mangroves reveals the coon oysters, which cling to the aerial mangrove roots and hang in clusters in the open air when the tide goes out. Coon oysters are very good to eat but hard to get out of their sharp-edged shells.

Another highly edible animal that sometimes gets into the edges of the mangroves is the spiny lobster. Once when my family and I were snorkeling in the mangrove islets of Florida Bay we found the whole submarine fringe of prop-root basketry around two islets to be crowded with young spiny lobsters, ensconced in the wall of roots, and with their antennae all thrust seaward. Most of them were under legal size.

Some were not, however, and these we tried to catch, but we were never able to extricate a single one from the wall of wickerwork.

Along with the hospitality they offer marine creatures, mangroves make another contribution to the fauna in this part of the world: they provide nesting places for the herons and other water birds without which Florida would be a very dismal landscape.

A water-bird rookery is one of the marvels of the natural world. The gregariousness of wading birds, the tendency for the different kinds to fraternize on a foraging ground, is not restricted to fishing time. It is even more dramatically displayed in their nesting assemblages—in the mixed rookeries they build.

There can be no doubt that most wading birds share a common notion of what kind of place makes a good nesting site. As disorderly and unplanned as a mixed rookery may appear, the species in it are obviously there because the place has met certain specifications: good lodgment for nests, a supply of twigs for nest-building, an accessible food supply that will meet the heavy demands of the fledgling period, and relative freedom from terrestrial predators. It is probably the latter need that explains why rookeries are so frequently located over water in swamps—significantly often over swamps with raccoon-scaring alligators in them—and why in the coastal fringes in southernmost Florida rookeries are set up so regularly on mangrove islands. Without insulation from raccoons, snakes, rats and wildcats, a bird rookery in Florida would probably not be feasible.

Mangrove rookeries seem more durable than those in fresh-water trees. In southern Florida, where hurricanes charge sporadically across tree swamps and mangrove islands, a rookery site can be destroyed by the wind in a few hours. The most famous and historic of all Florida rookeries, that in Cuthbert Lake in Everglades National Park, lasted for decades, only to be almost wiped out of existence by Hurricane Donna.

Most of the common water birds nest impartially in a number of different kinds of trees; but in Florida brown pelicans, which are rare and endangered everywhere else, nest almost exclusively in mangroves. Their east coast rookeries occur mainly in black mangroves, while on the Gulf Coast they are all in red-mangrove swamp except for the northernmost colony, located on Sea Horse Island off Cedar Key.

To insert oneself silently into the dynamic, reeking, cacophonic midst of a croaking, keening, contesting, vomiting, defecating melange of superbly graceful adult birds and monstrously unfinished young in a mixed water-bird rookery is surely one of the most memorable of all wilderness experiences. But most rookeries are too frail to withstand visitors. Wood storks or great blue herons nesting in tall cypresses will put up with a tactful intrusion beneath them, but where the nests are clustered in the low trees and bushes that most smaller herons usually favor, even an unobtrusive visitor can cause dire confusion and distress, with parent birds squawking and flapping, fledglings tumbling, and watchful, avid fish crows diving down to raid the untended nests.

The only rookeries I know in southern Florida that you can get close to without doing damage are on mangrove islands. Cuthbert Island in Cuthbert Lake—what Hurricane Donna left of it—is one. Various little mangrove islands in eastern Florida Bay support nesting colonies, some mixed, some mostly pelicans, some roseate spoonbills, and these colonies seem to take no offense at the discreet approach of a boat.

Not long ago my wife and I went through Everglades National Park again, and our last stop was Everglades City at the western entrance to the park. We took the short evening cruise on Chokoloskee Bay to see half a dozen kinds of birds nesting on an archipelago of little mangrove islands. Some of the islands were separate trees and some were little clumps. All of them were round green domes, varying only in size and stringing out in a quarter-mile arc that was silhouetted against the setting sun and a bank of purplish storm clouds. And each island was the roost or nesting place of a host of water birds.

The boat drew up quietly to within a hundred feet or so of the middle of the island arc. The captain shut off the engine, and for nearly an hour we drifted there, listening to the croaking, gurgling comment of the birds and tallying their kinds. There were cormorants and five kinds of herons in the rookeries. Two roseate spoonbills came in to roost and settled separately in little mangrove trees. The white ibises had finished nesting the month before, and now were coming in to pass the night, each separate flock appearing as a dim, wavering line in the northeast, then slowly condensing into a chain of white birds. As the flocks arrived they circled to locate empty islands, then banked steeply and came to rest in the branches. As the little, dark green islands received their birds they flowered, as if with magnolia blooms, against the dark storm clouds out in the Gulf.

The Pioneering Red Mangrove

PHOTOGRAPHS BY DAN MC COY

The red mangroves rimming the Everglades along Florida Bay and the Gulf of Mexico are among the most aggressive trees in nature. When Christopher Columbus saw their like off the coast of Hispaniola in 1494 they were "so thick a rabbit could scarcely pass through," the ship's doctor reported in a letter back home to his native Spain.

Their aggressiveness is not only a matter of density; like Columbus himself they are pioneer voyagers in waters unvisited by less intrepid stock. For the red mangrove propagates itself by sending its seedlings out to sea—after they have germinated on the parent tree (right). And as the human explorer is followed first by conquerors and later by settlers, so it is with the red mangrove. The seedlings often plant themselves in shoals that have no other vegetation. Once they have fortified the site—which they do by virtually creating land where there was none —other colonizing trees move in behind them—black and white mangroves, then oak and mahogany—to provide a new habitat for creatures ranging from root-clinging oysters to treetop-nesting birds.

As it coalesces, a mangrove forest acquires a lush, glossy canopy overhead; below, twisted and intermeshing trunks and prop roots form an intricate maze. The water lapping at the roots at high tide is often stained red from tannin—the natural dye in the trees' bark that gives the red mangrove its name.

Being a voyager, the mangrove appears everywhere in the tropics: in Africa, on both coasts of Central and South America, and on Melanesian and Polynesian shores. The seedlings can survive afloat for a year until they find a hospitable sandbar to light on. Some travel thousands of miles from their parent trees before coming to rest; the New World mangroves are thought to have originated in Africa.

A view from most places on the Gulf Coast of Florida will show a slender mangrove sapling here, another two or three there, and in the distance full-blown islands of varying dimensions. A visit to the same site another year may show quite different formations of trees and islands, for they are constantly being altered by autumn storms. But even when a cataclysmic hurricane wipes out a whole forest, the irrepressible red mangrove is the first plant to return to the scene and build up the land all over again.

A red mangrove tree dips toward the Gulf of Mexico, heavy with string-bean-shaped seedlings that it will soon deliver to the water below it. There some will take root; others will ride out with the tide to root elsewhere. From the falling of such seedlings come tangled masses of trees that spread to form islands like the one on the horizon.

Clusters of sweet-scented flowers—here magnified five times—begin the tree's life cycle.

The Birth of a Seedling

The life cycle of the red mangrove tree begins with a spring flowering that turns it into a blaze of yellow *(left)*. The flowers, about an inch in diameter, with cottony white nectar-filled centers that attract bees, bloom for a few weeks and then drop off, making way in the summer for a sweet-tasting berry that squirrels and birds feed on. The fruit sprout elongated green appendages *(right)* that are the red mangrove's principal distinction. These seedling shoots are a rarity among plant growths; by the time a seedling is ready to drop from the tree it is itself already a rudimentary tree.

This form of viviparous propagation—the production of living young direct from a parent—is a dramatic instance of environmental adaptation. The seeds of most trees germinate in soil; but since the saline coastal soil that supports the adult red mangrove is too hostile for proper germination, the tree holds its seeds until they are ready to grow.

The mangrove lets the seedlings go in late August or early September —storm season, when higher-than-usual tides provide the seedlings with easy transportation away from home. If they do not root below the parent in a day or two, they drift away to implant themselves elsewhere. In a few years a sapling will be yielding its own fruit, and in about five years' time an open shoal can acquire a whole new arbor of mangroves *(pages 146-147)*.

Strawberry-sized fruit follow the flowers and sprout foot-long seedlings that drop in late summer, to take root in offshore shallows.

In this developing mangrove forest, the center tree is from three to five years old; the nearby seedlings range in age from a few days to

about a year. The upright seedlings have taken root; those that are horizontal may drift off to right themselves and take root elsewhere.

Mangrove prop roots, bending in graceful arcs, serve to brace the tree, give it air and entrap debris that decomposes to provide nourishm

How the Mangrove Forest Grows

In its second year of life the mangrove starts to develop its major underpinnings—prop roots *(left)* that serve the dual purpose of reinforcing the tree against storms and helping transmit nourishment, moisture and oxygen from the air and soil to the trunk and branches. The prop roots are also the means by which the tree builds land; they enmesh all sorts of natural rubbish, from the leaves shed by the tree itself, to the sand, grasses and shells that are daily swept in by the sea *(right)*. As this detritus thickens and decays, it metamorphoses into soil, which further supports the growing tree and gives the advancing prop roots room and depth to perform their functions.

In a fully developed mangrove forest *(pages 150-151)* the roots form a jumble of arches so intertwined that the human eye can hardly discern where one begins and another ends. Such a forest, though hospitable to many creatures *(pages 152-153)*, is almost impenetrable to those that do not crawl or scramble, for many prop roots are too high to climb over and others are too low to stoop under.

Though mangrove forests lose ground to the ravages of storms from time to time, they have made a net gain in the past 30 to 40 years; during that period the land area around Florida and Biscayne Bays has been increased by approximately 1,500 acres, and once-open shoals have been transformed into heavily forested patches of land.

The mangrove's shed leaves are among its first soil builders.

Grasses, shells and other debris help form supportive muck.

A mature mangrove forest, with 20- to 30-foot-high trunks and a network of prop roots, fringes a Florida shore. Under ideal conditions

—meaning an absence of catastrophic hurricanes—a colony of this size and density can grow from pioneer seedlings in half a century.

Its belly bulging, a corn snake digests a meal while napping in a mangrove.

A Bower for Wildlife

Every part of the mangrove forest —from the prop roots, which alternately submerge and emerge with the tides, to the topmost branches, which may tower as high as 80 feet —provides shelter or food for a multitude of creatures. This population ranges from the tiny sand fly flitting among the leaves to the 250-pound tarpon lurking offshore.

Of the bird species that find homes among the mangroves, white pelicans appear in such abundance that during the winter the trees look snow-covered from the air. Their cousin, the brown pelican (*far right*), rare and endangered everywhere except Florida, shares the rookeries in neighborly amity with egrets, herons, wood storks, ospreys, bald eagles and cormorants.

A host of other creatures come down from higher land to forage. Raccoons favor the oysters that live off the prop roots (*left*). Sir Walter Raleigh, exploring the New World for Queen Elizabeth I in the late 16th Century, also found them agreeable, reporting that they were "very salt and well tasted." Snakes slither up the tree trunks after birds' eggs and nestlings; cormorants, which dine chiefly on the fish in the nearby waters, even the score by catching a napping snake now and then. Fiddler crabs scuttling about in low tide perform a large service: aerating the soil as they probe for food, they increase the supply of oxygen to the trees that attract all the creatures.

Coon oysters, a principal food of scavenging raccoons, cling to the prop roots.

A wary cormorant dries its wings on a perch in a mangrove treetop.

A brown pelican rests on a low branch between dives for fish.

A Violent End, a New Beginning

The equinoctial storms of autumn, with their especially high tides, are for the most part a blessing to the mangrove tree. They bring it nutriments that it needs for its well-being; they carry its young away to establish the beginnings of new mangrove colonies in other places.

But every quarter century or so an epic hurricane comes like a curse instead. It hurls winds close to 200 miles an hour across the land, tearing the bark from the trees and exposing their tender cores to the desiccating salt spray of the sea. Such a storm churns the waves to heights of 20 feet; on Florida's flat terrain this can cause the waters to spill inland more than 10 miles. The backwash sucks out the supporting soil from among the prop roots of the mangroves and the winds then fell even the giants of the forest. Of the major hurricanes that have ravaged Florida during this century, one, in 1960, destroyed from 50 to 75 per cent of the mature mangroves along the Shark River (right), until then the site of some of the tallest mangroves in the world.

But the mangrove tree has a remarkable ability to regenerate. It sprouts new life in the very center of a hurricane's devastation. When the storm subsides, gentler tides return and deposit seedlings gathered from healthy trees elsewhere—and so begins again the process that keeps the shape of the Florida shoreline ever new and ever changing.

The dead hulk of a mangrove felled by Hurricane Donna in 1960 sprawls in the Shark River, among seedlings that presage a new forest.

7/ A Wilderness Besieged

No state is under greater pressure from all the forces that place demands upon land, water and life....The United States begins or ends in Florida. RAYMOND F. DASMANN/ *NO FURTHER RETREAT*

You used to hear an unkind definition of a government African expert as a man who had made a flight over the continent of Africa. The gibe was no doubt justified, but actually if you want to visualize the anatomy of a region in a short while the best possible means of travel is by a plane flown sympathetically, searchingly and at an elevation from which one kind of vegetation can be told from another.

I made such a flight over the whole southern tip of Florida not long ago, and though I had covered most of the ground before by car, boat, airboat or small plane, nothing ever put the country together for me like that journey in a jet. The flight was one of the field trips offered at the Second National Biological Congress at Miami Beach. When I saw "Overflight of South Florida" on the list of excursions, my first thought was that I had flown over the place a hundred times already. But then I saw the flight plan they had, with a jet snaking through the whole southern end of the peninsula 1,000 feet up, missing no major feature of the country, and with Dr. Frank Craighead, consultant for Everglades National Park and the ranking authority on the region, explaining what was being flown over. I quickly signed up for my wife and myself.

The plane climbed out over western Miami into the half-world of suburbs, farms and limerock mines where the city is spreading into the Everglades. As we went into a slow southward turn I could barely make out the thin line in the west where Florida Highway 27 emerges from farms and mango groves, crosses the Tamiami Trail, and angles off northwest toward Lake Okeechobee. The road was visible so far away only because of the outlandish strips of cajeput, Brazilian peppers and casuarinas that grow along its shoulders.

There are more ways to pollute a landscape than by loading it with sewage, smog and beer cans. You can load it with exotic plants and animals. Whether brought in intentionally or accidentally, these are likely to change the landscape. The changes they make are rarely good, and often are atrocious. The droll armadillo, for instance—introduced into Florida only a few decades ago—is modifying the woodlands by its rooting for the small animals that inhabit the leaf mold. The walking catfish, which caused national excitement when it established itself in Florida a few years ago, is apparently doing no harm so far; but it may, once it gets the feel of the land. And so may any of the foreign birds, fishes, reptiles, insects and plants that now number in hundreds.

The most conspicuous changes produced by exotic organisms in southern Florida are the brand-new types of landscape dominated by the three foreign trees I mentioned: cajeput, Brazilian pepper and casuarina. The most widespread are the casuarinas, brought long ago from Australia, and now driving out or inhibiting many other trees. Cajeput is a handsome Asian relative of the eucalyptus, with cream-smooth bark that curls off in thin layers like birch bark. Being fireproof, and catholic in its habitat selection, it has invaded thousands of acres of cutover flatwoods. Cajeput tends to form biologically sterile communities, practically devoid of animal life—perhaps because the secretion the tree produces is offensive to animals. Local naturalists tell me that when cajeput comes in around a gator hole the gator will move away. The Brazilian pepper, an attractive ornamental tree or shrub with bright red berries that appeal to birds, is now growing in spreading copses all through the frost-free parts of the state.

I started to regale my wife with a small jeremiad on the subject of the new plants and animals that have been brought to this part of the state; but that seemed a bad way to start the flight, and I made up my mind to try to do better—to concentrate on happier sights below our windows.

This was not easy. From the plane, U.S. Highway 1 was a sharp line running down the Rock Rim. Greater Miami was crowding south, shoving aside the last of the pinewoods and hammocks and flooding into country where bare limerock has been smashed into truck farms.

The limestone floor of southern Florida is profoundly involved in the ecological organization of the landscape, both natural and urban. The

Rock Rim interrupts the eastward flow of surface water to the Atlantic, and impounds the low head that sets the River of Grass off in its creeping flow southwestward. The peculiar properties of this floor of fissured rock, covered and calked by muck, bear as much on the welfare of man in Miami as they do on otters and Everglades kites. The rock is the aquifer—the underground water storage and delivery system—for the Gold Coast's wells. The recharging of this system depends on the capacity of the muck to hold water. The muck in turn is the debris of an integrated biological community that is dependent upon protracted flooding. As drainage, farming and fire destroy this covering of muck, the annual dry season lengthens, the sporadic droughts become more severe, the fauna thins out in the River of Grass; and to the east of it, in the cities of the Rock Rim, the salt water rises in the fresh-water wells. There could be no more graphic proof of the interdependence of man and nature than the predicament of the metropolitan lower east coast of Florida. There, for decades, agricultural and urban development has been progressively destroying the hydrologic system that makes life possible both in the Everglades and in the cities. The realization of that fact is the greatest single hope for saving any wilderness in southern Florida, and perhaps for saving the cities themselves.

Just below Miami the plane crossed Black Point, so called for its fringe of tall dark mangroves, and turned eastward over Biscayne Bay to give us a look at Elliott Key. I knew my plan to stay cheerful would receive a setback there. Elliott Key is near the northern end of the archipelago of the upper Florida Keys and is the nucleus of the Biscayne National Monument, which is being developed to save the superb tropical reef-and-key country between Miami and Key Largo. Elliott Key is covered by tropical hammock, a dense low forest of diverse West Indian trees. The vegetation is not virgin; the island once was largely under cultivation. But even though the forest is second growth, it has had half a century or so in which to regenerate, and has come back in a continuous even stand, and in what probably is close to its original diversity of species.

"Notice the clean strip bulldozed down the center of the island," said Frank Craighead over the intercom, "right through the heart of the hammock. It came close to destroying the last known stand of Sargent's palm in Florida." Sargent's palm, known also as cherry palm, hog cabbage or buccaneer palm, is a West Indian species that grows to a height of about 25 feet, and looks a little like a small royal palm. Everybody crowded to the windows and looked down at the wide band cut straight through the woods. A wave of muttering spread through the cabin. All up and down the aisle people who had never heard of Sargent's palm asked each other what kind of vandal would wreck a piece of rare wild country that way. Then the answer started passing from seat to seat: "To kill the preservation scheme—to ruin the key as a natural area and make the conservationists give up the project."

That marred group morale badly—until somebody passed the word that the bulldozer-happy chaps were being sued for the expense of re-planting the strip, and for all the costs involved in growing a mature stand again. That cheered us up a little.

Back over the mainland, we headed for the tip of the peninsula and the mangrove shores of eastern Florida Bay. On the way we flew by the infamous C-111, the "Aerojet Canal," built in 1964-1965 to provide access to the sea for the barges of a solid-fuel plant—that has since shut down. Frank Craighead summarized the complicated story of that bloodletting exercise and its threat to the vital eastern section of Everglades National Park and the ecology of Taylor Slough.

The slough is not clearly discernible from the air as a topographic feature. It is a linear complex of ponds, marshes and sawgrass glades in a broad, shallow depression of the limestone floor of the eastern Everglades. In the wet season it carries water southward into Florida Bay, flowing into Everglades National Park, across the Hole-in-the-Doughnut—the private agricultural holdings that scar the eastern section of the park—and into the midsection of the Florida Bay shore. In former times, in the wet season, small boats could be paddled all the way from Homestead through Taylor Slough to Florida Bay. In recent decades, however, with all the farming and development at its headwaters, the slough has dried out. The uproar over the recent digging in this region was stirred up by the probability that the canal complex involved would further lower the slough's headwaters. This would increase the duration of drought and the threat of fire, make the eastern section of the park more vulnerable to invasion in the dry season by salt water from Barnes Sound, and disrupt the ecologic stability of this section of the park. But court orders, generated by efforts of the National Audubon Society, have lessened the danger. Gated culverts have been installed in C-111 to permit the flow of water into Barnes Sound but prevent salt water from backing up into Taylor Slough. And work on auxiliary canals of the system has been halted.

Soon after passing C-111, we were over the zone of northeastern Florida Bay where salt and fresh water meet. From the air the irregular mosaic of lagoons and saline vegetation looked as if buckets of paint—tan, beige, chartreuse and olive—had been poured together on a perfectly smooth surface. We crossed Taylor Slough where it spreads into Little Madeira Bay, famous for its crocodiles, mahogany and mosquitoes, and for a while continued on west along the wavering saline zone with its broad band of intermingled glades and salt-tolerant vegetation. Then we turned southwestward, passing Coot Bay and coming out abruptly over Cape Sable, an obviously separate and very different kind of country, cut off from the Everglades by the vast lagoon known as Whitewater Bay. We circled over Flamingo, once a remote little fishing village, now site of the southern headquarters of Everglades National Park. Looking down on that tactful intrusion of organized humanity, I thought of my own earliest visit there with my brother in the early '30s. The first living thing we had seen at the end of our five-hour trip in a Model A Ford down the ruinous road of those days was a bobcat in a garbage can behind a tall, teetery, weather-beaten house. The rear end of a bobcat it actually was, sticking out of the can he was foraging in. I even recalled what the lady of that house said when she gave us a drink of water and we spoke of the bobcat. "They're a nuisance around here," she said. "They eat our house cats so bad we can't keep none."

I also remembered seeing a man skinning a crocodile at the old Coot Bay alligator camp, and I recalled losing a lot of plugs to baby tarpon that jumped around in a narrow creek like crazy and threw our lures up into the mangroves. Most vividly I thought of the mosquitoes, of driving back to Homestead after dark with a broken spring at three miles an hour the whole way. For most of the trip back my brother sat out on the hood of the car, in the wan hope that the whip of the overhanging trees would brush some of the mosquitoes away. But as it turned out the trees were mostly poisonwood, and the next day my brother's eyes were swollen shut and his face was like a pumpkin.

Flamingo is located at the bottom of Cape Sable, which actually consists of three subcapes: East Cape, Middle Cape and Northwest Cape, connected by surf-built beaches. The best beach is at East Cape, the southernmost projection of the mainland United States. There is an important nesting colony of the loggerhead turtle on Cape Sable. Along with all other kinds of sea turtles, the loggerhead is declining the world over. Its reproduction is increasingly hindered by the loss of wild seashore and by the egg hunting that still goes on in parts of the nesting range. Although Cape Sable suffers frequent hurricane damage it is good loggerhead nesting shore, and because the beaches there are bet-

Thick with tropical hardwoods, Elliott Key predominates in this air view looking north at the keys of upper Biscayne Bay. The zigzag line down the middle of the key is the survey line for a roadbed that was bulldozed in 1968 as a prelude to real-estate development. The project was thwarted when the island was included as the nucleus of Biscayne National Monument, and the abandoned roadbed is now being reclaimed by tropical vegetation.

ter shielded from human intrusion than most of the mainland coast, they deserve careful attention as a sea-turtle sanctuary.

The only serious natural menace to the Cape Sable turtles is the raccoon. Coons love turtle eggs, and at Cape Sable the coons are so abundant that it is hard to see how the loggerhead nests there. The big coon population may not be natural, but another sign of man's disruption of ecological balance, in this case by his reduction of the panthers and alligators, the two most important coon predators.

A conspicuous feature of Cape Sable is a broad crescent of marl prairie that spreads inland behind the beaches. These prairies are not residual sea bottom, but wave-built land. Although a slow rise of sea level has occurred at the cape during the last 5,000 years or so, at the same time the land has been repeatedly built up by wave-deposition during the sporadic hurricanes. That process has created a series of ridges, which can clearly be seen from the air, running parallel with the shore. This slightly elevated land makes a barrier to the flow of the Everglades' water and diverts it westward into the Gulf of Mexico.

To keep the geography in view, our pilot held a course straight up the cape, flying along Lake Ingraham, on the prairie behind the clean ocean beach, and passing over old canals that mark the dashed hopes of early real-estate men. We turned out over the Gulf again at Middle Cape, where a ragged stand of palms is all that remains of a huge coconut plantation that was set out in the 1880s and soon abandoned.

The land beneath us was as wild as any in Florida. As far as we could see in any direction the old coco palms were the only sign that man had ever tried to tame it. From the days of the earliest explorers the conspicuous geographic position of Cape Sable, jutting into the Gulf, brought it to the attention of travelers. But the cape escaped the pandemic of development because of its remoteness—and its mosquitoes.

Thank the Lord for the mosquitoes. The world owes them a lot for their part in preserving Cape Sable. A heroic statue of a mosquito in bronze ought to be set up on a hurricane-proof pedestal, a huge plinth of Key Largo limestone perhaps, at some commanding point on the cape. There might be a little trouble deciding what kind of mosquito the statue ought to represent. As I understand it, three kinds have borne the main burden of keeping people out. One is *Psorophora*, known locally as the Everglades mosquito. Another is the salt-marsh mosquito or, as the conchs call it, mangrove mosquito—*Aedes taeniorhyncus*. The third is *Aedes sollitans*, commonly known as the New Jersey mosquito.

Apart from the deterrent influence of mosquitoes on development, they deserve attention as one of the really imposing biologic phenomena of the region. Their abundance at certain seasons—I think of June with most uneasiness—surpasses belief, or used to. Madeira Bay stands out in my memory as the mosquito capital of the world; but the whole crescent from Shark River down the cape and around the shore of Florida Bay to Key Largo probably has more mosquitoes than any place on earth. People from New Jersey, Labrador or Alaska will tell you that nobody has seen mosquitoes till he visits their area; but this must be mere regional chauvinism. The abundance of mosquitoes in June at Madeira Bay is controlled only by the amount of space there is to hold them.

Madeira Bay mosquitoes do more than punch countless holes in your skin—they interfere with your breathing. There are authenticated cases of people succumbing to mosquito attack in former days. In telling of these events it is customary for the narrator to say, "Sucked him dry, poor devil." But according to James S. Haeger of the Entomological Research Center at Vero Beach, the mosquitoes probably did more than that. In his view, while loss of juices might have been a factor, reaction to the saliva a mosquito injects probably made trouble also, and there was also probably respiratory damage resulting from both mechanical obstruction and the irritation that the wing scales of mosquitoes produce in mucous membrane. When you add to all this the panic that sometimes overcomes the victim—as it did one man who had a flat tire on Key Largo one night and tried to run to Homestead through a cloud of salt-marsh mosquitoes—no wonder fatalities have occurred. The wonder is that in the old days there weren't more victims, with railroad workers getting drunk on rotgut on Saturday nights and passing out on the roadside. One of the standing mysteries of Florida is what took place in the biochemistry of the Indians, when they came down into this country, that let them live without screens or bug spray.

A short way beyond Northwest Cape our plane banked and headed northeast, moving over the complex of sloughs and mangrove islands around Ponce de Leon Bay. To the degree that the River of Grass is, in more than a metaphoric sense, a river, this country is its mouth and delta. It is obviously a drowned shoreline, with no beach anywhere in sight, only eroding islets partly stabilized by red mangroves.

As we zigzagged up the Shark River distributaries to Tarpon Bay and on into the lower Shark River Slough, the mangroves slowly dropped out and were replaced by the Pahayokee landscape, the grass-and-tree-island country of the typical Everglades. The hundreds of little separate, insular heads and hammocks set about on the sawgrass plain were mainly elongate-teardrop in shape, with the big ends upstream and the thin ends drawn out toward the southwest. The shape is supposed to have been molded by running water, no doubt during times when currents flowed much stronger than they do now. Most of the tree-islands also have a rock outcrop at the upper end. Some people believe that all of the larger islets in this lower section of the Shark River valley were inhabited by Indians—the aborigines, that is, not the Seminoles; there are more tree-islands in the Glades than there ever were Seminoles in southern Florida.

Heading on up the valley, we flew over the Shark Valley Observation Tower and followed the tower road up to the Tamiami Trail, crossing it just east of Forty-Mile Bend—the dogleg made when the two construction crews, one building out from Miami, the other from the west coast, failed by a bit to come together. From there it was only a moment before we were over the vast, raw rectangular patches of bulldozed lifelessness where a major catastrophe had lately been so narrowly averted when the federal government halted further construction on a training-flight strip at the planned site of an international jetport. It was good to leave this unhallowed place behind and cruise out over the Big Cypress Swamp into Seminole country, and to hear Frank Craighead saying that we were flying over the traditional site of the Green Corn Dance, the major springtime ceremony of the Indians.

Turning back southwestward over the swampland, we moseyed out along the Loop Road, the old route to the settlement of Pinecrest, which runs through a marvelously rich and varied country where cypress swamp, bayheads, hammocks and pineland alternate with tracts of saw-grass glade. All through this part of the country the apparition of a Boeing 727 a thousand feet up kept stirring up flocks of white water birds. I couldn't make out whether they were common egrets, snowy egrets, cattle egrets or immature little blues; but they were there in comforting numbers. The westerly course took us back into the salt zone once again, the cypresses gave way to salt marsh and ponds bordered with mangrove, and flocks of water birds became so frequent you could almost fancy you were looking down into the Everglades of the 1930s. Then we crossed a broad belt of mangrove swamp and suddenly came out over the Gulf of Mexico and the Ten Thousand Islands.

From the air this is the most striking landscape in Florida. It is a mosaic of separate mangrove islets, spaced evenly but widely random in their shapes. The outer ones have white sand beaches; the rest are clean-edged patches of what looks like green felt, laid out like a vast jigsaw puzzle that has been assembled but has all its pieces pulled evenly apart. This bewilderingly redundant archipelago begins at Cape Romano and extends southward for some 20 miles to Pavilion Key, where it gradually merges with the slightly less wildly convoluted mangrove patchwork that continues to Cape Sable.

We circled out over the Gulf and came in again over Chokoloskee Island, once an important community of the Calusa Indians, who predated the Seminoles. The whole island is essentially a shell mound, covering some 135 acres and 20 feet high—the highest land, except for Marco Island, anywhere in the Ten Thousand Islands. After circling over Chokoloskee we headed inland, and Everglades City appeared below the plane. This is the western entrance to the national park. The ranger station there is where you record your travel plan if you aim to cruise the marked boat route of the 100-mile-long Wilderness Waterway to Flamingo. You have only to look at the twisting route from the air to see why telling somebody your travel plans is a good precaution to take.

Beyond Everglades City the spartina marsh grass and mangroves gave way to sawgrass sprinkled with little cypress trees, and then to big cypress heads and strands. Cutting back over the Tamiami Trail, we were quickly over the little town of Copeland and from there over the Fahkahatchee Strand, the main drainage slough of the Big Cypress Swamp. After some searching the pilot found Deep Lake, located in Deep Lake Strand, which runs east of the Fahakatchee. Deep Lake, a lime-sink pond 95 feet deep, is the deepest natural body of fresh water in southern Florida. It is a solution sink formed by surface water percolating down through fissured limestone that once stood much higher above sea level and ground-water level than the present lake does.

From there we turned toward the Gulf again and into a ghastly gridwork of canals where a vast real-estate project was recently laid out in uninhabitable swampland that in the long run would have been worth more as intact wilderness than all the assets of the developers involved in ruining it. When we came out over the Tamiami Trail again, we could see where the spillway of the main canal running alongside that melancholy undertaking was bleeding the water of the Big Cypress Swamp out to the Gulf of Mexico by the millions of gallons a day.

Northward we flew to Marco, largest of the Ten Thousand Islands, and now prominent as the site of the state's most recent and most imposing instant metropolis. Marco Island is about six miles long and three miles wide. It was built up by the combined action of storm seas building sand dunes and of Calusa Indians accumulating clam shells. One archeological site there, excavated by Frank Hamilton Cushing in 1895, yielded a diverse array of incredibly well-preserved wooden masks, tools and ornaments. The material came from muck-filled areas between a series of shell ridges, and was preserved by the water-soaked muck that covered it. The articles were made of a number of kinds of wood, including pine, cypress, mangrove and other species not yet identified. The trees were felled and cut into lengths with shell axes, then shaped with adzes made of sawfish teeth, scrapers made of barracuda jaws, or chisels made from the heavy columellas—the central spines —of big conch shells. The smooth finish of some of the articles suggests that they were sanded with sharkskin.

The beds of huge quahog clams that once thrived in the surrounding waters were evidently one important reason for the Calusas' being there. The clams were still extant when I first visited Marco in the '30s and were, in fact, the main reason I went there. Soon afterward they were wiped out, probably because of overexploitation.

As we moved in over the $500-million development that now spreads over Marco Island I remembered the strange little lost-looking salt-water hamlet that once was there, the gray-shingled, pile-supported houses with racked-out fishing nets before them; the clam factory; and the quiet, ponderous quahogs, bedded like cobblestones in the shallows, straining the pristine water of those Depression days as they had when the oldest Indian shellfish cultures thrived there. Suddenly it felt curious to see 60 people bending their necks to look down through the windows of a jet on a dozen square miles of streets and urban canals that seemed laid out to test the maze-running wits of the inhabitants of the fine homes spaced out along them. If there is one point of sharpest focus for the agonizing problems southern Florida faces, it is in that luxurious city that has arisen overnight by developers' fiat in the utterly remote jumping-off place that the Ten Thousand Islands once were.

After meditating on the numbing spectacle of Marco Island for a while, we left it and headed northward. We flew along nine miles of uninhabited Gulf beach, marred only by a continuous strip of volunteer casuarinas, which have the habit of springing up in new seaside groves when seeds wash ashore with hurricanes. We passed offshore of Rookery Bay where, by a famous *tour de force* of regional planning, a wilderness of mangroves, fishes, birds and water has, for the time at least, been saved at the edge of metropolitan Naples. We loafed around over the Gulf looking at the Naples skyline while Frank Craighead told us how the people there created a worldwide stir when they made of the Rookery Bay project a model of man-land harmony.

The project came about when people began tossing in their sleep over dreams of Naples and Marco running together. The long-range scheme for the region included a highway down through the Ten Thousand Islands, and south of that a causeway across Florida Bay to Key West. That was for the future; but explosive development between Naples and Marco was imminent, and it was to try to control this that the Collier County Conservancy was organized. This extraordinarily forceful group defeated a move to open Rookery Bay to automobiles. With the help of the Nature Conservancy of Washington and the National Audubon Society, it bought private lands with which to buffer the 1,500 acres of public lands in and around the Bay, and the 4,100-acre Rookery Bay Sanctuary was formed. But to protect the delicate ecologic balance within the sanctuary, control over the whole landscape was vital; and in 1967 the Conservation Foundation embarked on a program of research and public relations to bring this about. As auspicious as the Rookery Bay project appears, the area is by no means ecologically self-contained. If in the long run the area is somehow to be kept clean and wild—a place where young sea fishes grow and where quiet people can watch waterfowl tend their clamorous nests—this will clearly have to be done under a growing siege from mankind and mankind's works.

North of Naples we flew along more miles of good beach, undeveloped for the nonce, though there were casuarinas behind it; and then we turned inland to Corkscrew Swamp. Corkscrew is the only sizable tract of the Big Cypress Swamp that remains uncut and, as I noted in Chapter 2, the Corkscrew Sanctuary harbors the most important remaining rookery of the beleaguered wood stork. Located north of the mayhem that developers are committing in the drainage pattern of much of the southern part of Big Cypress, Corkscrew seems at the moment to be one of the most stable samples of original landscape under preservation anywhere in southern Florida.

From Corkscrew we skimmed over mixed cypress swamp and pinelands to the town of Immokalee, which stands 40 feet above sea level —higher than any place south of Lake Okeechobee except Marco Island. All the land is laid out in the rectangles of farms and ranches.

A short way to the northeast we entered the strange spread of coun-

In a nest dug on a Cape Sable beach, a loggerhead turtle lays her eggs (above), generally numbering 100 or more, then uses her flippers to cover them with sand (right). The infants, which hatch within two months and take to the water immediately, are two-inch-long miniatures of their ponderous parents, which may weigh up to 500 pounds.

try known as the Devil's Garden, a wild hodgepodge of flatwoods, hammocks, bayheads and water that suddenly here and there gives way to a geometric landscape of circular ponds strung out in patterns of straight lines. Many of the ponds are rings of water surrounding central islands. The geologic origin of Devil's Garden seems not to be known. Somebody suggested that a shower of meteorites made it, as they are said to have made a somewhat similar landscape in North Carolina. The region is probably some special kind of karst topography—a sunken limestone landscape, in which the solution ponds follow the course of old surface or subsurface drainage flows.

I had driven through the Devil's Garden several times, but this was my first good look at it from the air, and I marveled that such dramatic terrain should all the time have lain out there among the little roads I had traveled on so often. Our altitude was just right to show off the geometry of the place and the flocks of herons that our crossing sent wafting about the countryside; we were also able to tell most of the kinds of trees apart. This strange land is now being rapidly lost to pasture, and as with most of the original biological landscapes of Florida, nothing has been done to save a sample of it.

Traveling on over pines, palm hammocks and flocks of flying water birds, we flew north into vast sugar-cane lands, on to the sugar town of Clewiston, at the southwestern shore of Lake Okeechobee, and out across that great inland sea. Along the eastern shore of the lake once stood one of the finest stands of tropical hammock in the state. It grew on a deep peat soil that proved its undoing soon after white men got there because it grew beans and cane too well. Two thirds of the way down the shore we turned southeastward over the lakeside town of Pahokee—the name is a variant of Pahayokee, the Seminole name for the sawgrass glades—and followed the West Palm Beach canal across ranches, farms and fruit groves into Water Conservation Area No. 1. This is the northernmost of the three big impoundments designed to control the water supply of the area. Farther southward we crossed Conservation Area No. 2A, a place notable for the huge catches of large-mouth bass that for some reason are made there from time to time.

We traveled eastward till Fort Lauderdale was under us—the city limits creeping westward into the Glades at a pace you could almost see. Then suddenly we were out over the Atlantic and the Gulf Stream, where charter boats towed the snow-white v's of their wakes across the indigo water. From there it was no time till we were streaking in toward the fabulous façade of Miami Beach, with the city behind it, its solid back to Biscayne Bay, and more city across on the far shore and on out into the western noontime haze as far as you could see.

With our flight nearly over, it seemed an appropriate time for more reminiscence, and I thought of the 1890s when Lieutenant Hugh Willoughby, about to begin a canoe trip across the Everglades, described Miami this way:

"What a change has been made in this place since the same time last year! . . . Of course, its splendid big hotel [The Royal Palm], with every modern convenience, will prove a great boon to the tourist, but for me the picturesqueness seemed to have gone; its wildness has been rudely marred by the hand of civilization.

"In all Florida I have never seen a more beautiful spot than where this deep, narrow river [the Miami River] suddenly opens into Biscayne Bay. . . . Of course it will all be very beautiful around the hotel. . . . I regret the change. . . . But in the nature of things the wilderness must be gradually encroached upon. . . . We must not look upon these things from the sentimental point of view. The romance and poetry must be suppressed for the sterner, material welfare of our fellow-man."

As we turned into our approach to the airport, I wondered idly what Willoughby would have thought about the balance of poetry and material welfare down there below us, and then my thoughts turned to the little burrowing owls that live in holes in the grass flats among the runways, and it occurred to me that I ought to find out how they had fared when the Boeing 747s first came to this airport.

Then we touched down, and a few minutes later the engines stopped, just where our trip had started 2 hours and 20 minutes before. When the doors of the plane opened no instant authorities on the southern Florida ecosystem emerged, but 60 people came out having seen a complicated country, with a treasure of wild creatures and wild landscapes, and with a heavy load of problems. To me the low-flown reconnaissance brought a new feeling of the oneness of the region. I went away confident that the choice that southern Florida faces is not between water for birds and water for people, as short-sighted boosters were proclaiming a little while ago. The question is, rather, whether both shall survive on a shared water ration in a magic but pitifully fragile land.

The Storm-haunted Shore

Like an ancient battlefield, Cape Sable at the southwestern tip of Florida, in the track of hurricanes, is a lonely place haunted by a history of violence. It is the cape's fate to keep reliving its turbulent past—to recover from one hurricane only to face another. And the awful, destructive force of tropical storms has turned this peninsula into a strange patchwork of desert and swamp.

The storms hit the cape hardest along its Gulf shore, a 30-mile arc of broad beaches broken by three "V"-shaped spits of land known as East Cape, Middle Cape and Northwest Cape. In many areas along this coast, stormy seas chew away great chunks of beach, indenting the shoreline by as much as 100 feet. Elsewhere waves build up huge mounds of sea shells, thick blankets of mud and seaweed and piles of shattered driftwood. Here and there lie young mangrove trees undermined by the waves or felled by winds of 100 miles an hour or more. Mature mangroves usually are strong enough to hold their ground, but many are stripped of their leaves and bark, enduring like skeletons in ghost forests behind the battered beach.

Farther inland, alternating belts of sand and swamp present curious proof of the storms' shaping force: as giant hurricane waves spill into the low-lying interior, the sand they sweep with them forms a low ridge that traps sea water in a trough on the inland side. The resulting brackish pools become overgrown by mangroves and other swamp vegetation. And growing incongruously on the dry sand ridges between the swamps are desert plants—agave, yucca, cactus—and cabbage palm. During the worst hurricanes, when waves sweep all the way over the peninsula, some of these plant communities are destroyed. But always new vegetation springs up in the same alternating patterns. And when pioneering red mangroves sprout at the edge of an eroded beach, the soil collected and created by their dense roots gradually extends the shoreline back out to sea.

The cape's recovery from a hurricane is always painfully slow. But as a matter of principle, the rangers of Everglades National Park—of which the cape is a unique part —make no attempt to hasten the process by man-made means, lest they risk altering the natural course of regeneration. So the cape is left wild and desolate to work out its own tempestuous evolution.

A DESOLATE BEACH AT MIDDLE CAPE

ROOTS OF DEAD MANGROVES EXPOSED BY EROSION AT NORTHWEST CAPE

A·CABBAGE PALM RISING ABOVE A CLUMP OF YUCCAS (RIGHT)

SPINES EDGING AN AGAVE LEAF

A MASS OF SEA SHELLS NEAR EAST CAPE

BRANCHES OF A WIND-STRIPPED MANGROVE

MOUNDS OF SHELLS PILED UP BY THE WAVES AT MIDDLE CAPE

Bibliography

*Also available in paperback.
†Available in paperback only.

*Bent, Arthur Cleveland, *Life Histories of North American Marsh Birds*. Peter Smith, 1963.

Carr, Archie, and Coleman J. Goin, *Guide to the Reptiles, Amphibians and Fresh-Water Fishes of Florida*. University of Florida Press, 1959.

*Caulfield, Patricia, *Everglades*. Sierra Club, 1970.

Conant, Roger, *A Field Guide to the Reptiles and Amphibians of the United States and Canada East of the 100th Meridian*. Houghton Mifflin Company, 1958.

†Craighead, Frank C., *Orchids and Other Air Plants of the Everglades National Park*. University of Miami Press, 1963.

Craighead, Frank C., *The Trees of South Florida, Vol. I: The Natural Environments and Their Succession*. University of Miami Press, 1971.

Dasmann, Raymond F., *No Further Retreat—The Fight to Save Florida*. The Macmillan Company, 1971.

†Davis, John H., Jr., *The Natural Features of Southern Florida*. The Florida Geological Survey, 1943.

Dimock, A. W. and Julian A., *Florida Enchantments*. The Outing Publishing Company, 1908.

*Douglas, Marjory Stoneman, *The Everglades—River of Grass*. Rinehart & Company, 1947.

Federal Writers' Project of the Work Projects Administration, *Florida—A Guide to the Southernmost State*. Oxford University Press, 1939.

Ford, Alice, *The Bird Biographies of John James Audubon*. University of Oklahoma Press, 1965.

Gantz, Charlotte Orr, *A Naturalist in Southern Florida*. University of Miami Press, 1971.

Hanna, Alfred Jackson and Kathryn Abbey, *Lake Okeechobee—Wellspring of the Everglades*. The Bobbs-Merrill Company, 1948.

*Harrar, Ellwood S. and J. George, *Guide to Southern Trees*, 2nd ed. Peter Smith, 1962.

†Hawkes, Alex D., *Guide to Plants of the Everglades National Park*. Tropic Isle Publishers Inc., 1965.

Howell, Arthur H., *Florida Bird Life*. Coward-McCann, Inc., 1932.

*Johnson, James Ralph, *The Southern Swamps of America*. David McKay Company, Inc., 1970.

Kennedy, Stetson, *Palmetto Country*. Duell, Sloan & Pearce, 1942.

Longstreet, R. J., ed., *Birds in Florida*. Trend House, 1969.

McIlhenny, E. A., *The Alligator's Life History*. The Christopher Publishing House, 1935.

Pough, Richard H., *Audubon Water Bird Guide—Water, Game and Large Land Birds; Eastern and Central North America from Southern Texas to Central Greenland*. Doubleday & Company, Inc., 1951.

†Robertson, William B., Jr., *Everglades—The Park Story*. University of Miami Press, 1959.

Safford, W. E., "Natural History of Paradise Key and the Near-By Everglades of Florida." *Smithsonian Report for 1917*. Government Printing Office, 1919.

Sanger, Marjory Bartlett, *Mangrove Island*. The World Publishing Company, 1963.

Simpson, Charles Torrey, *In Lower Florida Wilds*. G. P. Putnam's Sons, 1920.

Tebeau, Charlton W., *Florida's Last Frontier—The History of Collier County*, rev. ed. University of Miami Press, 1970.

Tebeau, Charlton W., *A History of Florida*. University of Miami Press, 1971.

*Tebeau, Charlton W., *Man in the Everglades—2000 Years of Human History in the Everglades National Park*, 2nd ed. University of Miami Press, 1968.

Acknowledgments

The author and editors of this book are particularly indebted to Donald Goodman, Assistant Professor of Biology, University of Florida, Gainesville. They also wish to thank the following persons at Everglades National Park, Homestead, Florida: Jack E. Stark, Superintendent; Ralph E. Miele; John C. Ogden; Robert L. Peterson; John Wesley Phillips; James Sanders; William W. Shenk; James E. Watters. At the University of Florida: Oliver Austin, Professor of Zoology; Thomas Emmel, Assistant Professor of Zoology; Daniel B. Ward, Associate Professor of Botany. At the National Audubon Society: Sam Dasher; Louise Donohue; Alexander Sprunt IV. At the New-York Historical Society: Mary C. Black; Richard J. Koke; Martin Leifer; Ellin Mathieu; Edward H. Santrucek. And also Ruth Annan, Miami, Florida; Herbert R. Axelrod, TFH Publications, Neptune City, New Jersey; Frank C. Craighead Sr., Naples, Florida; George E. Dail Jr., Executive Director, Central and South Florida Flood Control District, West Palm Beach; Edward H. Dwight, Director, Munson-Williams-Proctor Institute, Utica, New York; James S. Haeger, Entomological Research Center, Vero Beach, Florida; Sidney S. Horenstein, Department of Invertebrate Paleontology, The American Museum of Natural History, New York, New York; Larry G. Pardue, New York Botanical Garden, New York, New York; Glen Simmons, Florida City, Florida; Frank N. Young, Professor of Zoology, Indiana University, Bloomington.

Picture Credits

Sources for the pictures in this book are shown below. Credits for the pictures from left to right are separated by commas; from top to bottom they are separated by dashes.

Cover—Patricia Caulfield. Front end papers 2, 3—Russell Munson. Front end paper 4, page 1—Patricia Caulfield. 2, 3—Patricia Caulfield. 4, 5—Dr. M. P. Kahl. 6, 7—Ed Cooper. 8, 9—Patricia Caulfield. 10, 11—William J. Bolte. 12, 13—James A. Kern. 18, 19—Map by R. R. Donnelley Cartographic Services. 22—Map by R. R. Donnelley Cartographic Services. 24—Karl Knaack from TFH Publications. 29—Patricia Caulfield. 32 through 40—Maps by Walter Johnson. 33 through 41—Russell Munson. 46—Patricia Caulfield. 51 —David Molchos. 54, 55—James H. Carmichael Jr. 63, 64, 65—Dan J. McCoy. 69—James A. Kern. 75—Fred Ward from Black Star. 76, 77—James A. Kern except top right Fred Ward from Black Star. 78, 79—Lynn Pelham from Kay Reese & Associates, Edward Slater. 83—James H. Carmichael Jr. 86, 87—Frederick A. Folger. 90, 91—Patricia Caulfield. 94—Nina Leen. 99 through 107—Paulus Leeser courtesy New-York Historical Society. 113—Jeff Simon. 117—Left Robert Lerner—Treat Davidson from National Audubon Society, right James A. Kern except bottom Patricia Caulfield. 120 through 131—Robert Walch. 137—Dan J. McCoy. 143 through 155—Dan J. McCoy. 160—McFadden Air Photos. 166, 167 —Dan J. McCoy. 171—John Zoiner. 172, 173—Dan J. McCoy. 174, 175, 176—John Zoiner. 177—Dan J. McCoy. 178, 179 —John Zoiner.

Index

*Numerals in italics indicate a
photograph or drawing of the subject
mentioned.*